BERKS

C000002926

STREET ATLAS

CONTENTS

REFERENCE

Motorway	M4	Posttown Boundary By arrangement with the Post Office	
A Road	A4	Postcode Boundary Within Posttowns	
Under Construction		Map Continuation	62
Proposed		Built Up Area	MILL ST
B Road	B471	Car Park Selected	P
Dual Carriageway		Church or Chapel	†
One Way Street Traffic flow on A Roads is indicated by a heavy line on the driver's left.	→	Fire Station	■
Pedestrianized Road		Hospital	H
Restricted Access		House Numbers A and B Roads only	113 98
Track		Information Centre	i
Footpath		National Grid Reference	$^1 75$
Railway	Level Crossing ╳ Station ■	Police Station	▲
County Boundary		Post Office	★
District Boundary		Toilet with disabled facilities	▽ ♿

SCALE

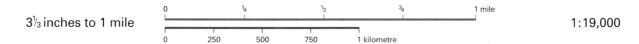

$3\frac{1}{3}$ inches to 1 mile

0	¼	½	¾	1 mile

| 0 | 250 | 500 | 750 | 1 kilometre |

1:19,000

Geographers' A-Z Map Company Ltd.

Head Office:
Fairfield Road, Borough Green, Sevenoaks, Kent, TN15 8PP
Telephone 01732 781000

Showrooms:
44 Gray's Inn Road, London, WC1X 8HX
Telephone 0171 242 9246

The Maps in the Atlas are based upon the Ordnance Survey 1:10,560 & 1:10,000 Maps with the permission of the Controller of Her Majesty's Stationery Office. © Crown Copyright.

Every possible care has been taken to ensure that the information given in this publication is accurate and whilst the publishers would be grateful to learn of any errors, they regret they cannot accept any responsibility for loss thereby caused.

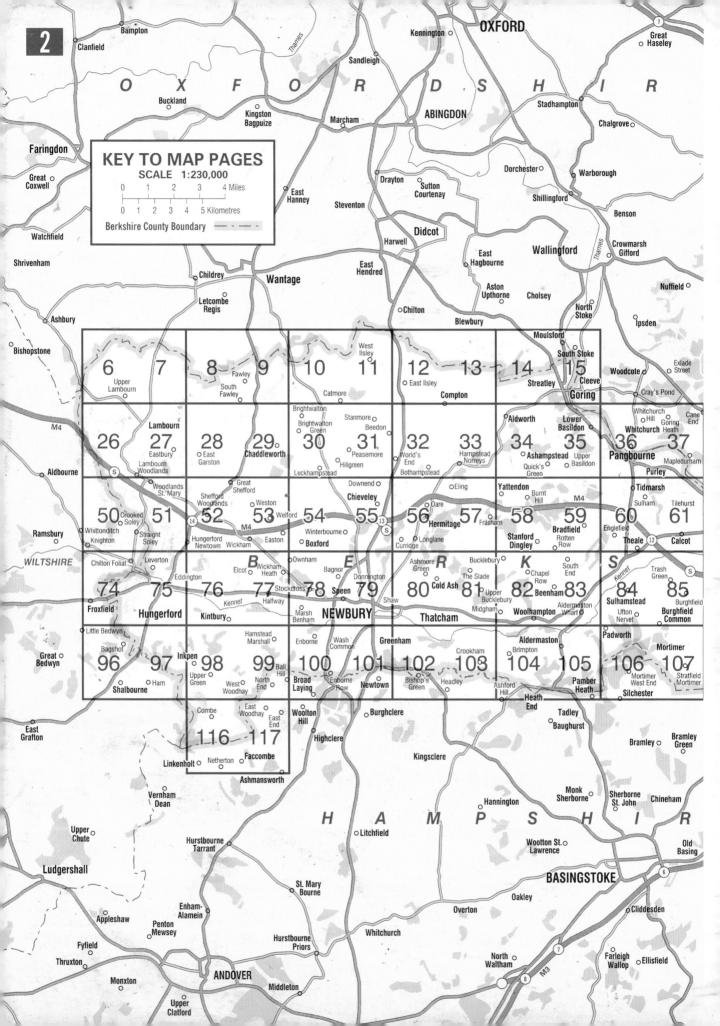

2

OXFORD

Bampton
Clanfield
Buckland
Kingston Bagpuize
Marcham
Sandleigh
Kennington

ABINGDON

OXFORDSHIRE

Faringdon
Great Coxwell
Watchfield
Shrivenham
Ashbury
Bishopstone

Childrey
Letcombe Regis
Wantage

Drayton
Steventon
Harwell
East Hendred
Chilton
Blewbury

Sutton Courtenay
East Hagbourne
Didcot

Dorchester
Shillingford
Wallingford
Aston Upthorne
Cholsey
North Stoke

Warborough
Benson
Crowmarsh Gifford
Nuffield

Stadhampton
Chalgrove
Exlade Street

Moulsford
South Stoke
Streatley
Goring
Cleeve

Woodcote
Cray's Pond
Ipsden

| 6 | 7 | 8 | 9 | 10 | 11 | 12 | 13 | 14 | 15 |

Upper Lambourn
Fawley
South Fawley
Catmore
West Ilsley
East Ilsley
Compton
Whitchurch Hill
Goring Heath
Cane End

| 26 | 27 | 28 | 29 | 30 | 31 | 32 | 33 | 34 | 35 | 36 | 37 |

Lambourn
Eastbury
Lambourn Woodlands
East Garston
Chaddleworth
Brightwalton
Brightwalton Green
Leckhampstead
Stanmore
Beedon
Peasemore
Hillgreen
World's End
Bothampstead
Hampstead Norreys
Aldworth
Ashampstead
Quick's Green
Lower Basildon
Upper Basildon
Pangbourne
Whitchurch
Mapledurham
Purley

Aldbourne

| 50 | 51 | 52 | 53 | 54 | 55 | 56 | 57 | 58 | 59 | 60 | 61 |

Woodlands St. Mary
Crooked Soley
Whittonditch
Knighton
Straight Soley
Shefford Woodlands
Great Shefford
Weston
Welford
Hungerford Newtown
Wickham
Easton
Winterbourne
Boxford
Downend
Chieveley
Oare
Hermitage
Longlane
Curridge
Eling
Frilsham
Yattendon
Burnt Hill
Stanford Dingley
Bradfield
Rotten Row
Englefield
Theale
Sulham
Tidmarsh
Tilehurst
Calcot

Ramsbury

WILTSHIRE

| 74 | 75 | 76 | 77 | 78 | 79 | 80 | 81 | 82 | 83 | 84 | 85 |

Chilton Foliat
Leverton
Eddington
Elcot
Wickham Heath
Kintbury
Halfway
Stockcross
Ownham
Bagnor
Speen
Donnington
Shaw
Ashmore Green
Cold Ash
Bucklebury
The Slade
Upper Bucklebury
Midgham
South End
Chapel Row
Beenham
Woolhampton
Aldermaston Wharf
Sulhamstead
Ufton Nervet
Trash Green
Burghfield
Burghfield Common

Froxfield
Hungerford
Kennet
Marsh Benham

NEWBURY
Thatcham

| 96 | 97 | 98 | 99 | 100 | 101 | 102 | 103 | 104 | 105 | 106 | 107 |

Little Bedwyn
Bagshot
Inkpen
Hamstead Marshall
Upper Green
Ham
West Woodhay
North End
Ball Hill
Broad Laying
Enborne
Wash Common
Enborne Row
Newtown
Greenham
Bishop's Green
Crookham
Headley
Aldermaston
Brimpton
Ashford Hill
Heath End
Pamber Heath
Padworth
Mortimer West End
Silchester
Mortimer
Stratfield Mortimer

Great Bedwyn
Shalbourne

| 116 | 117 |

Combe
East Woodhay
East End
Woolton Hill
Highclere
Burghclere
Linkenholt
Netherton
Faccombe
Ashmansworth

Tadley
Baughurst
Bramley
Bramley Green
Chineham

East Grafton
Vernham Dean

Upper Chute

Ludgershall

HAMPSHIRE

Hurstbourne Tarrant
St. Mary Bourne
Litchfield
Kingsclere
Hannington
Monk Sherborne
Sherborne St. John
Wootton St. Lawrence

BASINGSTOKE

Appleshaw
Penton Mewsey
Enham-Alamein
Hurstbourne Priors
Whitchurch
Overton
Oakley
Cliddesden

Fyfield
Thruxton
Monxton
Old Basing

ANDOVER
Middleton
Upper Clatford

North Waltham
Farleigh Wallop
Ellisfield

M4
M3

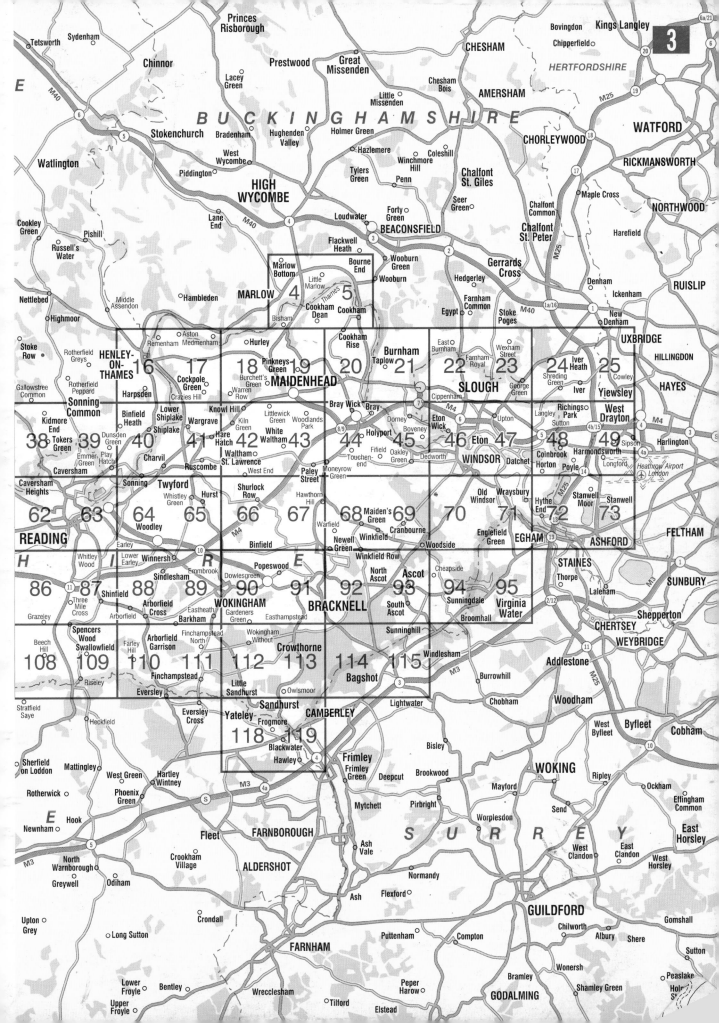

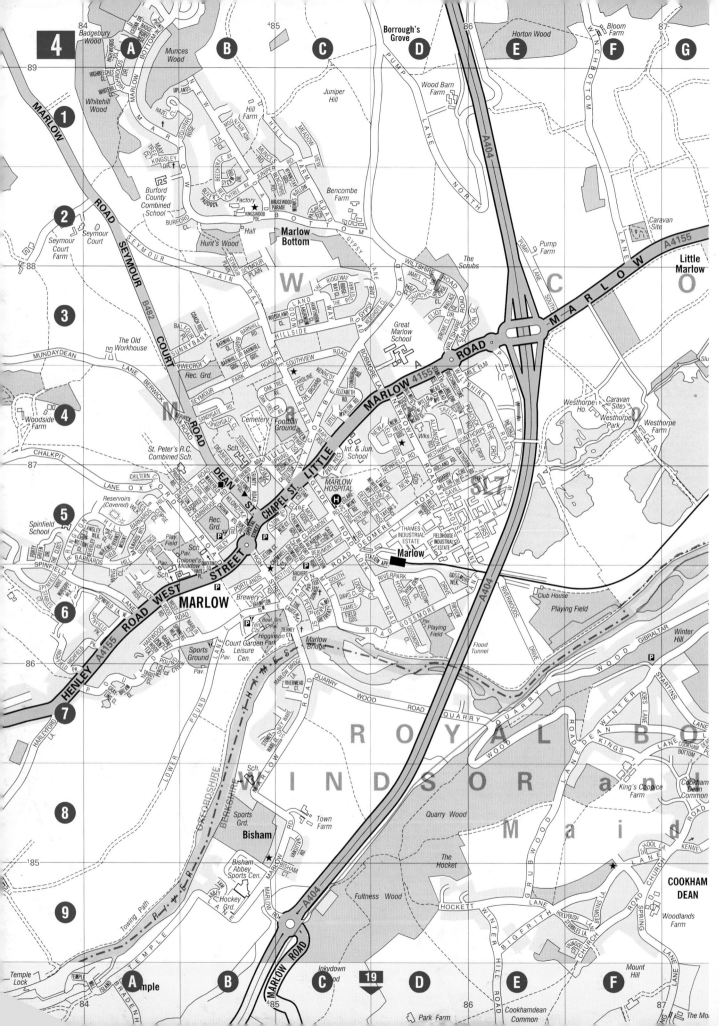

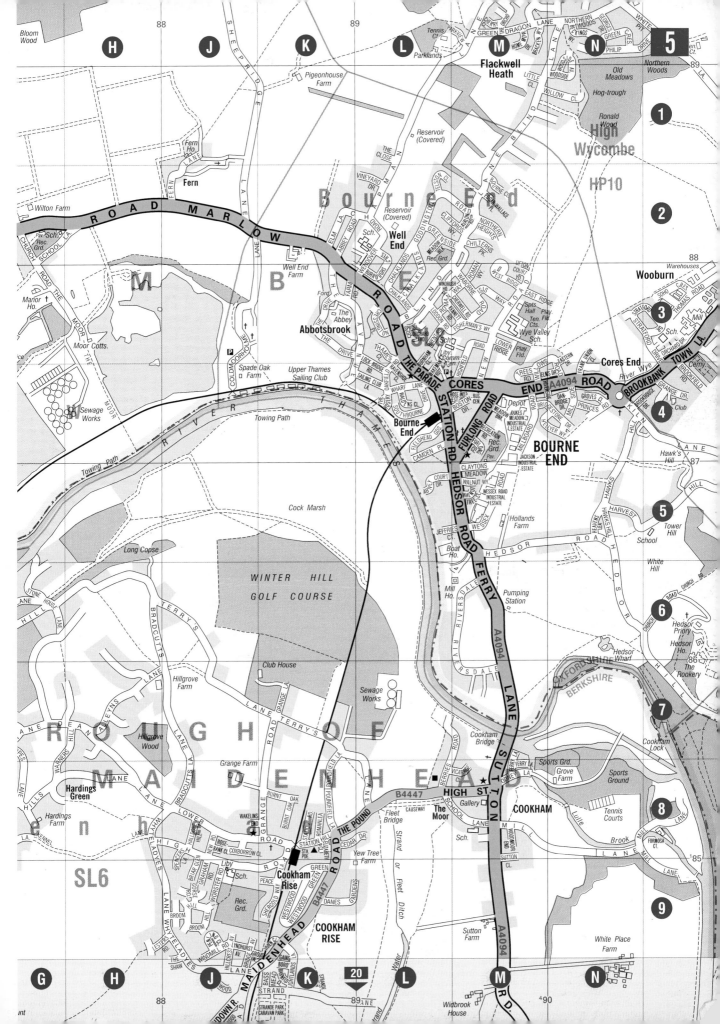

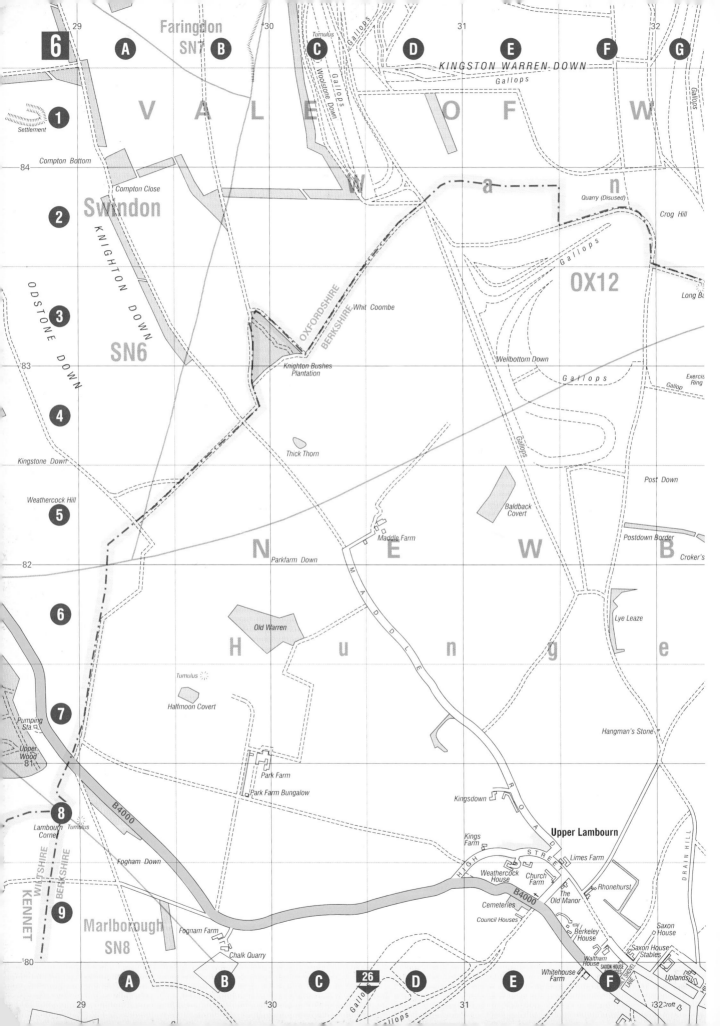

6

29   **A**   Faringdon   **B**   30   Turnulus   **C**   31   **D**   **E**   **F**   32   **G**

SN7

KINGSTON WARREN DOWN

1

Settlement

V A L E   O F   W

Gallops

Gallops

Woolstone Down

Gallops

Gallops

84   Compton Bottom

Compton Close

2

Swindon

W

Quarry (Disused)

Crog Hill

KNIGHTON DOWN

a   n

ODSTONE DOWN

3

OXFORDSHIRE

BERKSHIRE

Whit Coombe

Gallops

OX12

SN6

83

Knighton Bushes
Plantation

Wellbottom Down

Gallops

Long B

4

Thick Thorn

Gallops

Exercis
Ring

Kingstone Down

Gallop

Post Down

Weathercock Hill

Baldback
Covert

5

Postdown Border

82   N   Parkfarm Down   E   W   B

Maddle Farm

Croker's

M
A
D
D
L
E

6

Lye Leaze

Old Warren

H   u   n   g   e

Tumulus

Halfmoon Covert

Hangman's Stone

7

Pumping
Sta.

Upper
Wood

81

Park Farm

R
O
A
D

Park Farm Bungalow

Kingsdown

8

B4000

Lambourn
Corner

Tumulus

Upper Lambourn

Kings
Farm

S
T
R
E
E
T

Limes Farm

Fogham Down

Weathercock
House

Church
Farm

Rhonehurst

D
R
A
I
N
 H
I
L
L

H
I
G
H

WILTSHIRE

BERKSHIRE

The
Old Manor

9

Marlborough

Cemeteries

B4000

Saxon
House

KENNET

SN8

Fognam Farm

Council Houses

Berkeley
House

Saxon House
Stables

80

Chalk Quarry

Waltham
House

Uplands

Whitehouse
Farm

Croft

A   **B**   **C**   **26**   **D**   **E**   **F**

29   30   Gallops   31   32

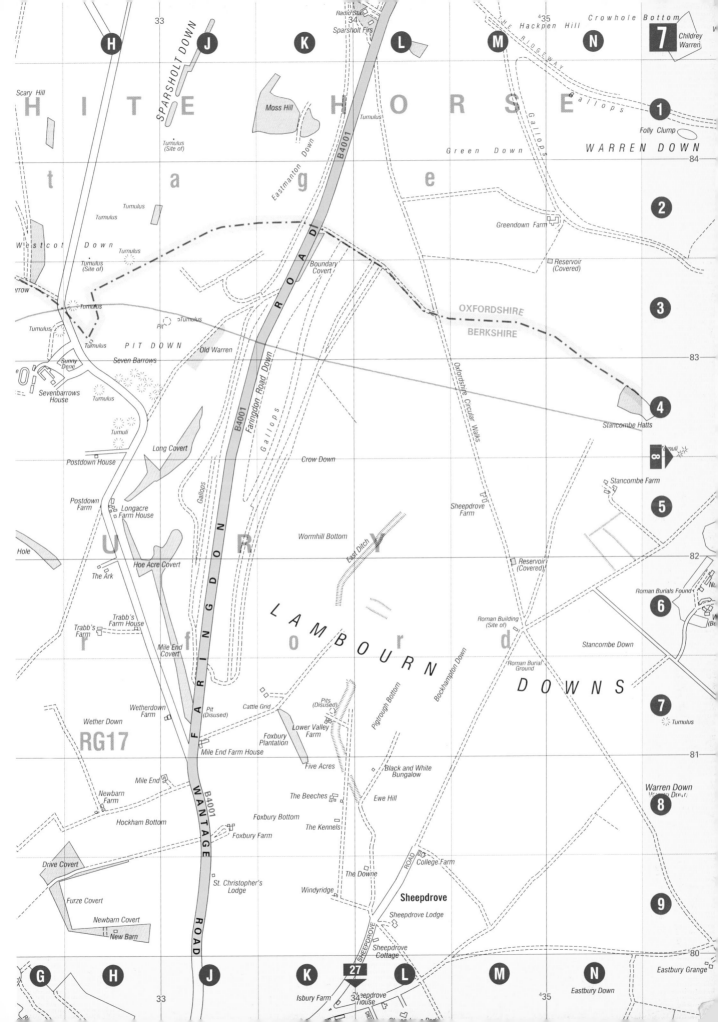

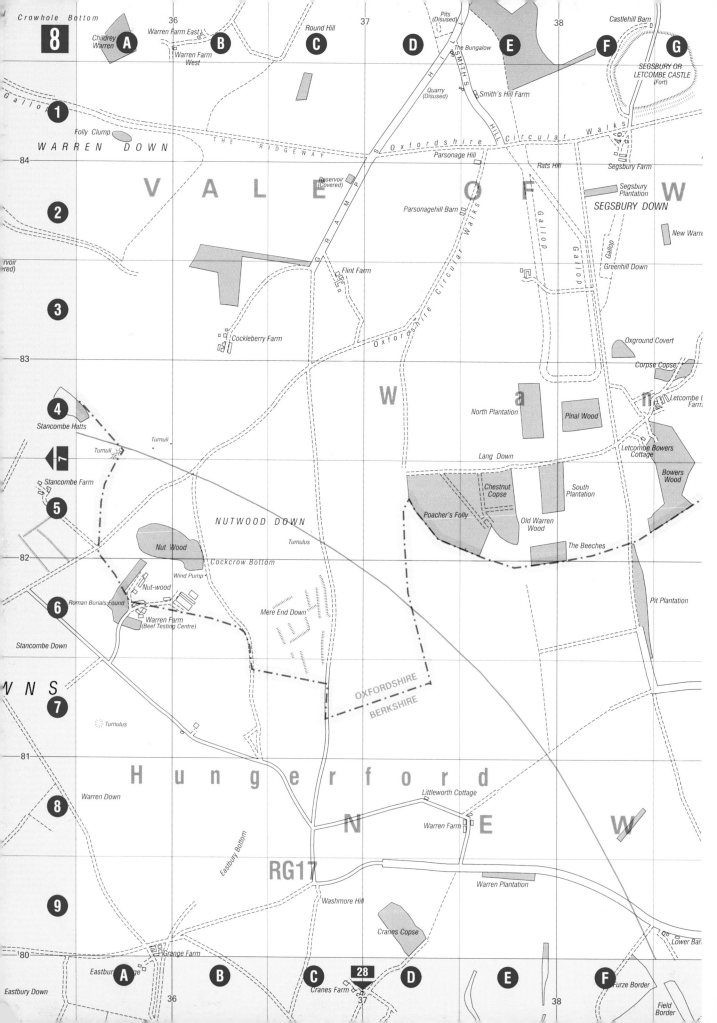

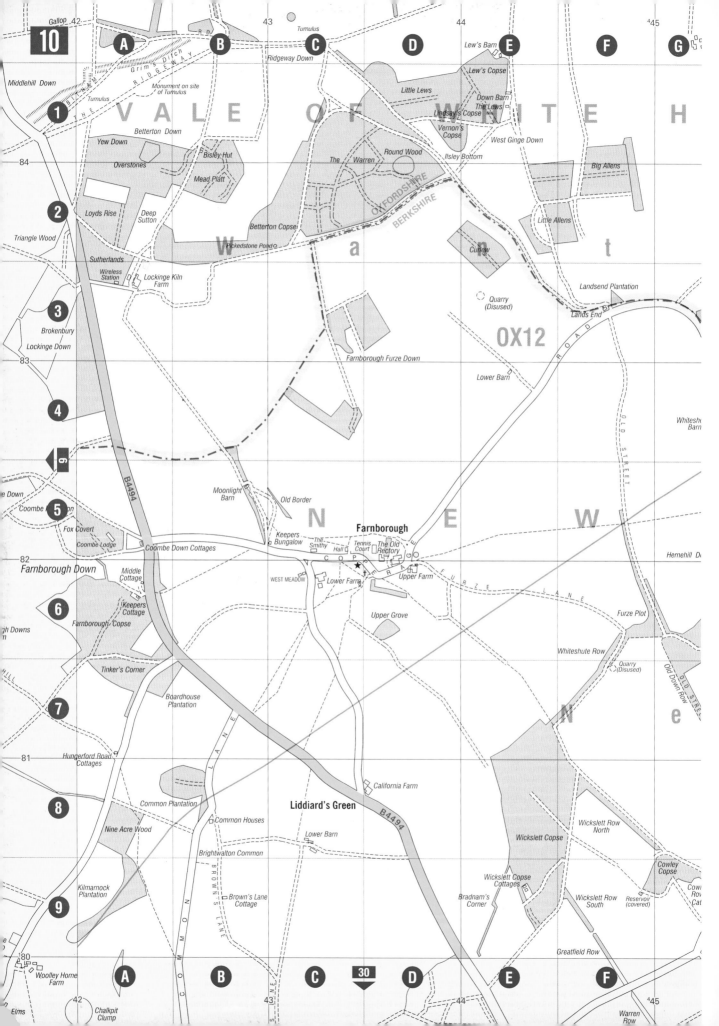

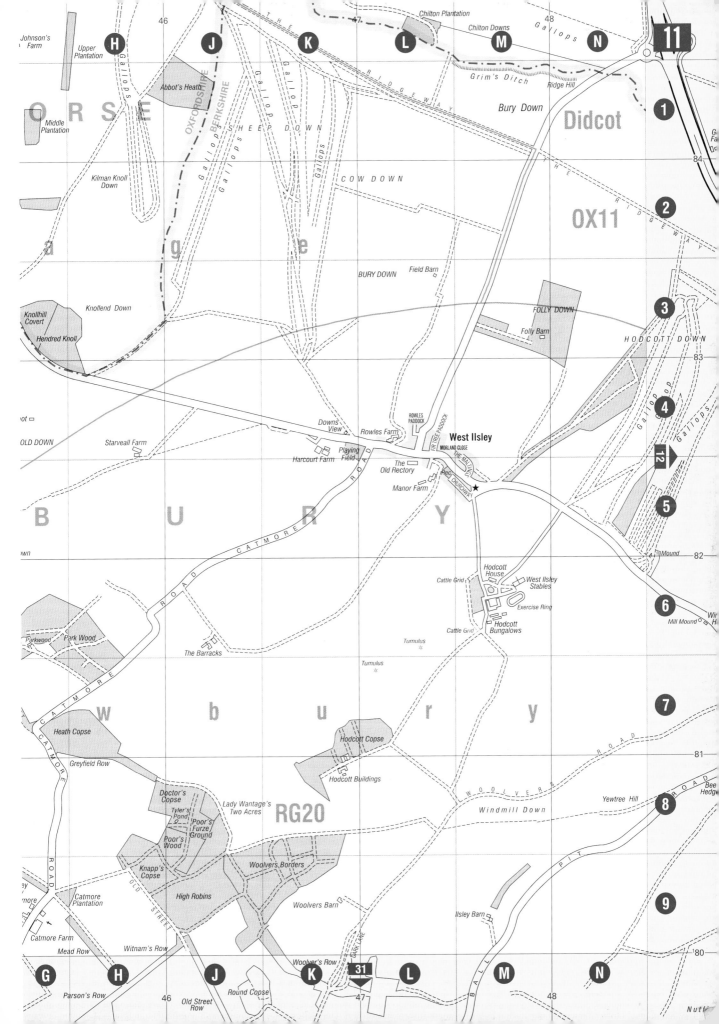

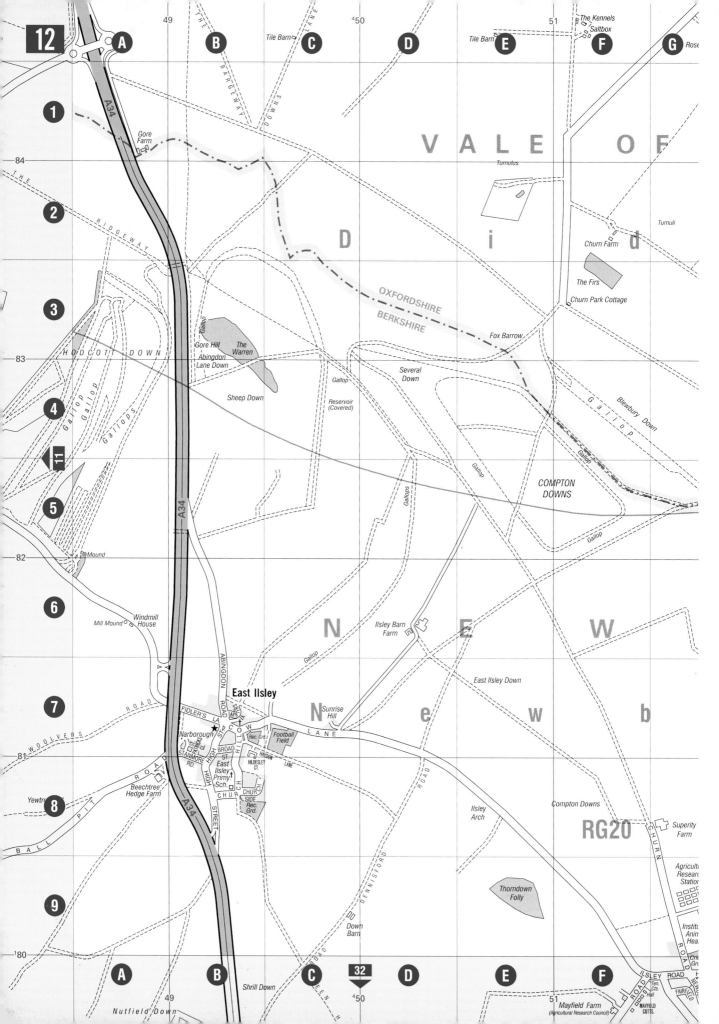

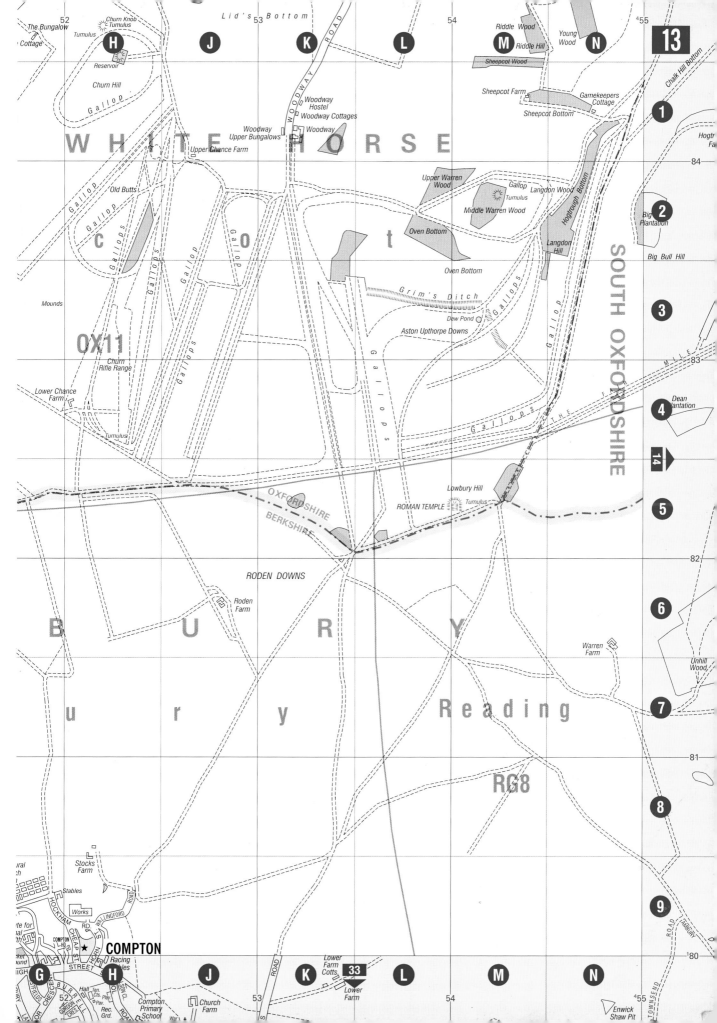

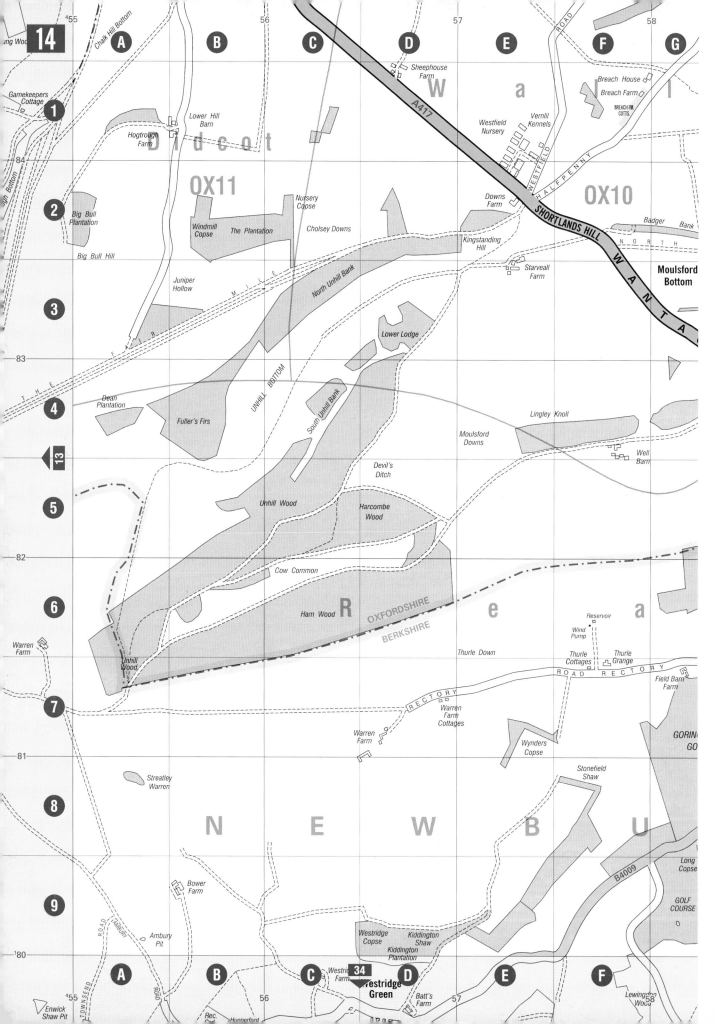

14

455

A   B   C   D   W   E   a   F   G

Chalk Hill Bottom

Gamekeepers Cottage

1   Lower Hill Barn

Hogtrough Farm   Didcot

OX11

Big Bull Plantation

2   Windmill Copse   The Plantation   Cholsey Downs   Downs Farm   OX10   Badger Bank

Big Bull Hill   Nursery Copse   Kingstanding Hill   Moulsford Bottom

Juniper Hollow   North Unhill Bank   Starveall Farm

3

Lower Lodge

83

Dean Plantation   Fuller's Firs   South Unhill Bank   Moulsford Downs   Lingley Knoll

4   UNHILL BOTTOM

Well Barn

13   Devil's Ditch

Unhill Wood   Harcombe Wood

5

82

Cow Common

Ham Wood   R   OXFORDSHIRE   e   a   Reservoir

6   BERKSHIRE   Wind Pump   Thurle Grange

Warren Farm   Unhill Wood   Thurle Down   Thurle Cottages   Field Barn Farm

ROAD   RECTORY

7   RECTORY   Warren Farm Cottages   Wynders Copse   GORING GO

81   Warren Farm   Stonefield Shaw

Streatley Warren

8   N   E   W   B   U

B4009   Long Copse

Bower Farm   GOLF COURSE

9

Ambury Pit

180   Westridge Copse   Kiddington Shaw

455   A   B   C   Westridge Farm   34   D   Kiddington Plantation   E   F

Enwick Shaw Pit   56   Westridge Green   Batt's Farm   57   Lewington Wood   58

Rec.

Hungerford

TOWNSEND ROAD   FAIRBURY

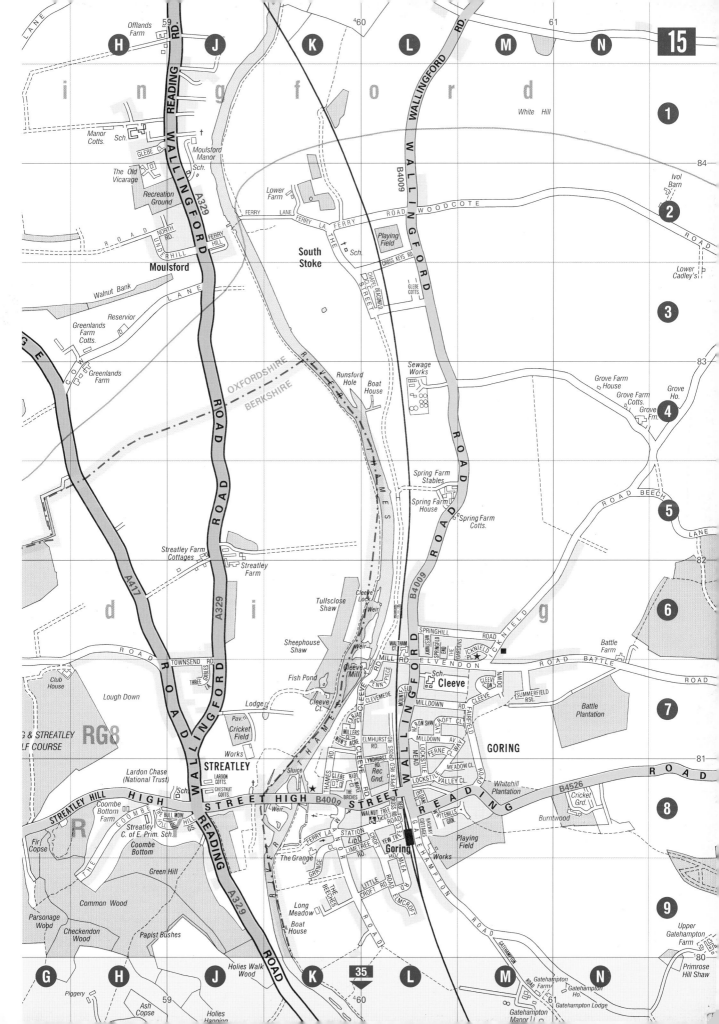

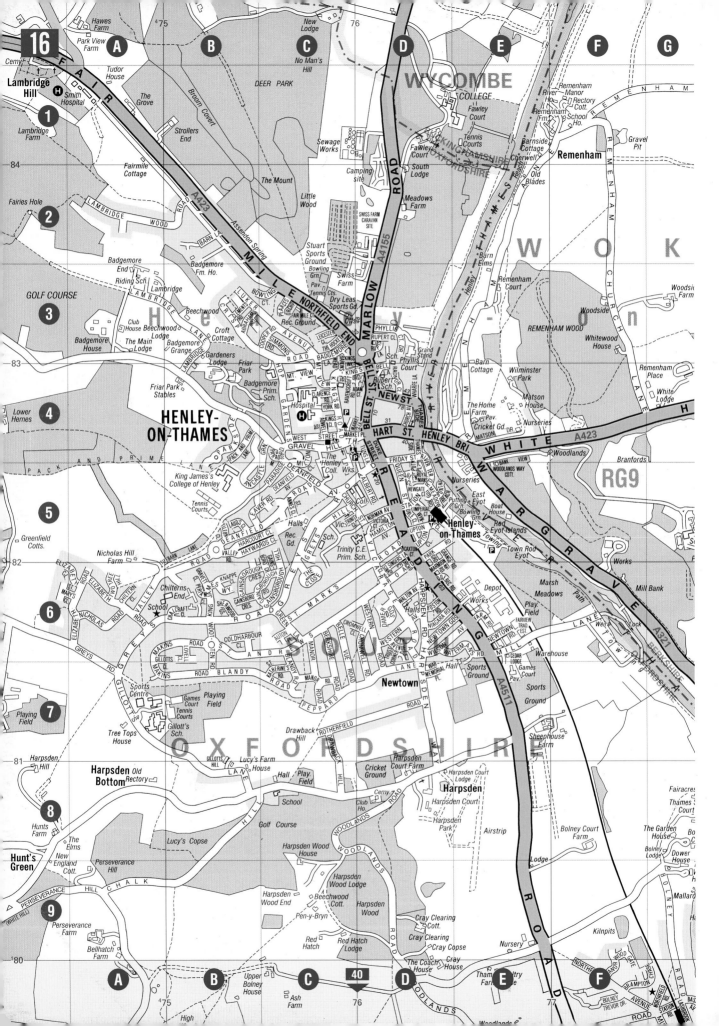

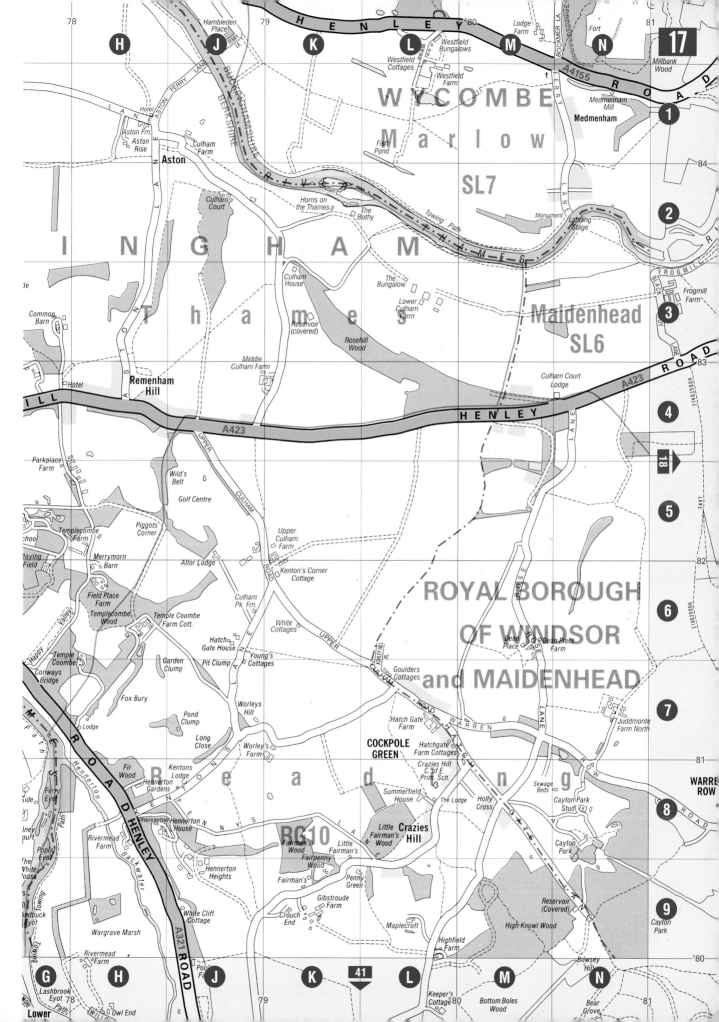

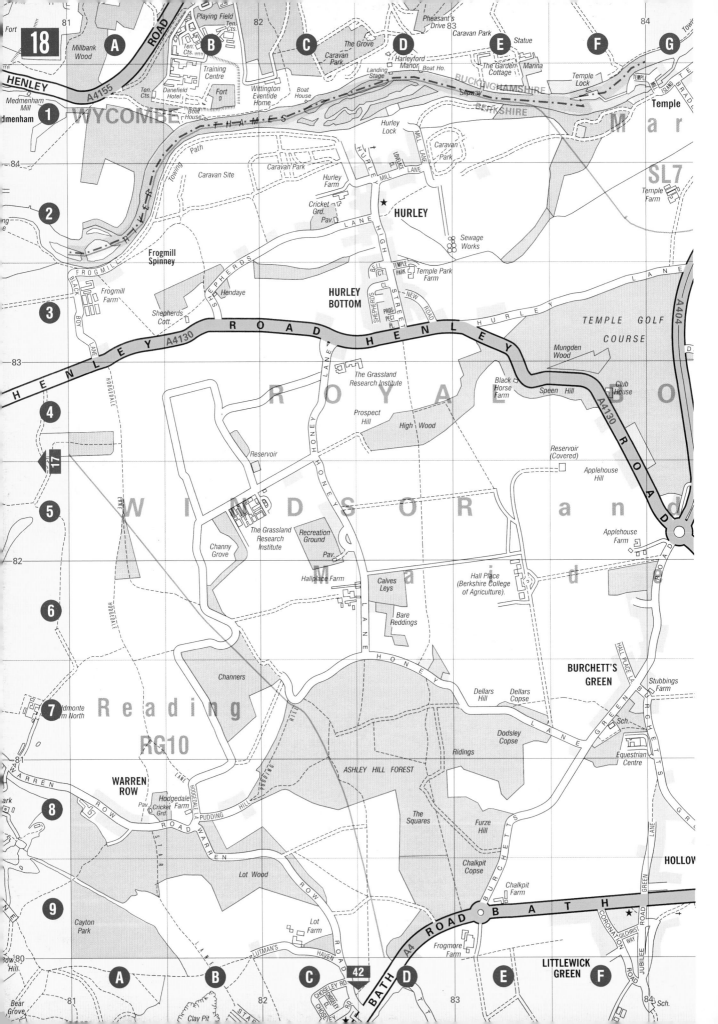

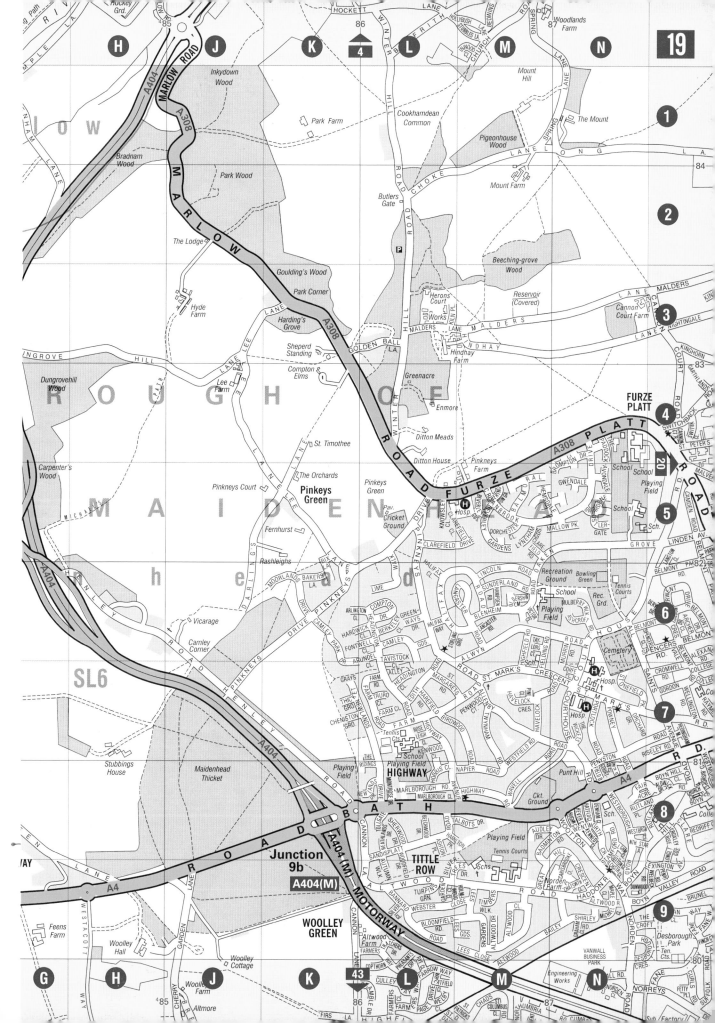

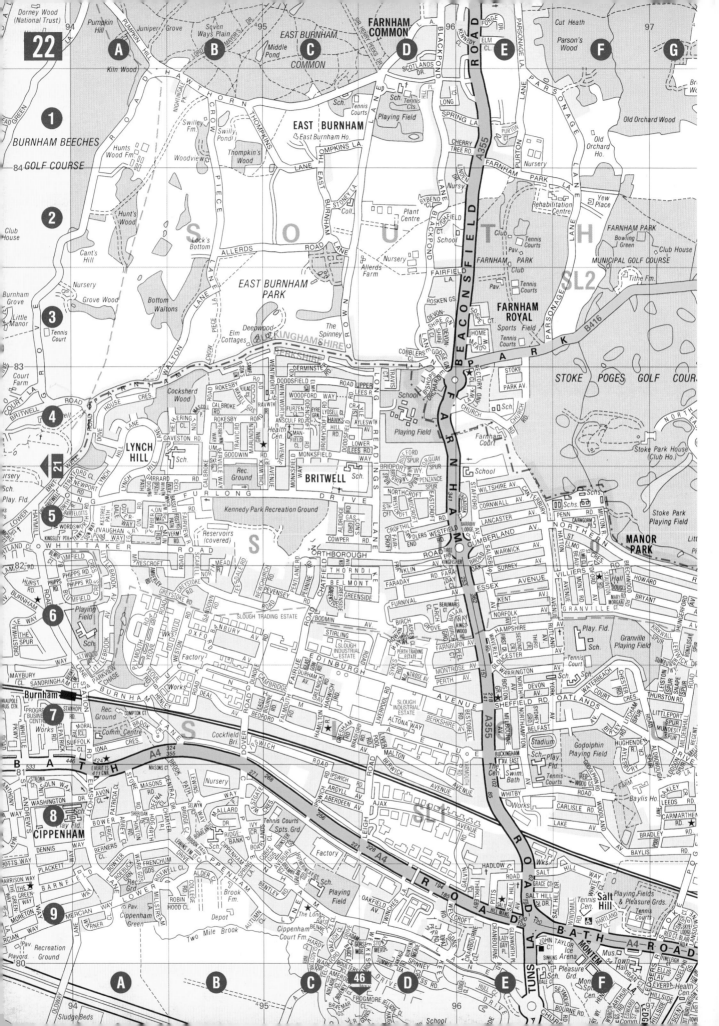

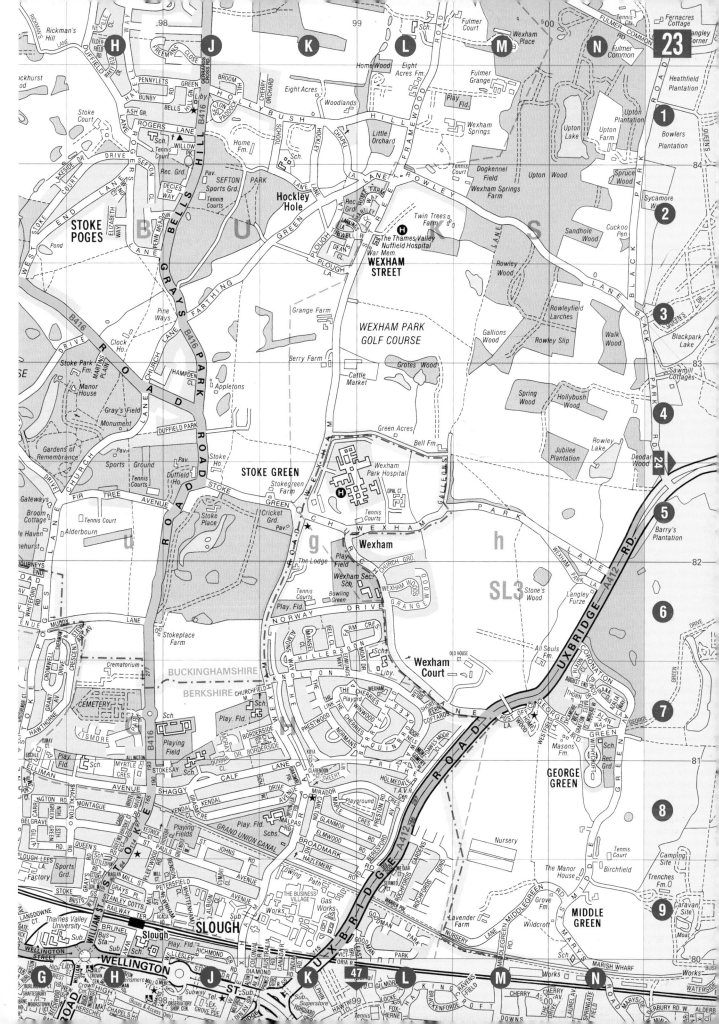

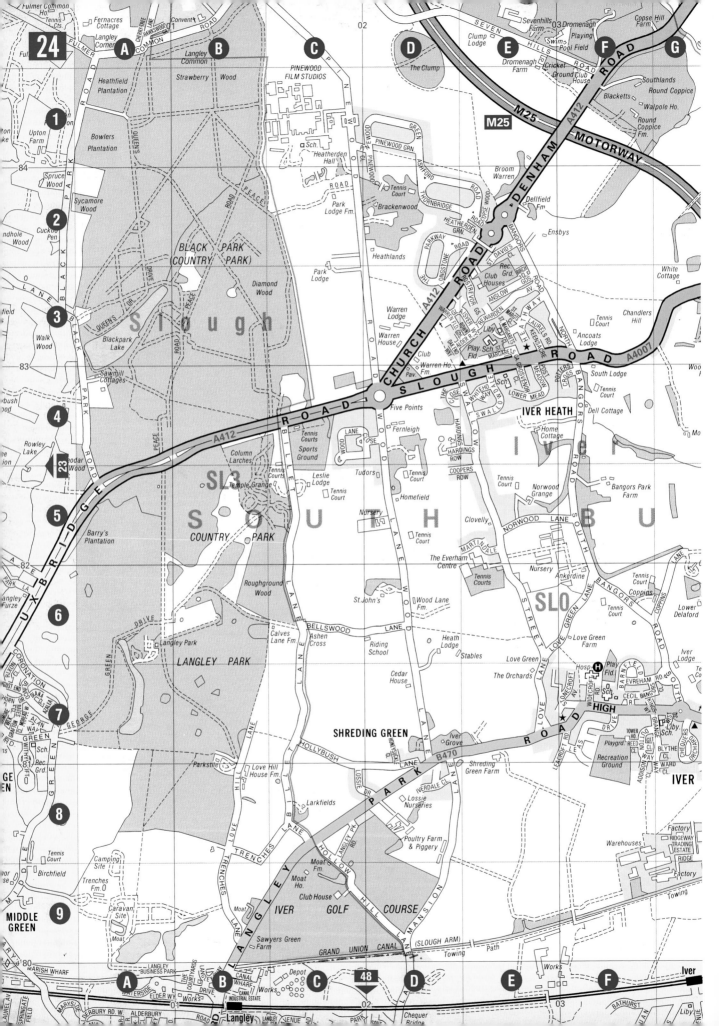

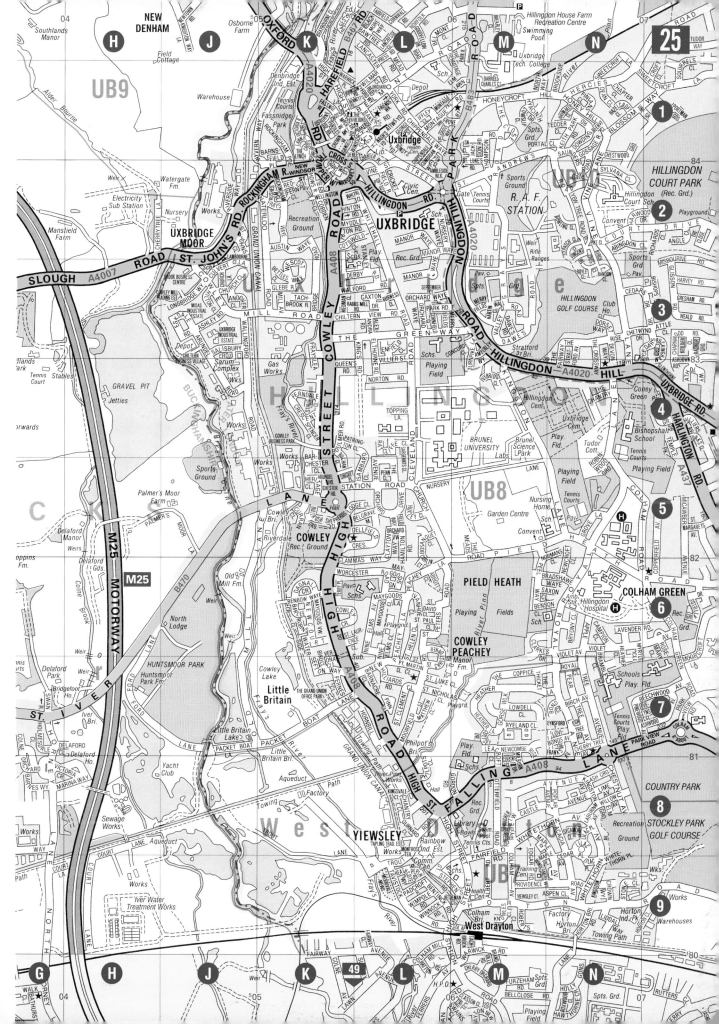

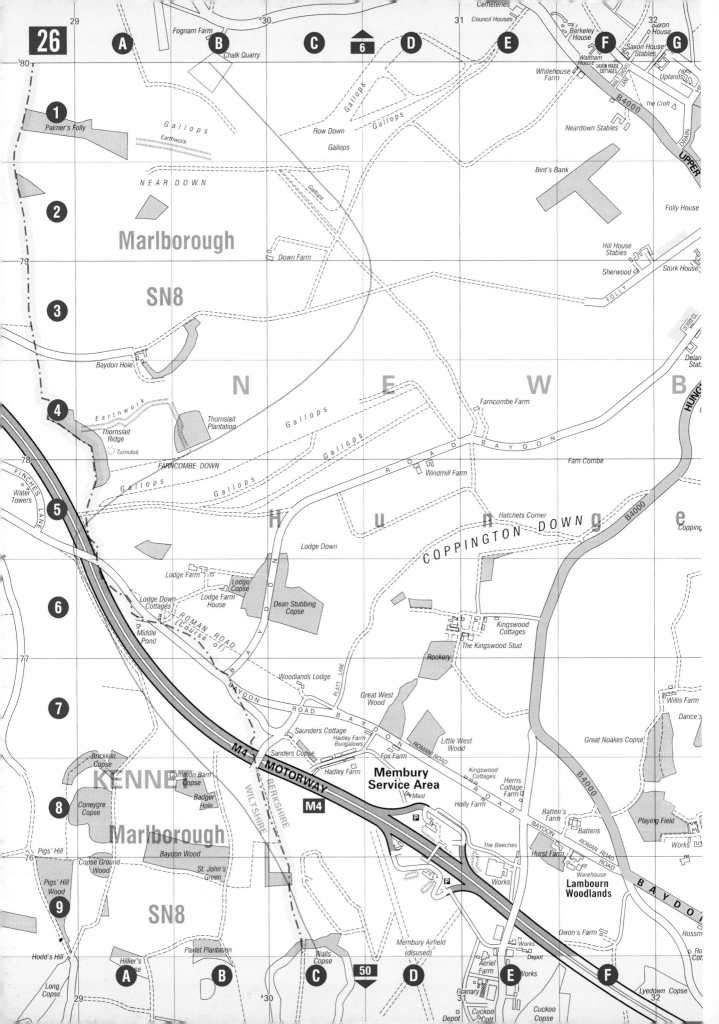

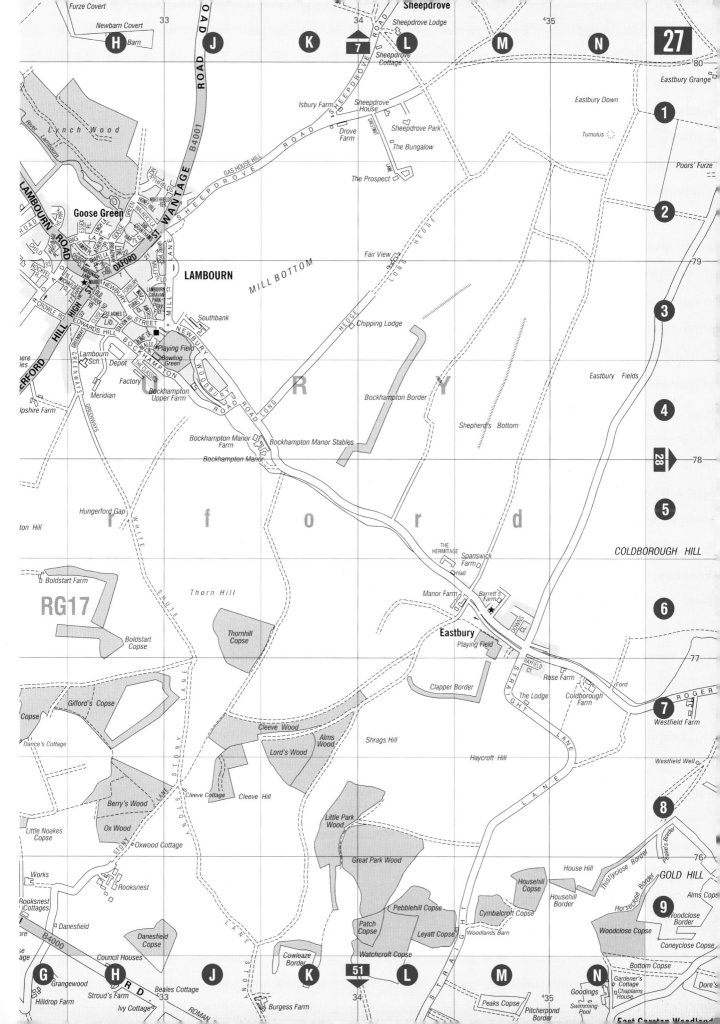

Washmore Hill

A   B   C   Cranes C   D   E   F   G   Bar
8

80
Grange Farm

Eastbury Grange

Eastbury Down

Cranes Farm

Furze Border

1

Tumulus

Poors' Furze

Pound's Farm

Field Border

2

79

Well Cop

Oakhedge Copse

N   E   W   B

3

Eastbury   Fields

Hasham Copse

Lady Copse

4

78   ◄ **27**

Winterdown Barn

H   u   n   g   e   r   f   o

Lodge Copse

5

COLDBOROUGH   HILL

Jimmy's Farm

Lone Barn Farm

Furze Border

RG17

6

Colett

Manor Farm

Glebe House

77

East Garston

The Old Vicarage

Ford

Idborough Farm

R O G E R ' S   L A N E   STATION RD   BURFORD'S   BACK   STREET   FRONT   LANE

7

Westfield Farm

Hall

College Farm

★

Westfield Well

STREET

8

Parsonage Farm

River Lambourn

Maidencourt Farm

Car

76

use Hill

Gallops

GOLD HILL

Thistlyclose Border

Peake's Border

Alms Copse

Woodclose Border

Woodclose Copse

Gallops

Shefford Prim. Sch

9

Coneyclose Copse

Woodclose Copse

River Mead

GREAT SHEFFORD

Bottom Copse

Gardener's Cottage   Chaplains House

A   Dore's Border   B   Dore's

C   Gallops   **52**   D   E   Manor Farm   F

Goodings   Swimming Pool

36   Dore's Copse   37   Manor Farm Cottages   38   CHURCH   STREET   FETTIPLACE

East Garston Woodlands

36   37   38

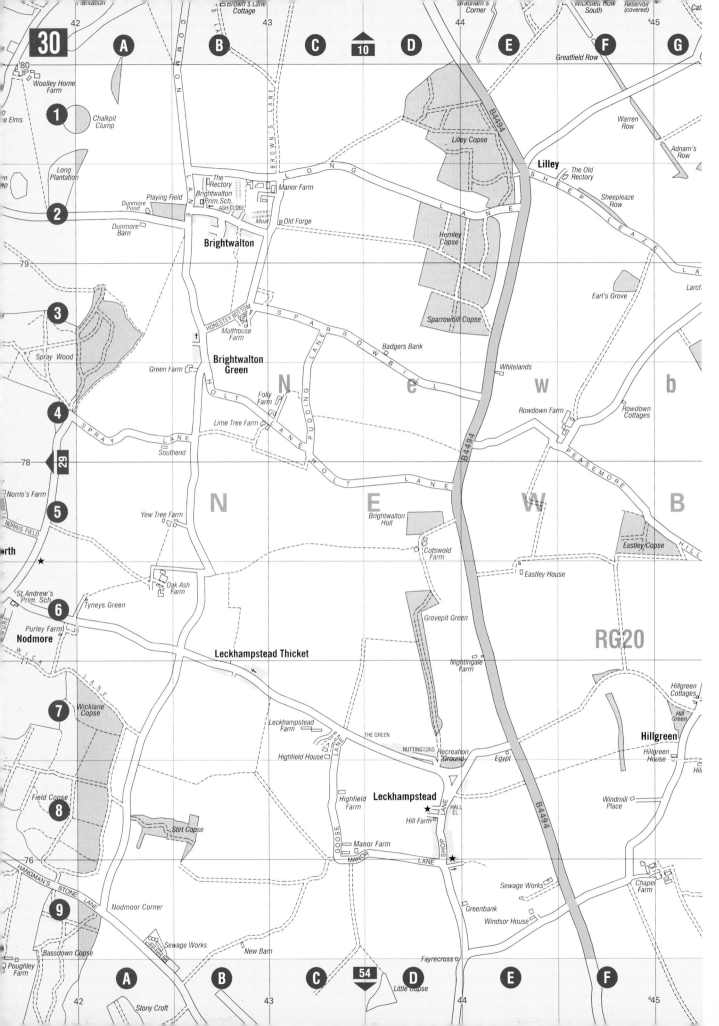

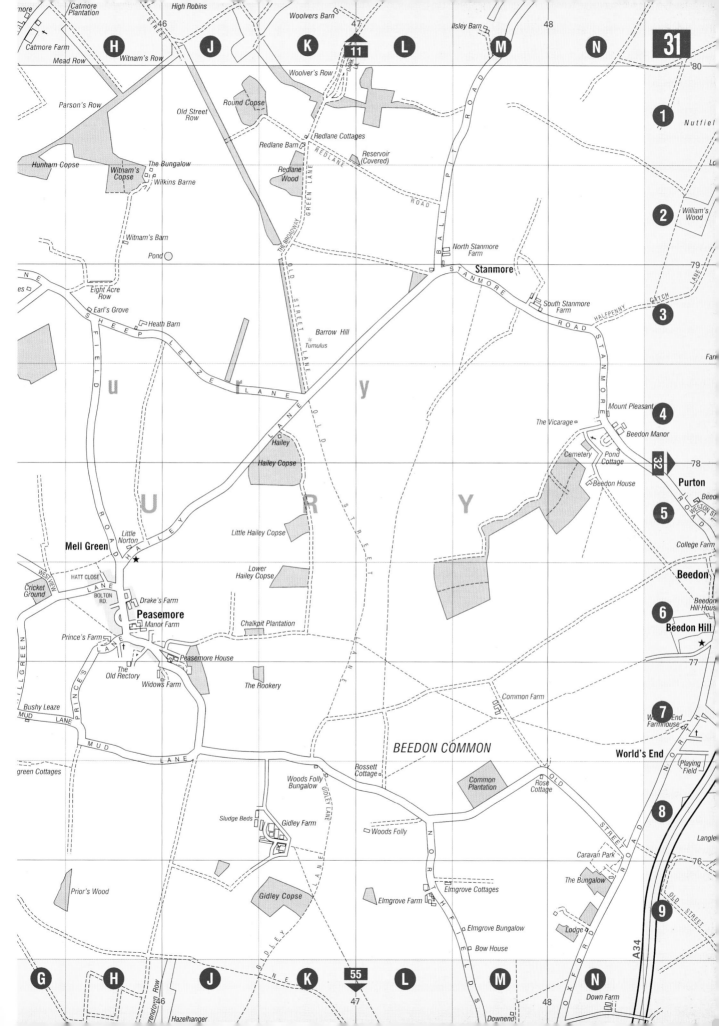

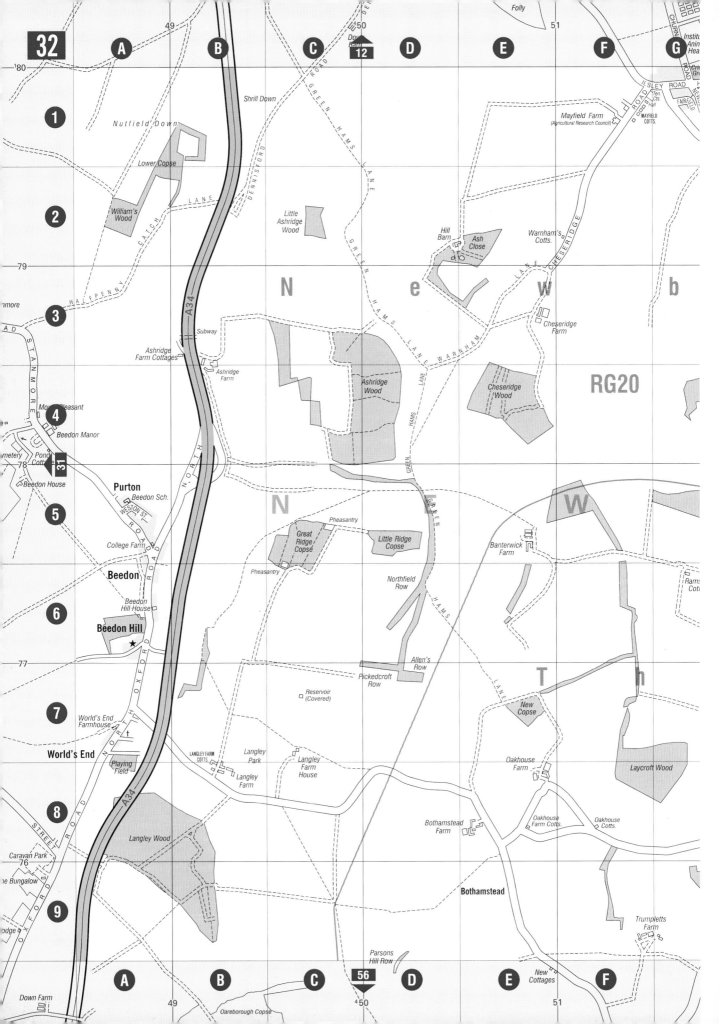

A · B · C · D · E · F · G

1
2
3
4
5
6
7
8
9

12

31

56

Folly

Nutfield Down

Lower Copse

William's Wood

CATCH LANE

HALFPENNY

STANMORE

Mo... Pleasant

Beedon Manor

...metery

Pond Cott...

Beedon House

Purton

Beedon Sch.

WESTON ST.

College Farm

Beedon

Beedon Hill House

Beedon Hill ★

World's End Farmhouse

World's End

Playing Field

Caravan Park

...e Bungalow

...odge 9

Down Farm

Shrill Down

DENNISFORD

A34

Subway

Ashridge Farm Cottages

Ashridge Farm

NORTH ROAD

OXFORD ROAD

STREET

Langley Wood

Langley Farm Cotts.

Langley Park

Langley Farm

Langley Farm House

Oareborough Copse

Little Ashridge Wood

GREEN HAMS LANE

N e

Ashridge Wood

GREEN HAMS LANE

WARNHAM LANE

N

Great Ridge Copse

Pheasantry

Pheasantry

Little Ridge Copse

GREEN

Northfield Row

Reservoir (Covered)

Pickedcroft Row

Allen's Row

Bothamstead Farm

Parsons Hill Row

New Cottages

Hill Barn

Ash Close

Warnham's Cotts.

Cheseridge Farm

e

CHESERIDGE

W

Cheseridge Wood

RG20

b

Mayfield Farm
(Agricultural Research Council)

ILSLEY ROAD

Ten. Cts.

Hall

MAYFIELD COTTS.

CHURN ROAD

FAIRFIELD

Cr... Gre...

Institute
Anim...
Hea...

Banterwick Farm

W

HAMS

T

New Copse

Oakhouse Farm

Oakhouse Farm Cotts.

Oakhouse Cotts.

Laycroft Wood

h

Bothamstead

Trumpletts Farm

Rams...
Cott...

'80

79

78

77

76

49

50

51

49

50

51

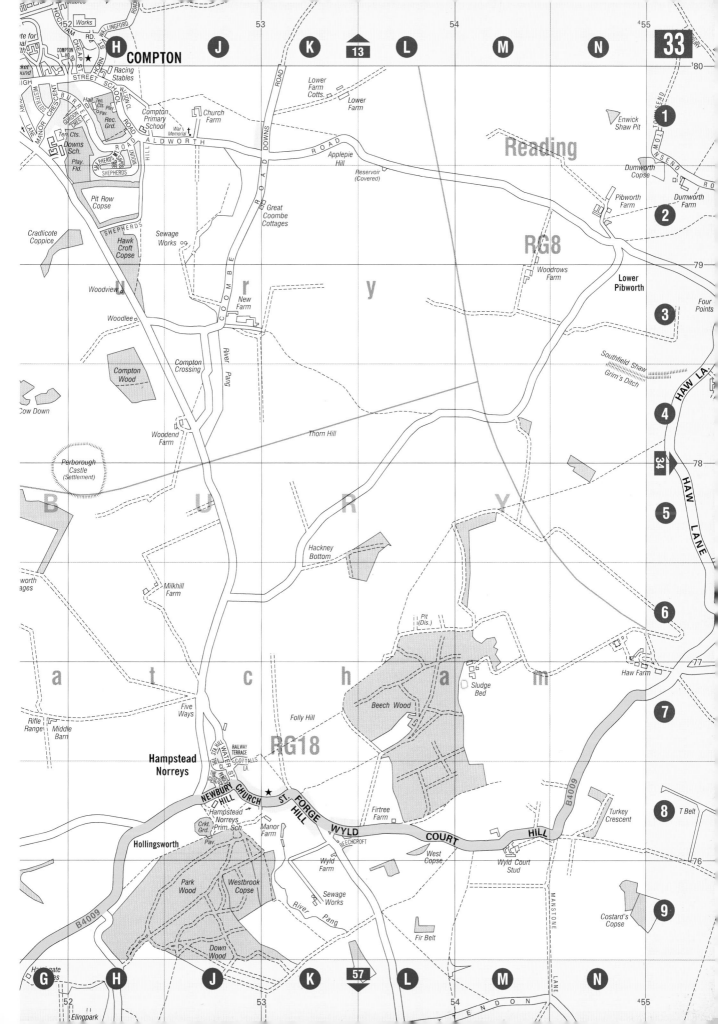

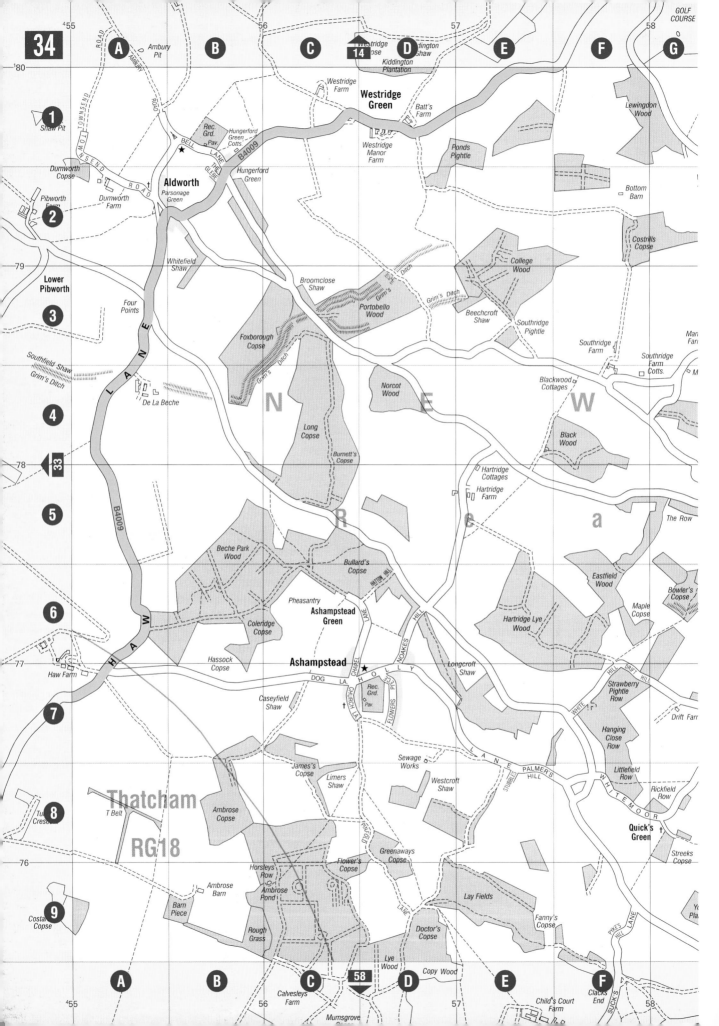

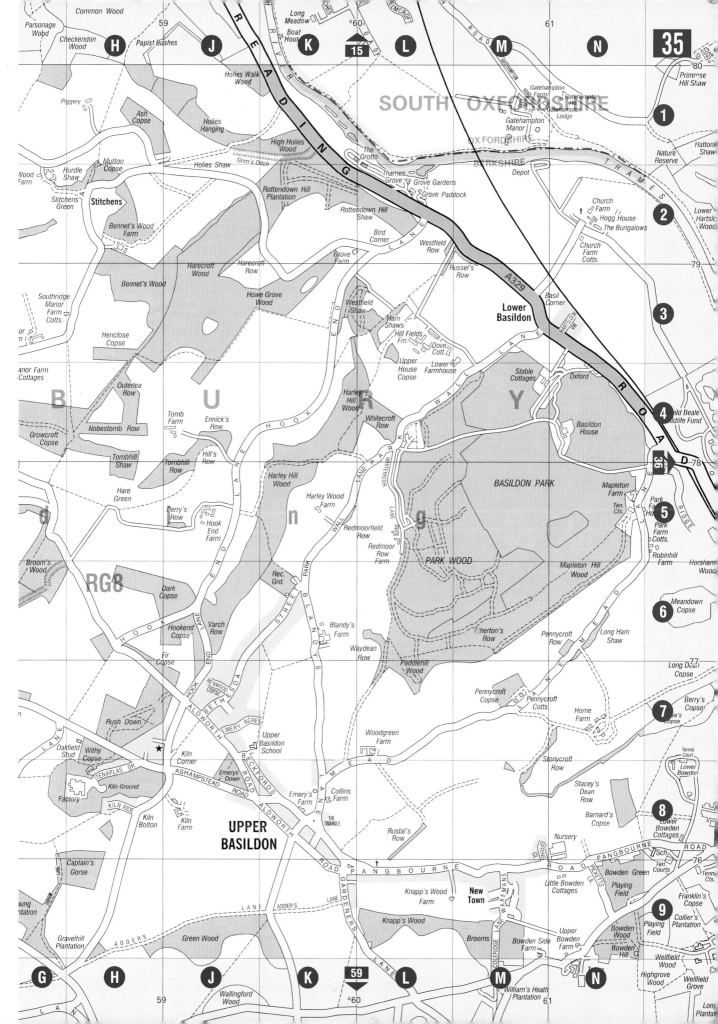

Common Wood
Parsonage Wood
Checkendon Wood
Papist Bushes
Piggery
Ash Copse
Holies Hanging
Mutton Copse
Hurdle Shaw
Wood Farm
Stitchens Green
Stitchens
Bennet's Wood Farm
Southridge Manor Farm Cotts.
Henclose Copse
Manor Farm Cottages
Outerlea Row
Nobestomb Row
Growcroft Copse
Tombhill Shaw
Tombhill Row
Hare Green
Broom's Wood
Dark Copse
Hookend Copse
Varch Row
Fir Copse
Rush Down
Oakfield Stud
Withy Copse
Factory
Kiln Ground
Kiln Ride
Kiln Bolton
Kiln Farm
Captain's Gorse
Young Plantation
Gravelhill Plantation
Green Wood

RIVER READING
Long Meadow
Boat House
Holies Walk Wood
High Holies Wood
Holies Shaw
Grim's Ditch
Rottendown Hill Plantation
Harecroft Wood
Harecroft Row
Howe Grove Wood
Bennet's Wood
Tomb Farm
Ennick's Row
Hill's Row
Berry's Row
Hook End Farm
Henwood Copse
Rec. Grd.
Blandy's Farm
Waydean Row
Harley Hill Wood
Harley Wood Farm
Redmoorfield Row
Redmoor Row Farm
Hookend Lane
Aldworth Lane
Emery Acres
Upper Basildon School
Kiln Corner
Emerys Down
Emery's Farm
Collins Farm
THE TRIANGLE
Rustal's Row
Knapp's Wood Farm
Knapp's Wood
Brooms
Bowden Side Farm
Wallingford Wood

SOUTH OXFORDSHIRE
OXFORDSHIRE
BERKSHIRE
The Grotto
Thames Grove
Grove Gardens
Grove Paddock
Rottendown Hill Shaw
Bird Corner
Grove Farm
Westfield Row
Westfield Shaw
Russel's Row
Ham Shaws
Hill Fields Fm.
Dove Cott.
Upper House Copse
Lower Farmhouse
Whitecroft Row
Paddlehill Wood
Woodgreen Farm
New Town
PANGBOURNE
William's Heath Plantation

Gatehampton Fm Farm
Gatehampton Ho Lodge
Gatehampton Manor
Church Farm
Hogg House
The Bungalows
Church Farm Cotts.
Basil Corner
Lower Basildon
Stable Cottages
Oxford
Basildon House
BASILDON PARK
Mapleton Farm
Ten. Cts.
Mapleton Hill Wood
PARK WOOD
Ftherton's Row
Pennycroft Row
Pennycroft Copse
Pennycroft Cotts.
Home Farm
Stonycroft Row
Nursery
Little Bowden Cottages
Bowden Green Playing Field
Upper Bowden Farm
Bowden Wood
Bowden Hill

Primrose Hill Shaw
80
Hatton Shaw
Nature Reserve
Lower Hartslc Wood
Church Farm Cotts.
79
Child Beale Wildlife Fund
Park Farm Ho
Park Farm Cotts.
Robinhill Farm
Horsham Wood
78
Meandown Copse
Long Ham Shaw
77
Long Dean Copse
Berry's Copse
ove's Copse
Tennis Court
Lower Bowden
Stacey's Dean Row
Barnard's Copse
Lower Bowden Cottages
Sch
Ten. Courts
76
Franklin's Copse
Collier's Plantation
Playing Field
Wellfield Wood
Highgrove Wood
Wellfield Grove
Long Plant

RIVER THAMES
A329
A329
Basil Corner
WALL LANE
BUR Y
HOOK END LANE
PARK LANE
WHITMOOR
MEAD LANE
SPRING CL.
PICKETTS LA.
WAKEMANS LANE
COLERIDGE LANE
SPRING RD
PANGBOURNE ROAD
ALDWORTH ROAD
BECKFORDS ROAD
ELIZABETH BESSDA
HENWOOD COPSE
SONNING LANE
KILN RIDE
TENAPLAS DR
ASHAMPSTEAD ROAD
GARDENERS LANE
ADDER'S LANE
MEAD LANE
RG8

UPPER BASILDON

d
B U R Y
d
n
g
36
RIDGE

Stitchens
Bennet's Wood

H J K 15 L M N
1
2
3
4
5
6
7
8
9
G H J K 59 L M N

59 60 61
59 60 61

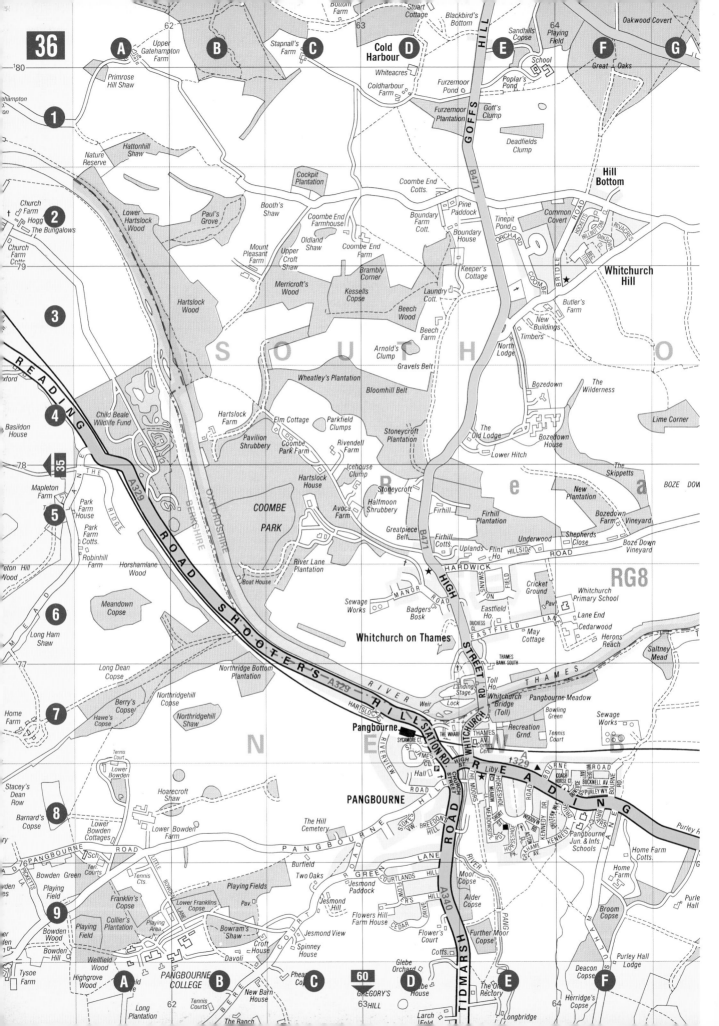

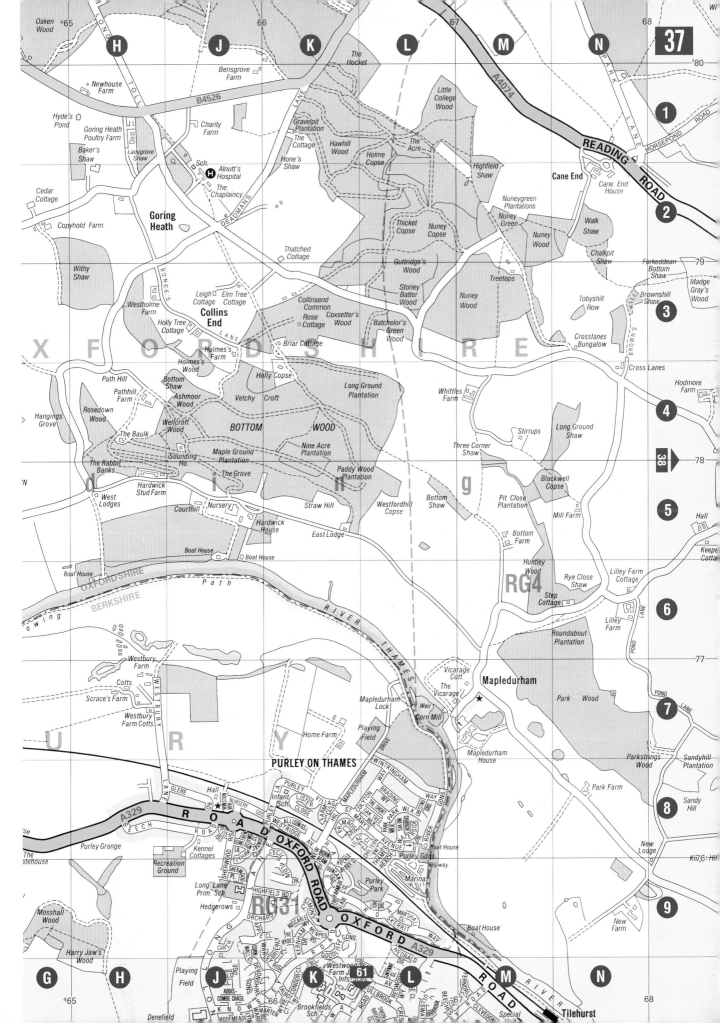

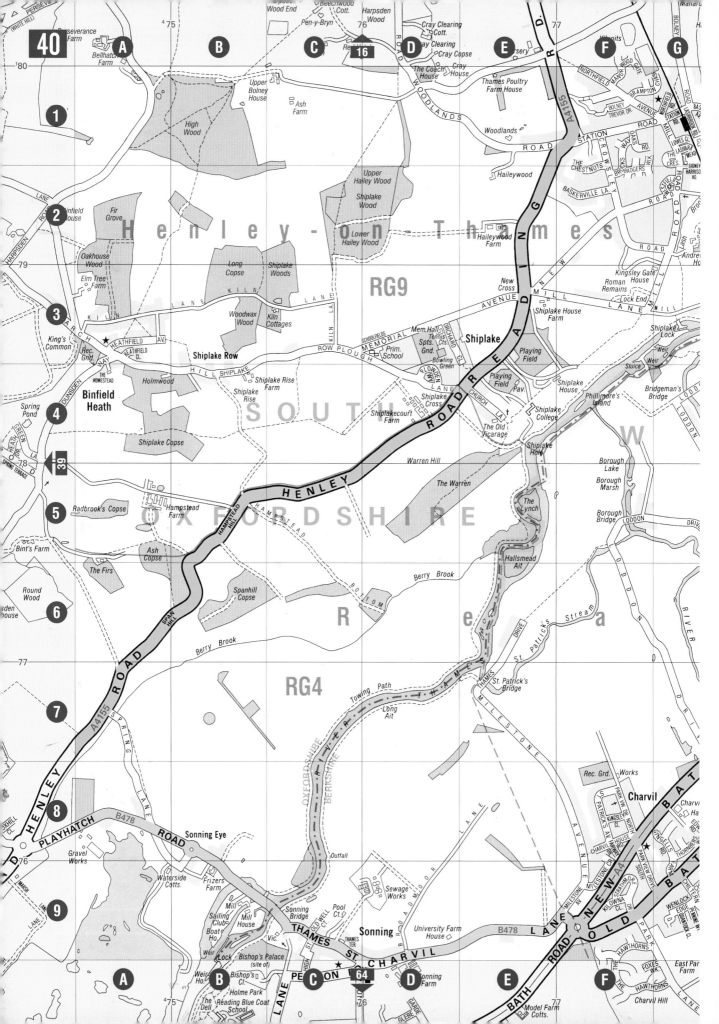

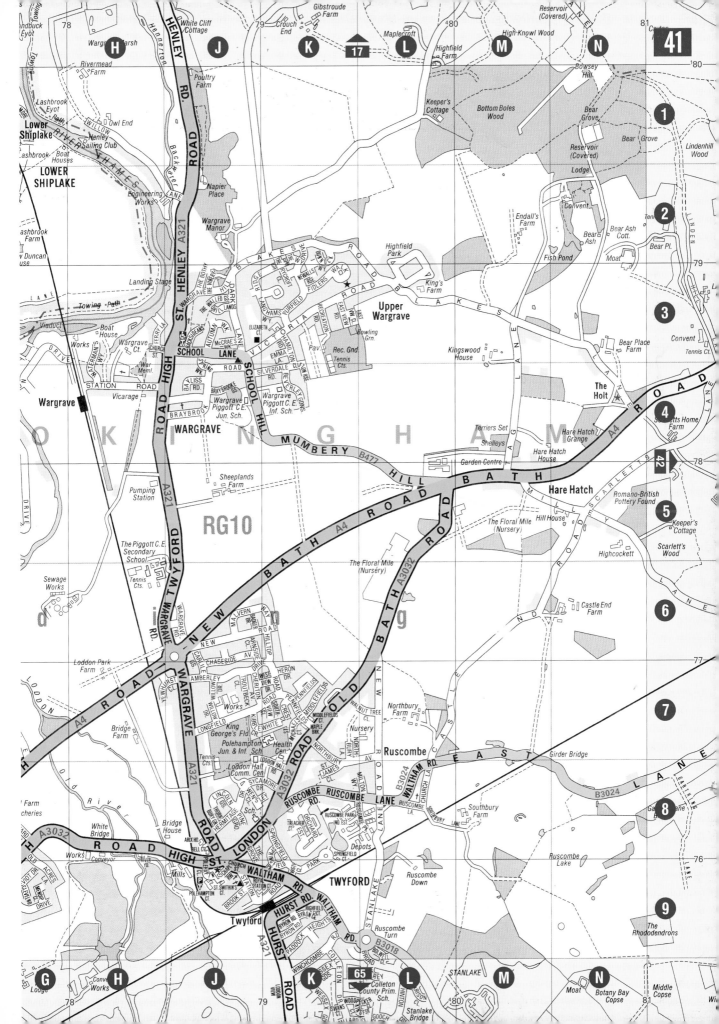

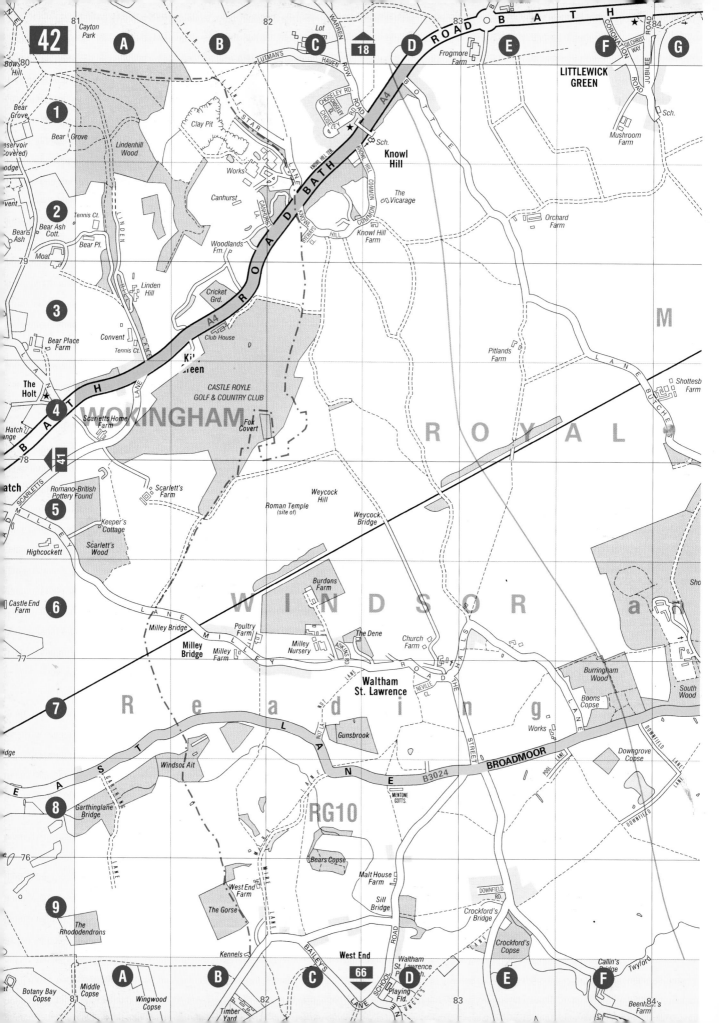

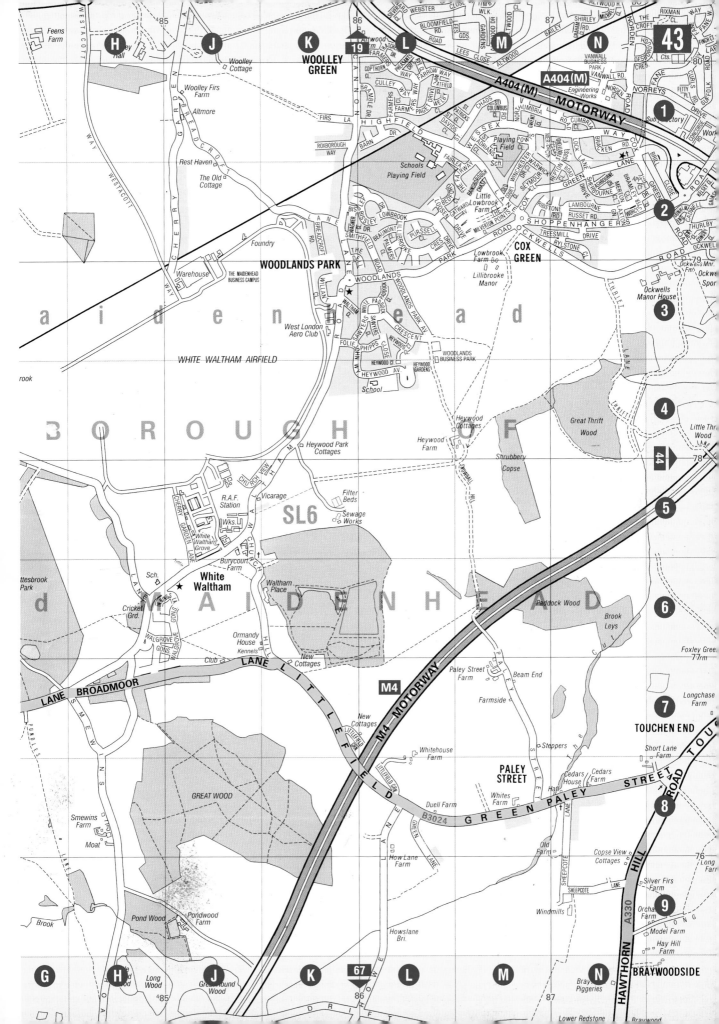

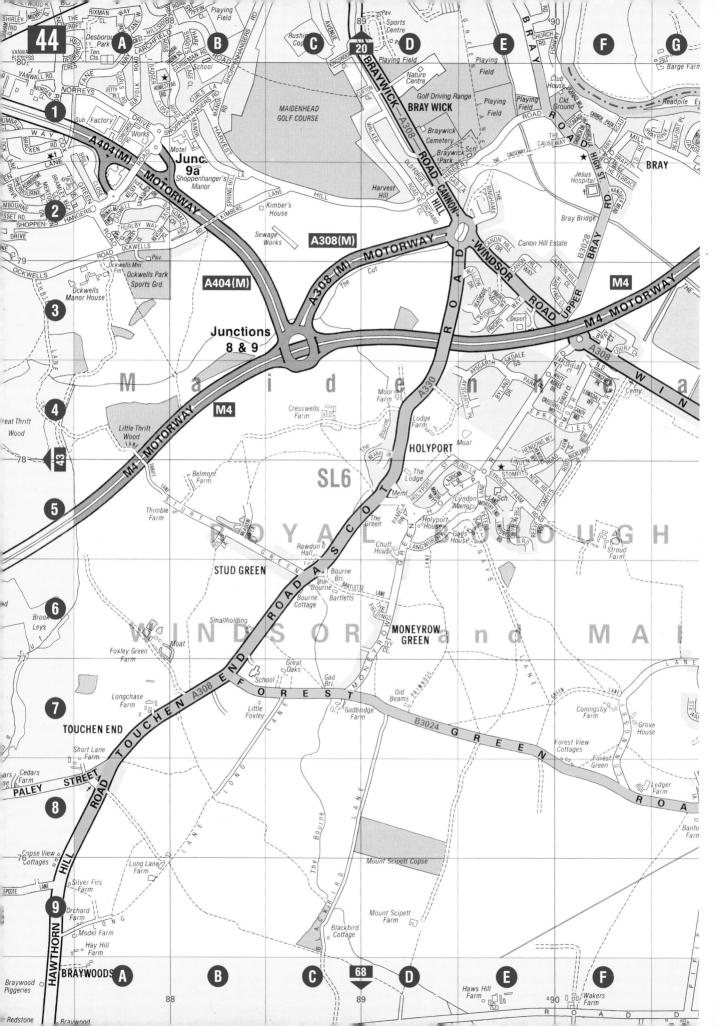

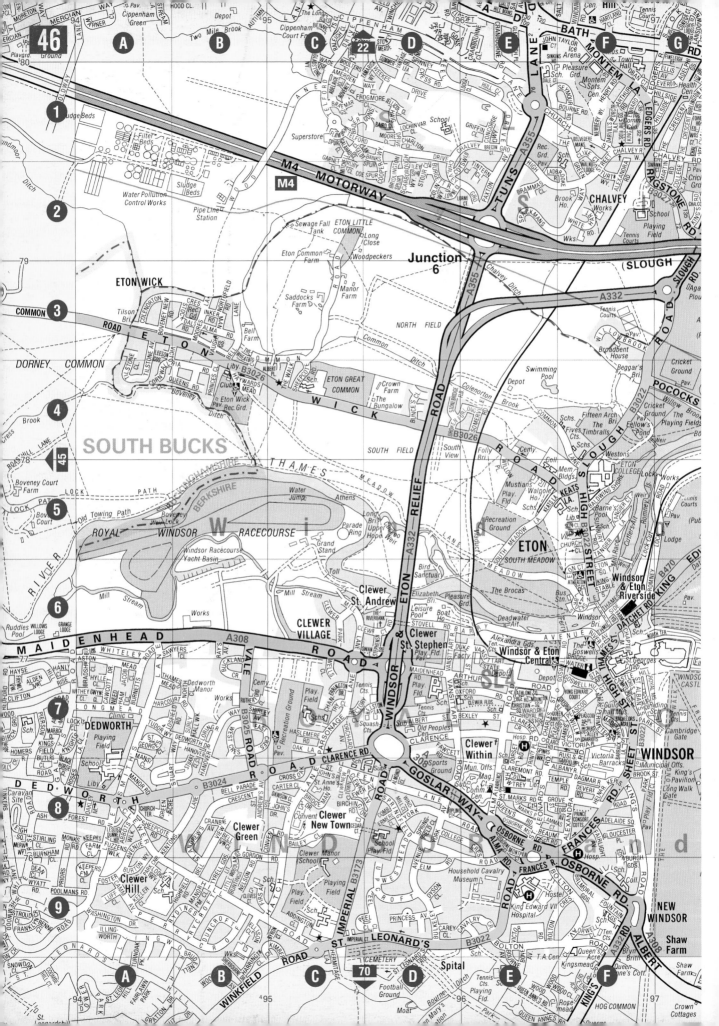

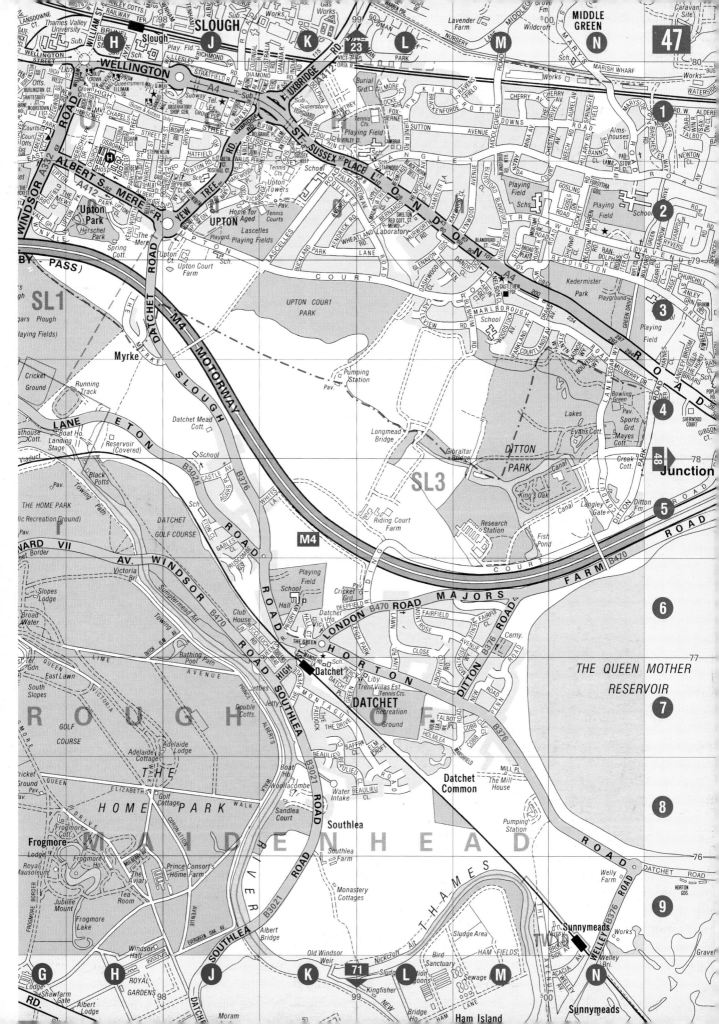

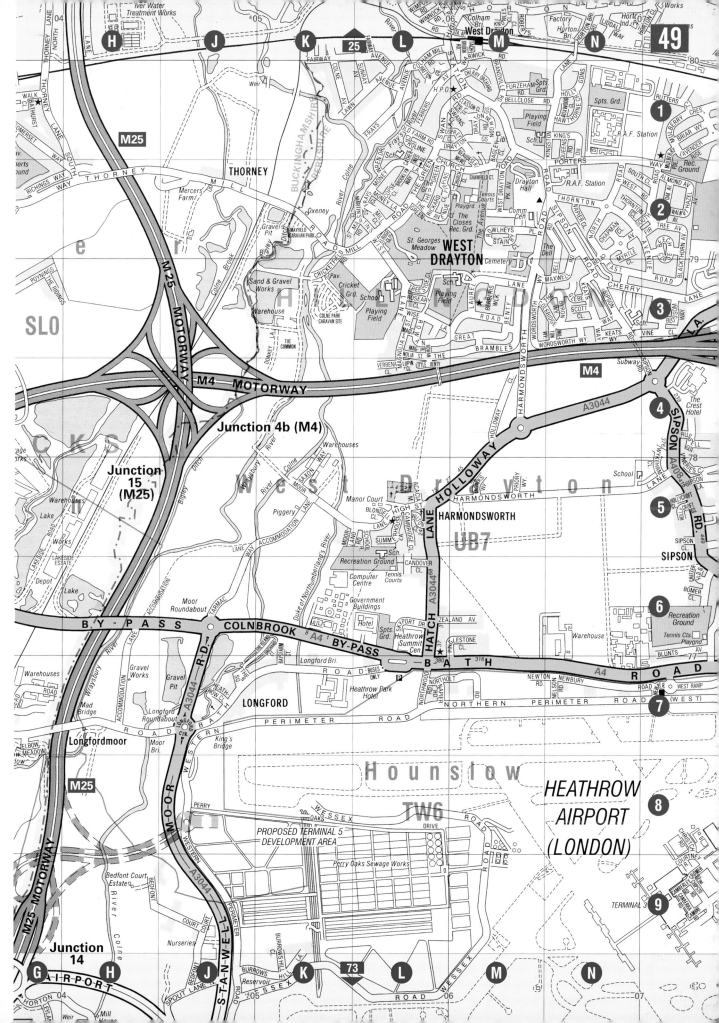

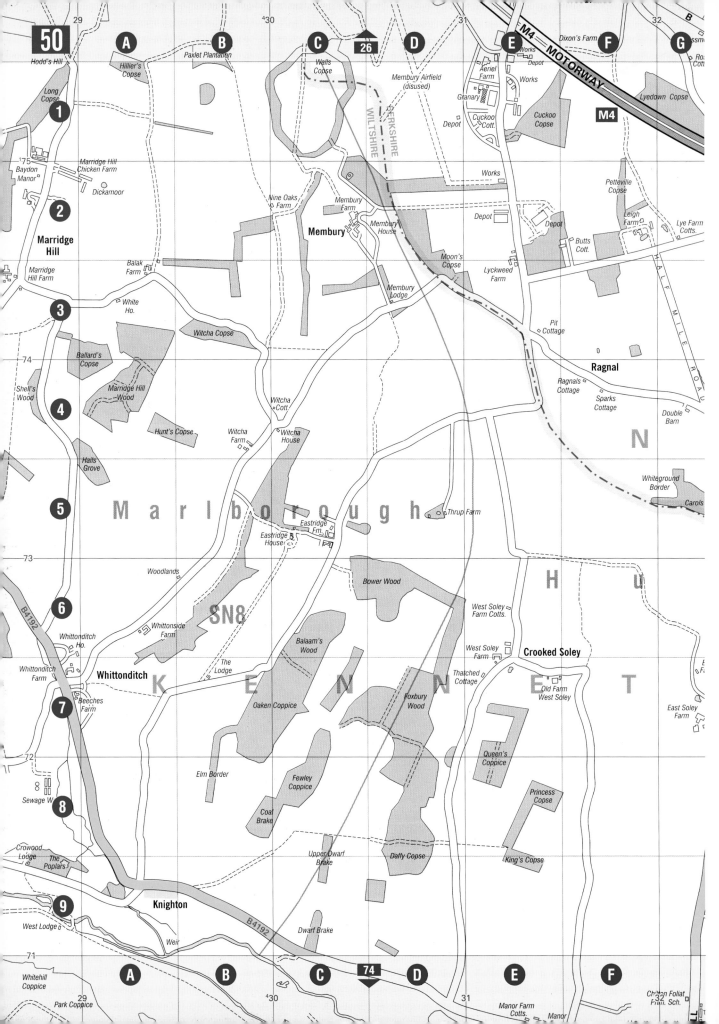

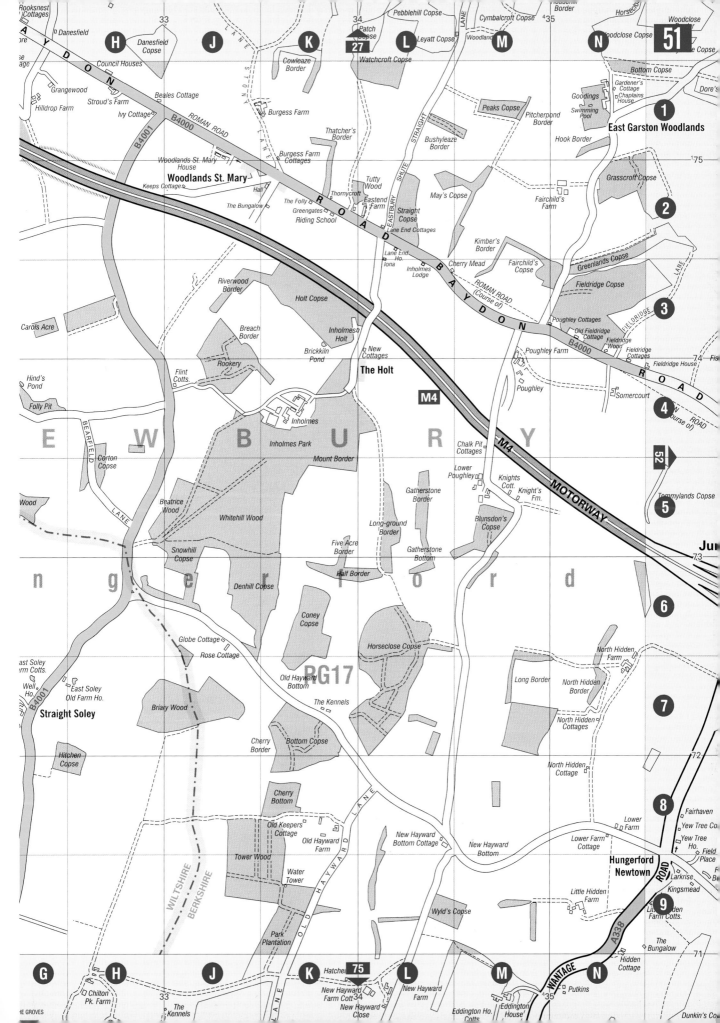

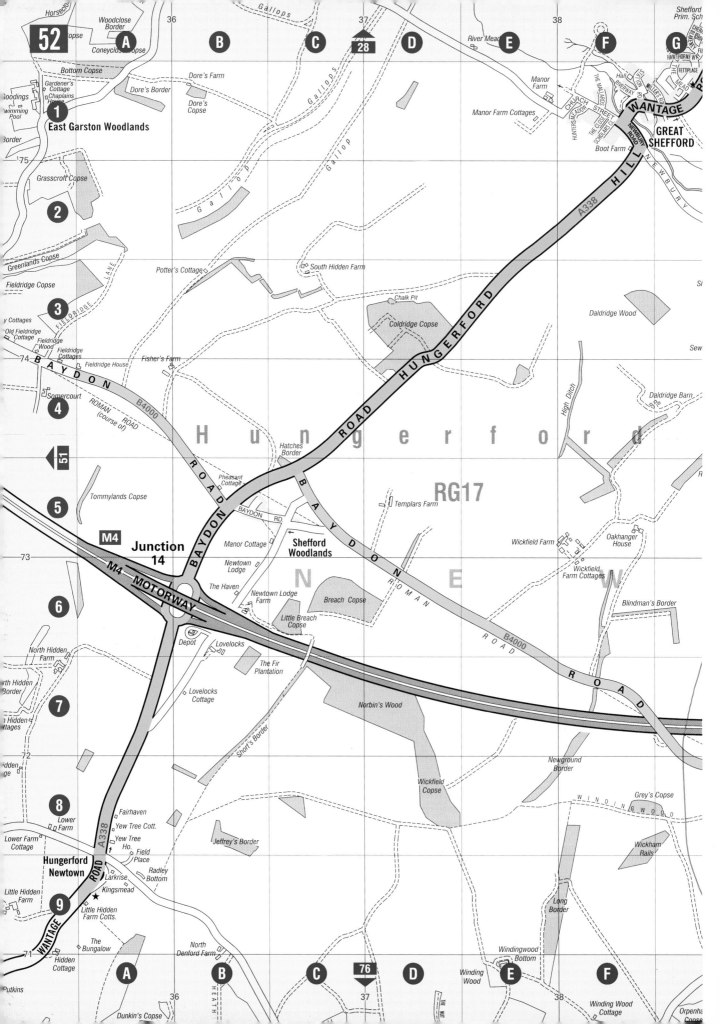

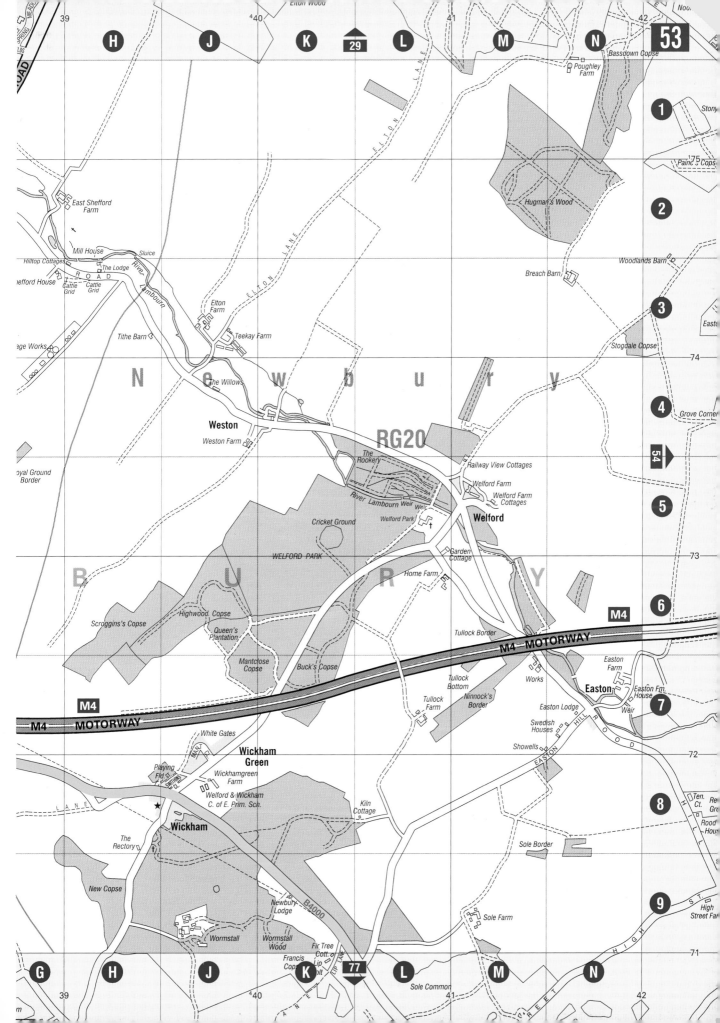

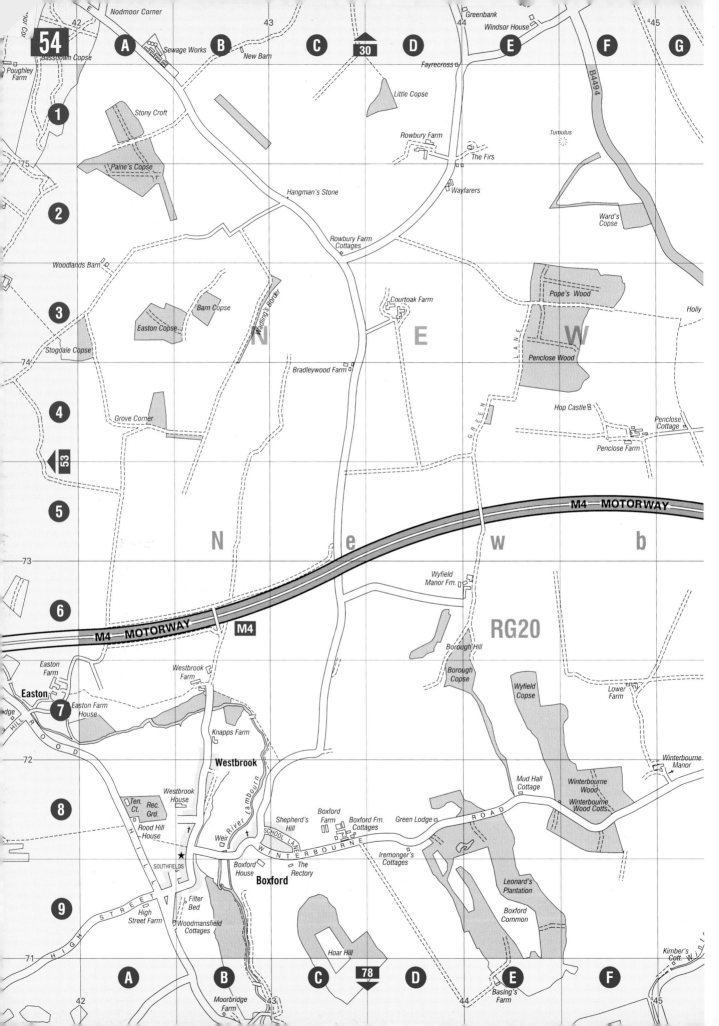

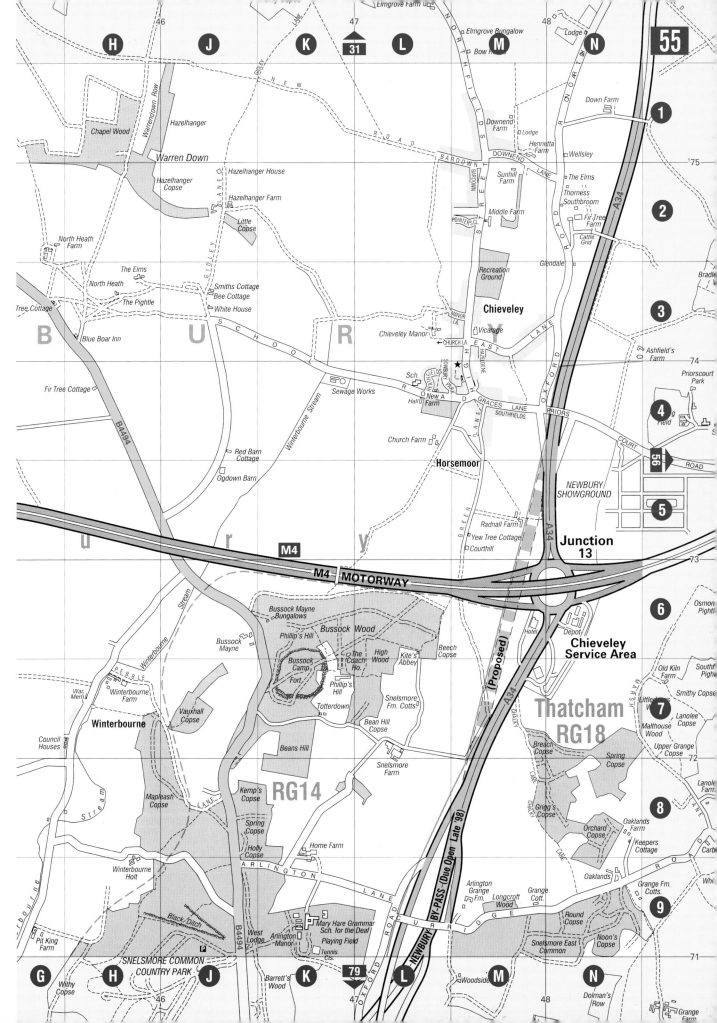

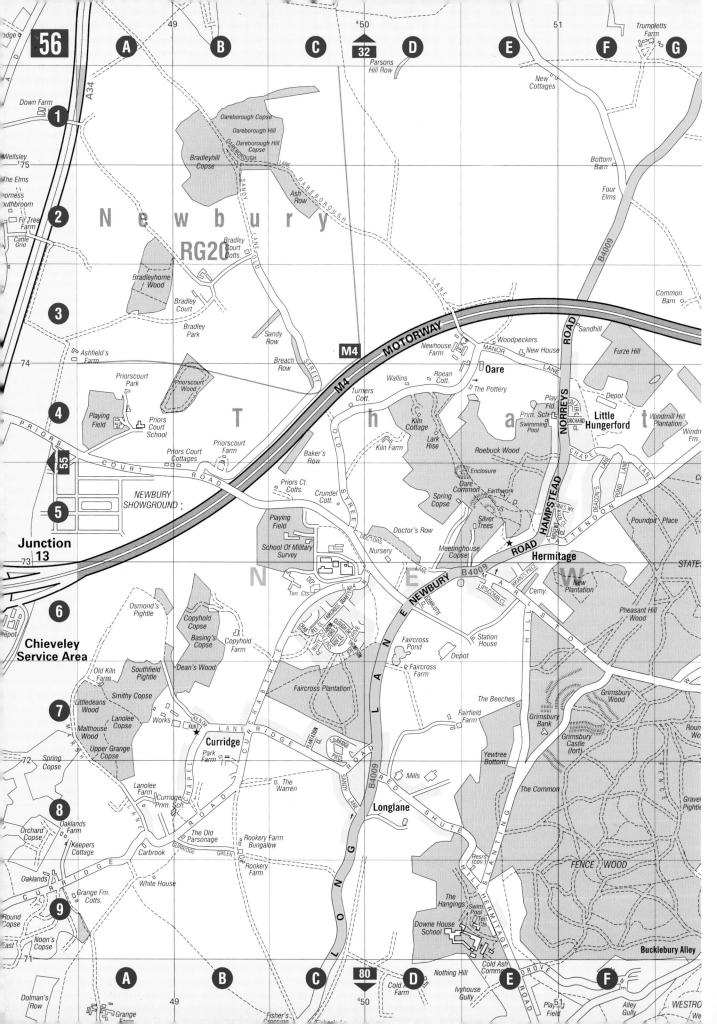

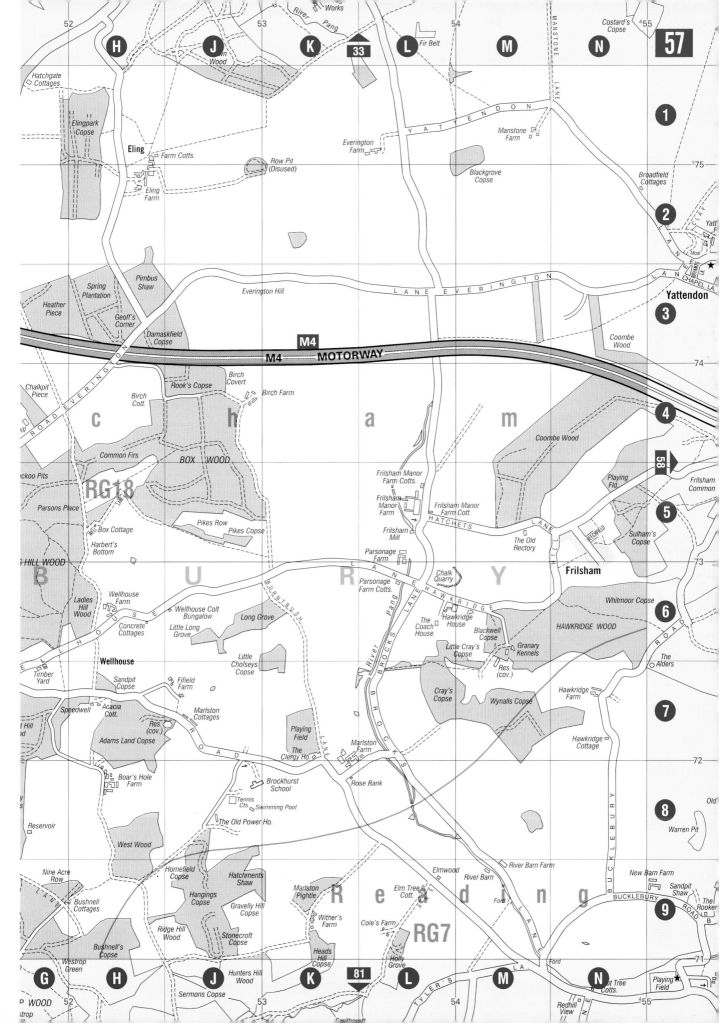

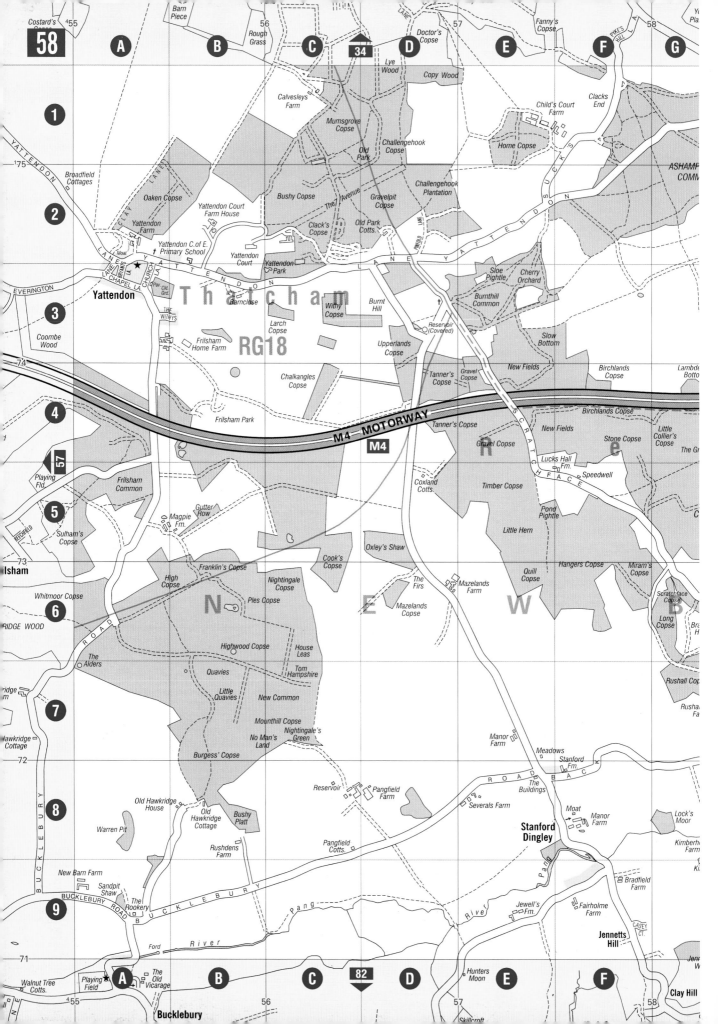

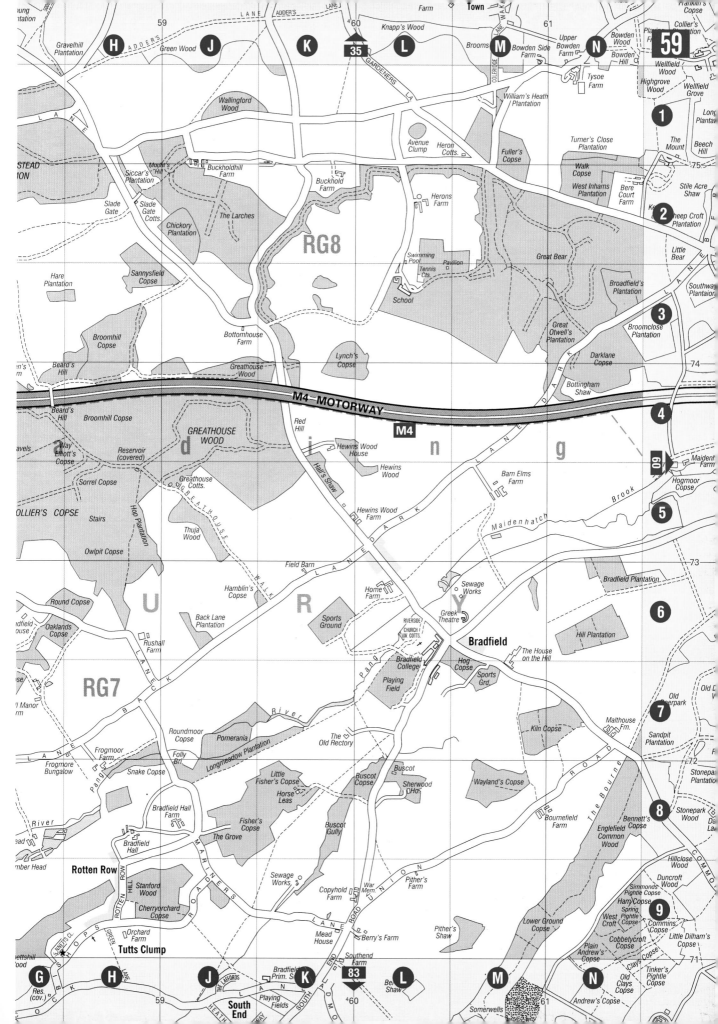

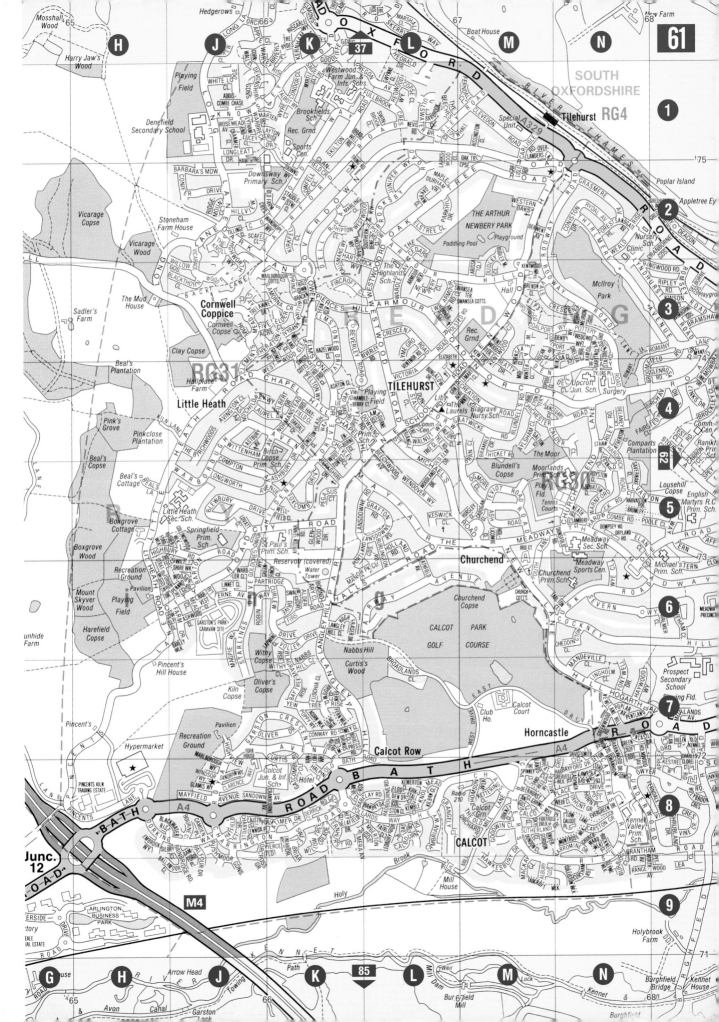

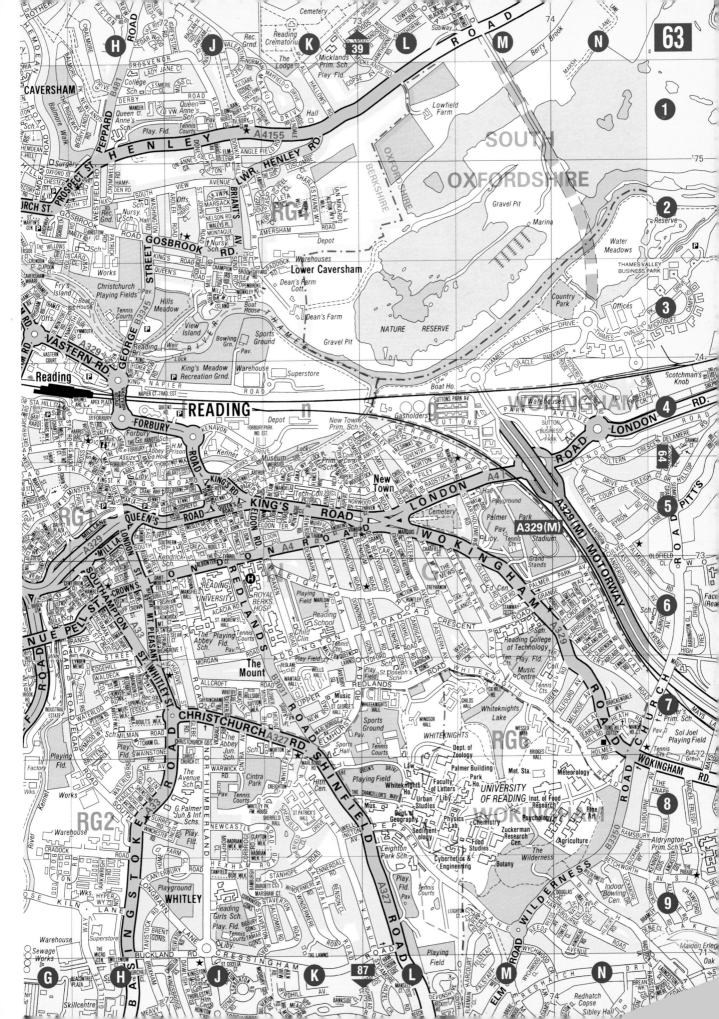

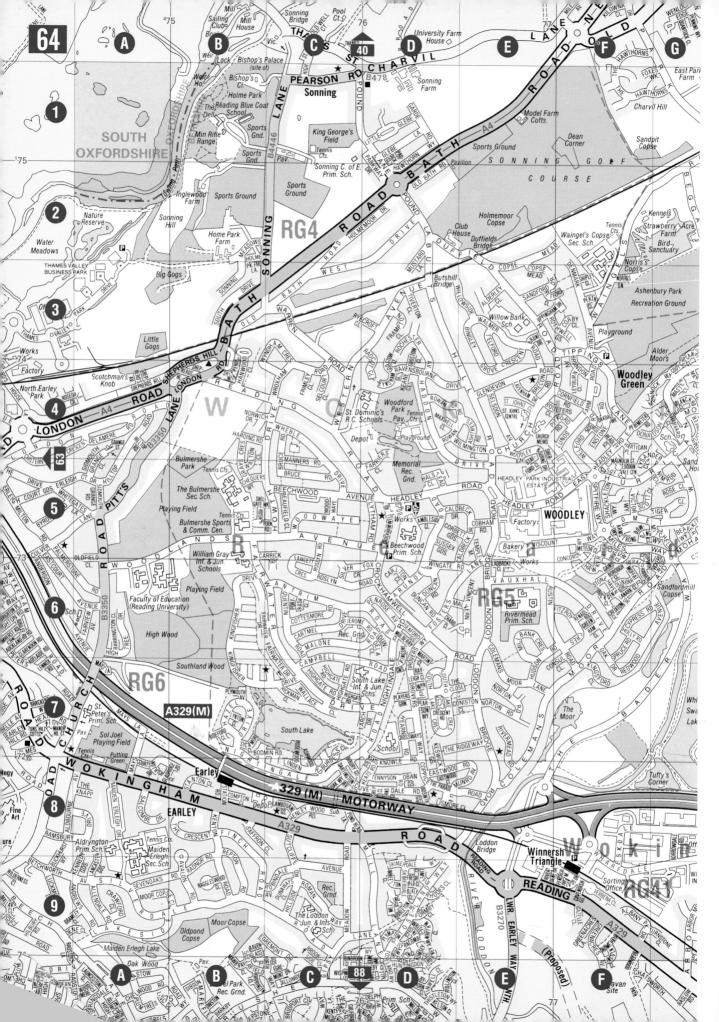

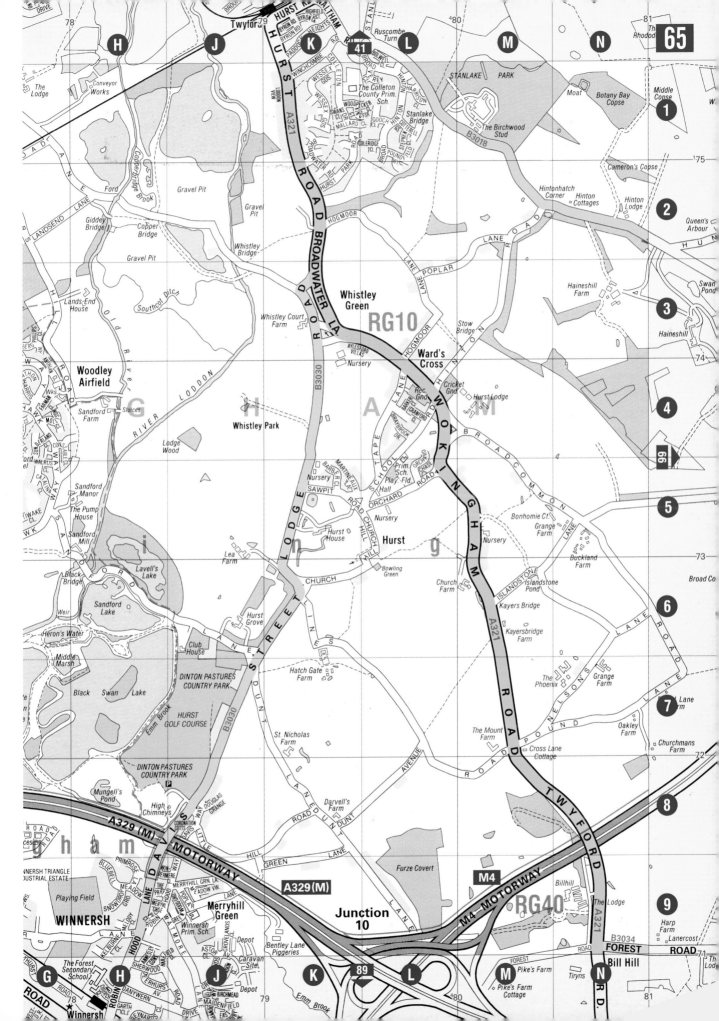

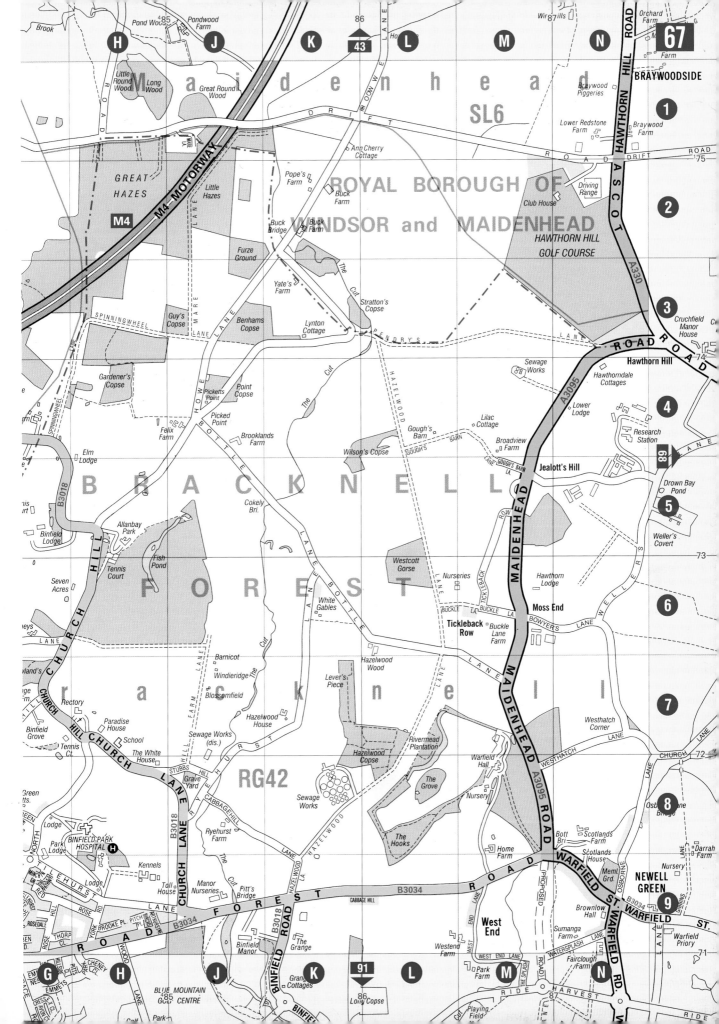

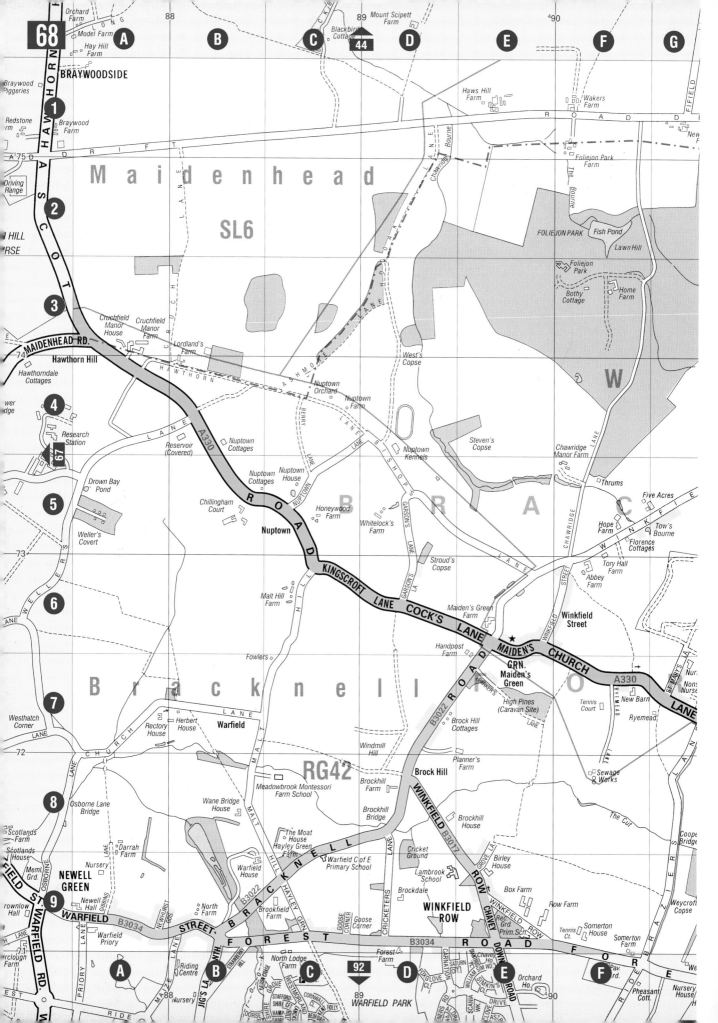

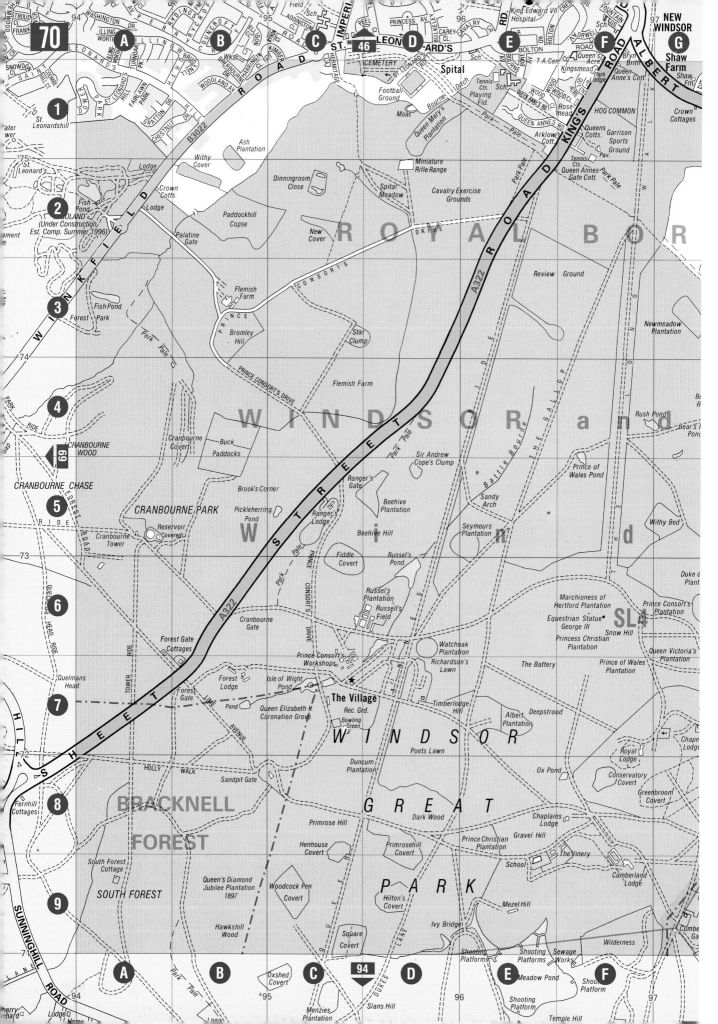

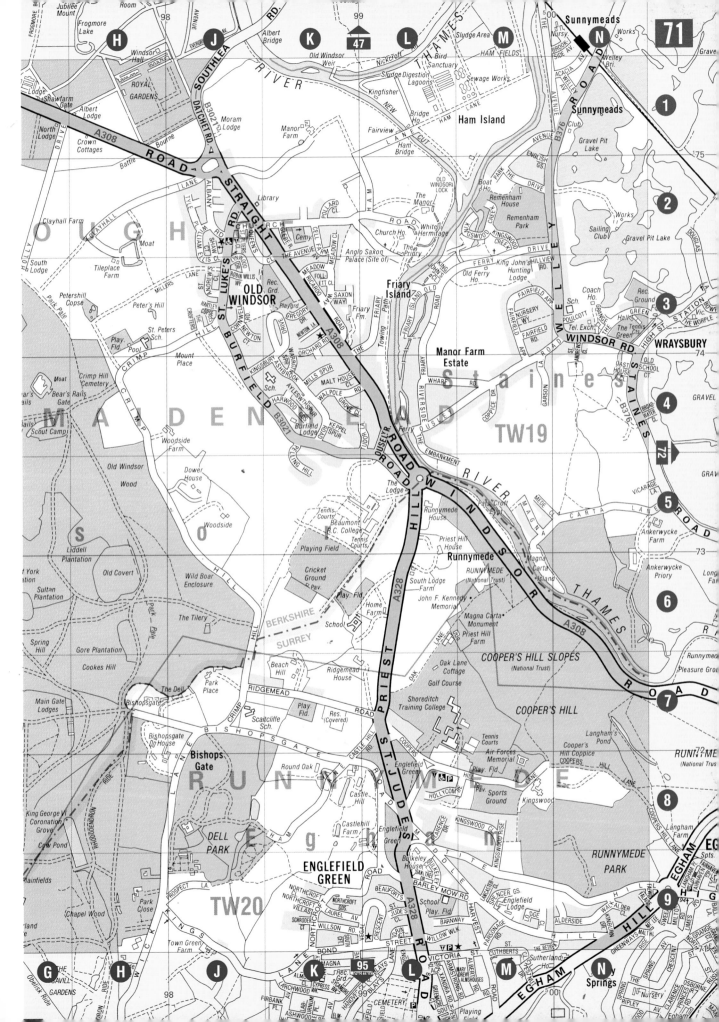

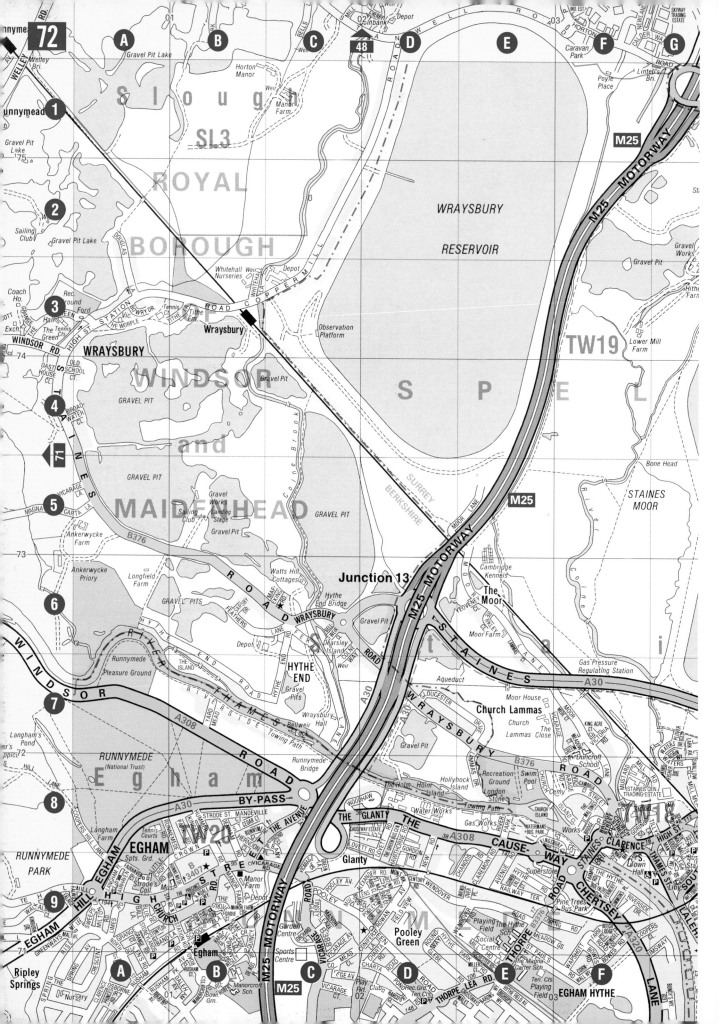

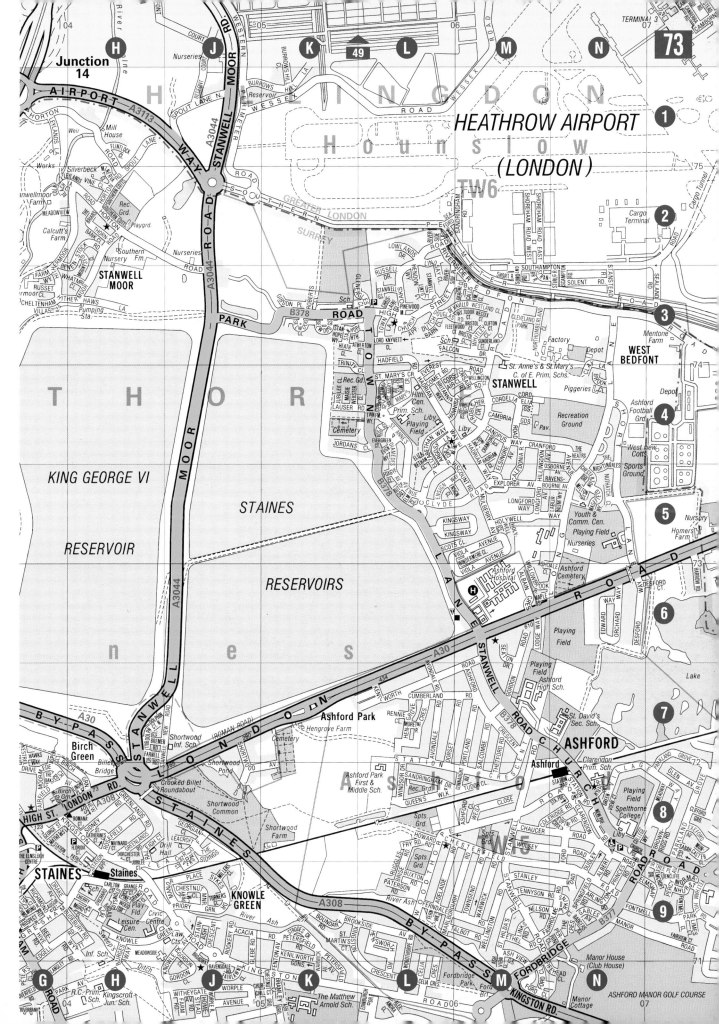

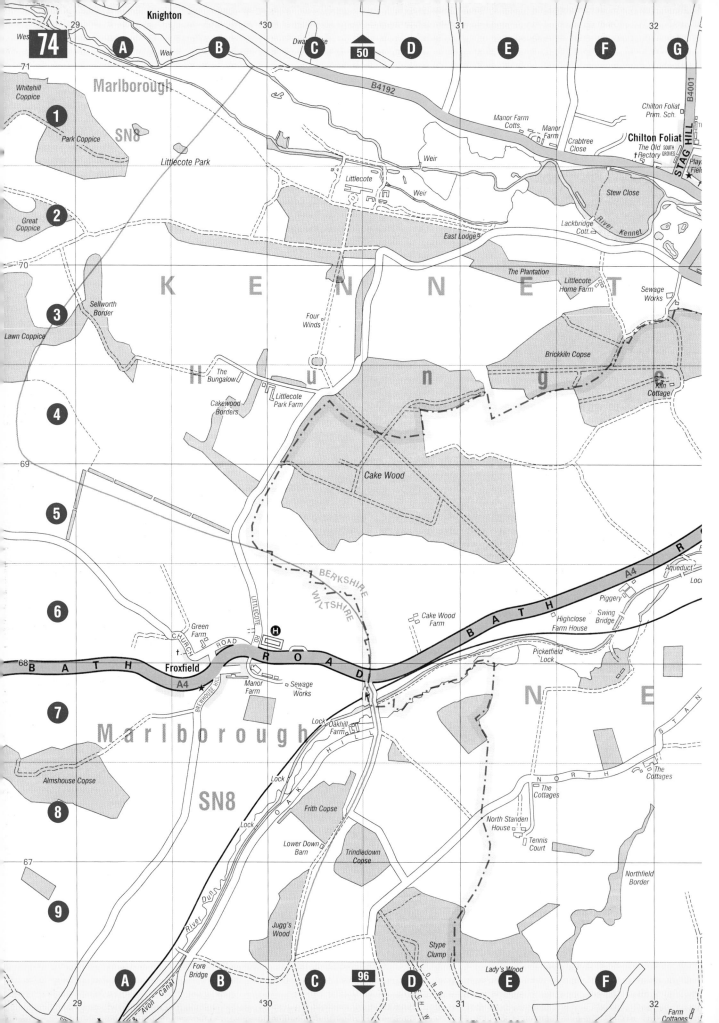

Knighton

A   B   C   **50**   D   E   F   G

West

Whitehill
Coppice

Marlborough

SN8

1

Park Coppice

Littlecote Park

2

Great
Coppice

70

3

Sellworth
Border

Lawn Coppice

The
Bungalow

Cakewood
Borders

Littlecote
Park Farm

4

5

6

Green
Farm

CHURCH

Froxfield

A4

BREWHOUSE HILL

Manor
Farm

Sewage
Works

7

Marlborough

Almshouse Copse

SN8

8

67

9

A   B   Fore
Bridge   C   **96**   D   E   F

29   30   31   32

Weir

Dwarfacre

B4192

Littlecote

Weir

Weir

East Lodge

Manor Farm
Cotts.

Manor
Farm

Crabtree
Close

Chilton Foliat
Prim. Sch.

Chilton Foliat

The Old SOUTH
† Rectory GROVES

STAG HILL

Play.
Field

Stew Close

River   Kennel

Lackbridge
Cott.

B4001

K   E   N   N   E   T

The Plantation

Littlecote
Home Farm

Sewage
Works

Four
Winds

H   u   n   g   e   r

Brickkiln Copse

Kiln
Cottage

Cake Wood

BERKSHIRE

WILTSHIRE

Cake Wood
Farm

Highclose
Farm House

Picketfield
Lock

Aqueduct

R

BATH   A4

Piggery

Swing
Bridge

N   E

N   O   R   T   H

Lock

Oakhill
Farm

OAK   HILL

Frith Copse

Lower Down
Barn

Jugg's
Wood

River   Dun

Fore
Bridge

Kennet & Avon Canal

Trindledown
Copse

North Standen
House

The
Cottages

Tennis
Court

Style
Clump

Lady's Wood

The
Cottages

Northfield
Border

S   T   A   N

Farm
Cottages

Lock

Lock

Lock

River

H LONG HEDGE

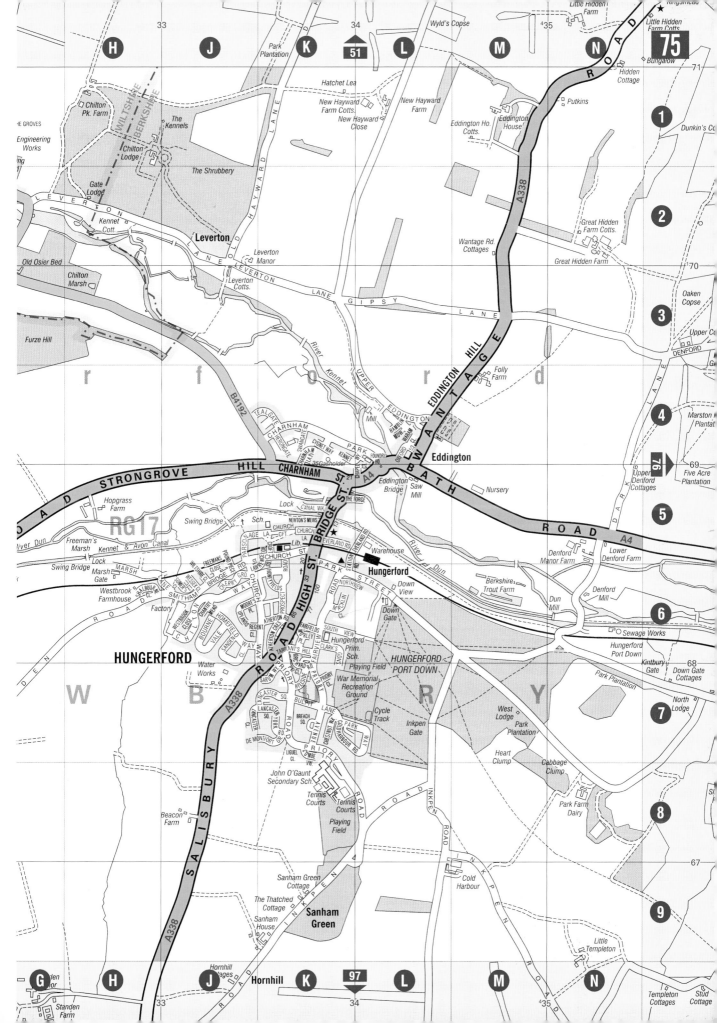

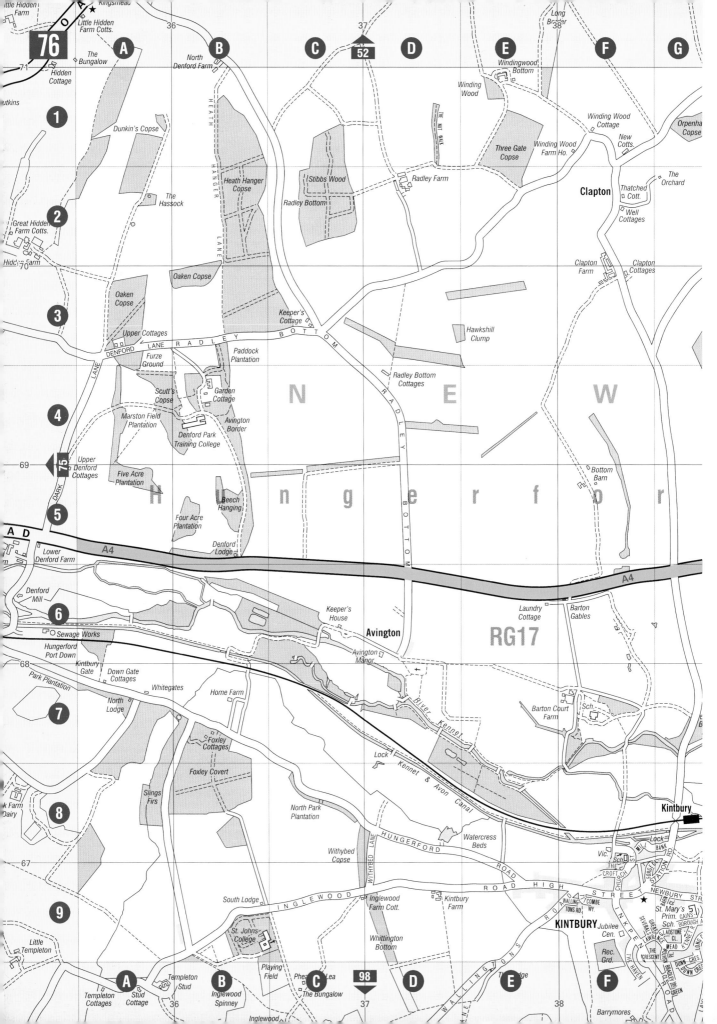

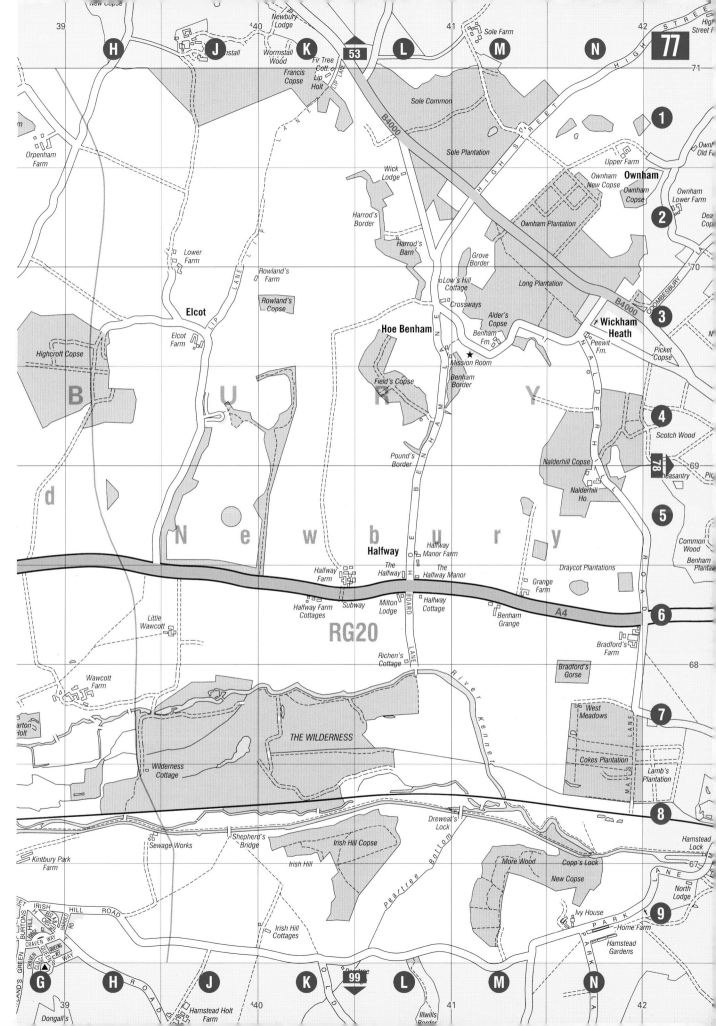

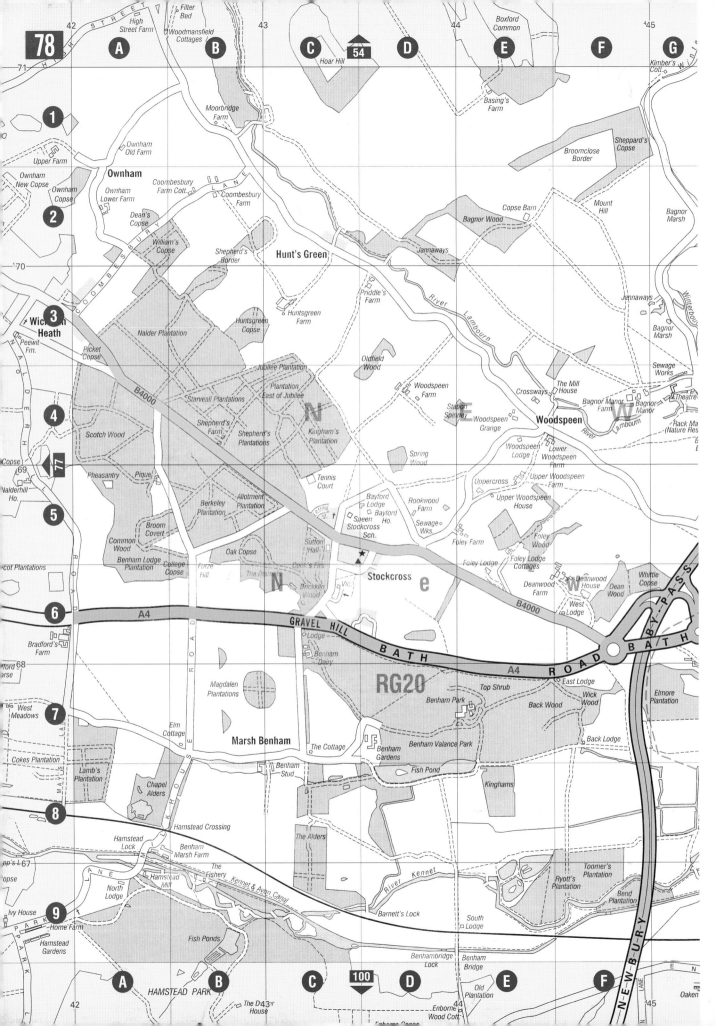

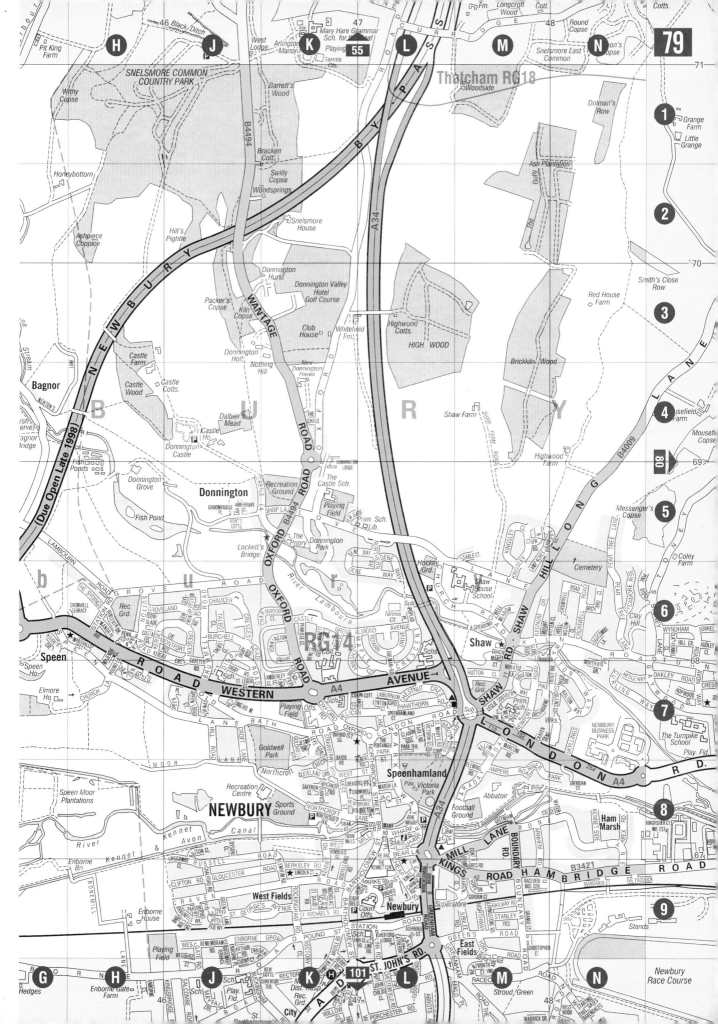

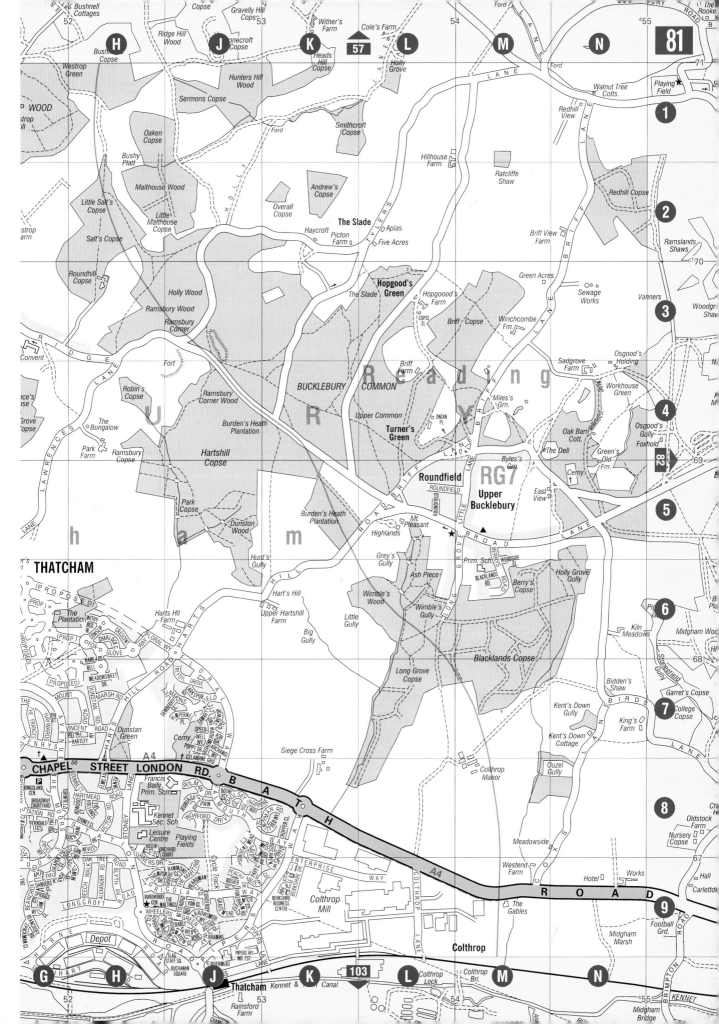

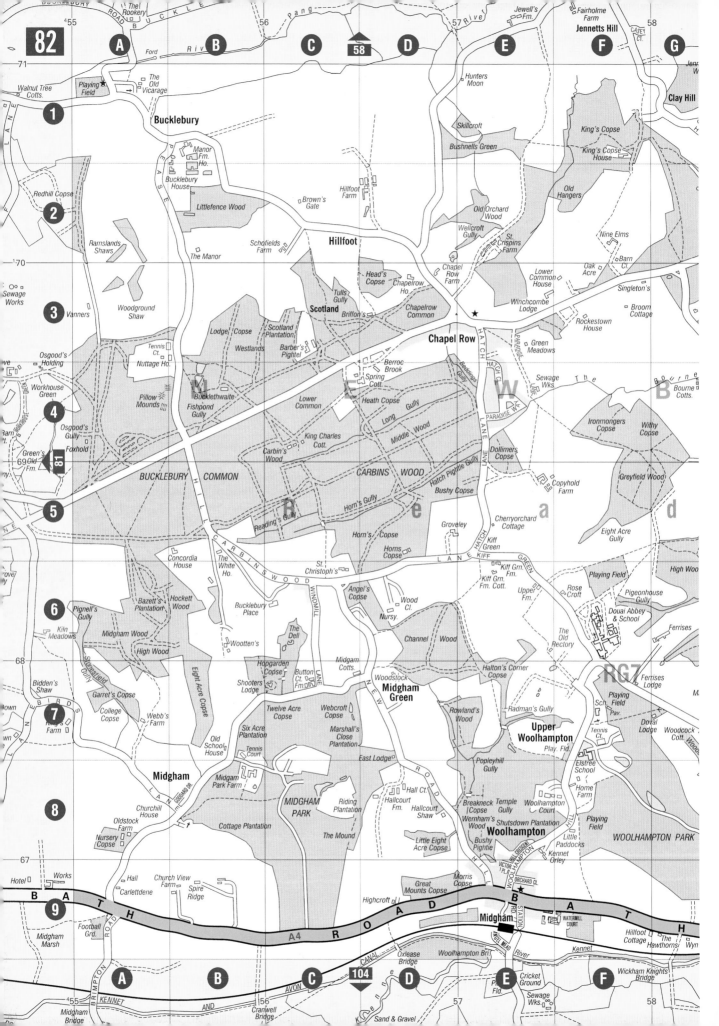

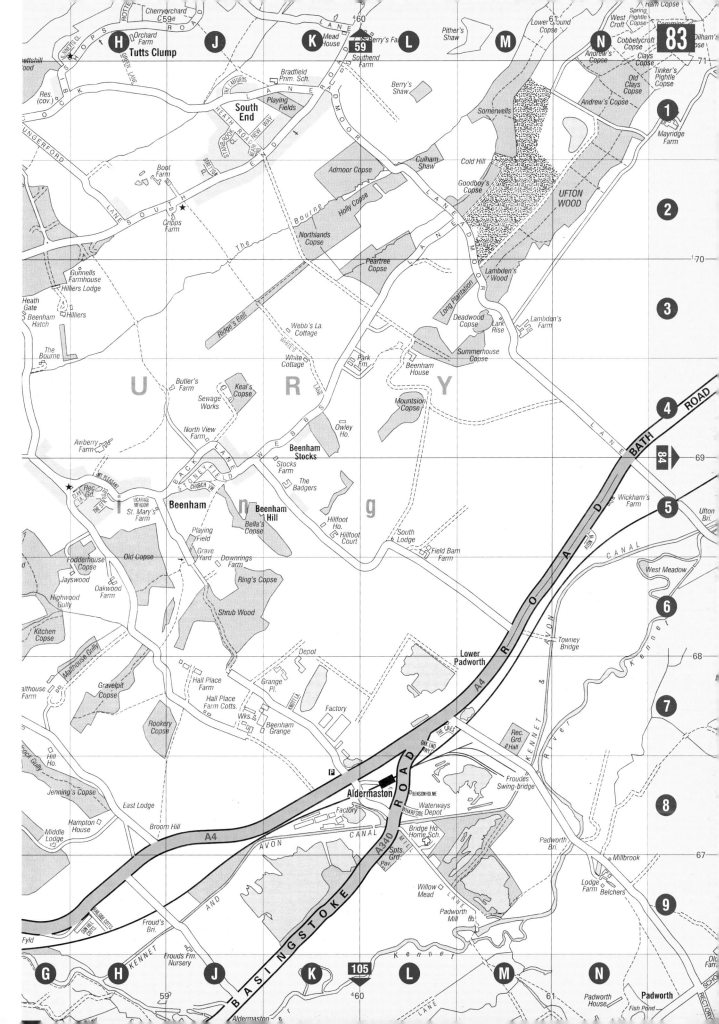

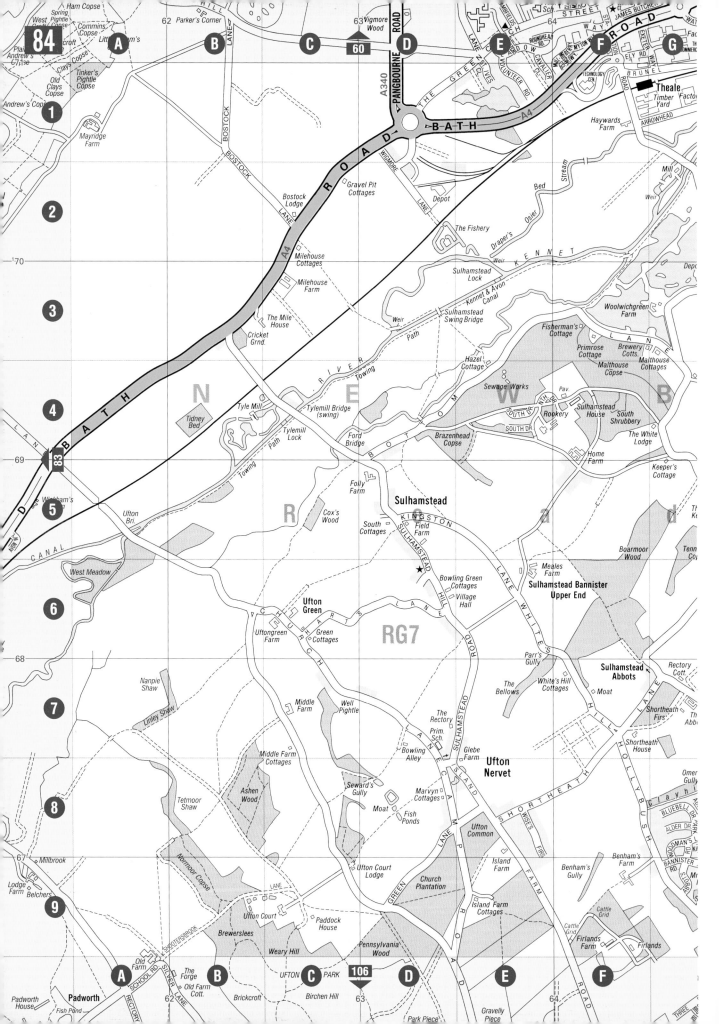

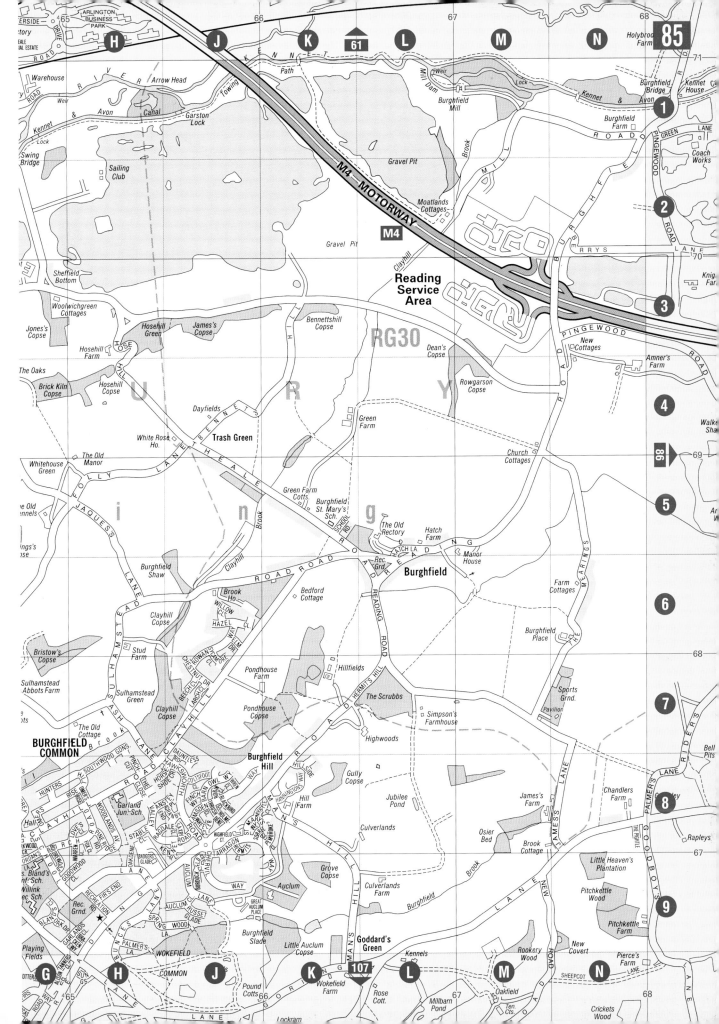

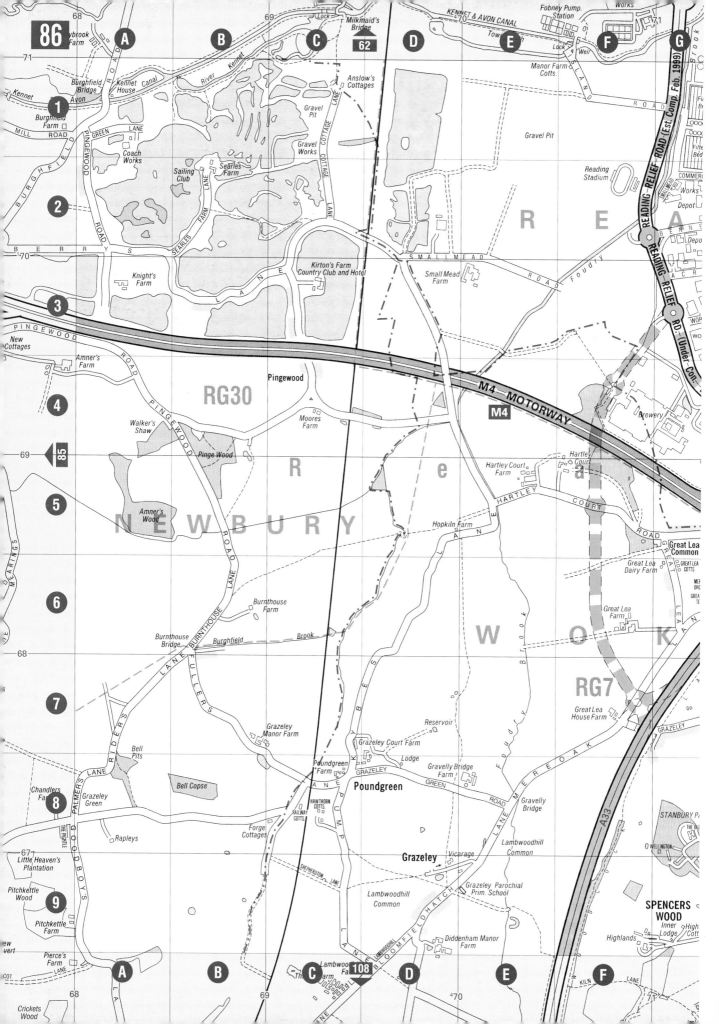

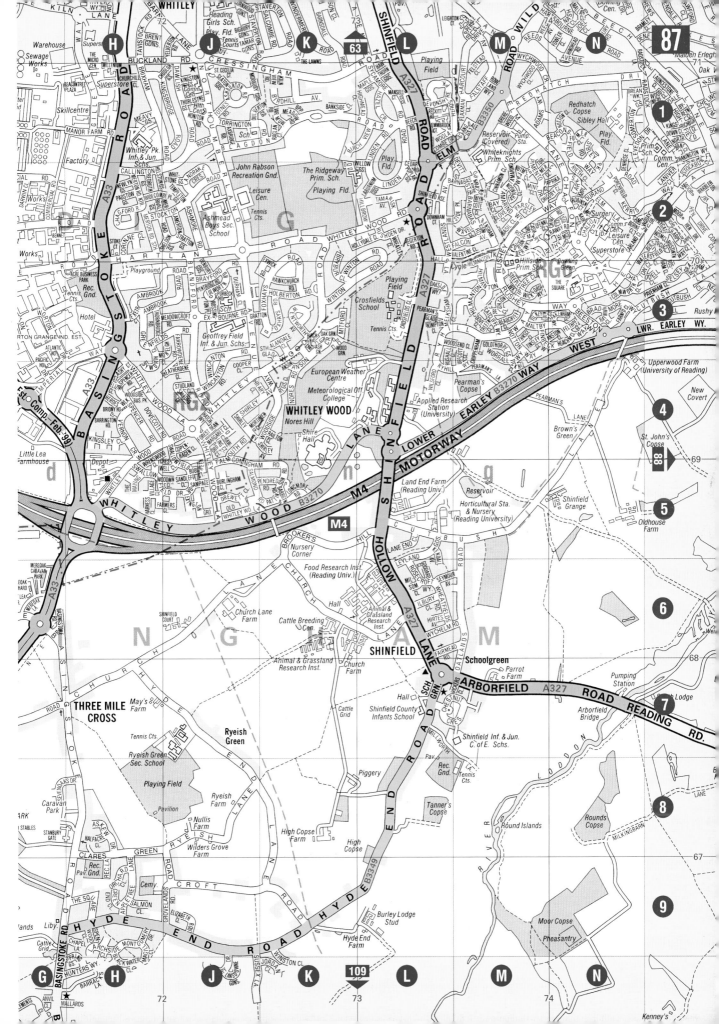

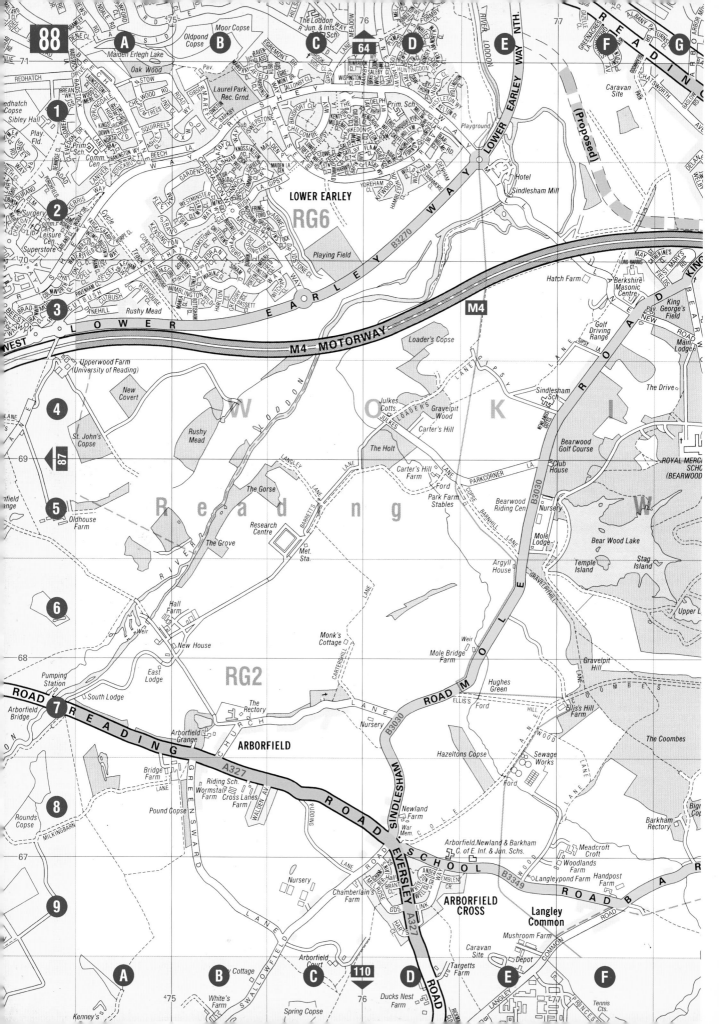

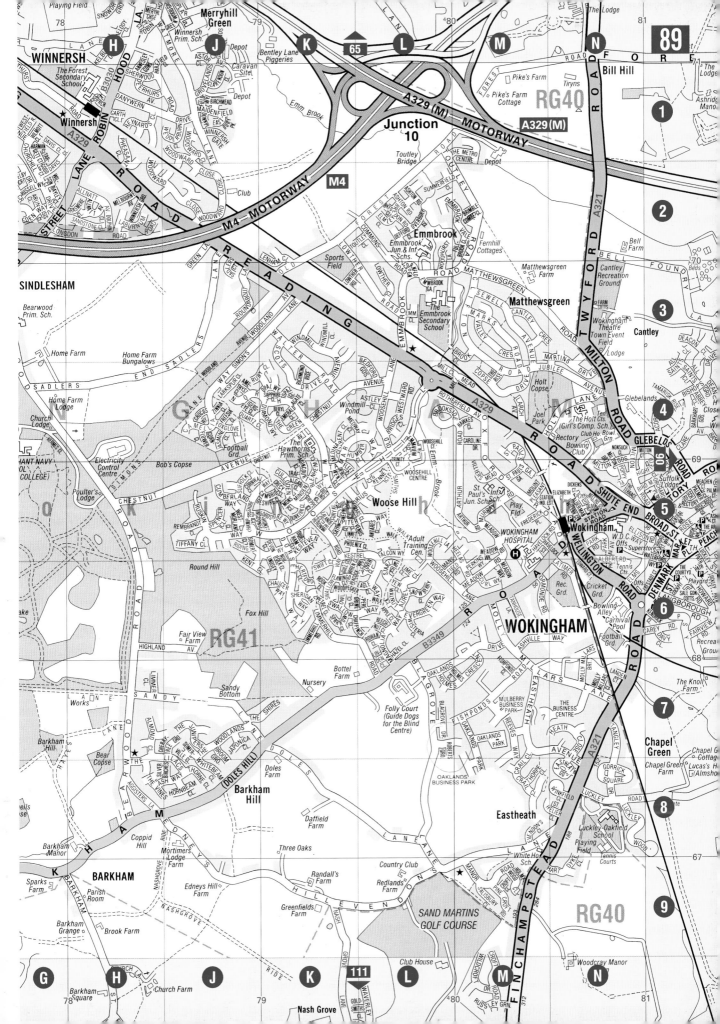

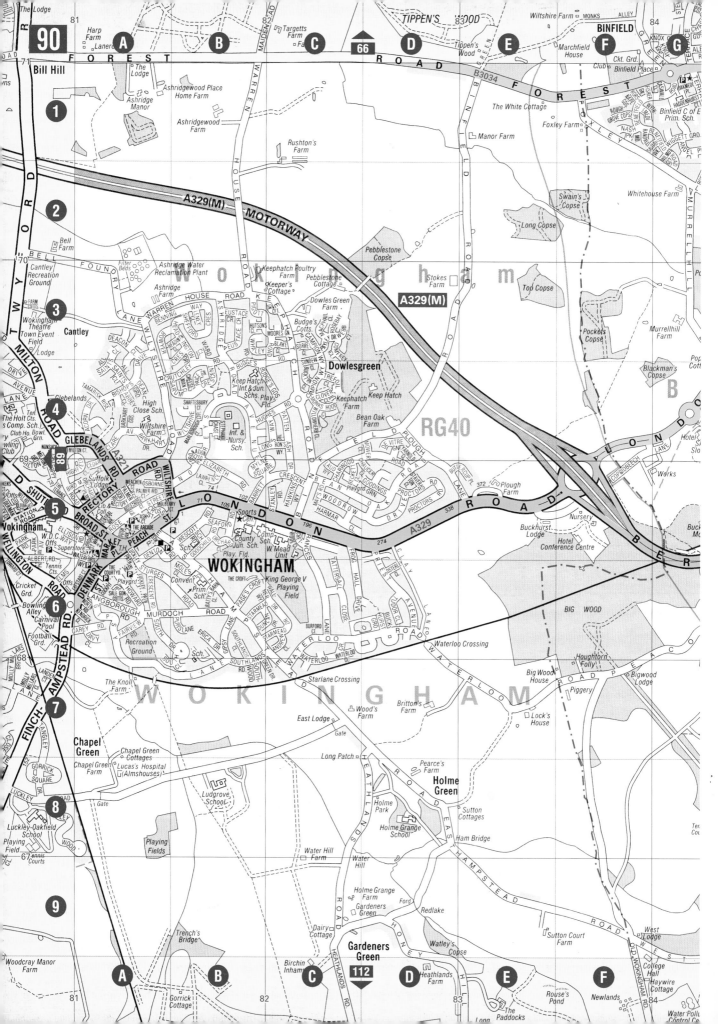

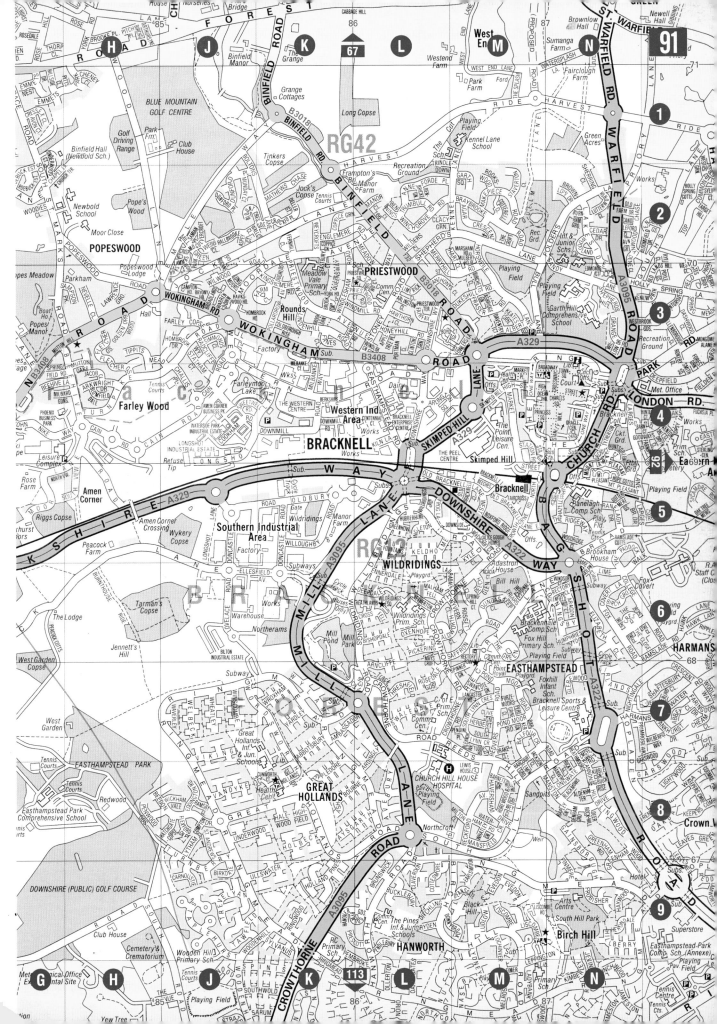

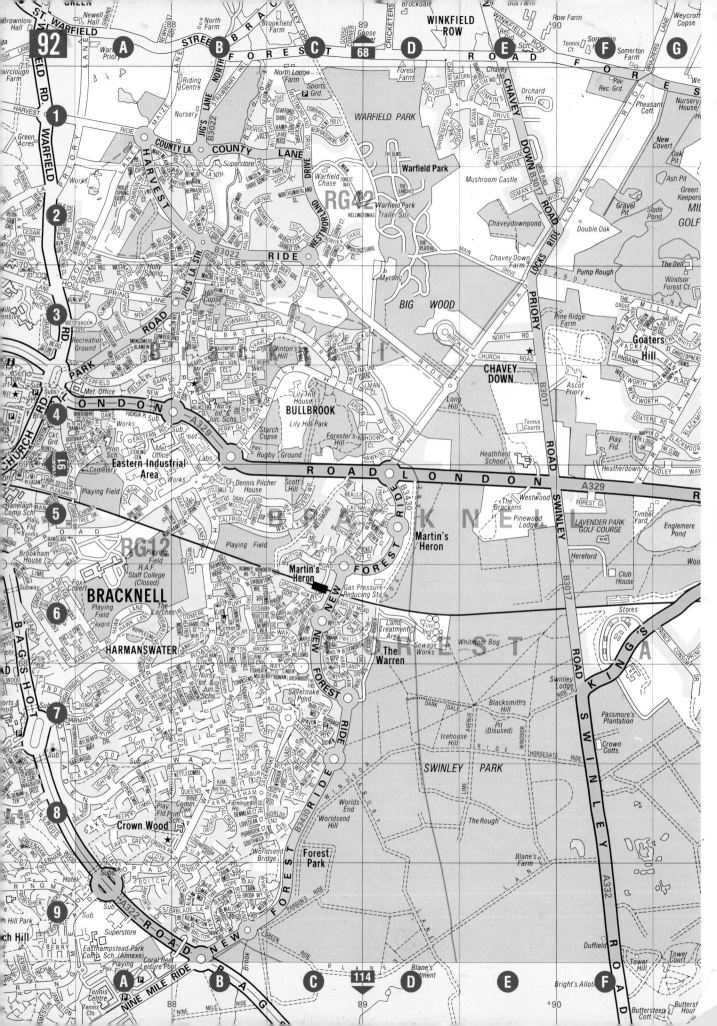

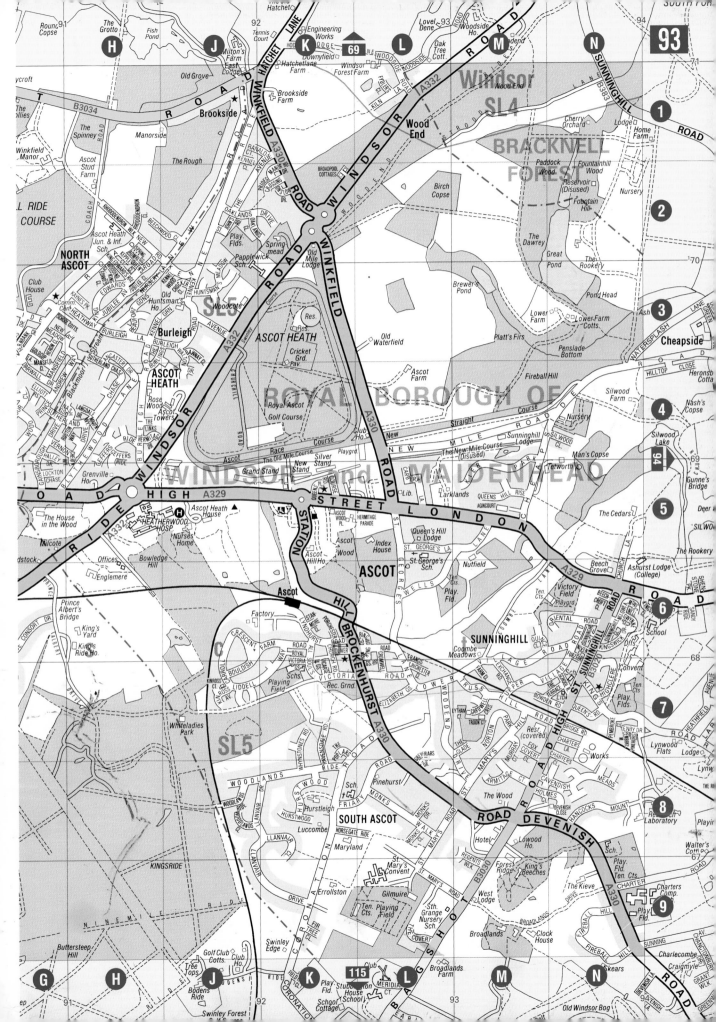

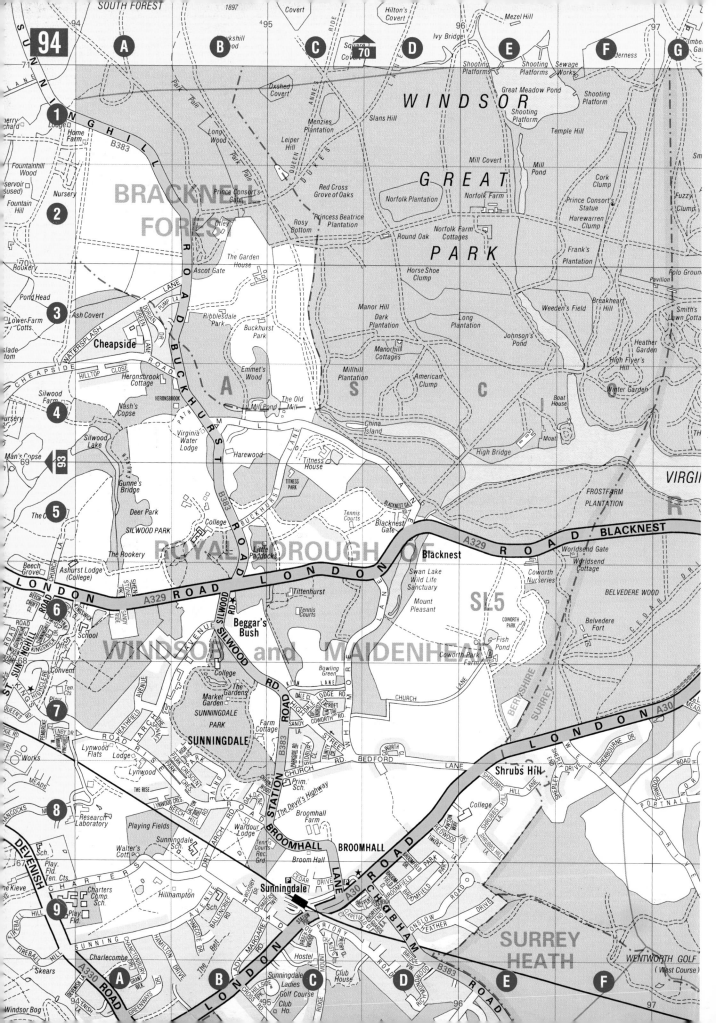

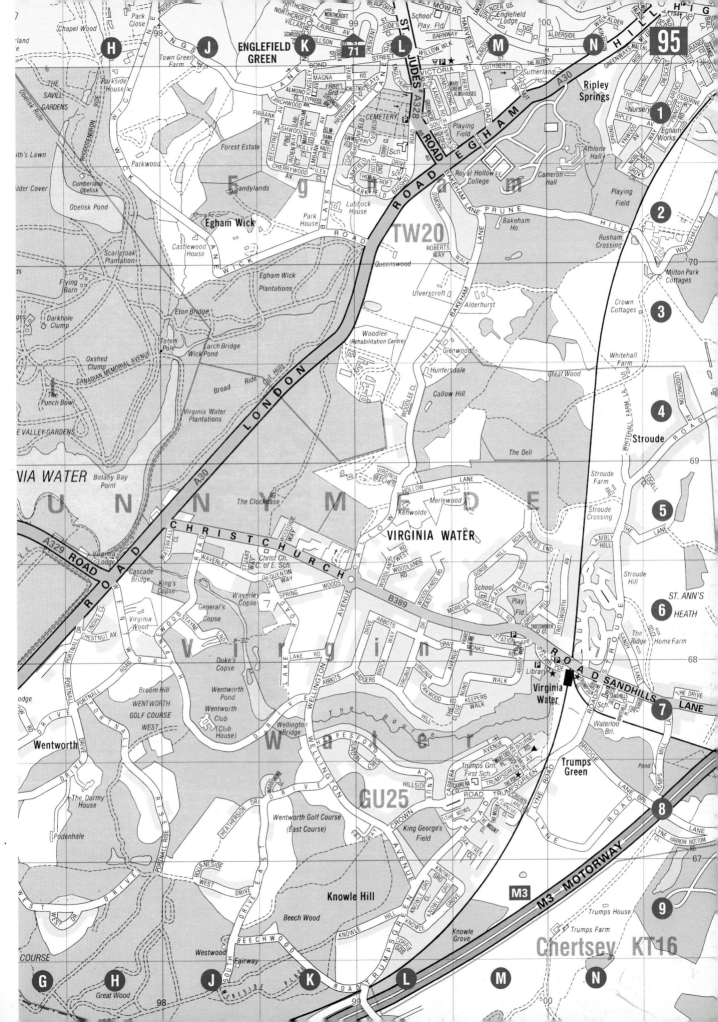

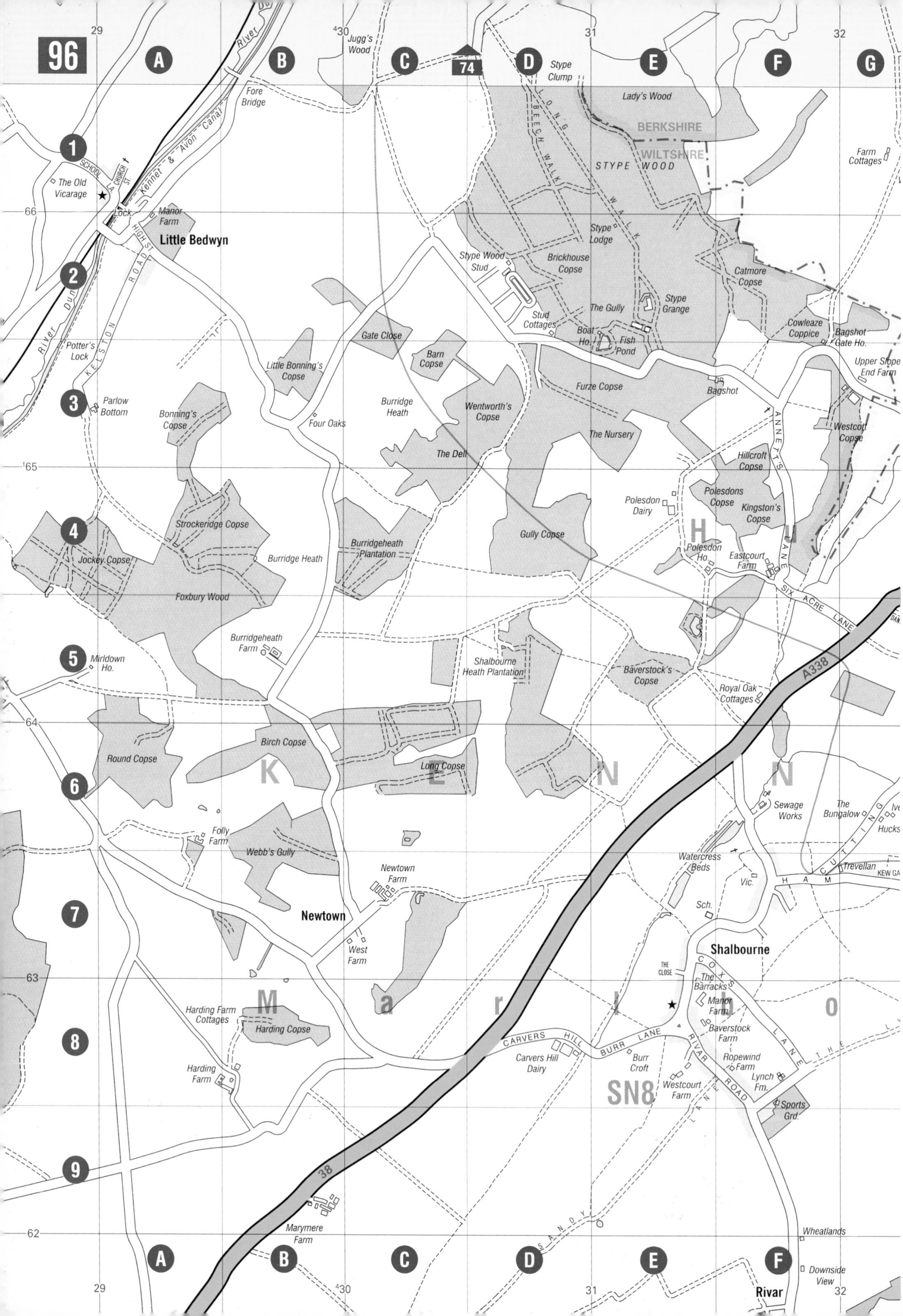

A B C D E F G

1

2

3

4

5

6

7

8

9

29   430   31   32

River Dun

Kennet & Avon Canal

Fore Bridge

Jugg's Wood

74

Stype Clump

Lady's Wood

BERKSHIRE

WILTSHIRE

STYPE WOOD

Farm Cottages

66

The Old Vicarage

School

Church St

Lock

HIGH ST

Manor Farm

Little Bedwyn

Stype Lodge

LONG BEECH WALK

Brickhouse Copse

Stype Wood Stud

Catmore Copse

River Dun

Potter's Lock

KELSTON ROAD

Gate Close

The Gully

Stype Grange

Cowleaze Coppice

Bagshot Gate Ho.

Parlow Bottom

Little Bonning's Copse

Barn Copse

Stud Cottages

Boat Ho.

Fish Pond

Bagshot

Upper Slope End Farm

3

Bonning's Copse

Burridge Heath

Wentworth's Copse

Furze Copse

Westcott Copse

65

Four Oaks

The Dell

The Nursery

Hillcroft Copse

Strockeridge Copse

Burridge Heath

Polesdon Dairy

Polesdons Copse

ANNETT'S LANE

4

Jockey Copse

Burridgeheath Plantation

Gully Copse

Polesdon Ho.

Kingston's Copse

H

Foxbury Wood

Eastcourt Farm

SIX ACRE LANE

Burridgeheath Farm

Shalbourne Heath Plantation

Baverstock's Copse

Royal Oak Cottages

A338

5

Mirldown Ho.

64

Round Copse

Birch Copse

K

L

Long Copse

N

N

Sewage Works

The Bungalow

Ivy

Hucks

6

Folly Farm

Webb's Gully

Watercress Beds

CUTTING

Trevellan

KEW GA

7

Newtown Farm

Sch.

Vic.

HAM

Newtown

West Farm

Shalbourne

THE CLOSE

The Barracks

COX'S LANE

Manor Farm

O

63

M

a

r

l

Baverstock Farm

THE LANE

8

Harding Farm Cottages

Harding Copse

CARVERS HILL

BURR LANE

Burr Croft

Ropewind Fm.

Lynch Fm.

Harding Farm

Carvers Hill Dairy

Westcott Farm

RIVAR ROAD

Sports Grd.

SN8

9

38

SANDY LANE

62

Marymere Farm

Wheatlands

29   430   31   32

A B C D E F

Rivar

Downside View

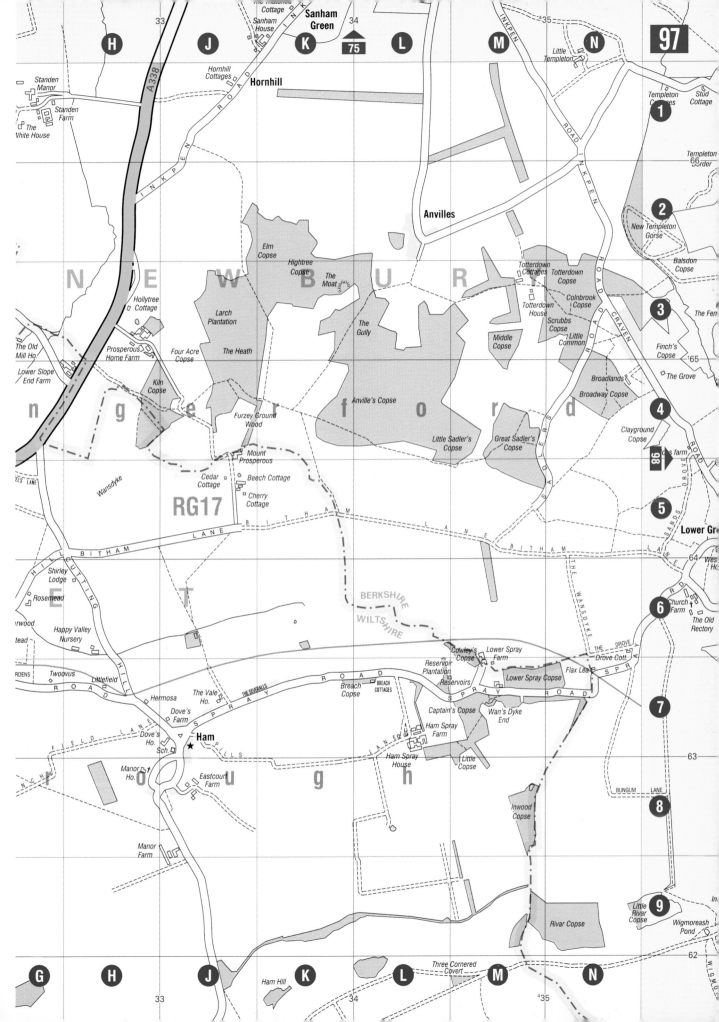

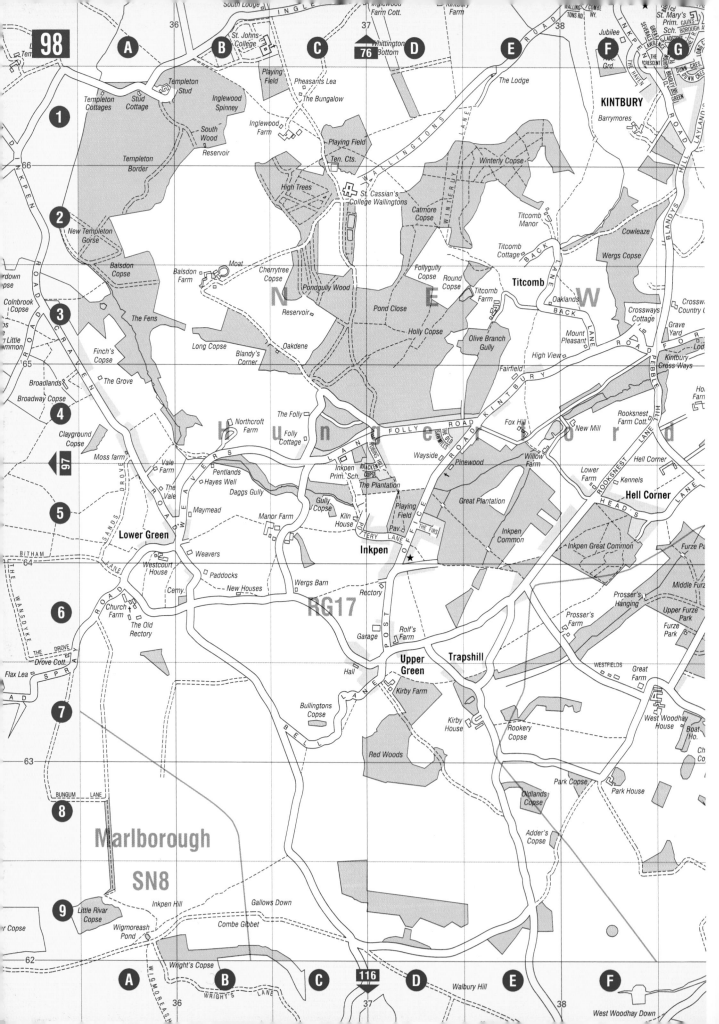

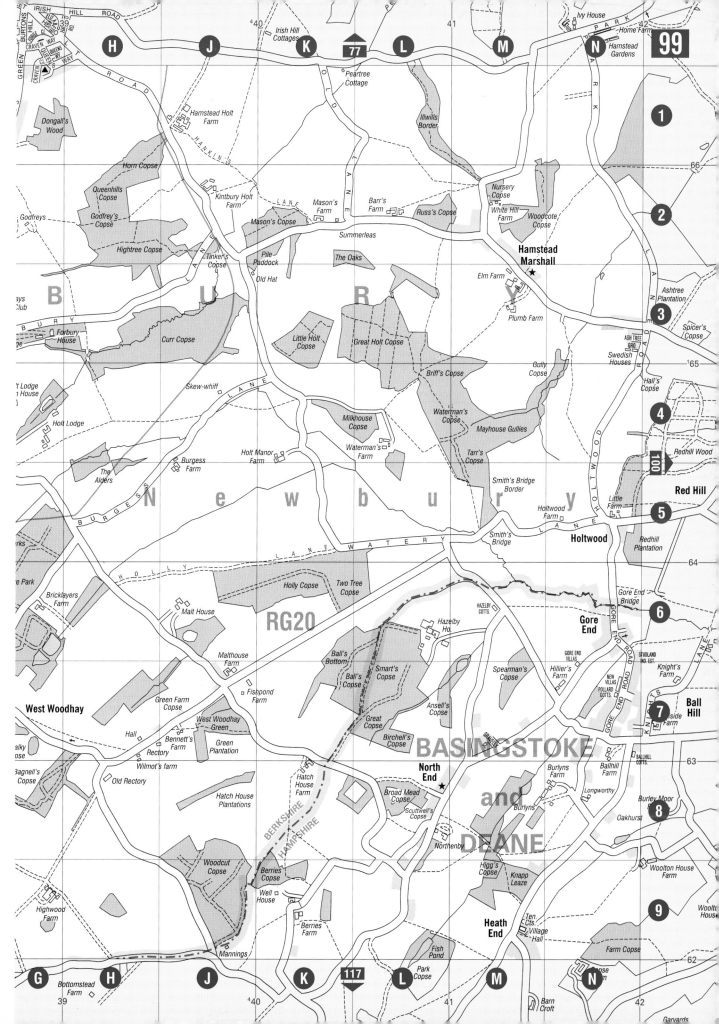

Ivy House
Home Farm
Hamstead Gardens

H   J   K   **77**   L   M   N

Irish Hill Cottages
Peartree Cottage

Dongall's Wood
Hamstead Holt Farm
Illwills Border

Horn Copse
Nursery Copse
White Hill Farm
Woodcote Copse

Queenhills Copse
Kintbury Holt Farm
Mason's Copse
Barr's Farm
Russ's Copse

Godfreys
Godfrey's Copse
Mason's Farm
Summerleas

Hightree Copse
Pile Paddock
The Oaks
Hamstead Marshall

Tinker's Copse
Old Hat
Elm Farm
Ashtree Plantation

B   U   R   Y
Plumb Farm
Spicer's Copse

ays Club
Forbury House
Curr Copse
Little Holt Copse
Great Holt Copse
Gully Copse
Swedish Houses
Hall's Copse

Holt Lodge
Skew-whiff
Briff's Copse
Waterman's Copse
Mayhouse Gullies
Redhill Wood

N   e   w   b   u   r   y
Burgess Farm
Milkhouse Copse
Waterman's Farm
Tarr's Copse
Smith's Bridge Border
Holtwood Farm
Little Farm
Red Hill

The Alders
Holt Manor Farm
100

B U R G E S S   L A N E
H O L L Y   L A N E   W A T E R Y
Smith's Bridge
Holtwood
Redhill Plantation

Gore End Bridge

Bricklayers Farm
Malt House
Holly Copse
Two Tree Copse
RG20
Gore End

Malthouse Farm
Ball's Bottom
Smart's Copse
Hazelby Ho.
Spearman's Copse
Hillier's Farm
Knight's Farm

West Woodhay
Green Farm Copse
Fishpond Farm
Ball's Copse
Great Copse
Ansell's Copse
Gore End Villas
New Villas
Pollard Cotts.

Hall
Bennett's Farm
Birchell's Copse
BASINGSTOKE
Ball Hill

Rectory
Green Plantation
North End
Burlyns Farm
Ballhill Farm

Wilmot's farm
and
Burley Moor

Bagnell's Copse
Old Rectory
Hatch House Farm
Broad Mead Copse
Scuttwell's Copse
Burlyns
Oakhurst
Woolton House Farm

Highwood Farm
Woodcut Copse
Berries Copse
Well House
Northenby
DEANE
Higg's Copse
Knapp Leaze

Berries Farm
Fish Pond
Park Copse
Heath End
Ten. Cts.
Village Hall
Farm Copse

G   H   J   K   **117**   L   M   N

Bottomstead Farm
Mannings
Barn Croft
Garvards

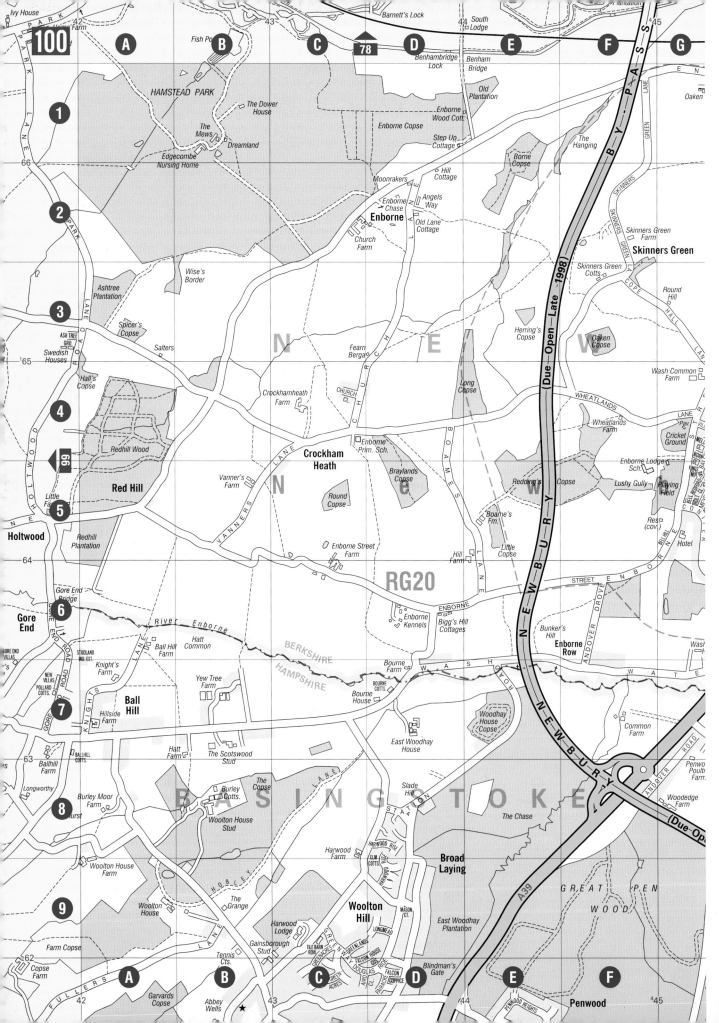

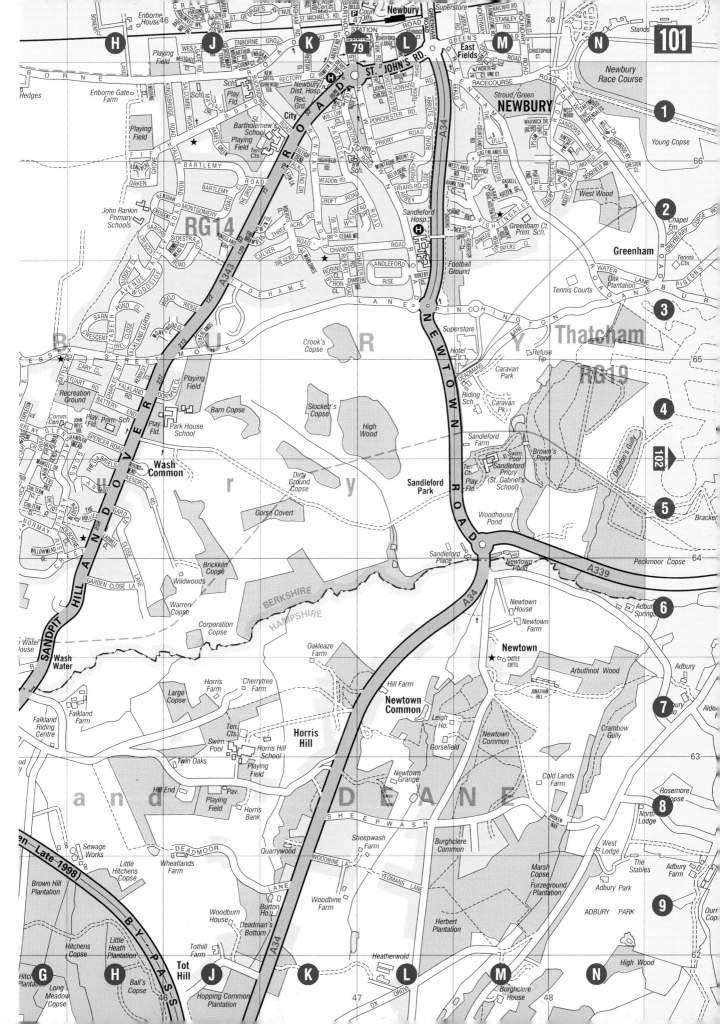

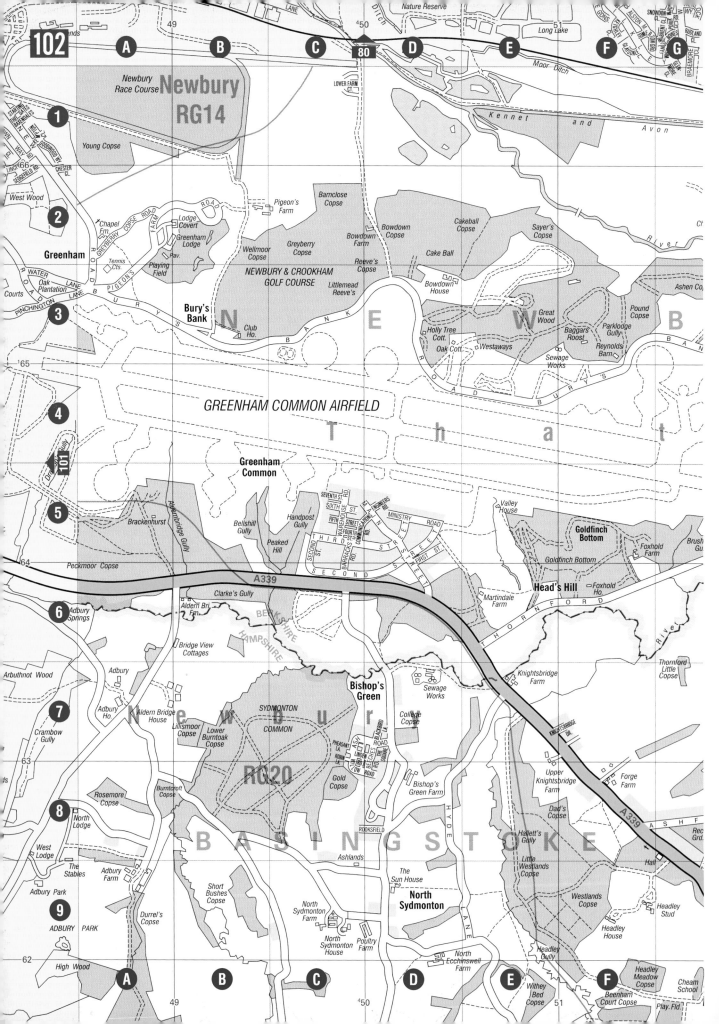

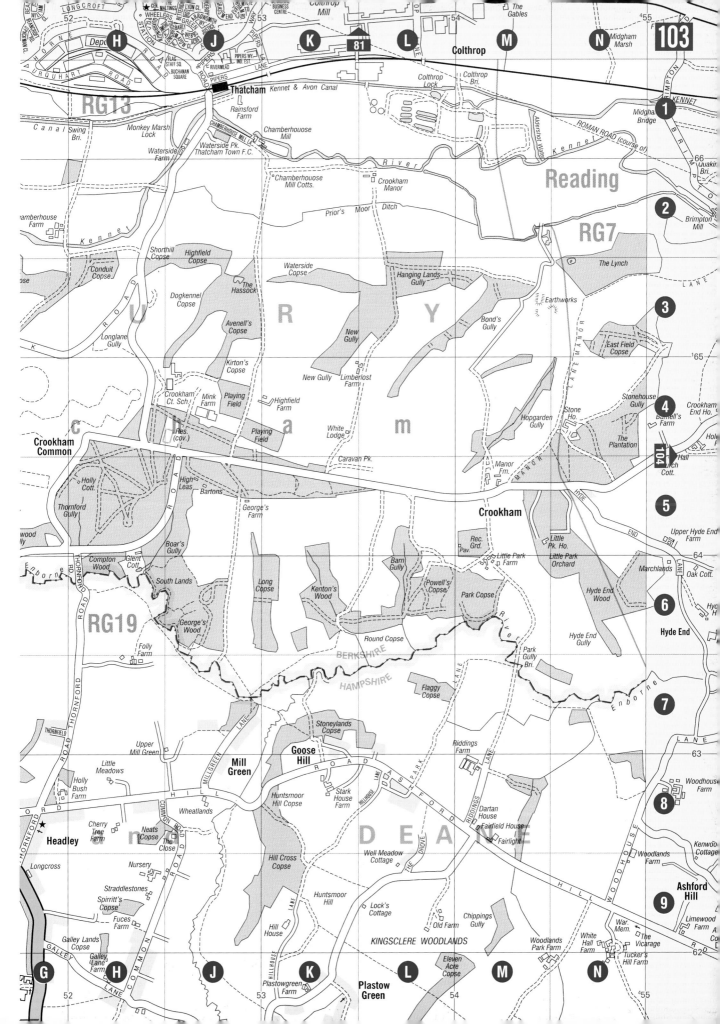

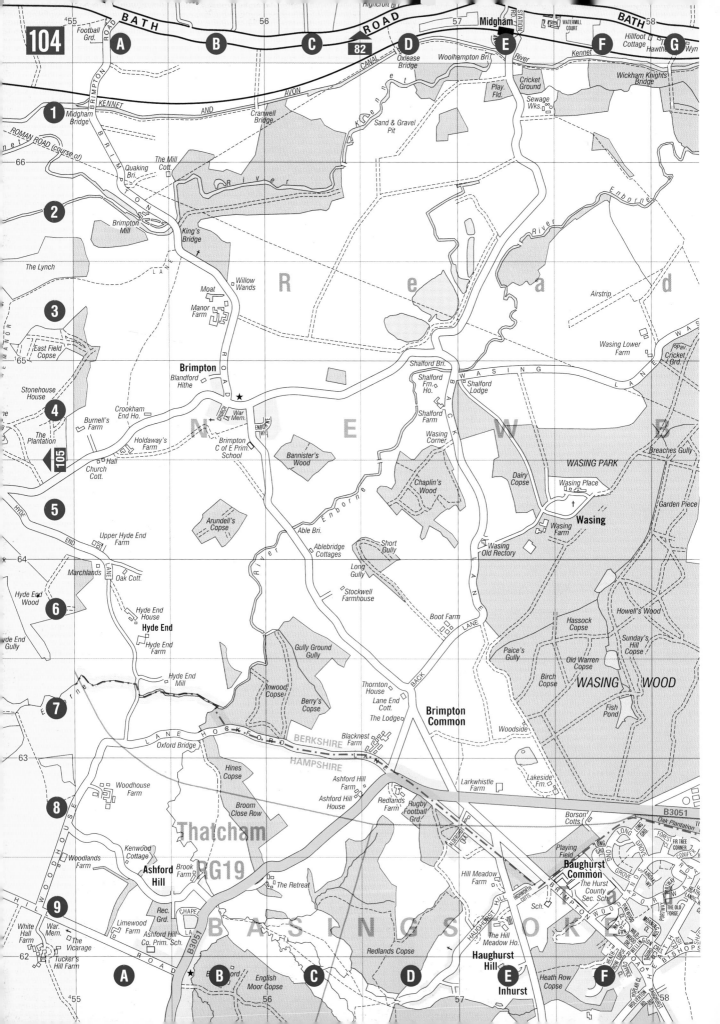

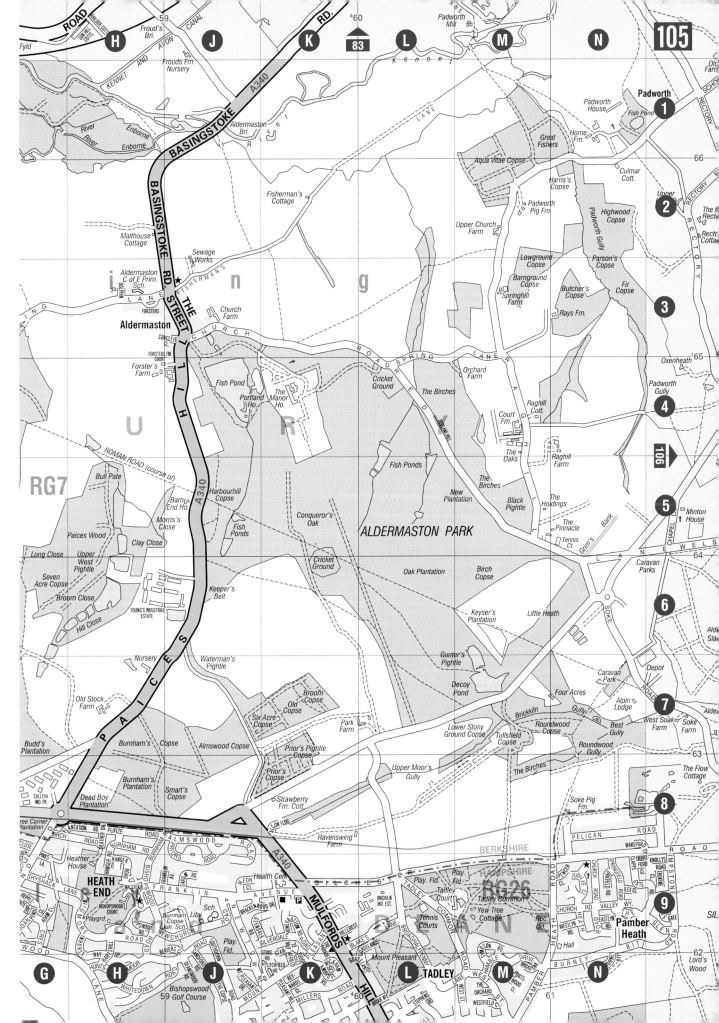

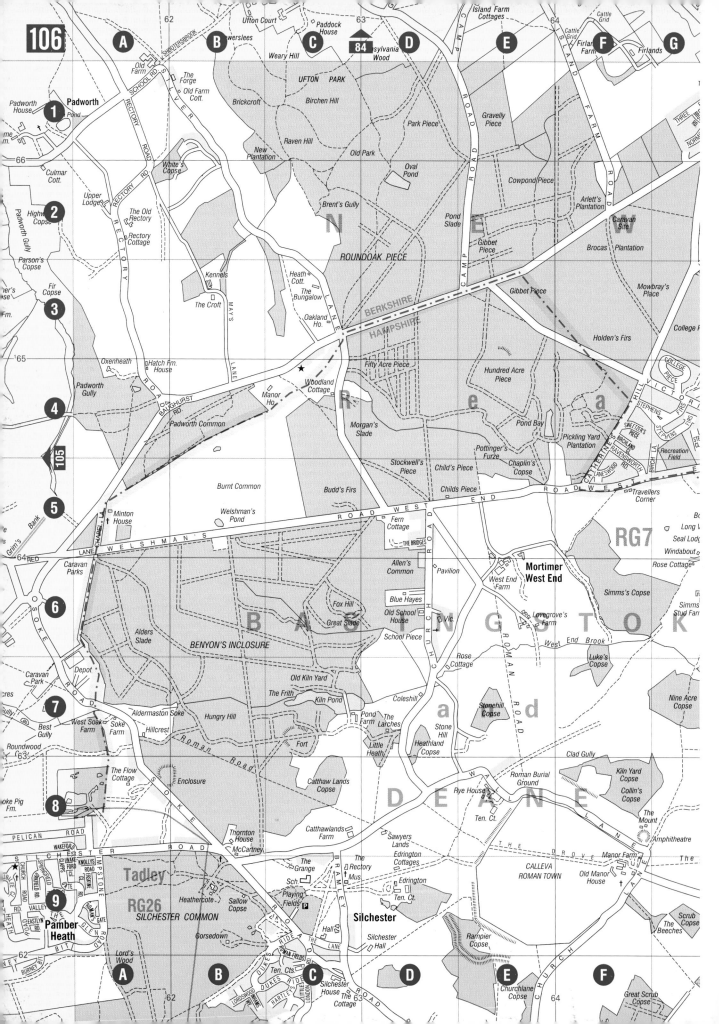

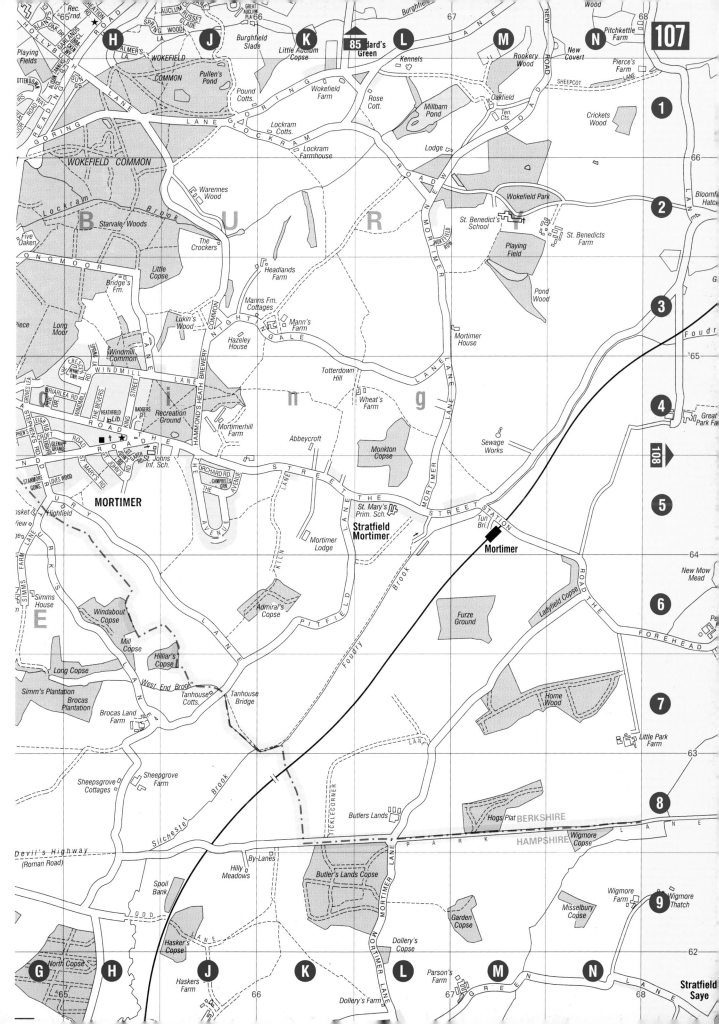

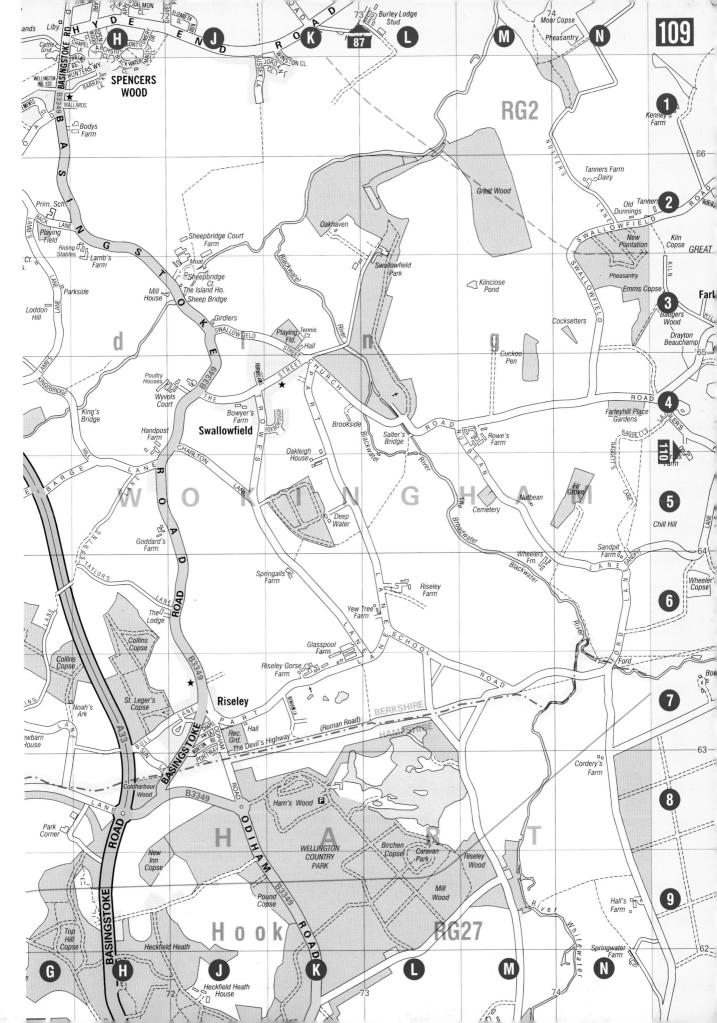

SPENCERS WOOD

RG2

Great Wood

Kenney's Farm

Tanners Farm Dairy

Old Dunnings

New Plantation

Kiln Copse

GREAT

Pheasantry

Swallowfield Park

Kilnclose Pond

Badgers Wood

Drayton Beauchamp

Emms Copse

Farl

Oakhaven

Sheepbridge Court Farm

Moat

Sheepbridge Ct.

The Island Ho.

Sheep Bridge

Girdlers

Mill House

Parkside

Loddon Hill

Lamb's Farm

Riding Stables

Prim. Sch.

Playing Field

BACK LANE

Cocksetters

Cuckoo Pen

Playing Fld.

Tennis Ct.

Hall

Swallowfield

Poultry Houses

Wyvols Court

Bowyer's Farm

Handpost Farm

King's Bridge

Kingsbridge

Brookside

Salter's Bridge

Rowe's Farm

Farleyhill Place Gardens

110

Nutbean

Fir Grove

Chill Hill

Cemetery

Oakleigh House

Deep Water

WOKINGHAM

Goddard's Farm

Springalls Farm

Riseley Farm

Yew Tree Farm

Wheelers Fm.

Blackwater

Sandpit Farm

Wheeler Copse

The Lodge

Collins Copse

Collins Copse

Noah's Ark

St. Leger's Copse

Riseley

Glasspool Farm

Riseley Gorse Farm

Hall

Rec. Grd.

(Roman Road)

The Devil's Highway

BERKSHIRE

HAMPSHIRE

Cordery's Farm

Coldharbour Wood

Ham's Wood

Park Corner

New Inn Copse

WELLINGTON COUNTRY PARK

Birchen Copse

Caravan Park

Riseley Wood

HART

Mill Wood

Hall's Farm

BASINGSTOKE ROAD

A33

ODIHAM ROAD

Pound Copse

Top Hill Copse

Heckfield Heath

Hook

RG27

Heckfield Heath House

Springwater Farm

River Whitewater

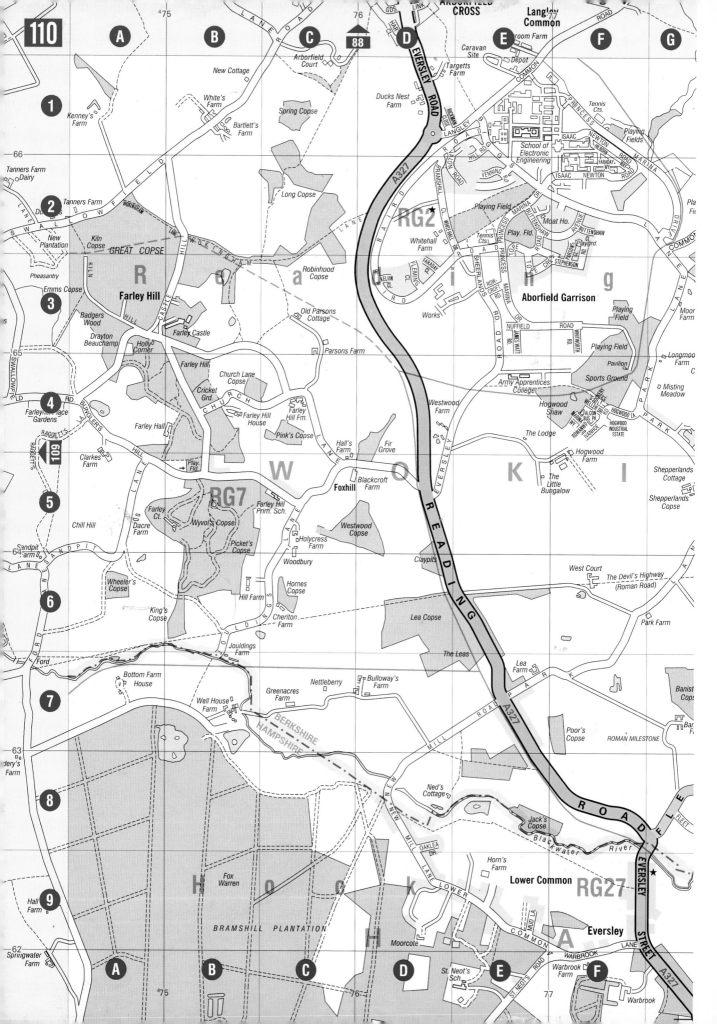

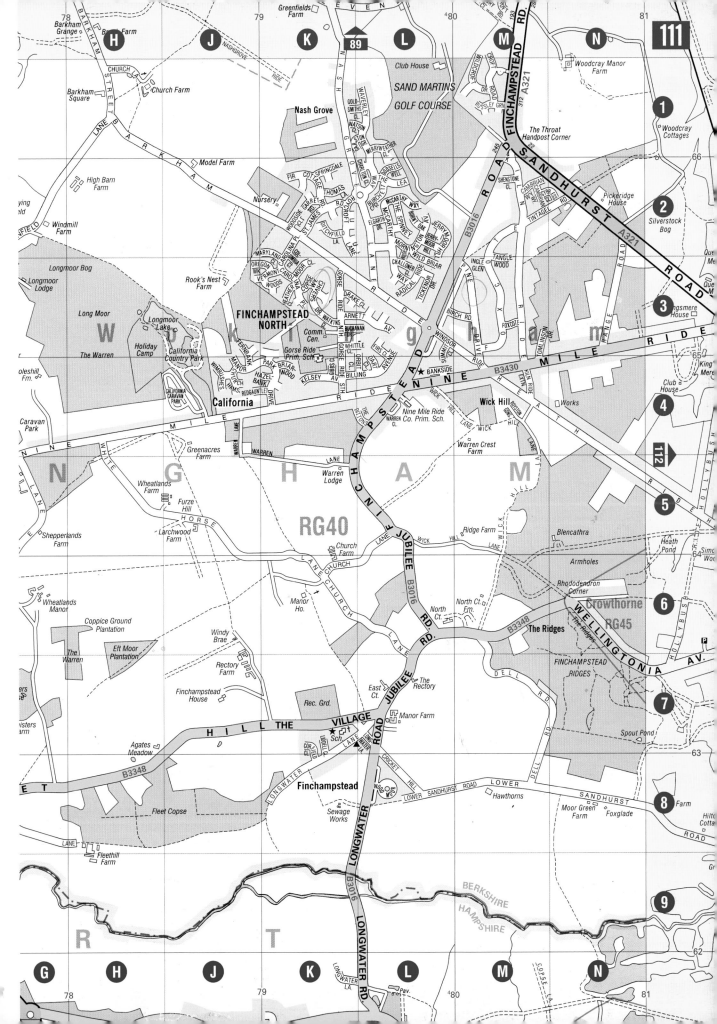

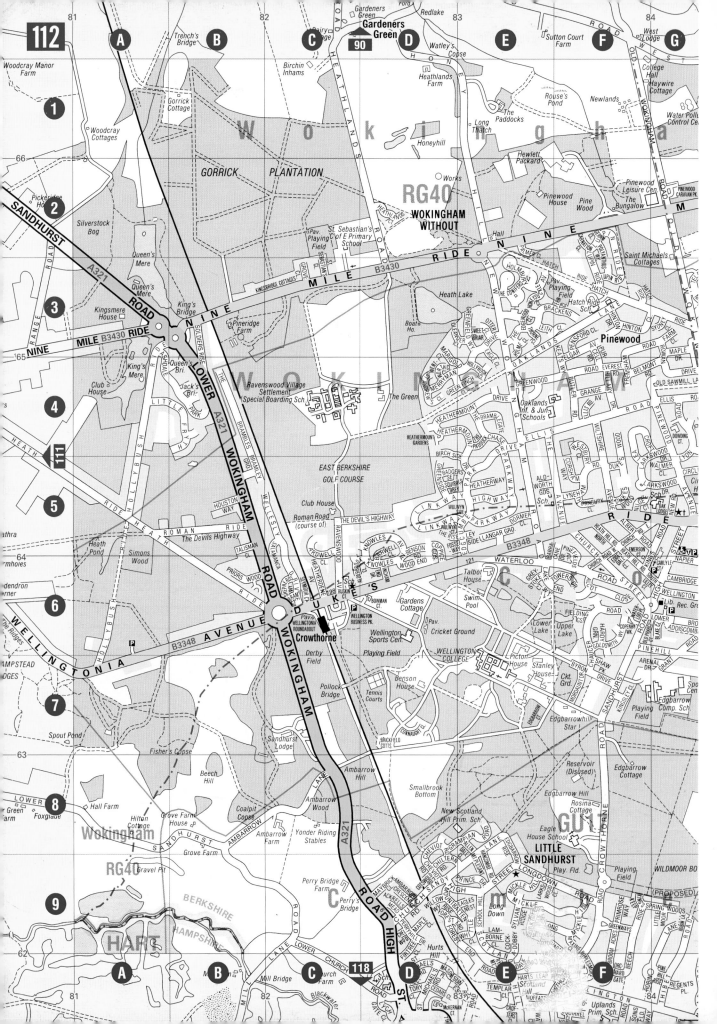

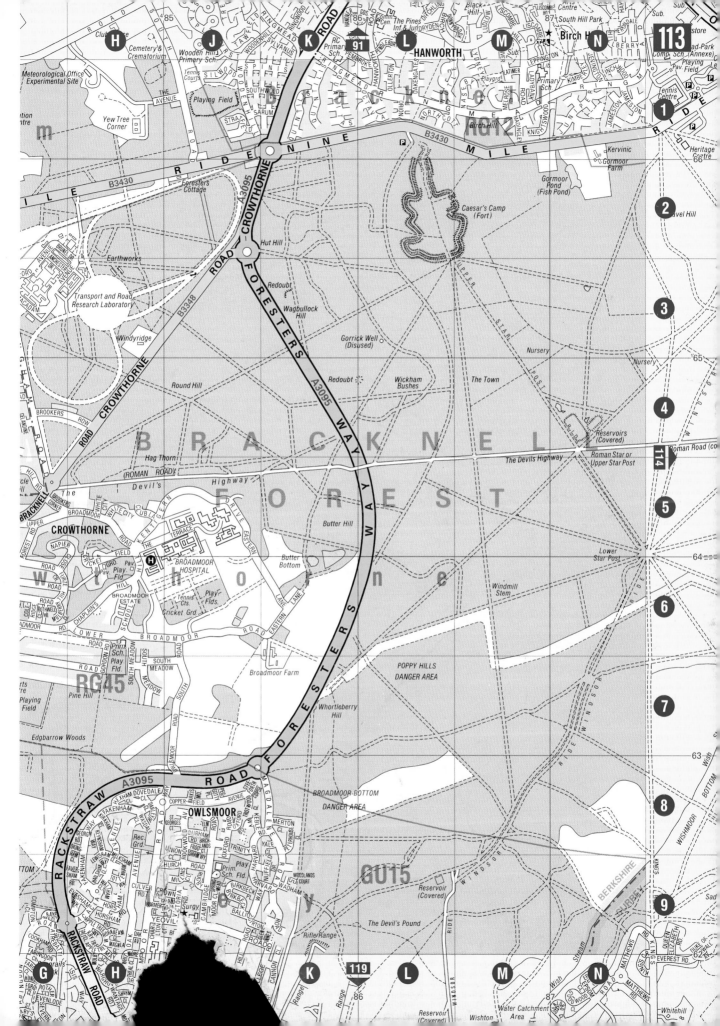

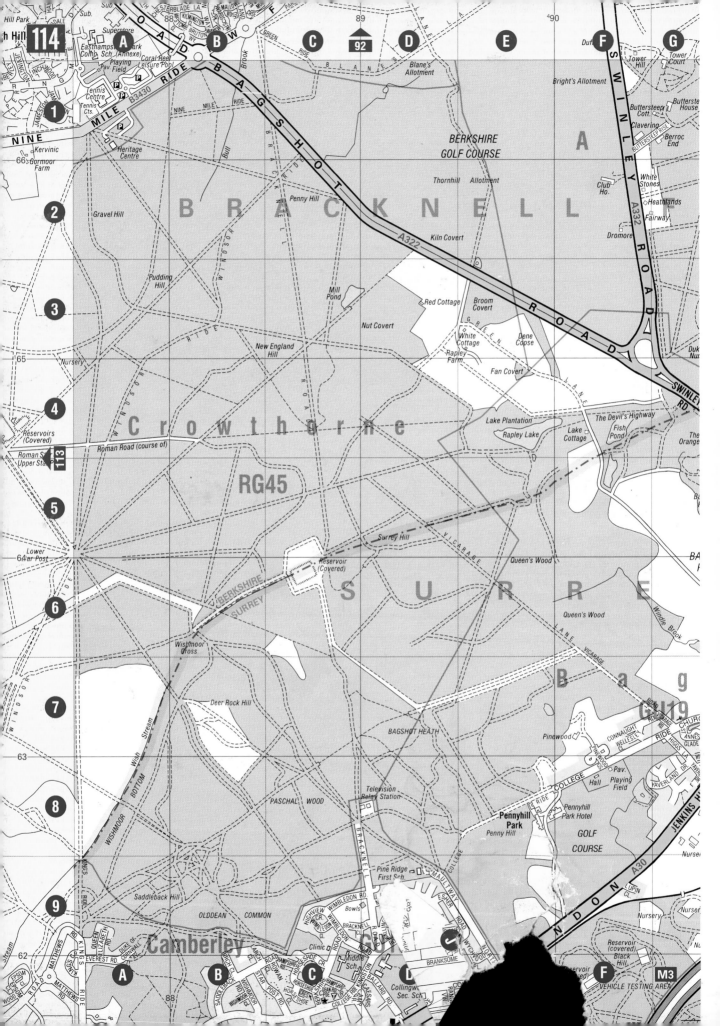

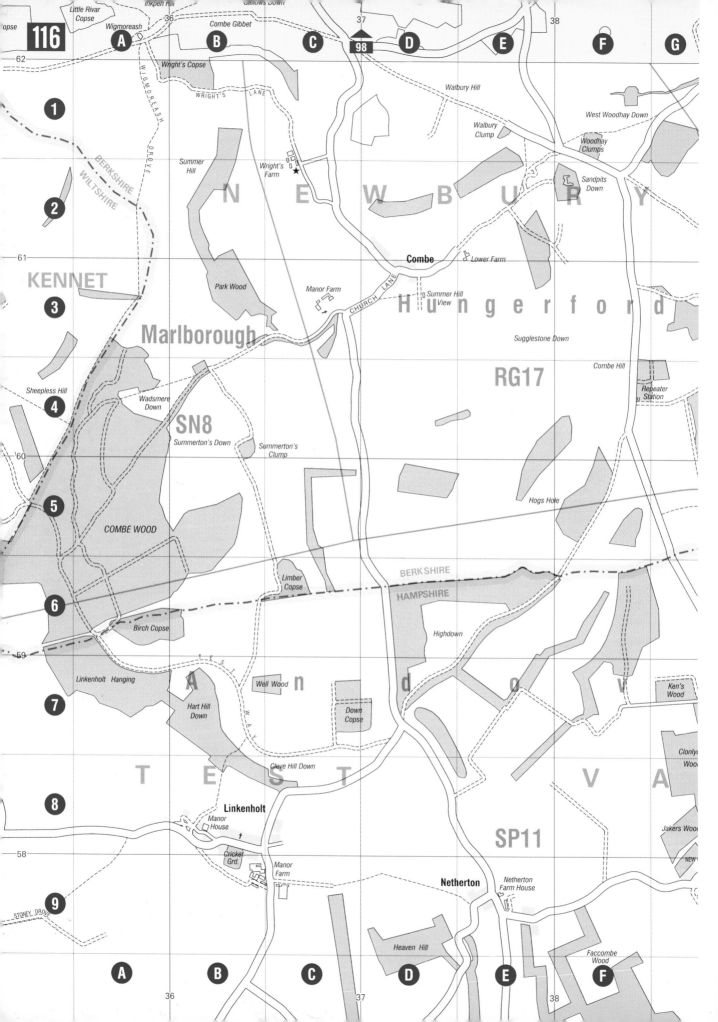

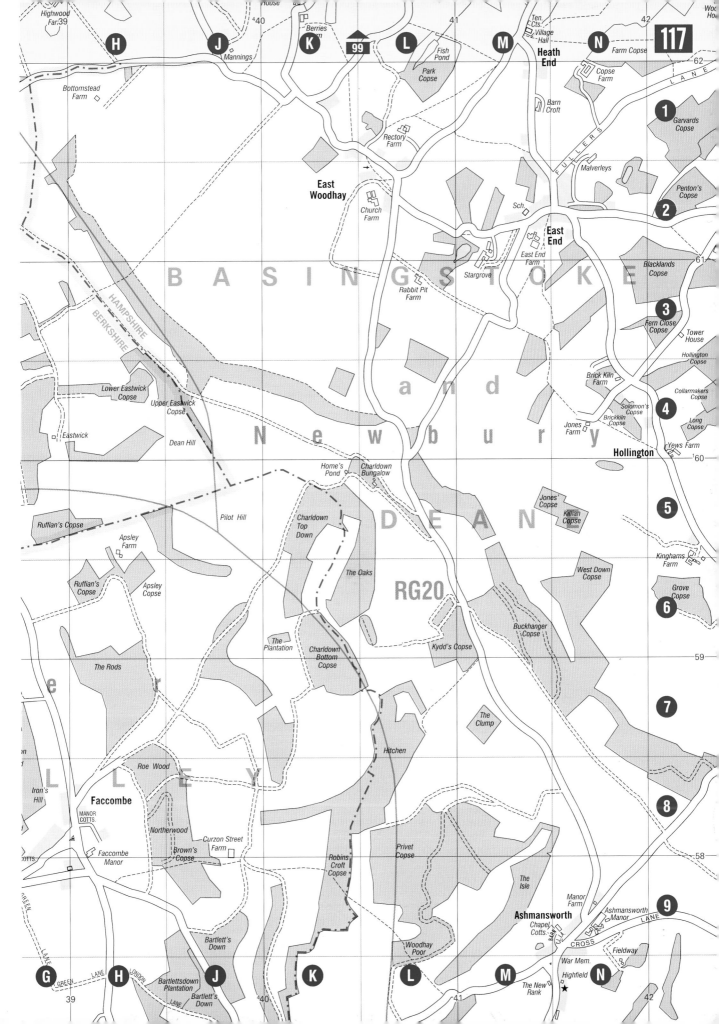

H **J** **K** **L** **M** **N**

99

Highwood Far. 39

Bottomstead Farm

BASINGSTOKE and Newbury

HAMPSHIRE
BERKSHIRE

Mannings

Berries

Rectory Farm

East Woodhay

Church Farm

Rabbit Pit Farm

Stargrove

Park Copse

Fish Pond

Ten. Cts.
Village Hall

Heath End

East End

East End Farm

Sch.

Malverleys

Copse Farm

Farm Copse

FULLERS LANE

62

Garvards Copse **1**

Penton's Copse **2**

Blacklands Copse

61

Fern Close Copse **3**

Tower House

Hollington Copse

Brick Kiln Farm

Collarmakers Copse

Solomon's Copse

Brickkiln Copse

Long Copse

Jones Farm

Yews Farm

Hollington

60

4

Lower Eastwick Copse

Upper Eastwick Copse

Eastwick

Dean Hill

NEW bury

Home's Pond

Charldown Bungalow

Jones' Copse

Killian Copse

5

Ruffian's Copse

Apsley Farm

Pilot Hill

Charldown Top Down

DEAN

West Down Copse

Kinghams Farm

Grove Copse **6**

Ruffian's Copse

Apsley Copse

The Oaks

RG20

Buckhanger Copse

The Rods

The Plantation

Charldown Bottom Copse

Kydd's Copse

59

7

Roe Wood

Hitchen

The Clump

Iron's Hill

Faccombe

MANOR COTTS.

Northerwood

Brown's Copse

Curzon Street Farm

Privet Copse

8

Faccombe Manor

Robins Croft Copse

The Isle

58

Manor Farm

Ashmansworth Manor

9

VALLEY

Bartlett's Down

Woodhay Poor

Ashmansworth

Chapel Cotts.

CROSS LANE

Fieldway

War Mem.

G **H** **J** **K** **L** **M** **N**

GREEN LANE
LONDON LANE

Bartlettsdown Plantation

Bartlett's Down

The New Rank

Highfield

39 40 41 42

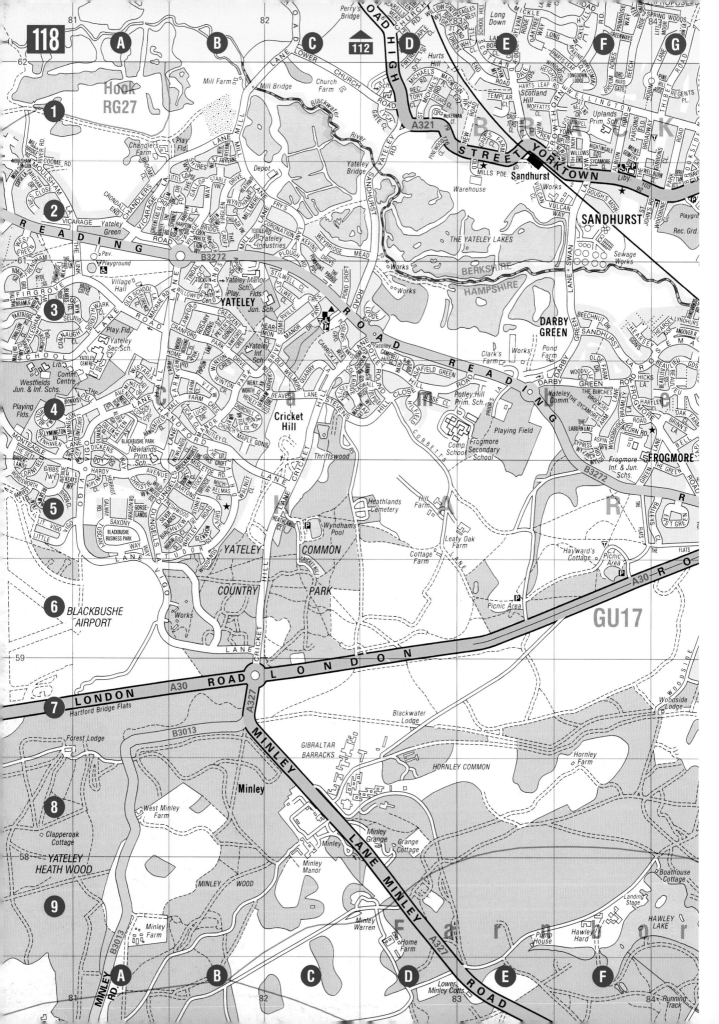

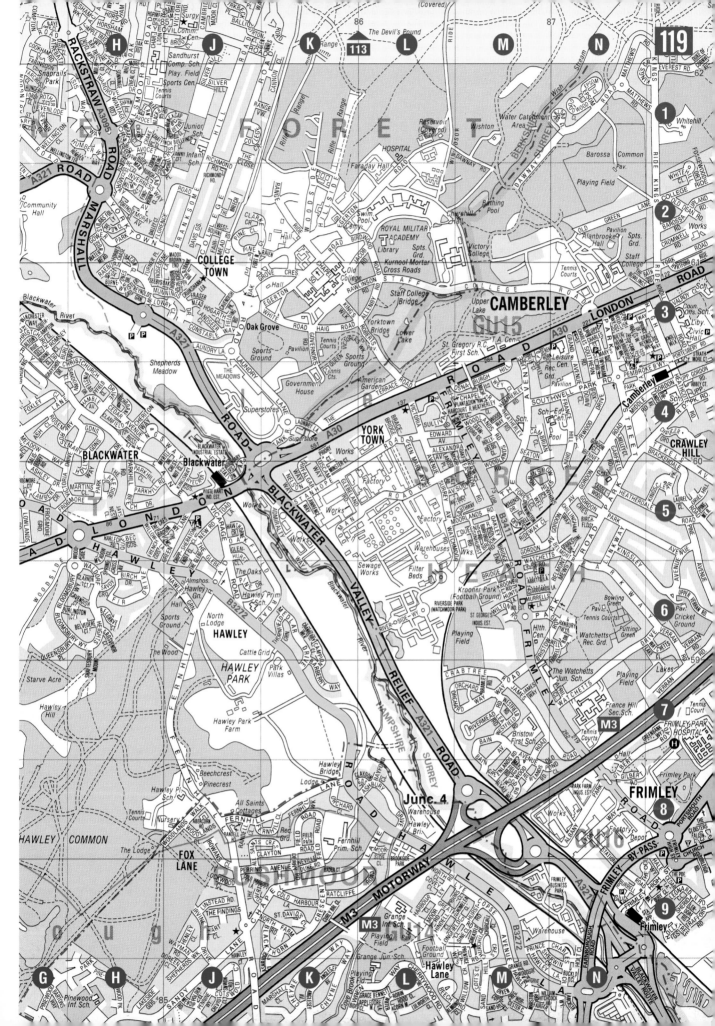

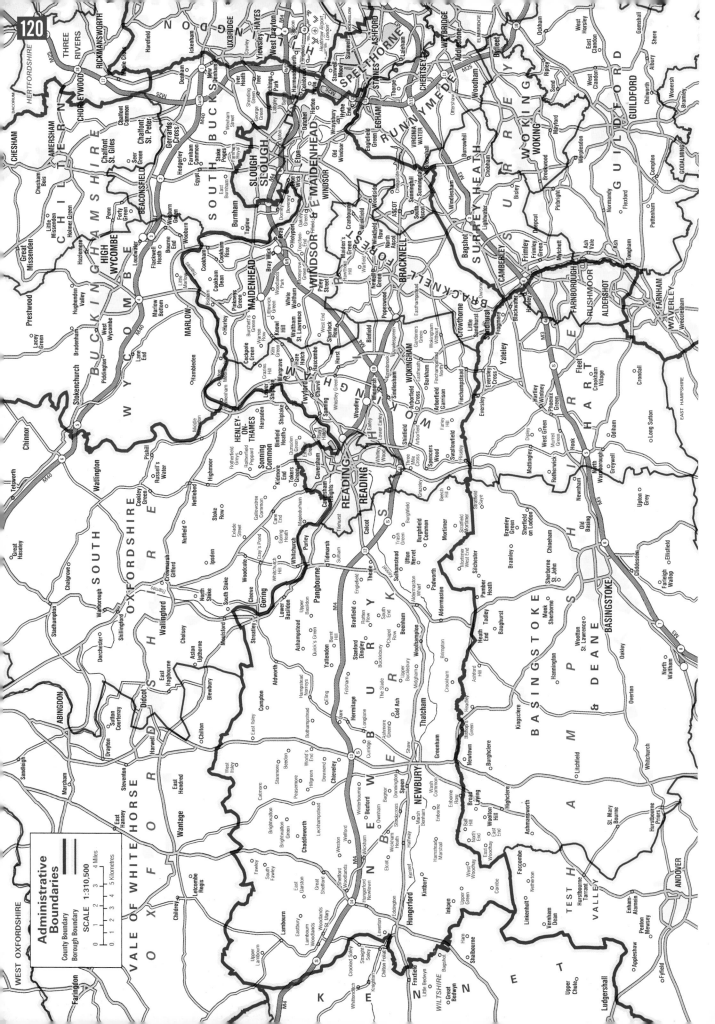

INDEX TO STREETS

HOW TO USE THIS INDEX

1. Each street name is followed by its Posttown or Postal Locality and then by its map reference; e.g. Abattoirs Rd. *Read* —4G **62** is in the Reading Posttown and is to be found in square 4G on page **62**. The page number being shown in bold type.
A strict alphabetical order is followed in which Av., Rd., St., etc. (though abbreviated) are read in full and as part of the street name; e.g. Ashcroft Clo. appears after Ash Ct. but before Ashcroft Ct.

2. Streets and a selection of Subsidiary names not shown on the Maps, appear in the index in *Italics* with the thoroughfare to which it is connected shown in brackets; e.g. *Abbotsbury Ho. Read —3J **87** (off Lulworth Rd.)*

3. With the now general usage of Postcodes for addressing mail, it is not recommended that this index is used for such a purpose.

GENERAL ABBREVIATIONS

All : Alley
App : Approach
Arc : Arcade
Av : Avenue
Bk : Back
Boulevd : Boulevard
Bri : Bridge
B'way : Broadway
Bldgs : Buildings
Bus : Business
Cen : Centre
Chu : Church
Chyd : Churchyard
Circ : Circle
Cir : Circus
Clo : Close
Comn : Common
Cotts : Cottages
Ct : Court
Cres : Crescent
Dri : Drive
E : East
Embkmt : Embankment
Est : Estate
Gdns : Gardens
Ga : Gate
Gt : Great
Grn : Green
Gro : Grove
Ho : House
Ind : Industrial
Junct : Junction
La : Lane
Lit : Little
Lwr : Lower
Mnr : Manor
Mans : Mansions
Mkt : Market
M : Mews
Mt : Mount
N : North
Pal : Palace
Pde : Parade
Pk : Park
Pas : Passage
Pl : Place
Rd : Road
S : South
Sq : Square
Sta : Station
St : Street
Ter : Terrace
Up : Upper
Vs : Villas
Wlk : Walk
W : West
Yd : Yard

POSTTOWN AND POSTAL LOCALITY ABBREVIATIONS

Aldermaston : *Aldm*
Aldworth : *Aldw*
Arborfield : *Arbor*
Arborfield Cross : *Arbor X*
Ascot : *Asc*
Ashampstead : *Ash'd*
Ashampstead Common : *Ash'd C*
Ashford : *Ashf*
Ashford Hill : *Ash H*
Ashmansworth : *Ashmw*
Ashmore Green : *Ashm G*
Aston : *Ast*
Bagnor : *Bagn*
Bagshot : *Bag*
Ball Hill : *Bal H*
Barkham : *B'ham*
Baughurst : *Baug*
Baydon : *Bay*
Beech Hill : *B Hill*
Beedon : *Beed*
Beenham : *Been*
Benham Hill : *Ben H*
Binfield : *Binf*
Binfield Heath : *Bin H*
Bisham : *Bish*
Bishops Green : *Bis G*
Blackwater : *B'water*
Blewbury : *Blew*
Bourne End : *Bour*
Boxford : *Box*
Bracknell : *Brack*
Bradfield : *Brad*
Bray : *Bray*
Brightwalton : *Bright*
Brimpton : *Brimp*
Brimpton Common : *Brimp C*
Bucklebury : *Bckby*
Burchetts Green : *Bur G*
Burghclere : *Burc*
Burghfield : *Bfld*
Burghfield Common : *Bfld C*
Burnham : *Burn*
Calcot : *Calc*
Camberley : *Camb*
Catmore : *Catm*
Caversham : *Cav*
Chaddleworth : *Chadw*
Chadwell Heath : *Chad*
Chalkhouse Green : *Chalk*
Chalvey : *Chalv*
Chapel Row : *Chap R*
Charvil : *Charv*
Chavey Down : *Chav D*
Chazey Heath : *Chaz H*
Chieveley : *Chvly*
Chilton Foliat : *Chilt F*
Cholsey : *Chol*
Cippenham : *Cipp*
Cockpole Green : *C Grn*
Cold Ash : *Cold A*
College Town : *Col T*
Colnbrook : *Coln*
Colthrop : *Colt*
Combe : *Combe*
Compton : *Comp*
Cookham : *Cook*
Cookham Dean : *Cook D*
Cowley : *Cow*
Crays Pond : *Cray P*
Crockham Heath : *Croc H*
Crookham Common : *Crook C*
Crowt : Crowthorne : *Crowt*
Curridge : *Cur*
Datchet : *Dat*
Denham : *Den*
Donnington : *Don*
Dorney : *Dor*
Dorney Reach : *Dor R*
Dunsden : *D'den*
Earley : *Ear*
East Garston : *E Gar*
East Ilsley : *E Ils*
East Woodhay : *E Wood*
Eastbury : *E'bury*
Easton : *E'ton*
Ecchinswell : *Ecc*
Eddington : *Edd*
Egham : *Egh*
Elcot : *Elc*
Emmer Green : *Emm G*
Enborne : *Enb*
Englefield : *Eng*
Eton : *Eton*
Eton College : *Eton C*
Eton Wick : *Eton W*
Eversley : *Eve*
Faccombe : *Fac*
Farley Hill : *Far H*
Farnborough (Hampshire) : *Farn*
Farnborough (Oxfordshire) : *Farnb*
Farnham Common : *Farn C*
Farnham Royal : *Farn R*
Feltham : *Felt*
Fifield : *Fif*
Finchampstead : *Finch*
Flackwell Heath : *F Hth*
Frilsham : *Fril*
Frimley : *Frim*
Frogmore (Surrey) : *Frogm*
Froxfield : *Frox*
Fulmer : *Ful*
Gallowstree Common : *Gall C*
George Green : *G Grn*
Goring : *Gor*
Goring Heath : *Gor H*
Grazeley : *Graz*
Great Shefford : *Gt Shef*
Greenham : *Green*
Halfway : *Half*
Ham : *Ham*
Hampstead Norreys : *Hamp N*
Hamstead Marshall : *Ham M*
Hare Hatch : *Hare H*
Harmondsworth : *Harm*
Harpsden : *Harp*
Hawley : *Hawl*
Headley (Berkshire) : *Hdly*
London Heathrow Airport : *H'row A*
Hedgerley : *Hedg*
Henley-on-Thames : *Hen T*
Henwick : *Henw*
Hermitage : *Herm*
Hillingdon : *Hil*
Holyport : *Holyp*
Hook : *Hook*
Horton : *Hort*
Hounslow : *Houn*
Hungerford : *Hung*
Hurley : *Hur*
Hurst : *Hurst*
Inkpen : *Ink*
Inkpen Common : *Ink C*
Iver : *Iver*
Kidmore End : *Kid E*
Kiln Green : *Kiln G*
Kintbury : *Kint*
Kintbury Holt : *Kint H*
Knowl Hill : *Know H*
L Bedwyn : *L Bed*
Lambourn : *Lamb*
Lambourn Woodlands : *Lamb W*
Lands End : *Land E*
Langley : *Langl*
Leckhampstead : *Leck*
Letcombe Bassett : *Let B*
Lightwater : *Light*
Linkenholt : *Link*
Little Marlow : *L Mar*
Little Sandhurst : *L Sand*
Littlewick Green : *L Grn*
Lockinge : *Lock*
Lower Basildon : *Lwr B*
Lower Earley : *Lwr Ear*
Lower Padworth : *Lwr P*
Lower Shiplake : *Lwr S*
Maidenhead : *M'head*
Mapledurham : *Map*
Marlow : *Mar*
Medmenham : *Medm*
Middlegreen : *Mid*
Midgham : *Midg*
Mortimer : *Mort*
Mortimer Common : *Mort C*
Mortimer West End : *Mort W*
Moulsford : *Moul*
Newbury : *Newb*
Newtown : *Newt*
Newtown Common : *Newt C*
North Ascot : *N Asc*
North End : *N End*
Nuptown : *Nup*
Oakley Green : *Oak G*
Old Windsor : *Old Win*
Owlsmoor : *Owl*
Padworth : *Pad*
Padworth Common : *Pad C*
Pamber Heath : *Pam H*
Pangbourne : *Pang*
Peasemore : *P'mre*
Penwood : *Pen*
Pingewood : *Ping*
Playhatch : *Play*
Purley on Thames : *Pur T*
Reading : *Read*
Remenham : *Rem*
Riseley : *Rise*
Ruscombe : *Rusc*
Sandhurst : *Sand*
Shalbourne : *Shalb*
Shaw : *Shaw*
Shefford Woodlands : *Shef W*
Shinfield : *Shin*
Shiplake : *S'lake*
Shiplake Cross : *S'lake X*
Shurlock Row : *Shur R*
Silchester : *Sil*
Sindlesham : *Sind*
Slough : *Slou*
Sonning : *Son*
Sonning Common : *Son C*
South Ascot : *S Asc*
South Fawley : *S Faw*
South Stoke : *S Sto*
Southend : *South*
Speen : *Speen*
Spencers Wood : *Spen W*
Staines : *Stai*
Stanford Dingley : *Stan D*
Stanwell : *Stanw*
Stockcross : *Stcks*
Stoke Poges : *Stoke P*
Stratfield Saye : *Strat S*
Streatley : *Streat*
Sulham : *Sul*
Sulhamstead : *Sul'd*
Sunningdale : *S'dale*
Sunninghill : *S'hill*
Swallowfield : *Swal*
Tadley : *Tadl*
Taplow : *Tap*
Thatcham : *That*
Theale : *Thea*
Three Mile Cross : *Three M*
Tidmarsh : *Tid*
Tilehurst : *Tile*
Tokers Green : *Tok G*
Tutts Clump : *Tut C*
Twyford : *Twy*
Ufton Nervet : *Uft N*
Upper Basildon : *Up Bas*
Upper Bucklebury : *Up Buck*
Upper Culham : *Up Cul*
Upper Lambourn : *Up Lamb*
Upper Woolhampton : *Up Wool*
Uxbridge : *Uxb*
Virginia Water : *Vir W*
Waltham St Lawrence : *Wal L*
Wantage : *Want*
Warfield : *Warf*
Warfield Park : *Warf P*
Wargrave : *Warg*
Warren Row : *War R*
Wash Water : *Wash W*
Water Oakley : *Water*
Wellington College : *Wel C*
West Drayton : *W Dray*
West Ilsley : *W Ils*
West Woodhay : *W Wood*
Weston : *W'ton*
Wexham : *Wex*
Whistley Green : *Whis G*
Whitchurch Hill : *Whit H*
Whitchurch on Thames : *Whit T*
White Waltham : *White*
Wickham : *Wick*
Windlesham : *W'sham*
Windsor : *Wind*
Winkfield : *Wink*
Winkfield Row : *Wink R*
Winnersh : *Winn*
Winterbourne : *Wint*
Wokingham : *Wokgm*
Wooburn Green : *Wbrn G*
Woodcote : *Woodc*
Woodlands St Mary : *Wood M*
Woodley : *Wdly*
Woodspeen : *Woods*
Woolhampton : *Woolh*
Woolton Hill : *Wool H*
Woosehill : *Woos*
Wraysbury : *Wray*
Yateley : *Yat*
Yattendon : *Yatt*
Yiewsley : *Yiew*

INDEX TO STREETS

Abattoirs Rd. Read —4G **62**
Abberbury Clo. Don —5J **79**
Abbetts La. Camb —6M **119**
Abbey Clo. Brack —7A **92**
Abbey Clo. Newb —2L **101**
Abbey Clo. Slou —8A **22**
Abbey Clo. Wokgm —4A **90**
Abbey Ct. Camb —4N **119**
Abbey Pk. Bfld C —8G **84**
Abbey Rd. Bour —2K **5**
Abbey Rd. Vir W —7M **95**
Abbey Sq. Read —5H **63**
Abbey St. Read —4H **63**
Abbey Way. Mar —9B **4**
Abbey Wood. S'dale —9C **94**
Abbotsbury. Brack —7K **91**
*Abbotsbury Ho. Read —3J **87***
(off Lulworth Rd.)
Abbots Dri. Vir W —7K **95**
*Abbots Ho. Read —4H **63***
(off Abbey St.)
Abbot's Rd. Bfld C —9G **84**
Abbots Rd. Newb —1L **101**
Abbots Wlk. Read —4H **63**
Abbots Wlk. Wind —8A **46**
Abbott's Clo. Uxb —6L **25**
Abbotts Way. Slou —9N **21**
Aberaman. Cav —7F **38**
Abercorn Ho. Hawl —8J **119**
Aberdeen Av. Slou —8C **22**
Aberford Clo. Read —5C **62**
Abex Rd. Newb —8L **79**
Abingdon Clo. Brack —7B **92**
Abingdon Clo. Uxb —2N **25**
Abingdon Dri. Cav —7J **39**
Abingdon Rd. E Ils —7B **12**
Abingdon Rd. Sand —1G **119**
Abingdon Wlk. M'head —3B **20**
Abney Ct. Dri. Bour —5L **5**
Abrahams Rd. Hen T —3B **16**
Abury La. Brack —8D **92**
Acacia Av. Owl —9H **113**
Acacia Av. W Dray —8N **25**
Acacia Av. Wray —1N **71**
Acacia Ct. Brack —6M **91**
Acacia Ho. Slou —9H **23**
Acacia M. W Dray —5L **49**
Acacia Rd. Read —6J **63**
Acacia Rd. Stai —9J **73**
Accommodation La. W Dray —7H **49**
Ackrells Mead. Sand —9D **112**
Acorn Dri. Wokgm —4A **90**
Acorn M. Farn —9L **119**
Acorn Rd. B'water —4F **118**
Acorn Wlk. Calc —7K **61**
Acre Bus. Pk. Read —3H **87**
Acre Pas. Wind —7F **46**
Acre Rd. Read —3G **86**
Acre, The. Mar —5D **4**
Adam Clo. Baug —9G **105**
Adam Clo. Slou —9C **22**
Adam Ct. Hen T —4D **16**
Adams Way. Ear —1M **87**
Adder's La. Up Bas —9H **35**
Addington Clo. Wind —9C **46**
Addington Rd. Read —6K **63**
Addiscombe Chase. Tile —1J **61**
Addiscombe Rd. Crowt —6G **112**
Addison Clo. Iver —8F **24**
Addison Ct. M'head —5E **20**
Addison Rd. Read —3G **62**
Adelaide Clo. Slou —1C **46**
Adelaide Rd. Ashf —9L **73**
Adelaide Rd. Read —7N **63**
Adelaide Sq. Wind —8F **46**
Adelphi Gdns. Slou —1G **46**
Adey's Clo. Newb —1M **101**
Adkins Rd. Wal L —6C **42**
Admiral Kepple Ct. Asc —2H **93**
Admiral's Ct. Read —7G **62**
Admiralty Way. Camb —5K **119**
Admoor La. South —1K **83**
Adwell Dri. Lwr Ear —2B **88**
Adwell Sq. Hen T —4C **16**
Adwood Ct. That —8H **81**
Agar Cres. Brack —2M **91**
Agars Pl. Dat —5J **47**
Agate Clo. Wokgm —4K **89**
Aggisters La. Wokgm —8H **89**
Agincourt. Asc —5M **93**
Agincourt Clo. Wokgm —5K **89**
Agricola Way. That —9H **81**
Ainsdale Cres. Read —8A **62**
Aintree. Lamb —3H **27**
Aintree Clo. Coln —7F **48**
Aintree Clo. Green —1N **101**
Aird Clo. Wool H —9C **100**
Airport Way. Stai —1H **73**
Ajax Av. Slou —8D **22**
Alandale Clo. Read —3K **87**
Alan Pl. Read —7A **62**
Alan Way. G Grn —7N **23**
Albain Cres. Ashf —6M **73**
Albany Pk. Coln —6E **48**
Albany Pk. Frim —8N **119**
Albany Pk. Dri. Winn —9F **64**
Albany Pl. Egh —8C **72**
Albany Rd. Old Win —2J **71**
Albany Rd. Read —5D **62**
Albany Rd. Wind —8F **46**
Alben Rd. Binf —9G **66**
Albert Clo. Slou —2H **47**
Albert Pl. Eton W —4C **46**
Albert Rd. Ashf —9N **73**
Albert Rd. Bag —9H **115**
Albert Rd. Brack —3M **91**
Albert Rd. Cav —9E **38**
Albert Rd. Crowt —5F **112**
Albert Rd. Egh —1M **95**
Albert Rd. Hen T —5D **16**
Albert Rd. Newb —7L **79**
Albert Rd. Old Win —9F **46**
Albert Rd. W Dray —9M **25**
Albert Rd. Wokgm —5N **89**
Albert St. M'head —8C **20**
(in two parts)
Albert St. Slou —2H **47**
Albert St. Wind —7D **46**
Albion Clo. Slou —9J **23**
Albion Ho. Langl —4C **48**
Albion Rd. Sand —1F **118**
Albion Ter. Read —6J **63**
Albury Clo. Read —3C **62**
Albury Gdns. Calc —9M **61**
Alcot Clo. Crowt —6F **112**
Aldborough Spur. Slou —7G **22**
Aldbourne Av. Ear —8N **63**
Aldbourne Rd. Burn —6L **21**
Aldeburgh Clo. Cav —5J **39**
Aldebury Rd. M'head —4B **20**
Aldenham Clo. Cav —7J **39**
Aldenham Ter. Brack —8N **91**
Alden View. Wind —7N **45**
Alderbrook Clo. Crowt —6C **112**
Alderbury Rd. Slou —1A **48**
Alderbury Rd. W. Slou —1A **48**
Alder Clo. Egh —9N **71**
Alder Clo. Slou —9B **22**
Alder Dri. Bfld C —8G **84**
Alder Dri. Tile —6K **61**
Alderfield Clo. Thea —8G **60**
Alder Gro. Yat —4A **118**
Alderley Clo. Wdly —3E **64**
Alderman Willey Clo. Wokgm —5N **89**
Alder Rd. Den —1K **25**
Alder Rd. Iver —3E **24**
Aldershot La. Baug —8D **104**
Alderside Wlk. Egh —9N **71**
Alders, The. That —7G **80**
Aldin Av. N. Slou —1J **47**
Aldin Av. S. Slou —1J **47**
Aldridge Pk. Wink R —1D **92**
Aldridge Rd. Slou —5C **22**
Aldwick Dri. M'head —8A **20**
Aldworth Clo. Brack —6L **91**
Aldworth Clo. Read —7C **62**
Aldworth Gdns. Crowt —5E **112**
Aldworth Rd. Comp —1H **33**
Aldworth Rd. Up Bas —7J **35**
Alexander Ct. Read —5F **62**
Alexander Rd. Egh —9D **72**
Alexander Rd. That —9H **81**
Alexander Wlk. Brack —7M **91**
Alexandra Av. Camb —4L **119**
Alexandra Clo. Stai —9L **73**
Alexandra Rd. Egh —1L **95**
Alexandra Rd. M'head —6A **20**
Alexandra Rd. Read —5K **63**
Alexandra Rd. Slou —2F **46**
Alexandra Rd. Uxb —3L **25**
Alexandra Rd. Wind —8F **46**
Alford Clo. Tile —4L **61**
Alfred St. Read —5F **62**
Alice Gough Homes. Brack —5M **91**
Alice La. Burn —5L **21**
Alison Clo. Bfld C —9G **85**
Alison Wlk. Cav —2K **63**
Allanson Rd. Mar —4D **4**
Allcroft Rd. Read —7J **63**
Allenby Rd. Camb —3L **119**
Allenby Rd. M'head —7M **19**
Allendale Clo. Sand —8E **112**
Allendale Rd. Ear —9A **64**
Allerds Rd. Farn R —2B **22**
Alleyns La. Cook —7H **5**
All Hallows Rd. Cav —1K **63**
Allington Ct. Slou —7H **23**
Allison Ct. Read —5F **62**
Allison Gdns. Pur T —8K **37**
Allnatt Av. Winn —2H **89**
Allonby Clo. Lwr Ear —1C **88**
All Saints Av. M'head —6N **19**
All Saints Clo. Wokgm —4A **90**
All Saints Cres. Farn —8J **119**
All Saints Rise. Warf —1A **92**
All Saints Rd. Light —9M **115**
Allsmore La. Brack —5C **92**
All Soul's Rd. Asc —6K **93**
Alma Ct. Burn —4M **21**
Alma Rd. Eton W —3B **46**
Alma Rd. Wind —8E **46**
Alma St. Read —4C **62**

Almond Av.—Bedford La.

Almond Av. Newb —6L 79
Almond Av. W Dray —2N 49
Almond Clo. Egh —1K 95
Almond Clo. Farn —9M 119
Almond Clo. Wind —8D 46
Almond Clo. Wokgm —7H 89
Almond Dri. Cav —9M 39
Almond Rd. Burn —3L 21
Almond Ville. Burn —4M 21
Almons Way. Slou —6K 23
Almshouses. Read —5G 62
(off Castle St.)
Almswood Rd. Tadl —8J 105
Alpha St. N. Slou —1J 47
Alpha St. S. Slou —2H 47
Alpine St. Read —6H 63
Alsace Wlk. Camb —8M 119
Alston Gdns. M'head —7B 20
Alston M. That —9F 80
Alston Wlk. Cav —2K 63
Altona Way. Slou —7D 22
Alton Ride. B'water —3G 119
Altwood Bailey. M'head —9M 19
Altwood Clo. M'head —9M 19
Altwood Clo. Slou —6A 22
Altwood Dri. M'head —9M 19
Altwood Rd. M'head —9L 19
Alvista Av. Tap —7L 21
Alwyn Rd. M'head —6M 19
Alyson Ct. M'head —5C 20
Amanda Ct. Slou —2M 47
Ambarrow Cres. Sand —9D 112
Ambarrow La. Sand —8B 112
Ambassador. Brack —7K 91
Amberley Clo. Newb —7K 79
Amberley Ct. M'head —3F 20
Amberley Dri. Twy —7J 41
Amberley Rd. Slou —6A 22
Amberley Way. Uxb —3M 25
Amblecote Rd. Tile —5B 62
Ambleside Clo. Wdly —5D 64
Ambleside Rd. Light —9K 115
Ambleside Wlk. Uxb —2L 25
(off Cumbrian Way)
Ambrook Rd. Read —3H 87
Ambrose Pl. Read —5F 62
Ambrose Rd. Tadl —9K 105
Ambury Rd. Aldw —9A 14
Amen Corner Bus. Pk. Binf —4J 91
Amerden Clo. Tap —7G 21
Amerden La. Bray —1H 45
Amerden La. Tap —7G 21
Amerden Way. Slou —1C 46
Amersham Clo. Calc —8K 61
Amersham Rd. Cav —2K 63
Amethyst Clo. Wokgm —4J 89
Amethyst La. Read —6C 62
Amherst Rd. Read —6N 63
Amity Rd. Read —5L 63
Amity St. Read —4L 63
Ammanford. Cav —8F 38
Ampere Rd. Newb —8M 79
Ancaster Dri. Asc —3H 93
Ancastle Grn. Hen T —5B 16
Andermans. Wind —7N 45
Anderson Av. Ear —6N 63
Anderson Cres. Arbor X —9D 88
Anderson Pl. Bag —6H 115
Andover Clo. Tile —3L 61
Andover Clo. Uxb —3J 25
Andover Drove. Wash W —6F 100
Andover Rd. B'water —3G 118
Andover Rd. Newb —5H 101
Andover Rd. Pen —8F 100
Andrew Clo. Wokgm —6C 90
Andrew's Clo. Thea —9F 60
Andrews Rd. Ear —9A 64
Angel Ct. Newb —7L 79
Angel Mead. Woolh —9E 82
Angel Pl. Binf —1G 90
Angle Clo. Uxb —2N 25
Angle Field Rd. Cav —1J 63
Anglers Way. Read —5K 63
Anglesey Av. Farn —9K 119
Angus Clo. Calc —8M 61
Anne Clo. M'head —4B 20
Anneforde Pl. Brack —2L 91
Annerdale. Cold A —2F 80
Annesley Gdns. Winn —1H 89
Annett's La. Hung —3F 96
Ansculf Rd. Slou —4C 22
Anslow Gdns. Iver —3E 24
Anslow Pl. Slou —6M 21
Anson Cres. Read —4K 87
Anson Wlk. Read —4K 87
Anstey Pl. Bfld C —8H 85
Anstey Rd. Read —5F 62
Anston Clo. Lwr Ear —3N 87
Antares Clo. Wokgm —5L 89
Anthian Clo. Wdly —4G 65
Anthony Way. Slou —8N 21
Antrim Rd. Wdly —6C 64
Anvil Ct. Langl —3B 48
Apex Plaza. Read —4H 63
Aplin Way. Light —9K 115
Appleby End. Read —5B 62
Apple Clo. Tile —9J 37
Apple Clo. Wokgm —6L 89
Apple Croft. M'head —2N 43
Appledore. Brack —8K 91
Appledore M. Farn —9L 119
Appleford Clo. That —9G 81
Appleford Rd. Read —8A 62
Apple Tree Av. Uxb & W Dray —6N 25
Appletree Clo. Brack —3L 91
Appletree La. Slou —2L 47
Appletree La. Spen W —9H 87
Appletree Pl. Brack —3L 91
Apple Tree Way. Owl —9H 113
Appley Ct. Camb —4M 119
Appley Dri. Camb —3M 119
Approach Rd. Tap —7H 21
April Clo. Camb —7N 119
Apsey Ct. Binf —2J 91
Aquila Clo. Wokgm —5K 89
Aragon Ct. Brack —6N 91
Aragon Rd. Yat —5A 118
Arborfield Clo. Slou —2G 47
Arborfield Rd. Shin —7M 87
Arbor La. Winn —9G 64
Arbor Meadows. Winn —9G 64
Arbour Clo. Read —7F 62
Arcade, The. Newb —8L 79
Arcade, The. Wokgm —5A 90
Archangel Way. That —7J 81
Archer Clo. M'head —6A 20
Archers Ct. Mar —6C 4
Archer Ter. W Dray —8M 25
Arch Hill. Bin H —3N 39
Archway Rd. Cav —2G 63
Arden Clo. Brack —4C 92
Ardingly. Brack —7L 91
Ardler Rd. Cav —2J 63
Ardwell Clo. Crowt —5C 112
Arenal Dri. Crowt —7F 112
Argosy La. Stai —4L 73
Argyle Rd. Newb —9K 79
Argyle Rd. Read —5E 62
Argyle St. Read —5E 62
Argyll Av. Slou —8C 22
Arix Ho. Twy —8J 41
Arkle Av. That —8C 80
Arkley Ct. M'head —4F 44
Arkwright Dri. Brack —4H 91
Arkwright Rd. Coln —8F 48
Arkwright Rd. Read —9H 63
Arlington Bus. Pk. Thea —9H 61
Arlington Clo. Brack —3L 91
Arlington Clo. M'head —6K 19
Arlington La. Newb —9J 55
Arlington Rd. Ashf —9N 73
Arlington Sq. Brack —4L 91
Armadale Ct. Read —6D 62
Armitage Ct. Asc —8M 93
Armour Hill. Tile —2L 61
Armour Rd. Tile —3L 61
Armour Wlk. Tile —3L 61
Armstrong Rd. Egh —1L 95
Armstrong Way. Wdly —5F 64
Arncliffe. Brack —7L 91
Arndale Way. Egh —9B 72
Arnett Av. Wokgm —3K 111
Arnhem Rd. Newb —8M 79
Arnside Clo. Twy —6J 41
Arrowhead Rd. Thea —1F 84
Arrowsmith Way. That —9J 81
Arthur Clark Home, The. Cav —1F 62
Arthur Clo. Bag —9H 115
Arthur Pl. Read —5J 63
Arthur Rd. Newb —9J 79
Arthur Rd. Slou —1F 46
Arthur Rd. Wind —7E 46
Arthur Rd. Wokgm —5M 89
Arthurstone Birches. Binf —9H 67
Arun Clo. Winn —2G 89
Arundel Clo. M'head —6L 19
Arundel Ct. Slou —3M 47
Arundel Ho. Uxb —5K 25
Arundel Rd. Uxb —3J 25
Arundel Rd. Wdly —6D 64
Ascot Clo. Green —2N 101
Ascot Rd. M'head & Brack —2N 67
Ascot Wood Pl. Asc —5K 93
Ashampstead Rd. Read —8A 62
Ashampstead Rd. Up Bas —8J 35
Ashbourne. Brack —8K 91
Ashbourne Gro. M'head —2N 43
Ashbourne Ho. Chalv —1G 47
Ashbourne Way. That —8E 80
Ashbrook Rd. Old Win —4K 71
Ashburton Rd. Read —1J 87
Ashbury Dri. B'water —8L 119
Ashbury Dri. Tile —5K 61
Ashby Ct. Read —4H 87
Ash Clo. B'water —4G 119
Ash Clo. Bright —2B 30
Ash Clo. Slou —2C 48
Ash Ct. Newb —7L 79
Ash Ct. Wokgm —5A 90
Ashcroft Clo. Cav —8E 38
Ashcroft Ct. Burn —3L 21
Ashcroft Rd. M'head —6N 19
Ashdale Clo. Stai —6M 73
Ashdale Pk. Wokgm —4A 112
Ashdown. M'head —3E 20
Ashdown Clo. Brack —4D 92
Ashdown Rd. Uxb —3N 25
Asher Dri. Asc —3F 92
Ashfield Grn. Yat —4D 118
Ashford Av. Son C —1E 38
Ashford Clo. Ashf —8M 73
Ashford Cres. Ashf —7M 73
Ashford Hill Rd. Hdly —8G 102
Ashford La. Dor —1L 45
Ashford Rd. Iver —1D 24
Ash Ga. That —7J 81
Ash Grn. Read —3K 87
Ash Gro. Stai —9K 73
Ash Gro. Stoke P —1H 23
Ash Gro. W Dray —8N 25
Ash La. Baug —9G 104
Ash La. Bfld C —7H 85
Ash La. Wind —8N 45
Ashley Clo. Ear —1A 88
Ashley Ct. M'head —7E 20
Ashley Dri. B'water —5G 119
Ashley Hill Pl. C Grn —6L 17
Ashley Pk. M'head —4E 20
Ashley Rd. Read —7E 62
Ashley Rd. Uxb —3J 25
Ashman Rd. That —8K 81
Ashmere Clo. Calc —8K 61
Ashmere Ter. Read —4E 62
Ashmore Grn. Rd. Cold A —4E 80
Ashmore La. Wind —4C 68
Ashmore Rd. Read —2J 87
Ashridge. Farn —9K 119
Ashridge Ct. Newb —9L 79
Ashridge Grn. Brack —3M 91
Ashridge Rd. Wokgm —3B 90
Ash Rd. Bis G —7C 102
Ash Rd. Tile —5M 61
Ash Ter. Ashm G —3E 80
Ashton Clo. Tile —4K 61
Ashton Pl. Kint —9G 76
Ashton Pl. M'head —8L 19
Ashton Rd. Wokgm —2L 89
Ash Tree Gro. Ham M —3N 99
Ashtrees Rd. Wdly —4E 64
Ash View Clo. Ashf —9M 73
Ash View Gdns. Ashf —9M 73
Ashville Way. Wokgm —6N 89
Ash Way. Wokgm —8H 89
Ashwood. Wdly —7C 64
Ashwood Av. Uxb —7N 25
Ashwood Clo. Tile —6J 61
Ashwood Dri. Newb —7A 80
Ashwood Rd. Egh —1K 95
Ashworth Dri. That —9F 80
Askew Dri. Spen W —8H 87
Aspen Clo. Slou —6D 22
Aspen Clo. Stai —7G 73
Aspen Clo. W Dray —9N 25
Aspin Way. B'water —4F 118
Astley Clo. Wokgm —4L 89
Aston Av. Tile —4J 61
Aston Clo. Pang —8E 36
Aston Ct. Read —7B 62
Aston Ferry La. Ast —1H 17
Aston La. Rem —4H 17
Aston Mead. Wind —6A 46
Astor Clo. M'head —8E 20
Astor Clo. Winn —9J 65
Astra Mead. Wink R —1E 92
Atfield Gro. W'sham —6N 115
Atherton Clo. Stai —3L 73
Atherton Clo. Tile —4N 61
Atherton Ct. Wind —6F 46
Atherton Cres. Hung —6K 75
Atherton Pl. Lamb —2H 27
Atherton Rd. Hung —6K 75
Athlone Clo. M'head —5B 20
Athlone Sq. Wind —7E 46
Athol Way. Uxb —4N 25
Atkinson's All. M'head —6C 20
Atlantic Ho. Read —3G 87
Atrebatti Rd. Sand —9G 113
Attle Clo. Uxb —3N 25
Auburn Ct. Cav —2G 62
Auckland Clo. M'head —6E 20
Auckland Rd. Read —6N 63
Auclum Clo. Bfld C —9J 85
Auclum La. Bfld C —9J 85
Audley Clo. Newb —6A 80
Audley Dri. M'head —8M 19
Audley St. Read —4D 62
Audley Way. Asc —5G 92
Augur Clo. Stai —9G 73
August End. G Grn —7N 23
August End. Read —4C 62
Augustine Clo. Coln —9F 48
Augustine Wlk. Warf —2B 92
Austen Gdns. Newb —2M 101
Austin Rd. Wdly —6E 64
Austin Waye. Uxb —2K 25
Australia Av. M'head —6C 20
Australia Rd. Slou —1K 47
Auton Pl. Hen T —6C 16
Autumn Clo. Cav —6K 39
Autumn Clo. Slou —9B 22
Autumn Wlk. M'head —9L 19
Autumn Wlk. Warg —3J 41
Avalon Rd. Bour —2M 5
Avalon Rd. Ear —9B 64
Avebury. Brack —8L 91
Avebury. Slou —8C 22
Avebury Sq. Read —7K 63
Aveley Wlk. Read —7H 63
Avenue Clo. W Dray —2L 49
Avenue Rd. M'head —9E 20
Avenue Rd. Stai —9E 72
Avenue Sucy. Camb —5M 119
Avenue, The. Asc —1K 93
Avenue, The. Bour —3K 5
Avenue, The. Camb —4M 119
Avenue, The. Cow —5L 25
Avenue, The. Crowt —5F 112
Avenue, The. Dat —7K 47
Avenue, The. Egh —8C 72
Avenue, The. Light —9K 115
Avenue, The. M'head —3F 20
Avenue, The. Mort —5J 107
Avenue, The. Old Win —2K 71
Avenue, The. Wokgm —1J 113
Avenue, The. Wray —1N 71
Averil Ct. Tap —7M 21
Avington Clo. Tile —4J 61
Avocet Cres. Col T —1H 119
Avon Clo. Calc —7N 61
Avon Clo. Slou —8A 22
Avon Ct. Binf —1G 91
Avondale. M'head —5N 19
Avondale Rd. Ashf —7L 73
Avon Gro. Brack —2N 91
Avon Pl. Read —4K 63
Avon Way. Newb —7A 80
Avon Way. Pad —5N 83
Axbridge. Brack —7B 92
Axbridge Rd. Read —1J 87
Aylesbury Cres. Slou —7F 22
Aylesford Vs. Whis G —3K 65
Aylesworth Av. Slou —4D 22
Aylesworth Spur. Old Win —4K 71
Aylsham Clo. Tile —4M 61
Ayrton Senna Rd. Tile —5K 61
Aysgarth. Brack —8K 91
Aysgarth Pk. M'head —4E 44
Azalea Way. G Grn —7N 23

Bachelors Acre. Wind —7F 46
Back La. Been —5J 83
Back La. Brimp C —7D 104
Back La. Kint —2E 98
Back La. Spen W —2G 109
Back La. Stan D —8F 58
Back La. Tile —3J 61
Backsideans. Warg —3J 41
Back St. E Gar —7B 28
Bacon Clo. Col T —2H 119
Bader Ct. Farn —9K 119
Bader Gdns. Slou —1C 46
Bader Way. Wdly —7F 64
Badgebury Rise. Mar —1A 4
Badgemore La. Hen T —3C 16
Badger Clo. M'head —1A 44
Badger Dri. Light —9K 115
Badger Dri. Twy —6J 41
Badgersbridge Ride. Wind —4L 69
Badgers Clo. Ashf —9N 73
Badgers Croft. Mort C —4H 107
Badgers Glade. Bfld C —9H 85
Badgers Hill. Vir W —7L 95
Badgers Rise. Cav —8G 38
Badgers Sett. Crowt —5D 112
Badgers Wlk. S'lake —2F 40
Badgers Way. Brack —3C 92
Bad Goodesberg Way. M'head —7C 20
Badminton Rd. M'head —8M 19
Bagley Clo. W Dray —1M 49
Bagnols Way. Newb —9J 79
Bagshot Grn. Bag —7H 115
Bagshot Rd. Asc —2L 115
Bagshot Rd. Brack & Crowt —5M 91
Bagshot Rd. Egh —2L 95
Baigents La. W'sham —6N 115
Bailey Clo. M'head —7C 20
Bailey Clo. Wind —8C 46
Baileys Clo. B'water —5G 118
Bailey's La. Wal L —9C 42
Baily Av. That —7E 80
Bain Av. Camb —7M 119
Bainbridge Rd. Calc —8J 61
Baird Clo. Slou —1D 46
Baird Rd. Arbor X —2D 110
Bakeham La. Egh —2M 95
Bakers La. M'head —6K 19
Bakers Rd. Uxb —1L 25
Baker St. Read —5F 62
Bakers Yd. Uxb —1L 25
Baldwin Rd. Burn —4M 21
Baldwins Shore. Eton —5F 46
Balfour Cres. Brack —7M 91
Balfour Cres. Newb —5G 100
Balfour Dri. Calc —8J 61
Balfour Pl. Mar —3B 4
Balintore Ct. Col T —1H 119
Ballamoor Clo. Calc —9H 61
Ballard Grn. Wind —6A 46
Ballard Rd. Camb —9D 114
Ballencrief Rd. S'dale —9B 94
Balliol Rd. Cav —1D 62
Balliol Way. Owl —9J 113
Ball Pit Rd. E Ils —2L 31
Ball Pit Rd. W Ils —9M 11
Balmoral. M'head —5M 19
Balmoral Clo. Slou —7A 22
Balmoral Gdns. Wind —9F 46
Balmore Dri. Cav —9H 39
Balmore Pk. Cav —9H 39
Bamburgh Clo. Read —9J 63
Bamford Pl. Calc —8J 61
Banbury. Brack —9B 92
Banbury Av. Slou —6B 22
Banbury Gdns. Cav —1J 63
Band La. Egh —9A 72
Bandon Clo. Uxb —3N 25
Bangors Clo. Iver —7F 24
Bangors Rd. N. Iver —2E 24
Bangors Rd. S. Iver —4F 24
Bankside. Wokgm —4L 111
Bankside Clo. Read —1K 87
Banks Spur. Chalv —1D 46
Bank View. Hen T —4E 16
Bannard Rd. M'head —9L 19
Bannister Clo. Slou —1N 47
Bannister Gdns. Yat —4D 118
Bannister Rd. Bfld C —9G 84
Barbara's Meadow. Tile —2J 61
Barber Clo. Hurst —5K 65
Barberry Way. B'water —7K 119
Barbrook Clo. Tile —1L 61
Barchester Clo. Uxb —4K 25
Barchester Rd. Slou —1A 48
Barclay Rd. Calc —8K 61
Barclose Av. Cav —1J 63
Bardney Clo. M'head —2A 44
Bardolph's Clo. Tok G —5D 38
Bardown. Chvly —1L 55
Barfield Rd. That —7D 80
Barge La. Swal —7F 108
Bargeman Rd. M'head —1B 44
Bargeway, The. Blew —1B 12
Barholme Clo. Lwr Ear —1D 88
Barkby. Lwr Ear —1B 88
Barker Ct. Hurst —4L 65
Barker Grn. Brack —7M 91
Barkham Ride. Wokgm —1H 111
Barkham Rd. B'ham & Wokgm —9G 89
Barkham St. B'ham —9H 89
Barkhart Dri. Wokgm —4A 90
Barkhart Gdns. Wokgm —4A 90
Barkis Mead. Owl —8J 113
Barkwith Clo. Lwr Ear —1D 88
Barlee Cres. Uxb —6K 25
Barley Clo. That —9J 81
Barley Mead. Warf —2B 92
Barley Mow Rd. Egh —9L 71
Barley Wlk. Tile —6J 61
Barnacre Clo. Uxb —7L 25
Barnard Clo. Cav —8J 39
Barnards Hill. Mar —5A 4
Barn Clo. Brack —4A 92
Barn Clo. Kint —9G 76
Barn Clo. M'head —4C 20
Barn Clo. Read —8D 62
Barn Clo. La. Ashmw —9M 117
Barn Cres. Newb —3H 101
Barn Dri. M'head —1L 43
Barnes Way. Iver —8G 25
Barnett Ct. Brack —4A 92
Barnett Grn. Brack —8M 91
Barnfield. Iver —7F 24
Barnfield. Slou —9N 21
Barn Field. Yat —4B 118
Barnfield Clo. Cook —1C 20
Barnhill Clo. Mar —3B 4
Barnhill Gdns. Mar —3B 4
Barnhill Rd. Mar —3B 4
Barn La. Hen T —2B 16
Barn Owl Way. Bfld C —8J 85
Barnsdale Rd. Read —9K 63
Barnsfield Pl. Uxb —1K 25
Barnway. Egh —9L 71
Barnwood Clo. Read —4E 62
Baron Ct. Read —5D 62
Baronsmead. Hen T —4C 16
Barons Way. Egh —9E 72
Barony Ho. Brack —3J 91
Barossa Rd. Camb —2N 119
Barracane Dri. Crowt —5F 112
Barrack La. Wind —7F 46
Barracks La. Spen W —9H 87
Barracks Rd. Green —5C 102
Barrett Cres. Wokgm —5B 90
Barrett's La. Arbor —5C 88
Barrington Clo. Ear —6A 64
Barrington Ho. Read —4H 87
Barrow Lodge. Slou —5E 22
Barr's Rd. Tap —7L 21
Barry Av. Wind —6E 46
Barry Pl. Read —4G 62
Bartelotts Rd. Slou —5N 21
Bartholomew Pl. Warf —2A 92
Bartholomew St. Newb —9K 79
Bartlemy Clo. Newb —2J 101
Bartlemy Rd. Newb —2J 101
Bartletts La. Holyp —6C 44
Barton Rd. Slou —1A 48
Barton Rd. Tile —6J 61
Bartons Dri. Yat —5B 118
Bartons Way. Farn —9G 119
Barwell Clo. Crowt —5D 112
Basemoors. Brack —4B 92
Basford Way. Wind —9N 45
Basil Clo. Ear —2M 87
Basingstoke Rd. Aldm —2H 105
Basingstoke Rd. Hook —9H 109
Basingstoke Rd. Read —5H 87
Basingstoke Rd. Rise —8H 109
Basingstoke Rd. Spen W & Swal —1G 109
Basingstoke Rd. Three M —6G 87
Baskerville La. S'lake —2F 40
Baskerville Rd. Son C —1E 38
Baslow Rd. Winn —1G 88
Basmore Av. Lwr S —1G 40
Bassett Clo. Lwr Ear —3B 88
Bassett Rd. Uxb —1K 25
Bassett Way. Slou —5B 22
Bass Mead. Cook —1C 20
Batcombe Mead. Brack —9B 92
Bates Clo. G Grn —7N 23
Bath Ct. M'head —8N 19
Bath Rd. Calc & Read —8H 61
Bath Rd. Camb —3N 119
Bath Rd. Coln —5C 48
(Brands Hill)
Bath Rd. Coln —7F 48
(Poyle)
Bath Rd. Colt —8J 81
Bath Rd. Edd —5L 75
Bath Rd. Frox —7A 74
Bath Rd. Hare H —5M 41
Bath Rd. Hung —6E 74
Bath Rd. M'head —8J 19
Bath Rd. Newb —6D 78
Bath Rd. Slou —7L 21
Bath Rd. Son —3B 64
Bath Rd. Tap —7F 20
Bath Rd. That —7C 80
Bath Rd. Thea —1D 84
Bath Rd. W Dray & Hay —7J 49
Bathurst Clo. Iver —1G 49
Bathurst Rd. Winn —1G 89
Bathurst Wlk. Iver —1F 48
Battery End. Newb —4H 101
Battle Clo. Speen —7H 79
Battlemead Clo. M'head —3F 20
Battle Rd. Gor —7N 15
Battle Rd. Newb —4G 101
Battle St. Read —4F 62
Batty's Barn Clo. Wokgm —6B 90
Baughurst Rd. Aldm —4A 106
Baughurst Rd. Baug —9F 104
Bawtree Rd. Uxb —1L 25
Baxendales, The. Green —1N 101
Bay Clo. Ear —2M 87
Baydon Dri. Read —7E 62
Baydon Rd. Lamb W —7B 26
Baydon Rd. Shef W —5B 52
Bay Dri. Brack —4B 92
Bayer Ho. Newb —7K 79
Bayford Clo. B'water —8L 119
Bayford Dri. Calc —8N 61
Bay Ho. Brack —4B 92
Bayley Ct. Winn —2G 89
Bayley Cres. Burn —6K 21
Baylis Pde. Slou —7G 22
Baylis Rd. Slou —8F 22
Bayliss Rd. Warg —4J 41
Bay Rd. Brack —3B 92
Baysfarm Ct. W Dray —7K 49
Baytree Ct. Burn —4M 21
Bay Tree Rise. Calc —7K 61
Beacon Ct. Read —5D 62
Beaconsfield Rd. Farn R —3E 22
Beaconsfield Way. Ear —1N 87
Beacontree Plaza. Read —1H 87
Beales Farm Rd. Lamb —3H 27
Beals La. Tile —5H 61
Beancroft Rd. That —9G 81
Bean Oak Rd. Wokgm —5C 90
Bearfield La. Hung —4H 51
Bear La. Newb —8L 79
Bearwood Path. Winn —9F 64
Bearwood Rd. Sind —3G 88
Beatty Dri. Read —4M 61
Beauchief Clo. Lwr Ear —3M 87
Beaudesert Rd. W Dray —1M 49
Beaufield Clo. Wdly —5C 64
Beaufort Clo. Mar —5C 4
Beaufort Gdns. Asc —3H 93
Beaufort Gdns. Mar —5C 4
Beaufort Pl. Bray —1G 44
Beauforts. Egh —9L 71
Beaulieu Clo. Brack —5C 92
Beaulieu Clo. Dat —7K 47
Beaulieu Gdns. B'water —4G 118
Beaumaris Ct. Slou —6D 22
Beaumont Clo. M'head —2L 43
Beaumont Gdns. Brack —7B 92
Beaumont Rise. Mar —5C 4
Beaumont Rd. Slou —5F 22
Beaumont Rd. Wind —8E 46
Beaver La. Yat —4C 118
Beavers Clo. Tadl —9J 105
Beaver Way. Wdly —5G 64
Beckett Clo. Wokgm —5C 90
Beckford Av. Brack —8M 91
Beckfords. Up Bas —7J 35
Beckings Way. F Hth —1N 5
Bec Tithe. Whit H —2F 36
Bede Wlk. Read —9J 63
Bedfont Ct. Stai —9H 49
Bedfont Rd. Stai —3M 73
Bedford Av. Slou —7B 22
Bedford Clo. M'head —2L 43
Bedford Clo. Newb —5G 100
Bedford Gdns. Wokgm —4L 89
Bedford La. Asc —7D 94

Bedford Rd. Read —4F **62**
(in two parts)
Bedfordshire Down. Warf —1C **92**
Bedfordshire Way. Wokgm —5J **89**
Bedwins La. Cook —9F **4**
Beecham Rd. Read —5C **62**
Beechbrook Av. Yat —4C **118**
Beech Clo. Bfld —7J **85**
Beech Clo. Stai —4L **73**
Beech Clo. W Dray —2N **49**
Beechcroft. Hamp N —8K **33**
Beechcroft Clo. Asc —6N **93**
Beechcroft Ct. Brack —5M **91**
Beech Dri. B'water —5H **119**
Beeches Rd. Bis G —7D **102**
Beeches, The. Gor —9K **15**
Beeches, The. Tile —1L **61**
Beechfield. Fril —5N **57**
Beech Glen. Brack —6M **91**
Beech Hill Rd. Asc —8B **94**
Beech Hill Rd. B Hill —5D **108**
Beechingstoke. Mar —4D **4**
Beech La. Ear —9N **63**
Beech La. Woodc —5N **15**
Beech Lodge. Stai —9F **72**
Beechmont Av. Vir W —7M **95**
Beechnut Clo. Wokgm —6L **89**
Beechnut Dri. B'water —3F **118**
Beech Ride. Sand —1F **118**
Beech Rd. Farn —9L **119**
Beech Rd. Pur T —8H **37**
Beech Rd. Read —1L **87**
Beech Rd. Slou —1N **47**
Beech Rd. Tok G —6D **38**
Beechtree Av. Egh —1K **95**
Beechtree Av. Mar —2B **4**
Beech Wlk. Hung —1D **96**
Beech Wlk. That —9H **81**
Beech Wlk. W'sham —6N **115**
Beechwood Av. Tile —4L **61**
Beechwood Av. Uxb —7N **25**
Beechwood Av. Wdly —5C **64**
Beechwood Clo. Asc —2H **93**
Beechwood Dri. M'head —8L **19**
Beechwood Rd. Slou —6F **22**
Beechwood Rd. Vir W —9J **95**
Beedon Dri. Brack —8H **91**
Beehive Clo. Uxb —1N **25**
Beehive La. Binf —4G **91**
Beehive Rd. Binf —4H **91**
Beehive Rd. Stai —9G **73**
Beggars Hill Rd. Land E —2G **64**
Beighton Clo. Lwr Ear —3M **87**
Belfast Av. Slou —7E **22**
Belgrave Ct. B'water —6H **119**
Belgrave M. Uxb —5L **25**
Belgrave Pl. Slou —1J **47**
Belgrave Rd. Slou —8G **23**
Belgravia Ct. Read —6D **62**
Bell Av. W Dray —3N **49**
Bell Clo. Slou —6K **23**
Bellclose Rd. W Dray —1M **49**
Bell Ct. Hur —3D **18**
Bell Ct. Twy —8J **41**
Belle Av. Read —7N **63**
Belleisle. Pur T —8J **37**
Belleisle Ct. Pur T —8J 37
(off Trenthams Clo.)
Belle Vue Rd. Hen T —6C **16**
Belle Vue Rd. Read —5F **62**
Belle Vue Ter. Read —5E **62**
Bell Foundry La. Wokgm —2N **89**
Bell Hill. Newb —5G **100**
Bell Holt. Newb —5G **100**
Bell Ho. Gdns. Wokgm —5N **89**
Bellingham Wlk. Cav —8G **39**
Bell La. Aldw —1B **34**
Bell La. B'water —4G **118**
Bell La. Eton W —3B **46**
Bell La. Hen T —4D **16**
Bell La. Ink —7C **98**
Bell Pde. Wind —8B **46**
Bell Pl. Bag —7J **115**
Bells Hill. Stoke P —2J **23**
Bells Hill Grn. Stoke P —1J **23**
Bells La. Hort —9C **48**
Bell St. Hen T —4D **16**
Bell St. M'head —8C **20**
Bellswood La. Iver —6C **24**
Bell View. Wind —9B **46**
Bell View Clo. Wind —8B **46**
Bellvue Pl. Slou —2H **47**
Bellweir Clo. Stai —6C **72**
Belmont. Slou —6C **22**
Belmont Clo. Uxb —1L **25**
Belmont Cres. M'head —6N **19**
Belmont Dri. M'head —6A **20**
Belmont M. Camb —6N **119**
Belmont Pk. Av. M'head —5A **20**
Belmont Pk. Rd. M'head —6A **20**
Belmont Rd. Camb —5N **119**
Belmont Rd. Crowt —4F **112**
Belmont Rd. M'head —6A **20**
Belmont Rd. Read —5D **62**
Belmont Rd. Uxb —1L **25**
Belmont Vale. M'head —6A **20**
Belvedere Ct. B'water —6H **119**
Belvedere Dri. Newb —2L **101**
Belvedere Dri. Winn —9F **64**
Belvedere Mans. Chalv —1F **46**
Bembridge Ct. Slou —2H **47**
Bembridge Pl. Read —5J **63**
Benbow Waye. Uxb —6K **25**
Benbricke Grn. Brack —2L **91**
Bencombe Rd. Mar —2C **4**
Benedict Grn. Warf —2B **92**
Benen-Stock Rd. Stai —2H **73**
Benetfield Rd. Binf —1F **90**
Benham La. Rise —7K **109**
Bennet Ct. Camb —4N **119**
Bennet Ct. Read —2G **87**
Bennet Rd. Read —2G **86**
Bennet's Hill. Bfld —4J **85**
Bennett Clo. Newb —6K **79**
Bennett Clo. Gdns. Newb —6K **79**
Bennetts Clo. Slou —9C **22**
Bennett's Yd. Uxb —1K **25**
Benning Clo. Wind —9N **45**
Bennings Clo. Brack —2L **91**
Benning Way. Wokgm —3A **90**
Benson Clo. Read —9K **63**
Benson Clo. Slou —9J **23**
Benson Clo. Uxb —6M **25**
Bensonholme. Pad —8L **83**
Benson Rd. Crowt —5D **112**
Bentinck Rd. W Dray —9L **25**
Bentley Pk. Burn —3N **21**
Bentley Rd. Slou —9C **22**
Benyon Ct. Read —6E **62**
(in two parts)
Benyon M. Read —6E **62**
Berberis Wlk. W Dray —3M **49**
Bere Ct. Rd. Pang —2A **60**
Bere Rd. Brack —8B **92**
Beresford Av. Slou —8L **23**
Beresford Rd. Read —4E **62**
Berkeley Av. Read —6E **62**
Berkeley Clo. M'head —6L **19**
Berkeley Ct. Read —6F **62**
Berkeley Dri. Wink —5K **69**
Berkeley M. Burn —7N **21**
Berkeley Rd. Newb —9K **79**
Berkley Clo. Stai —6E **72**
Berkshire Av. Slou —7D **22**
Berkshire Bus. Cen. That —9K **81**
Berkshire Ct. Brack —4K **91**
Berkshire Dri. That —9K **81**
Berkshire Dri. Tile —5K **61**
Berkshire Rd. Camb —9C **114**
Berkshire Rd. Hen T —6C **16**
Berkshire Way. Wokgm & Brack —5F **90**
Bernadine Clo. Warf —2B **92**
Bernard Ct. Camb —5M **119**
Berners Clo. Slou —8A **22**
Bernersh Clo. Sand —9G **113**
Berries Rd. Cook —8L **5**
Berrybank. Col T —3J **119**
Berrycroft. Brack —3A **92**
Berryfield. Slou —7L **23**
Berry Hill. Tap —7G **21**
Berrylands Rd. Cav —1H **63**
Berry La. Brack —4C **68**
Berrys La. Read —2N **85**
Berrys Rd. Up Buck —5M **81**
Berstead Clo. Lwr Ear —2A **88**
Berwick Av. Slou —7D **22**
Berwick La. Mar —4B **4**
Berwick Rd. Mar —4A **4**
Beryl Clo. Wokgm —4K **89**
Bestobell Rd. Slou —7E **22**
Beswick Gdns. Brack —3C **92**
Betam Rd. Read —5K **63**
Betchworth Av. Ear —9N **63**
Bethesda St. Up Bas —7J **35**
Betjeman Ct. W Dray —9L **25**
Betjeman Wlk. Yat —5A **118**
Betteridge Rd. That —9J **81**
Bettles Clo. Uxb —3K **25**
Bettoney Vere. Bray —1F **44**
Beverley Clo. Mar —5A **4**
Beverley Clo. That —7F **80**
Beverley Ct. Slou —1K **47**
Beverley Gdns. M'head —5M **19**
Beverley Gdns. Warg —4K **41**
Beverley Rd. Tile —3K **61**
Bevers, The. Mort C —4H **107**
Bexley Ct. Read —6D **62**
Bexley St. Wind —7E **46**
Bibury Clo. Wdly —8C **64**
Bideford Clo. Farn —9K **119**
Bideford Clo. Wdly —7B **64**
Bideford Spur. Slou —4D **22**
Bietigheim Way. Camb —3N **119**
Big Barn Gro. Warf —2B **92**
Bigbury Gdns. Read —9J **63**
Bigfrith La. Cook —9E **4**
Biggs La. Arbor & Finch —1E **110**
Big La. Lamb —2H **27**
Biko Clo. Uxb —6K **25**
Biko Ct. Read —5J **63**
Billet La. Iver & Slou —4C **24**
Billet Rd. Stai —7H **73**
Billing Av. Finch —4K **111**
Billingbear La. Binf —7F **66**
Bilton Clo. Coln —8F **48**
Bilton Ind. Est. Brack —6J **91**
Binbrook Clo. Lwr Ear —1C **88**
Binfield Rd. Brack —1K **91**
Binfield Rd. Wokgm —1E **90**
Bingham Rd. Burn —6K **21**
Binghams, The. M'head —2E **44**
Bingley Gro. Wdly —3E **64**
Binstead Dri. B'water —4H **119**
Birch Av. Tile —4A **62**
Birch Av. W Dray —7N **25**
Birch Clo. Camb —9B **114**
Birch Clo. Iver —3E **24**
Birch Clo. Son C —1F **38**
Birch Cres. Uxb —2N **25**
Birch Dri. B'water —6H **119**
Birches, The. B'water —4F **118**
Birches, The. Gor —8K **15**
Birchetts Clo. Brack —3M **91**
Birchfields. Camb —5N **119**
Birch Grn. Stai —8H **73**
Birch Gro. Brack —6N **91**
Birch Gro. Slou —6D **22**
Birch Gro. Wind —7N **45**
Birch Hill Rd. Brack —9M **91**
Birchington Rd. Wind —8C **46**
Birchland Clo. Mort W —4F **106**
Birchlands Ct. Owl —8J **113**
Birch La. Asc —3D **92**
Birch La. Mort C —5G **106**
Birchmead. Winn —1J **89**
Birch Rd. Bfld C —8G **85**
Birch Rd. Tadl —8G **105**
Birch Rd. W'sham —6N **115**
Birch Rd. Wokgm —3L **111**
Birch Side. Crowt —4D **112**
Birch Tree View. Light —9K **115**
Birch View. Read —1K **87**
Birchview Clo. Yat —5A **118**
Birchwood Clo. Cav —7J **39**
Birchwood Dri. Light —9M **115**
Birchwood Rd. Newb —7A **80**
Birchwoods, The. Tile —4J **61**
Birdhill Av. Read —1K **87**
Bird M. Wokgm —5N **89**
Birds La. Midg —7N **81**
Bird Wood Ct. Son C —1G **39**
Birdwood Rd. Col T —2K **119**
Birdwood Rd. M'head —7L **19**
Birkbeck Pl. Owl —9J **113**
Birkdale. Brack —9J **91**
Birkhall Clo. Calc —7K **61**
Birley Rd. Slou —7F **22**
Bisham Ct. Bish —9C **4**
Bisham Ct. Slou —1H **47**
Bishop Ct. M'head —8A **20**
Bishopdale. Brack —6L **91**
Bishops Clo. Uxb —3N **25**
Bishop's Dri. Wokgm —4A **90**
Bishops Farm Clo. Oak G —8L **45**
Bishopsgate Rd. Egh —7J **71**
Bishops Gro. W'sham —6N **115**
Bishop's La. Brack —4D **68**
Bishops Orchard. Farn R —4D **22**
Bishop's Rd. Read —6N **63**
Bishops Rd. Slou —1J **47**
Bishops Rd. Tut C —1G **83**
Bishops Way. Egh —9E **72**
Bishopswood Ct. Baug —9H **105**
Bishopswood La. Baug —9G **104**
Bishopswood Rd. Tadl —9H **105**
Bispham Ct. Read —6J **63**
Bissley Dri. M'head —2K **43**
Bitham La. Hung —5H **97**
Bitham Rd. Lock —1N **9**
Bittern Clo. Col T —1H **119**
Bitterne Av. Tile —6J **61**
Bix La. M'head —5K **19**
Blackamoor La. M'head —5D **20**
Blackbird Clo. Bfld C —8J **85**
Blackbird Clo. Col T —1H **119**
Blackbird La. Bis G —7D **102**
Blackbird La. M'head —9C **44**
Black Boy La. Hur —3A **18**
Blackbushe Airport. B'water —6A **118**
Blackbushe Bus. Pk. Yat —5A **118**
Blackbushe Pk. Yat —4A **118**
Blackcap Pl. Col T —1J **119**
Blackdown Way. That —9F **80**
Black Horse Clo. Wind —8N **45**
Blacklands Rd. Up Buck —6M **81**
Blackley Clo. Ear —9D **64**
Blackmeadows. Brack —8N **91**
Blackmoor Clo. Asc —4G **92**
Blackmoor Wood. Asc —4G **92**
Blackmore La. Son C —1G **38**
Blackmore Way. Uxb —1L **25**
Blacknest Ga. Rd. Asc —5D **94**
Blacknest Rd. S'dale & Vir W —5F **94**
Black Pk. Rd. Wex —3N **23**
Blackpond La. Farn C —1D **22**
Blacksmith Row. Slou —3B **48**
Blackstroud La. E. Light —9N **115**
Blackstroud La. W. Light —9N **115**
Blackthorn Av. W Dray —3N **49**
Blackthorn Clo. Tile —3J **61**
Blackthorn Cres. Farn —9K **119**
Blackthorn Dell. Slou —2L **47**
Blackthorne Cres. Coln —8F **48**
Blackthorne Ind. Est. Coln —9F **48**
Blackthorne Rd. Coln —9F **48**
Blackwater Clo. Cav —9L **39**
Blackwater Clo. Spen W —9H **87**
Blackwater Ind. Est. B'water —4J **119**
Blackwater Rise. Calc —8H **61**
Blackwater Valley Relief Rd. Camb —5K **119**
Blackwater Valley Route. Farn —9N **119**
Blaenant. Cav —8F **38**
Blaenavon. Cav —8F **38**
Blagdon Rd. Read —1J **87**
Blagrave Farm La. Cav —8C **38**
Blagrave La. Cav —1C **62**
Blagrave Rise. Tile —6K **61**
Blagrave St. Read —4H **63**
Blagrove Dri. Wokgm —7L **89**
Blagrove La. Wokgm —7L **89**
Blair Rd. Slou —9G **22**
Blake Clo. Crowt —6G **112**
Blake Clo. Wokgm —3C **90**
Blakeney Ct. M'head —5C **20**
Blakeney Fields. Gt Shef —9G **28**
Blakes Cotts. Read —5J **63**
Blakes La. Hare H —3L **41**
Blake's La. Tadl —9K **105**
Blakes Ride. Yat —3A **118**
Blakes Rd. Warg —3J **41**
Blanchard Clo. Wdly —4G **64**
Blandford Clo. Slou —2M **47**
Blandford Ct. Slou —2M **47**
Blandford Rd. Read —3J **87**
Blandford Rd. N. Slou —2M **47**
Blandford Rd. S. Slou —2M **47**
Bland's Clo. Bfld C —9G **85**
Blandy Rd. Hen T —7B **16**
Blandys Hill. Kint —2G **98**
Blandy's La. Up Bas —6K **35**
Blane's La. Brack & Asc —1C **114**
Blatches Clo. Thea —9E **60**
Blay's Clo. Egh —1L **95**
Blay's La. Egh —2K **95**
Bledlow Clo. Newb —5H **101**
Blenheim Clo. Wokgm —5K **89**
Blenheim Gdns. Read —6L **63**
Blenheim Pl. Read —6G 62
(off Castle St.)
Blenheim Rd. Cav —9G **38**
Blenheim Rd. M'head —6M **19**
Blenheim Rd. Newb —9K **79**
Blenheim Rd. Read —5K **63**
Blenheim Rd. Slou —3M **47**
Blenheim Ter. Read —6G 62
(off Castle St.)
Blewburton Wlk. Brack —6B **92**
Blewbury Dri. Tile —5J **61**
Blinco La. G Grn —7N **23**
Blind La. Bour & F Hth —3L **5**
Blind La. Holyp —5D **44**
Blind La. Lamb —3H **27**
Blomfield Dale. Brack —4H **91**
Blondell Clo. W Dray —5L **49**
Bloomfield Dri. Brack —2A **92**
Bloomfieldhatch La. Graz —2B **108**
Bloomfield Rd. M'head —9L **19**
Bloomsbury Way. B'water —6G **119**
Blossom Av. Thea —9F **60**
Blossom La. Thea —9F **60**
Blossom Way. Uxb —1N **25**
Blossom Way. W Dray —3N **49**
Blount Cres. Binf —2J **91**
Blount's Ct. Rd. Son C —1H **39**
Bloxworth Clo. Brack —6C **92**
Blue Ball La. Egh —9A **72**
Bluebell Dri. Bfld C —8G **84**
Bluebell Hill. Brack —3B **92**
Bluebell Meadow. Winn —9H **65**
Bluecoats. That —7G **80**
Blue Coat Wlk. Brack —7A **92**
Bluethroat Clo. Col T —1J **119**
Blumfield Ct. Slou —5N **21**
Blumfield Cres. Slou —6N **21**
Blundell's Rd. Tile —4M **61**
Blunts Av. W Dray —6N **49**
Blyth Av. That —9H **81**
Blythe Clo. Iver —7G **24**
Blythewood La. Asc —5H **93**
Blyth Wlk. Read —7H 63
(off Charndon Clo.)
Boames La. Enb —4D **100**
Board La. Half —6L **77**
Boarlands Clo. Slou —8B **22**
Boarlands Path. Cipp —8B **22**
Boathouse Reach. Hen T —5D **16**
Bobgreen Ct. Read —5J **87**
Bobmore La. Mar —3C **4**
Bockhampton Rd. Lamb —3H **27**
Bockmer La. Medm —1N **17**
Boden's Ride. Asc —2G **115**
Bodmin Av. Slou —6C **22**
Bodmin Clo. That —9F **80**
Bodmin Rd. Wdly —7B **64**
Body Rd. Read —5G **62**
Bog La. Brack —7C **92**
Bolderwood. Bfld C —8G **85**
Boleyn Clo. Stai —9F **72**
Bolingbroke Way. That —8J **81**
Bolney Rd. Lwr S —9G **16**
Bolney Trevor Dri. Lwr S —1F **40**
Bolton Av. Wind —9F **46**
Bolton Cres. Wind —9E **46**
Bolton Pl. Newb —8L **79**
Bolton Rd. P'mre —6H **31**
Bolton Rd. Wind —9E **46**
Boltons La. Binf —1J **91**
Bolwell Clo. Twy —9L **41**
Bomer Clo. W Dray —6N **49**
Bomford Clo. Herm —6C **56**
Bond Clo. W Dray —7N **25**
Bond St. Egh —9K **71**
Bone La. Newb —8M **79**
Bonemill La. Enb —9H **79**
Bones La. Bin H —2N **39**
Bonsey's Yd. Uxb —1L **25**
Borderside. Slou —7J **23**
Borrowdale Rd. Winn —8G **64**
Bosanquet Clo. Uxb —5L **25**
Boscawen Way. That —8K **81**
Bosham Clo. Ear —3A **88**
Bosman Dri. W'sham —3L **115**
Bostock La. Thea —1C **84**
Boston Av. Read —7F **62**
Boston Dri. Bour —4M **5**
Boston Gro. Slou —7E **22**
Boston Rd. Hen T —6D **16**
Bosworth Gdns. Wdly —8D **64**
Botany Clo. That —8J **81**
Bothy, The. Warg —3J **41**
Botmoor Way. Chad —7K **29**
Bottisham Clo. Lwr Ear —3B **88**
Bottle La. L Grn —1D **42**
Bottle La. Warf —4J **67**
Bottom Ho. Son C —1F **38**
Bottom La. Sul'd —4D **84**
Bouldish Farm Rd. Asc —7J **93**
Boulmer Rd. Uxb —4K **25**
Boulters Clo. M'head —5F **20**
Boulters Clo. Slou —1C **46**
Boulters Clo. Wdly —4E **64**
Boulters Ct. M'head —5F **20**
Boulters Gdns. M'head —5F **20**
Boulters Ho. Brack —6B **92**
Boulters La. M'head —5F **20**
Boulton Rd. Read —9G **63**
Boult St. Read —5J **63**
Boult's Wlk. Read —7H **63**
Boundary Clo. Tile —6K **61**
Boundary La. Cav —1E **62**
Boundary Rd. Ashf —9K **73**
Boundary Rd. Newb —8M **79**
Boundary Rd. Tap —5H **21**
Boundary Vs. B'water —5J **119**
Bourn Clo. Lwr Ear —2B **88**
Bourne Arch. That —7E **80**
Bourne Av. Read —8H **63**
Bourne Av. Wind —9E **46**
Bourne Clo. Bour —2M **5**
Bourne Clo. Calc —8J **61**
Bourne Cotts. Wool H —7D **100**
Bourne End Bus. Cen. Bour
(off Cores End Rd.) —4M 5
Bourne Rd. Pang —8E **36**
Bourne Rd. Slou —1F **46**
Bourne Rd. That —7E **80**
Bourne Rd. Vir W —7M **95**
Bourneside. Vir W —9J **95**
Bourne Vale. Hung —6J **75**
Bourton Clo. Tile —5N **61**
Bouverie Way. Slou —4N **47**
Boveney Clo. Slou —1C **46**
Boveney New Rd. Eton W —3A **46**
Boveney Rd. Dor —4M **45**
Bowden Rd. Asc —7M **93**
Bower Cres. Wokgm —3A **90**
Bower Way. Slou —8A **22**
Bowes-Lyon Clo. Wind —7E 46
(off Alma Rd.)
Bowes Rd. Stai —9F **72**
Bowes Rd. That —9G **80**
Bowfell Clo. Tile —2K **61**
Bowland Dri. Brack —9B **92**
Bowling Clo. Uxb —2N **25**
Bowling Ct. Hen T —3C **16**
Bowling Grn. La. Pur T —8J **37**
Bowling Grn. Rd. That —6D **80**
Bowlings, The. Camb —3N **119**
Bowman Ct. Wel C —6D **112**
Bowmans Clo. Burn —3L **21**
Bowry Dri. Wray —3A **72**
Bowyer Cres. Wokgm —3A **90**
Bowyer Dri. Slou —9A **22**
Bowyer's La. Brack —6M **67**
Boxford Ridge. Brack —5M **91**
Boxwood Clo. W Dray —1N **49**
Boyd Ct. Brack —3L **91**
Boyle Clo. Uxb —3N **25**
Boyndon Rd. M'head —7A **20**
Boyn Hill Av. M'head —8A **20**
Boyn Hill Clo. M'head —8A **20**
Boyn Hill Rd. M'head —9N **19**
Boyn Valley Rd. M'head —9N **19**
Bracebridge. Camb —4L **119**
Bracken Bank. Asc —3F **92**
Bracken Clo. Tile —3K **61**
Bracken Copse. Ink —5D **98**
Brackendale Rd. Camb —4N **119**
Brackendale Way. Read —7N **63**
Brackenforde. Slou —1L **47**
Bracken Rd. M'head —1N **43**
Brackens, The. Crowt —3E **112**
Bracken Way. Bfld C —9H **85**
Bracken Way. F Hth —1M **5**
Brackenwood Dri. Tadl —9J **105**
Bracknell Beeches. Brack —5M **91**
Bracknell Clo. Camb —9C **114**
Bracknell Enterprise Cen. Brack —4L **91**
Bracknell Rd. Bag —4G **115**
Bracknell Rd. Camb —8D **114**
Bracknell Rd. Crowt —5G **113**
Bracknell Rd. Crowt —1C **114**
(Penny Hill)
Bracknell Rd. Warf —9B **68**
Bradcutts La. Cook —6H **5**
Bradenham La. Mar —1G **18**
Bradfields. Brack —7A **92**
Bradford Rd. Slou —7C **22**
Brading Way. Pur T —8L **37**
Bradley Clo. Kint —1G **98**
Bradley Rd. Slou —8F **22**
Bradmore Way. Lwr Ear —3N **87**
Bradshaw Clo. Wind —7A **46**
Bradshawe Waye. Uxb —6N **25**
Bradwell Rd. Tile —1K **61**
Braemar Gdns. Slou —1C **46**
Braemore Clo. That —1G **102**
Bramber Ct. Slou —9C **22**
Bramber M. Cav —9L **39**
Bramble Clo. Uxb —7N **25**
Bramble Cres. Tile —4M **61**
Bramble Dri. M'head —1L **43**
Bramblegate. Crowt —4E **112**
Brambles, The. Crowt —4B **112**
Brambles, The. Newb —2J **101**
Brambles, The. W Dray —3M **49**
Bramblings. Cav —7E **38**
Bramley Clo. Ear —9N **63**
Bramley Clo. M'head —2N **43**
Bramley Clo. Stai —9K **73**
Bramley Ct. Crowt —6C **112**
Bramley Gro. Crowt —5B **112**
Bramley La. B'water —4F **118**
Bramley Rd. Camb —7M **119**
Bramley Rd. Sil —9C **106**
Bramling Av. Yat —3A **118**
Brammas Clo. Slou —2E **46**
Brampton Chase. Lwr S —1F **40**
Brampton Ct. M'head —6E **20**
Brampton M. Mar —6B **4**
Bramshaw Rd. Read —3A **62**
Bramshill Clo. Arbor —2D **110**
Bramwell Clo. That —9J **81**
Bran Clo. Tile —4M **61**
Brandon Av. Wdly —3F **64**
Brands Rd. Slou —5C **48**
Brandville Rd. W Dray —1M **49**
Branksome Ct. Read —5F **62**
Branksome Hill Rd. Col T —2J **119**
Brant Clo. Arbor X —9D **88**
Brants Bri. Brack —4B **92**
Braunfels Wlk. Newb —9J **79**
Braybank. Bray —1F **44**
Braybourne Clo. Uxb —1K **25**
Braybrook Dri. Hurst —4L **65**
Braybrooke Gdns. Warg —4J **41**
Braybrooke Rd. Brack —2M **91**
Braybrook Rd. Warg —4J **41**
Bray Clo. Bray —2F **44**
Bray Ct. M'head —3F **44**
Braye Clo. Sand —9G **113**
Brayfield Rd. Bray —1F **44**
Brayford Rd. Read —3J **87**
Bray Rd. M'head —8E **20**
Bray Rd. Read —8B **62**
Braywick Rd. M'head —8C **20**
Braywood Av. Egh —9A **72**
Braziers La. Wink R —9G **68**
Breach Cotts. Ham —7L **97**
Breach Sq. Hung —7K **75**
Breadcroft La. M'head —1J **43**
Breadcroft Rd. M'head —2K **43**
Bream Clo. Mar —7A **4**
Brean Wlk. Ear —1N **87**
Brearley Clo. Uxb —1M **25**
Brechin Ct. Read —6J 63
(off Kendrick Rd.)
Brecon Ct. Chalv —1E **46**
Brecon Rd. Wdly —4E **64**
Bredon Rd. Wokgm —2L **89**
Bredward Clo. Burn —4L **21**
Breech, The. Col T —2J **119**
Breedon's Hill. Pang —8D **36**
Bremer Rd. Stai —7H **73**
Brendon Clo. Tile —3M **61**
Brent Clo. That —9G **80**
Brent Gdns. Read —9H **63**
Brent Rd. Bour —3L **5**
Brerewood. Ear —1M **87**
Brewery Comn. Mort —4J **107**
Brewhouse Hill. Frox —7B **74**
Briant's Av. Cav —2J **63**
Briants Piece. Herm —6E **56**
Briar Clo. Cav —8G **38**
Briar Clo. Tap —7L **21**
Briardene. M'head —5N **19**
Briar Glen. Cook —9J **5**
Briarlea Rd. Mort C —4G **107**
Briars Clo. Pang —8E **36**

Briars, The—Cedar Ct.

Briars, The. Slou —4A 48
Briars, The. Stai —3H 73
Briar Way. Slou —6D 22
Briar Way. Tadl —9L 105
Briar Way. W Dray —1N 49
Briarwood. Finch —4K 111
Brickfield Cotts. Crowt —7D 112
Brickfield La. Burn —2K 21
Brickiln Ind. Est. Tadl —9L 105
Bridge Av. Cook —1B 20
Bridge Av. M'head —7D 20
Bridge Clo. Slou —8B 22
Bridge Clo. Stai —8F 72
Bridge End. Camb —5M 119
Bridge Ho. Read —4H 63
Bridge La. Vir W —7N 95
Bridgeman Dri. Wind —8C 46
Bridgemead. Frim —9N 119
Bridge Rd. Asc —7N 93
Bridge Rd. Bag —7H 115
Bridge Rd. Camb —6M 119
Bridge Rd. M'head —7D 20
Bridge Rd. Uxb —3K 25
Bridges Clo. Wokgm —4L 89
Bridges Hall. Read —7M 63
Bridges, The. Mort W —5D 106
Bridgestone Dri. Bour —4M 5
Bridge St. Cav —2G 62
Bridge St. Coln —6E 48
Bridge St. Hung —5K 75
Bridge St. M'head —7D 20
Bridge St. Newb —8L 79
Bridge St. Read —5G 63
Bridge St. Stai —8F 72
Bridge St. Plaza. Read —5G 63
Bridge View. S'dale —9D 94
Bridge Wlk. Yat —2B 118
Bridgewater Clo. Read —3C 62
Bridgewater Ct. Slou —3B 48
Bridgewater Ter. Wind —7F 46
Bridle Clo. M'head —5B 20
Bridle Rd. M'head —5B 20
Bridle Rd. Whit H —3F 36
Bridlington Spur. Slou —2D 46
Bridport Clo. Lwr Ear —1C 88
Bridport Way. Slou —5D 22
Brierly Pl. Tile —9K 37
Briff La. Been —5L 81
Briff La. Up Buck —5L 81
Brigham Rd. Read —3G 63
Brighton Pl. Read —6N 63
Brighton Rd. Read —6N 63
Brighton Spur. Slou —5D 22
Brill Clo. Cav —9G 38
Brill Clo. M'head —1A 44
Brill Clo. Mar —5A 4
Brimblecombe Clo. Wokgm —2M 89
Brimpton Rd. Baug —9F 104
Brimpton Rd. Brimp —1A 104
Brimpton Rd. Read —8B 62
Brinn's La. B'water —4G 118
Briony Ho. Read —4H 87
Brisbane Rd. Read —4B 62
Bristol Clo. Stai —3M 73
Bristol Ct. Stanw —3M 73
Bristol Way. Slou —9H 23
Bristow Ct. Cav —2H 63
Bristow Rd. Camb —6M 119
Britannia Ct. W Dray —2L 49
(off Green, The)
Britannia Ind. Est. Coln —8F 48
Britannia Way. Stai —4L 73
Brittain Ct. Sand —2G 118
Britten Rd. Read —8H 63
Britwell Rd. Burn —4M 21
Brixham Rd. Read —1H 87
Broadacre. Stai —9H 73
Broadcommon Rd. Hurst —4M 65
Broadhalfpenny La. Tadl —9L 105
Broad Hinton. Twy —1L 65
Broadlands Clo. Calc —7L 61
Broadlands Ct. Brack —3J 91
Broadlands Dri. S Asc —9M 93
Broad La. Brack —5N 91
Broad La. Up Buck —5M 81
Broadley Grn. W'sham —7N 115
Broadmark Rd. Slou —8K 23
Broadmeadow End. That —7J 81
Broadmoor Est. Crowt —6H 113
Broadmoor La. Son —9D 40
Broadmoor La. Wal L & White —8E 42
Broad Oak. Slou —5E 22
Broadoak. Tadl —9M 105
Broadoak Ct. Slou —5E 22
Broad Platts. Slou —2M 47
Broadpool Cotts. Asc —2K 93
Broadrick Heath. Warf —2A 92
Broad St. E Ils —7B 12
Broad St. Read —5G 62
Broad St. Wokgm —5A 90
Broad St. Mall, The. Read —5G 62
Broad St. Wlk. Wokgm —5A 90
Broadwater Clo. Wray —4N 71
Broadwater La. Twy —2K 65
Broadwater Pk. M'head —4H 45
Broadwater Rd. Twy —1K 65
Broadway. Brack —4M 91
Broadway. M'head —7C 20
Broadway. Stai —9J 73
Broadway. That —8G 80
Broadway. Wink —5L 69
Broadway Courtyard. That —8G 81
Broadway Rd. Light & W'sham —9M 115
Broadway, The. Lamb —2H 27
Broadway, The. P'mre —2K 31
Broadway, The. Sand —1F 118
Brocas Rd. Bfld C —1G 106
Brocas St. Eton —6F 46
Brockenhurst Dri. Yat —5B 118
Brockenhurst Rd. Asc —6K 93
Brockenhurst Rd. Brack —5C 92
Brock Gdns. Read —4C 62
Brocklands. Yat —5A 118
Brock La. M'head —7C 20
Brockley Clo. Tile —4A 62
Brockmer La. Medm —1N 17
Brocks La. Fril & Bckby —7L 57
Brocks Way. S'lake —2F 40
Brock Way. Vir W —7L 95
Brockway Ho. Langl —4C 48
Broken Furlong. Eton —4D 46
Broken Way. Newt —8N 101
Bromley Wlk. Tile —5N 61
Brompton Clo. Lwr Ear —2C 88
Brompton Dri. M'head —5N 19
Bromycroft Rd. Slou —4C 22
Bronte Rise. Green —2M 101
Brookbank. Wbrn G —4N 5
Brook Bus. Cen. Cow —3J 25
Brook Clo. Owl —9J 113
Brook Clo. Stai —4N 73
Brook Clo. Wokgm —3M 89
Brook Cotts. Yat —3A 118
Brook Cres. Slou —7A 22
Brookdene Clo. M'head —4C 20
Brook Dri. Brack —6B 92
Brooke Pl. Binf —9H 67
Brookers Corner. Crowt —5G 113
Brooker's Hill. Shin —5K 87
Brookers Row. Crowt —4G 113
Brookfield Rd. Wbrn G —4N 5
Brook Grn. Brack —3K 91
(in two parts)
Brookhouse Dri. Wbrn G —4N 5
Brook La. Wal L —2C 66
Brook Lea. Cav —3J 63
Brooklyn Dri. Emm G —6H 39
Brooklyn Way. W Dray —2L 49
Brookmill, The. Read —8E 62
Brook Path. Slou —8B 22
(in two parts)
Brook Rd. Bag —8H 115
Brook Rd. Camb —5M 119
Brooksby Clo. B'water —4F 118
Brooksby Rd. Tile —2L 61
Brookside. Calc —8N 61
(off Millers Gro.)
Brookside. Coln —6D 48
Brookside. Sand —2G 118
Brookside. Uxb —1N 25
Brookside. Wokgm —4L 89
Brookside Av. Ashf —9K 73
Brookside Av. Wray —9N 47
Brookside Clo. Ear —9C 64
Brookside Pk. Farn —8L 119
Brooks Rd. That —7H 81
Brook St. Twy —9J 41
Brook St. Wind —8F 46
Brook St. W. Read —6G 62
Brookway. Newb —9B 80
Broom Acres. Sand —1F 118
Broom Clo. Calc —7K 61
Broome Clo. Yat —2A 118
Broomfield Clo. Asc —9D 94
Broomfield Dri. Asc —8D 94
Broomfield Pk. Asc —9D 94
Broomfield Rd. Tile —4N 61
Broom Gro. Wokgm —7J 89
Broomhall La. Asc —8C 94
Broom Hill. Cook —9J 5
Broom Hill. Stoke P —1J 23
Broom Ho. Langl —3A 48
Broomsquires Rd. Bag —8J 115
Broom Way. B'water —5J 119
Broughton Clo. Read —3C 62
Brownfield Gdns. M'head —9B 20
Browning Clo. That —7F 80
Brownlow Dri. Brack —2N 91
Brownlow Rd. Read —5E 62
Brownrigg Cres. Brack —3B 92
Brownrigg Rd. Ashf —8N 73
Brownsfield Rd. That —7F 80
Brown's La. Bright —9B 10
Bruan Rd. Newb —2K 101
Bruce Clo. Slou —9C 22
Bruce Rd. Wdly —5C 64
Bruce Wlk. Wind —8N 45
Brucewood Pde. Mar —2C 4
Brudenell. Wind —9B 46
Brummell Rd. Newb —7J 79
Brunel Arc. Read —4H 63
Brunel Clo. M'head —9B 20
Brunel Dri. Crowt —2G 113
Brunel Dri. Wdly —3E 64
Brunel Rd. M'head —9A 20
Brunel Rd. Read —8A 62
Brunel Rd. Thea —1F 84
Brunel Way. Slou —9H 23
Brunswick. Brack —9L 91
Brunswick Hill. Read —5E 62
Brunswick Lodge. Read —5E 62
(off Brunswick Hill)
Brunswick St. Read —5E 62
Bruton Way. Brack —9B 92
Bryant Av. Slou —6F 22
Bryants La. Yatt —3A 58
Brybur Clo. Read —2K 87
Bryer Pl. Wind —9N 45
Bryony Clo. Uxb —6N 25
Bryony Ho. Brack —3J 91
Buccaneer Clo. Wdly —4G 64
Buccleuch Rd. Dat —6J 47
Buchanan Sq. That —1J 103
Buchan Clo. Uxb —4K 25
Buchannan Dri. Wokgm —3K 111
Buckden Clo. Wdly —6F 64
Buckham Hill. Gt Shef & Chadw —7H 29
Buckhurst Gro. Wokgm —6D 90
Buckhurst Hill. Brack —6C 92
Buckhurst La. Asc —5B 94
Buckhurst Rd. Asc —4B 94
Buckhurst Way. Ear —9N 63
Buckingham Av. Slou —7A 22
Buckingham Av. E. Slou —7E 22
Buckingham Dri. Emm G —9H 39
(in three parts)
Buckingham Gdns. Slou —1H 47
Buckingham Gro. Uxb —3N 25
Buckingham Rd. Newb —1J 101
Buckland Av. Slou —3K 47
Buckland Clo. Farn —9N 119
Buckland Cres. Wind —7B 46
Buckland Rd. Read —9H 63
Bucklebury. Brack —9L 91
Bucklebury Clo. Holyp —4F 44
Bucklebury Rd. Bckby —9N 57
Buckle La. Warf —6L 67
(in two parts)
Bucknell Av. Pang —8F 36
Bucknell Clo. Read —8N 61
Buckside. Cav —2G 62
Buckthorn Clo. Wokgm —4C 90
Buckthorns. Brack —2J 91
Budebury Rd. Stai —9H 73
Budge's Gdns. Wokgm —4B 90
Budge's Rd. Wokgm —4B 90
Buffins. Tap —5H 21
Bulkeley Av. Wind —9D 46
Bulkeley Clo. Egh —9L 71
Bullbrook Dri. Brack —3B 92
Bullbrook Row. Brack —4B 92
Bullfinch Clo. Col T —1J 119
Bull La. Brack —3M 91
Bull La. Rise —7F 108
(in two parts)
Bull Meadow, The. Streat —8H 15
Bullrusgh Gro. Uxb —5K 25
Bulmershe Rd. Read —5L 63
Bulpit La. Hung —7K 75
Bunby Rd. Stoke P —1H 23
Bunce's Clo. Eton W —4D 46
Bunces La. Bfld C —9H 85
Bunce's La. Gor H —3H 37
Bundy's Way. Stai —9G 72
Bungalow Dri. Tile —4L 61
Bungler's Hill. Far H —4A 110
Bungum La. Ham —8N 97
Bunkers Hill. Newb —5G 101
Bunten Meade. Slou —9D 22
Burbage Grn. Brack —7C 92
Burbidge Clo. Calc —9N 61
Burchell Rd. Newb —6J 79
Burchett Coppice. Wokgm —2L 111
Burchetts Grn. La. Bur G —7F 18
Burchetts Grn. Rd. L Grn —9E 18
Burcombe Way. Emm G —9H 39
Burcot Gdns. M'head —3B 20
Burdett Ct. Read —9J 63
Burdock Clo. Bfld C —9J 85
Burdwood Cen. That —9H 81
Burfield Rd. Old Win —3J 71
Burford Clo. Mar —2A 4
Burford Ct. Read —4F 62
Burford Ct. Wokgm —6C 90
Burford Gdns. Slou —6M 21
Burford Rd. Camb —5M 119
Burford's. E Gar —7B 28
Burgess Clo. Wdly —8C 64
Burgess La. Kint H —5H 99
Burges Way. Stai —9H 73
Burgett Rd. Slou —2D 46
Burghead Clo. Col T —2H 119
Burghfield Rd. Read —2N 85
Burleigh La. Asc —3H 93
Burleigh M. Cav —7J 39
Burleigh Rd. Asc —4H 93
Burleigh Rd. Frim —9N 119
Burley Way. B'water —3G 119
Burlingham Clo. Read —5J 87
Burlings, The. Asc —3H 93
Burlington Av. Slou —1G 46
Burlington Ct. B'water —6H 119
Burlington Ct. Slou —1G 47
Burlington Rd. Burn —5L 21
Burlington Rd. Slou —1G 47
Burlington Rd. Tile —5L 61
Burlsdon Way. Brack —3B 92
Burne-Jones Dri. Col T —3H 119
Burness Clo. Uxb —3L 25
Burnetts Rd. Wind —7A 46
Burney Bit. Pam H —9N 105
Burney Bit Rd. Tadl —9N 105
Burnham Clo. Bour —3L 5
Burnham Clo. Wind —8N 45
Burnham Gro. Brack —2N 91
Burnham La. Slou —6N 21
Burnham Rise. Emm G —6J 39
Burnham Rd. Tadl —8H 105
Burnistone Clo. Lwr Ear —1D 88
Burn Moor Chase. Brack —9B 92
Burns Clo. Wdly —8D 64
Burns Wlk. That —7F 80
Burntbush La. Fril —6K 57
Burnt Ho. Gdns. Warf —2B 92
Burnthouse La. Ping —6B 86
Burnthouse Ride. Brack —6H 91
Burnt Oak. Cook —8K 5
Burnt Oak. Wokgm —2L 111
Burnt Pollard La. Light —9N 115
Burn Wlk. Burn —4L 21
Burrcroft Ct. Read —7A 62
Burrcroft Rd. Read —7A 62
Burrell Rd. Comp —1H 33
Burrell Rd. Frim —9N 119
Burr La. Shalb —8E 96
Burroughs Cres. Bour —3L 5
Burroway Rd. Slou —2C 48
Burrows Hill Clo. Houn —9K 49
Burrows Hill La. Houn —1J 73
Burton Clo. W'sham —6N 115
Burtons Hill. Kint —9G 77
Burton Way. Wind —9A 46
Burwell Clo. Lwr Ear —2B 88
Bury's Bank Rd. Green —3A 102
Bush Wlk. Wokgm —5A 90
Business Cen., The. Wokgm —7N 89
Business Village, The. Slou —9K 23
Butchers La. White —4F 42
Bute St. Read —7B 62
Butler Rd. Bag —8J 115
Butler Rd. Crowt —4F 112
Butlers Clo. Wind —7N 45
Butler's Orchard. Kid E —2D 38
Butson Clo. Newb —8J 79
Buttenshaw Av. Arbor —2E 110
Buttenshaw Clo. Arbor —2F 110
Buttercup Clo. Wokgm —5D 90
Buttercup Sq. Stai —5L 73
Butter Mkt. Read —5H 63
Buttermere Av. Slou —6M 21
Buttermere Gdns. Brack —5N 91
Buttersteep Rise. Asc —1F 114
Butts Cen. Read —5G 62
(off Castle St.)
Buttsfield Rd. Chad —4K 29
Butts Hill Rd. Son & Wdly —2D 64
Buxton Av. Cav —9F 38
Buxton Rd. Ashf —9L 73
Bybend Clo. Farn R —2D 22
Byefield Rd. Read —8B 62
Byeways Clo. Know H —2C 42
Byland Dri. M'head —4E 44
Byreton Clo. Ear —1A 88
Byron Av. Mar —4D 4
Byron Clo. Newb —3K 101
Byron Clo. Twy —9K 41
Byron Clo. Yat —5A 118
Byron Ct. Wind —9C 46
Byron Dri. Crowt —7F 112
Byron Ho. Langl —4C 48
Byron Rd. Ear —5N 63
Byron Rd. Twy —9K 41
Byron Way. W Dray —3N 49
Bythorn Clo. Lwr Ear —1D 88
Byways. Burn —6K 21
Byways. Yat —4A 118
Bywood. Brack —9K 91
Byworth Clo. Read —4H 87
Cabbage Hill. Warf —9K 67
Cabbagehill La. Warf —8J 67
Cabin Moss. Brack —9B 92
Cabrera Av. Vir W —8L 95
Cabrera Clo. Vir W —8M 95
Caddy Clo. Egh —9B 72
Cadogan Clo. Cav —9K 39
Cadogan Clo. Holyp —5D 44
Cadogan Clo. Tile —5M 61
Cadwell Dri. M'head —2A 44
Caesars Camp Rd. Camb —9D 114
Caesars Ga. Warf —3B 92
Cain Rd. Brack —4H 91
Cairngorm Pl. Slou —5F 22
Cairngorm Rd. That —9G 80
Caistor Clo. Calc —8J 61
Calard Dri. That —6D 80
Calbourne Dri. Calc —8L 61
Calbroke Rd. Slou —5B 22
Calbrooke Rd. Slou —4B 22
Calcot Pl. Dri. Calc —8M 61
Caldbeck Dri. Wdly —5D 64
Calder Clo. M'head —5B 20
Calder Clo. Tile —4N 61
Calder Ct. Langl —4A 48
Calder Ct. M'head —5A 20
Calder Way. Coln —9F 48
Caldwell Rd. W'sham —5N 115
Caledonia Rd. Stai —5M 73
Caleta Clo. Cav —2K 63
Calfridus Way. Brack —5B 92
California Caravan Pk. Finch —4J 111
Calleva Ind. Pk. Aldm —8G 105
Callington Rd. Read —2H 87
Callin's La. Been —1F 66
Callis Farm Clo. Stai —3M 73
Callow Hill. Vir W —5L 95
Calshot Pl. Calc —8L 61
Camberley Rd. Houn —9N 49
Cambourne Clo. Lwr Ear —2N 87
Cambourne Rd. Houn —9N 49
Cambria Ct. Slou —1L 47
Cambria Ct. Stai —8F 72
Cambria Gdns. Stai —4M 73
Cambrian Clo. Camb —4M 119
Cambrian Way. Calc —8L 61
Cambrian Way. Wokgm —2M 111
Cambridge Av. Burn —3L 21
Cambridge Av. Slou —7C 22
Cambridge Clo. W Dray —5L 49
Cambridge Ho. Wind —7E 46
Cambridge Rd. Crowt —6G 112
Cambridge Rd. Mar —5B 4
Cambridge Rd. Owl —9J 113
Cambridge Rd. Uxb —1L 25
Cambridgeshire Clo. Warf —2C 92
Cambridgeshire Clo. Wokgm —5K 89
Cambridge St. Read —4E 62
Cambridge Wlk. Camb —3N 119
Camden Pl. Bour —4L 5
Camden Pl. Calc —8J 61
Camden Rd. M'head —5A 20
Camellia Way. Wokgm —4J 89
Camley Gdns. M'head —6L 19
Camley Pk. Dri. M'head —6K 19
Camm Av. Wind —9A 46
Campbell Clo. Yat —3D 118
Campbell Rd. Wdly —7C 64
Campbells Grn. Mort C —5J 107
Camperdown. M'head —5E 20
Campion Clo. B'water —6K 119
Campion Clo. Uxb —6N 25
Campion Ho. Brack —3J 91
Campion Way. Wokgm —3C 90
Camp Rd. Uft N —8D 84
Canad Rd. Slou —1K 47
Canadian Memorial Av. Asc —4H 95
Canal Ind. Est. Langl —1B 48
Canal Wlk. Hung —5K 75
Canal Way. Read —5K 63
Canal Wharf. Langl —1B 48
Canberra Rd. Houn —9N 49
Candleford Clo. Brack —2N 91
Candover Clo. W Dray —6L 49
Canford Ct. Read —5D 62
Canhurst La. Know H —2B 42
Cannock Clo. M'head —8E 20
Cannock Way. Lwr Ear —2B 88
Cannon Clo. Col T —1K 119
Cannon Ct. Rd. M'head —3A 20
(in two parts)
Cannondown Rd. Cook —1B 20
Cannon Hill. Brack —8N 91
Cannon Hill Clo. M'head —3F 44
Cannon La. M'head —8L 19
Cannon St. Read —4E 62
Canon Hill Dri. M'head —2D 44
Canon Hill Est. M'head —2E 44
Canon Hill Way. M'head —3E 44
Canopus Way. Stai —4M 73
Cansfield End. Newb —8K 79
Canterbury Av. Slou —5E 22
Canterbury Rd. Read —9H 63
Cantley Cres. Wokgm —3M 89
Caraway Rd. Ear —2N 87
Carbery La. Asc —5L 93
Carbinswood La. Woolh —5B 82
Cardiff M. Read —3F 62
Cardiff Rd. Read —3E 62
Cardigan Gdns. Read —7L 63
Cardigan Rd. Read —6L 63
Cardinal Clo. Cav —2H 63
Cardinals, The. Brack —6M 91
Cardinals Wlk. Tap —7M 21
Cardwell Cres. Asc —7M 93
Carew Clo. Tile —9J 37
Carey Clo. Wind —9D 46
Carey Rd. Wokgm —6A 90
Carey St. Read —5F 62
Cariad Ct. Gor —7K 15
Carisbrooke Clo. Cav —7J 39
Carisbrooke Clo. M'head —9N 19
Carisbrooke Ct. Slou —8H 23
Carland Clo. Lwr Ear —2N 87
Carlile Gdns. Twy —6J 41
Carlisle Rd. Slou —8F 22
Carlisle Rd. Tile —2M 61
(in two parts)
Carlton Clo. Wdly —6D 64
Carlton Ct. Stai —9H 73
Carlton Ct. Uxb —6L 25
Carlton Rd. Cav —8D 38
Carlton Rd. Slou —8K 23
Carlyle Ct. Crowt —6G 112
Carmarthen Rd. Slou —8G 22
Carnarvon Rd. Read —5L 63
Carnation Clo. Crowt —2F 112
Carnation Dri. Wink R —1D 92
Carnegie Rd. Newb —9L 79
Carnoustie. Brack —9J 91
Carnoustie Ct. Read —5K 63
(off Muirfield Clo.)
Carolina Pl. Wokgm —3K 111
Caroline Clo. W Dray —1L 49
Caroline Ct. Mar —4C 4
Caroline Ct. Read —6E 62
Caroline Dri. Wokgm —4M 89
Caroline St. Read —4F 62
Carrick Gdns. Wdly —5B 64
Carrick La. Yat —3C 118
Carrington Rd. Slou —8G 23
Carroll Cres. Asc —7J 93
Carron Clo. Tile —5A 62
Carsdale Clo. Read —7F 62
Carshalton Rd. Camb —9D 114
Carshalton Way. Lwr Ear —2B 88
Carston Gro. Calc —8N 61
Carter Clo. Wind —8C 46
Carter's Hill. Wokgm & Brack —8C 66
Cartershill La. Arbor —7C 88
Carters Rise. Calc —8M 61
Cartmel Dri. Wdly —6C 64
Carvers Hill. Shalb —8D 96
Cary Clo. Newb —4H 101
Casey Ct. South —9F 58
Cassia Dri. Ear —2M 87
Castle Av. Dat —5J 47
Castle Av. W Dray —8M 25
Castle Cotts. Newt —7M 101
Castle Ct. M'head —7A 20
Castlecraig Ct. Col T —2H 119
Castle Cres. Read —6F 62
Castle Dri. M'head —7A 20
Castle End Rd. Rusc —7L 41
Castle Farm Caravan Site. Wind
(off White Horse Rd.) —8N 45
Castle Gro. Newb —6K 79
Castle Hill. Far H —3A 110
Castle Hill. M'head —7B 20
Castle Hill. Read —6F 62
Castle Hill. Wind —7F 46
Castle Hill Rd. Egh —7K 71
Castle Hill Ter. M'head —7B 20
Castle La. Don —5J 79
Castle M. M'head —7B 20
Castle St. Read —5G 62
Castle St. Slou —2H 47
Castleton Ct. Mar —5C 4
Castleview Pde. Slou —3M 47
Castleview Rd. Slou —3L 47
Caswall Clo. Binf —1G 90
Caswall Ride. Yat —4D 118
Catalina Clo. Wdly —5G 65
Catcliffe Way. Lwr Ear —3M 87
Catena Rise. Light —9K 115
Catherine Rd. Newb —9L 79
Catherines Clo. W Dray —1L 49
Catherine's Hill. Mort —5F 106
Catherine St. Read —4D 62
Catmore Rd. W Ils —7G 11
Caunter Rd. Speen —7H 79
Causeway. Cook —8L 5
Causeway Est. Stai —8C 72
Causeway, The. Bray —1E 44
(in two parts)
Causeway, The. Mar —6C 4
Causeway, The. Stai —8E 72
Causmans Way. Tile —3K 61
Cavalier Clo. Thea —9E 60
Cavalry Cres. Wind —9E 46
Cavendish Clo. Tap —7K 21
Cavendish Ct. B'water —6H 119
Cavendish Ct. Coln —7F 48
Cavendish Ct. Mar —5C 4
Cavendish Ct. Newb —6B 80
Cavendish Gdns. Winn —9F 64
Cavendish Meads. Asc —8N 93
Cavendish Pk. Col T —3J 119
Cavendish Rd. Cav —7J 39
Caversham Pk. Dri. Cav —8J 39
Caversham Pk. Rd. Cav —7J 39
Caversham Rd. Read —4G 62
Caversham Wharf. Read —3G 63
Caves Farm Clo. Sand —1E 118
Cawcott Dri. Wind —7A 46
Cawsam Gdns. Cav —9J 39
Caxton Clo. Read —3C 62
Caxton Ct. Hen T —5D 16
Caxton Dri. Uxb —3L 25
Cecil Aldin Dri. Tile —8K 37
Cecil Rd. Iver —7F 24
Cecil Way. Slou —5B 22
Cedar Av. B'water —4H 119
Cedar Av. W Dray —8N 25
Cedar Chase. Tap —5G 21
Cedar Clo. Bag —7H 115
Cedar Clo. Burn —5N 21
Cedar Clo. Wokgm —5A 90
Cedar Ct. Egh —8B 72
Cedar Ct. Mar —5C 4

Cedar Ct.—Coleridge La.

Cedar Ct. Wind —8C 46
Cedar Dri. Asc —9C 94
Cedar Dri. Brack —2N 91
Cedar Dri. Cook —8K 5
Cedar Dri. Mar —1A 4
Cedar Dri. Pang —9D 36
Cedar Dri. S'hill —6F 94
Cedar Gro. That —8F 80
Cedar La. Frim —9N 119
Cedar Lodge. Hen T —6E 16
Cedar Mt. Newb —2K 101
Cedar Rd. Read —2L 87
Cedars. Brack —6C 92
Cedars Clo. Sand —1D 118
Cedars Dri. Uxb —3N 25
Cedars Rd. M'head —7D 20
Cedars, The. Tile —2L 61
Cedar Way. Slou —4N 47
Cedar Wood Cres. Cav —9H 39
Celandine Clo. Crowt —4G 113
Celandine Gro. That —7J 81
Celia Cres. Ashf —9L 73
Cell Farm Av. Old Win —2K 71
Centennial Ct. Brack —4L 91
Central Dri. Slou —8B 22
Central La. Wink —5L 69
Central Wlk. Wokgm —5A 90
Central Way. Wink —5L 69
Centre Rd. Wind —6M 45
Centurion Clo. Col T —1H 119
Centurion Clo. Read —6G 63
Century Rd. Stai —9D 72
Chaffinch Clo. Col T —1H 119
Chaffinch Clo. Tile —5J 61
Chaffinch Clo. Wokgm —6K 89
Chagford Rd. Read —2H 87
Chain St. Read —5G 63
Chalcott. Chalv —2G 46
Chalcraft Clo. Hen T —6B 16
Chalfont Clo. Ear —2N 87
Chalfont Way. Ear —2N 87
Chalford Rd. Newb —9J 79
Chalgrove Clo. M'head —8E 20
Chalgrove Way. Emm G —7J 39
Chalk Hill. Harp —9A 16
Chalkhouse Grn. La. Chalk (in two parts) —4G 38
Chalkhouse Grn. Rd. Kid E —2D 38
Chalklands. Bour —3L 5
Chalkpit Cotts. Hung —4M 51
Chalk Pit La. Burn —1L 21
Chalkpit La. Mar —4A 4
Chalky La. Cur —7M 55
Challis Pl. Brack —4J 91
Challoner Clo. Wokgm —3L 111
Challow Ct. M'head —5A 20
Chalvey Gdns. Slou —1G 46
Chalvey Gro. Slou —2D 46
Chalvey Pk. Slou —1G 47
Chalvey Rd. E. Slou —1G 46
Chalvey Rd. W. Slou —1F 46
Chamberhouse Mill La. That —1J 103
Chamberlains Gdns. Arbor X —9D 88
Chambers, The. Read —5H 63 (off East St.)
Champion Rd. Cav —3J 63
Chancellor's Way, The. Ear —8L 63
Chancery M. Read —5F 62
Chanctonbury Dri. Asc —9A 94
Chandlers La. Yat —2A 118
Chandos Mall. Chalv —1H 47
Chandos Rd. Newb —2K 101
Chandos Rd. Stai —9E 72
Chantry Clo. W Dray —8L 25
Chantry Clo. Wind —7C 46
Chantry Mead. Hung —6J 75
Chantry Rd. Bag —8G 115
Chantry, The. Uxb —4N 25
Chapel Clo. S Sto —3L 15
Chapel Ct. Hung —5L 75
Chapel Dri. B Hill —5D 108
Chapel Hill. Tile —4K 61
Chapel La. Ash H —9B 104
Chapel La. Ash'd —7C 34
Chapel La. Bag —8G 115
Chapel La. Binf —2G 91
Chapel La. Cur —8B 56
Chapel La. Farn & B'water —9K 119
Chapel La. Herm —4F 56
Chapel La. Lamb —2H 27
Chapel La. Mort —5A 106
Chapel La. Rise —7J 109
Chapel La. Spen W —9H 87
Chapel La. Stoke P —1K 23
Chapel La. Yatt —3A 58
Chapel Rd. Camb —4M 119
Chapel Row. Twy —9J 41
Chapel St. Mar —5B 4
Chapel St. Slou —1H 47
Chapel St. That —8G 81
Chapel St. Uxb —2K 25
Chapel View. Lamb —3H 27
Chaplain's Hill. Crowt —6H 113
Chapman Clo. W Dray —2N 49
Chapman La. Bour & F Hth —2L 5
Chapman Wlk. That —7E 80
Chapter Clo. Uxb —1N 25
Chapter M. Wind —6F 46
Chard Clo. Wdly —6D 64
Charfield Ct. Read —5L 63
Chariots Pl. Wind —7F 46
Charlbury Clo. Brack —6C 92
Charles Clore Ct. Read —8A 62
Charles Evans Way. Cav —2K 63
Charles Gdns. Slou —7K 23
Charles Ho. Wind —7E 46
Charles Sq. Brack —4N 91
Charles St. Newb —4H 101
Charles St. Read —4F 62
Charles St. Wind —7E 46
Charlock Clo. That —6H 81
Charlotte Clo. Herm —6D 56
Charlton. Wind —8M 45
Charlton Clo. Slou —1D 46
Charlton Clo. Wokgm —2L 111
Charlton Ct. Owl —9H 113
Charlton La. Swal —4J 109
Charlton Pl. Newb —7L 79
Charlton Sq. Wind —8M 45
Charlton Wlk. Wind —8M 45
Charmwood Clo. Newb —6K 79
Charndon Clo. Read —7H 63
Charnham La. Hung —4K 75
Charnham Pk. Hung —4K 75
Charnham St. Hung —5K 75
Charnwood. Asc —8B 94
Charnwood Rd. Uxb —3N 25
Charrington Rd. Calc —8J 61
Charta Rd. Egh —9D 72
Charter Clo. Slou —2H 47
Charterhouse Clo. Brack —7B 92
Charter Pl. Uxb —1L 25
Charter Rd. Newb —3K 101
Charter Rd. Slou —8A 22
Charters Clo. Asc —7N 93
Charters La. Asc —7N 93
Charters Rd. Asc —9N 93
Charters Way. Asc —9B 94
Charvil Ho. Rd. Charv —8F 40
Charvil La. Son —1D 64
Charville Dri. Calc —8J 61
Charwood Rd. Wokgm —5C 90
Chase Gdns. Binf —9G 66
Chaseside Av. Twy —6J 41
Chase, The. Calc —8L 61
Chase, The. Crowt —4E 112
Chase, The. Don —4K 79
Chase, The. Mar —4E 4
Chatfield. Slou —6C 22
Chatham St. Read —4F 62
Chatsworth Av. Winn —1F 88
Chatsworth Clo. Cav —7J 39
Chatsworth Clo. M'head —9N 19
Chatteris Way. Lwr Ear —2A 88
Chatton Clo. Lwr Ear —3N 87
Chaucer Clo. Emm G —8G 39
Chaucer Clo. Wokgm —5D 90
Chaucer Cres. Newb —6J 79
Chaucer Gro. Camb —4N 119
Chaucer Rd. Ashf —8M 73
Chaucer Rd. Crowt —6F 112
Chaucer Way. Wokgm —6K 89
Chauntry Clo. M'head —8F 20
Chauntry Rd. M'head —8E 20
Chavey Down Rd. Wink R —9E 68
Chawridge La. Wink —5F 68
Chazey Clo. Chaz H —5C 38
Chazey Rd. Cav —9D 38
Cheam Clo. Brack —7A 92
Cheapside. Read —4G 62
Cheapside Rd. Asc —5M 93
Cheap St. Comp —9H 13
Cheap St. Newb —9L 79
Cheddington Clo. Tile —6N 61
Cheeseman Clo. Wokgm —4B 90
Chelford Way. Cav —9F 38
Chelsea Clo. Tile —3N 61
Cheltenham Vs. Stai —3G 73
Chelwood Dri. Sand —9D 112
Chelwood Rd. Ear —1A 88
Cheney Clo. Binf —1H 91
Cheniston Ct. S'dale —9C 94
Cheniston Gro. M'head —7K 19
Chepstow Rd. Tile —2L 61
Chequer La. Strat S —8D 108
Chequers Orchard. Iver —7G 24
Chequers Sq. Uxb —1K 25
Chequers Way. Wdly —5B 64
Cherbury Clo. Brack —6B 92
Cherington Ga. M'head —5M 19
Cherington Way. Asc —4H 93
Cheriton Av. Twy —7J 41
Cheriton Clo. Newb —2M 101
Cheriton Ct. Read —6G 62
Cheriton Pl. Son C —1F 38
Cheriton Way. B'water —4H 119
Cherries, The. Slou —7K 23
Cherry Av. Slou —1M 47
Cherry Clo. Cav —5J 39
Cherry Clo. F Hth —1M 5
Cherry Clo. Newb —6K 79
Cherry Garden La. M'head —2J 43
Cherry Garden La. White —5J 43
Cherry Gro. Hung —6J 75
Cherry La. W Dray —3N 49
Cherry Orchard. Gt Shef —9G 28
Cherry Orchard. Stai —9H 73
Cherry Orchard. Stoke P —1K 23
Cherry Orchard. W Dray —1M 49
Cherry Tree Av. W Dray —7N 25
Cherry Tree Clo. Owl —9H 113
Cherry Tree Dri. Brack —5A 92
Cherrytree Gro. Wokgm —7H 89
Cherry Tree La. Ful —1A 24
Cherrytree La. Iver —2H 25
Cherry Tree Rd. Farn R —1E 22
Cherry Way. Hort —9D 48
Cherrywood Av. Egh —2K 95
Cherrywood Rd. Farn —9L 119
Chertsey La. Stai —9F 72
Chertsey Rd. W'sham & Chob —6N 115
Chervil Way. Bfld C —9J 85
Cherwell Clo. M'head —6D 20
Cherwell Clo. Slou —5C 48
Cherwell Cres. Read —5F 62 (off Trinity Pl.)
Cherwell Rd. Bour —3M 5
Cherwell Rd. Cav —7G 38
Cheshire Ct. Slou —1K 47
Cheshire Pk. Warf —1B 92
Chesseridge Rd. Comp —2F 32
Chesterblade La. Brack —9A 92
Chester Clo. Green —2N 101
Chesterfield Rd. Ashf —8M 73
Chesterfield Rd. Newb —1L 101
Chester Ho. Uxb —5K 25
Chesterman St. Read —6H 63
Chester Rd. Slou —7F 22
Chester St. Cav —2G 63
Chester St. Read —4D 62
Chesterton Dri. Stai —5N 73
Chesterton Rd. That —6F 80
Chestnut Av. Cav —9L 39
Chestnut Av. Slou —1N 47
Chestnut Av. Vir W —6H 95
Chestnut Av. W Dray —8N 25
Chestnut Av. Wokgm —5H 89
Chestnut Clo. B'water —5J 119
Chestnut Clo. Egh —1K 95
Chestnut Clo. M'head —5E 20
Chestnut Clo. Thea —8F 60
Chestnut Cotts. Streat —8J 15
Chestnut Ct. Newb —7L 79 (off Victoria Gdns.)
Chestnut Cres. Newb —7L 79
Chestnut Cres. Shin —7L 87
Chestnut Dri. Bfld —7J 85
Chestnut Dri. Egh —1M 95
Chestnut Dri. Wind —1A 70
Chestnut Gro. Pur T —8L 37
Chestnut Gro. Stai —9K 73
Chestnut Mnr. Clo. Stai —9J 73
Chestnuts, The. S'lake —2F 40
Chestnut Wlk. Hung —7K 75
Chestnut Wlk. Read —5H 63
Chestwood Gro. Uxb —1N 25
Chetwode Clo. Wokgm —5C 90
Chetwynd Dri. Uxb —3N 25
Cheviot Clo. Farn —9J 119
Cheviot Clo. M'head —8E 20
Cheviot Clo. Newb —5G 101
Cheviot Dri. Charv —9G 40
Cheviot Rd. Sand —8D 112
Cheviot Rd. Slou —4B 48
Chevley Gdns. Burn —3M 21
Chewter Clo. Bag —7J 115
Chewter La. W'sham —4L 115
Cheyne Way. Farn —9K 119
Chichester Ct. Slou —2K 47
Chichester Rd. Tile —4M 61
Chicory Clo. Ear —2M 87
Chievley Clo. Tile —4K 61
Chilcombe Way. Lwr Ear —1C 88
Childrey Way. Tile —4J 61
Childs Hall. Read —7M 63
Child St. Lamb —2G 27
Chillingham Way. Camb —5N 119
Chiltern Bus. Village. Uxb —3J 25
Chiltern Clo. Hen T —6A 16
Chiltern Clo. Mar —5A 4
Chiltern Clo. Newb —5G 101
Chiltern Ct. Emm G —7G 39
Chiltern Cres. Ear —5N 63
Chiltern Dri. Charv —9G 40
Chiltern Rd. Burn —6L 21
Chiltern Rd. Cav —9J 39
Chiltern Rd. M'head —8E 20
Chiltern Rd. Sand —9D 112
Chilterns Pk. Bour —2M 5
Chiltern View. Pur T —8L 37
Chiltern View Rd. Uxb —3K 25
Chiltern Wlk. Pang —8E 36
Chilton Ct. Tap —7M 21
Chilton Way. Hung —6J 75
Chilwick Rd. Slou —5B 22
Chippendale All. Uxb —1L 25
Chippendale Clo. Baug —9G 105
Chippendale Clo. B'water —6J 119
Chippendale Waye. Uxb —1L 25
Chippenham Clo. Lwr Ear —3M 87
Chipstead Rd. Houn —9N 49
Chisbury Clo. Brack —8B 92
Chitterfield Ga. W Dray —6N 49
Chittering Clo. Lwr Ear —2B 88
Chive Rd. Ear —2N 87
Chivers Dri. Wokgm —3K 111
Chives Pl. Warf —2A 92
Chobham Rd. S'dale & Wok —9D 94
Choke La. M'head —2L 19
Cholmeley Pl. Read —5L 63
Cholmeley Rd. Read —4L 63
Cholmeley Ter. Read —5L 63
Cholsey Clo. That —8J 81
Choseley Clo. Know H —1C 42
Choseley Rd. Know H —1C 42
Chrislaine Clo. Stai —3L 73
Christchurch Ct. Read —7J 63
Christchurch Dri. B'water —3G 119
Christchurch Gdns. Read —7J 63
Christchurch Rd. Houn —8N 49
Christchurch Rd. Read —7J 63
Christchurch Rd. Vir W —5J 95
Christian Sq. Wind —7E 46
Christie Clo. Light —9M 115
Christie Heights. Green —2M 101
Christie Wlk. Yat —5A 118
Christopher Ct. Newb —9M 79
Chudleigh Gdns. Read —1J 87
Church App. Stanw —3L 73
Church Av. Hen T —4D 16
Church Clo. Croc H —4C 100
Church Clo. Eton —5F 46
Church Clo. Lamb —2H 27
Church Clo. M'head —8A 20
Church Clo. Uxb —3J 25
Church Clo. W Dray —2M 49
Church Clo. Winn —1H 89
Church Cotts. Read —6M 61
Church Croft. Hung —5K 75
Church Dri. Bray —1F 44
Church End La. Tile —5N 61
Churchfield M. Slou —7J 23
Church Ga. That —8G 80
Church Gro. Wex —6L 23
Church Hams. Finch —4J 111
Church Hill. Brack —7G 67
Church Hill. E Ils —8B 12
Church Hill. Hurst —6K 65
Church Hill. White —5J 43
Churchill Clo. Farn —9M 119
Churchill Clo. Read —1H 87
Churchill Ct. Stai —9J 73
Churchill Cres. Farn —9M 119
Churchill Cres. Yat —4B 118
Churchill Dri. Mar —3D 4
Churchill Dri. Winn —1G 89
Churchill Rd. Asc —4J 93
Churchill Rd. Slou —3A 48
Church Island. Stai —8E 72
Church La. Arbor —7B 88
Church La. B'ham —1H 111
Church La. Binf —9J 67
Church La. Bray —1F 44
Church La. Brimp —4B 104
Church La. Chvly —3M 55
Church La. Combe —3C 116
Church La. Croc H —4C 100
Church La. Far H —4B 110
Church La. Finch —6K 111
Church La. Hung —5K 75
Church La. Rusc —8L 41
Church La. S'lake —4E 40
Church La. Sil —9E 106
Church La. Speen —7H 79
Church La. Stoke P —5H 23
Church La. Streat —7C 34
Church La. S'dale —7D 94
Church La. S'hill —6N 93
Church La. That —8G 80
Church La. Three M & Shin —7H 87
Church La. Uft N —6C 84
Church La. Uxb —3J 25
Church La. Warf —7A 68
Church La. Wex —5K 23
Church La. Wind —7F 46
Church La. Wink —7F 68
Church La. Yatt —3A 58
Church M. Pur T —8L 37
Church M. Wdly —4E 64
Church Pde. Ashf —8N 73
Church Path. Bray —1F 44
Church Path. S'hill —5A 94
Church Rd. Aldm —3J 105
Church Rd. Asc —6K 93
Church Rd. Ashf —7N 73
Church Rd. Bag —7G 114
Church Rd. Bour —6N 5 (in two parts)
Church Rd. Brack —4N 91
Church Rd. Cav —2F 62
Church Rd. Chav D —3E 92
Church Rd. Cook D —9F 4
Church Rd. Ear —7A 64
Church Rd. Egh —9A 72
Church Rd. Farn R —4E 22
Church Rd. Frim —8N 119
Church Rd. Frox —6B 74
Church Rd. Iver —4D 24
Church Rd. M'head —9E 20
Church Rd. Mar —2G 5
Church Rd. Mort —6D 106
Church Rd. Old Win —2J 71
Church Rd. Owl —9J 113
Church Rd. Pang —8D 36
Church Rd. Sand —9D 112
Church Rd. Shaw —6L 79
Church Rd. S'dale —8C 94
Church Rd. Swal —4K 109
Church Rd. Tadl —9N 105
Church Rd. Uxb —5L 25
Church Rd. W Dray —2L 49
Church Rd. W'sham —6L 115
Church Rd. Wdly —4E 64
Church Rd. E. Crowt —5F 112
Church Rd. W. Crowt —6F 112
Church Side. E Ils —8B 12
Church St. Burn —5M 21
Church St. Cav —2G 62
Church St. Chalv —1E 46
Church St. Crowt —5F 112
Church St. Gt Shef —1F 52
Church St. Hamp N —8J 33
Church St. Hen T —5C 16
Church St. Hung —5K 75
Church St. Kint —9F 76
Church St. L Bed —1A 96
Church St. Read —6H 63
Church St. Slou —1H 47
Church St. Stai —8E 72
Church St. Thea —9E 60
Church St. Twy —9J 41
Church St. Warg —3H 41
Church St. Wind —7F 46
Church Ter. Binf —2G 91
Church Ter. Read —6G 62 (off Dover St.)
Church Ter. Wind —8A 46
Church View. Been —5J 83
Church View. White —5J 43
Church View. Yat —2B 118
Church View Cotts. Brad —6L 59
Church Wlk. Burn —5L 21
Churchward Wlk. Calc —8N 61
Church Way. Hung —6J 75
Churchway. W Ils —5M 11
Churn Rd. Comp —8G 12
Cinnamon Clo. Ear —2M 87
Cintra Av. Read —8J 63
Cippenham Clo. Slou —8B 22
Cippenham La. Slou —8B 22
Circle Hill Rd. Crowt —5G 112
Circuit La. Read —7B 62
City Rd. Tile —6J 61
Clacy Grn. Brack —2L 91
Clammas Way. Uxb —6K 25
Clanfield Cres. Tile —2K 61
Clanfield Ride. B'water —4H 119
Clappers Meadow. M'head —5E 20
Clapps Ga. Rd. Pam H —9N 105
Clare Av. Wokgm —4A 90
Clarefield Clo. M'head —5L 19
Clarefield Ct. S'dale —9C 94
Clarefield Dri. M'head —5L 19
Clarefield Rd. M'head —5M 19
Clare Gdns. Egh —9B 72
Claremont Gdns. Mar —5C 4
Claremont Rd. Mar —5C 4
Claremont Rd. Stai —9E 72
Claremont Rd. Wind —8E 46
Clarence Cres. Wind —7E 46
Clarence Dri. Egh —9A 72
Clarence Rd. Hen T —4C 16
Clarence Rd. Wind —7C 46
Clarence St. Egh —9A 72
Clarence St. Stai —8F 72
Clarence Way. Calc —8J 61
Clarendon Clo. Winn —1J 89
Clarendon Ct. B'water —6H 119
Clarendon Ct. Slou —8K 23
Clarendon Gdns. Newb —7L 79
Clarendon Rd. Ashf —8N 73
Clarendon Rd. Read —6N 63
Clare Rd. M'head —8A 20
Clare Rd. Stai —5L 73
Clare Rd. Tap —7M 21
Clares Grn. Spen W —8H 87
Clarke Cres. Col T —2J 119
Clarkes Dri. Uxb —6M 25
Clark's Gdns. Hung —6K 75
Classics, The. Lamb —4H 27
Classon Clo. W Dray —1M 49
Claverdon. Brack —9L 91
Clay Clo. Tile —3J 61
Claydon Ct. Cav —3G 63
Claydon Gdns. B'water —8L 119
Clayhall La. Old Win —2H 71
Clay Hill. Been —3F 108
Clayhill Clo. Brack —5C 92
Clay Hill Cres. Newb —6A 80
Clayhill Rd. Bfld C & Bfld —8G 85
Clay La. Been —5H 83
Clay La. Stanw —4N 73
Clay La. Wokgm —5D 90
Clayton Ct. Langl —2B 48
Clayton Gro. Brack —3B 92
Clayton Rd. Farn —8K 119
Claytons Meadow. Bour —5M 5
Clayton Wlk. Read —8J 63
Clayton Way. Uxb —5L 25
Clearsprings. Light —9K 115
Cleeve Ct. Streat —7K 15
Cleeve Down. Gor —7M 15
Cleeve Rd. Gor —7K 15
Clemants Clo. Slou —1K 47
Clements Clo. Spen W —1G 109
Clements Mead. Tile —4J 61
Clements Rd. Hen T —3B 16
Clent Rd. Read —8H 63
Cleopatra Pl. Warf —2B 92
Clevedon Dri. Ear —1N 87
Clevedon Rd. Tile —1M 61
Cleve Ho. Brack —6B 92
Cleveland. Charv —9G 41
Cleveland Clo. M'head —8E 20
Cleveland Gro. Newb —8K 79
Cleveland Pk. Stai —3M 73
Cleveland Rd. Uxb —5L 25
Clevemede. Gor —7L 15
Cleves Ct. Wind —9B 46
Clewer Av. Wind —8C 46
Clewer Ct. Rd. Wind —6D 46
Clewer Fields. Wind —7E 46
Clewer Hill Rd. Wind —8A 46
Clewer New Town. Wind —8C 46
Clewer Pk. Wind —6C 46
Clifford Gro. Ashf —8N 73
Cliffords Way. Bour —2L 5
Clifton Clo. M'head —1D 44
Clifton Ct. Stanw —3M 73
Clifton Pk. Rd. Cav —1F 62
Clifton Rise. Warg —4K 41
Clifton Rise. Wind —7N 45
Clifton Rd. Newb —9J 79
Clifton Rd. Slou —1K 47
Clifton Rd. Wokgm —3M 89
Clifton St. Read —5F 62
Clintons Grn. Brack —3L 91
Clive Ct. Slou —1F 46
Clivedale Rd. Wdly —8D 64
Cliveden Mead. M'head —4E 20
Cliveden Rd. Tap —5G 21
Clive Grn. Brack —7M 91 (in two parts)
Clivemont Rd. M'head —5C 20
Cloister M. Thea —9F 60
Cloisters, The. Cav —1G 62
Cloisters, The. Frim —8N 119
Clonmel Way. Burn —4L 21
Close End. Lamb —3H 27
Close, The. Asc —4G 92
Close, The. Bour —1L 5
Close, The. Brack —6N 91
Close, The. Bfld C —8H 85
Close, The. Col T —1J 119
Close, The. Frim —9N 119
Close, The. Gt Shef —1F 52
Close, The. Hamp N —8J 33
Close, The. Hen T —6C 16
Close, The. Iver —4D 24
Close, The. Light —9K 115
Close, The. Mar —5A 4
Close, The. Shalb —7E 96
Close, The. Slou —8N 21
Close, The. That —7E 80
Close, The. Uxb —2N 25 (Court Dri.)
Close, The. Uxb —1M 25 (Honeycroft Hill)
Close, The. Vir W —7M 95
Close, The. Wdly —7D 64
Clough Dri. Herm —6C 56
Clove Clo. Lwr Ear —2M 87
Clover Clo. Wokgm —4C 90
Club La. Crowt —5H 113
Clyde Rd. Stai —5L 73
Coach Horse Ct. Pang —8F 36
Coachmans Ct. Newb —6M 79
Coach Ride. Mar —3B 4
Coach Rd. Asc —2H 93
Coalport Way. Tile —3M 61
Cobb Clo. Dat —7M 47
Cobbett's La. Yat —4D 118
Cobblers Clo. Farn R —3D 22
Cobden Clo. Uxb —2K 25
Cobham Rd. Wdly —5E 64
Cochrane Clo. That —8H 81
Cochrane Pl. W'sham —5N 115
Cock-A-Dobby. Sand —9E 112
Cockett Rd. Slou —2N 47
Cock La. South —1G 83
Cockney Hill. Tile —6N 61
Cockpit Path. Wokgm —6A 90
Cock's La. Warf —6D 68
Cody Clo. Wdly —4G 64
Coe Spur. Slou —2D 46
Coftards. Slou —7L 23
Cold Ash Hill. Cold A —2F 80
Coldborough Rise. Brack —3K 91
Coldharbour Clo. Hen T —6B 16
Cold Harbour La. Farn —9J 119
Coldharbour Rd. Hung —7K 75
Coldicutt St. Cav —3J 63
Coldmoorholme La. Bour —4J 5
Cole La. Arbor X —8D 88
Colemans Moor La. Wdly —6E 64
Colemans Moor Rd. Wdly —8E 64
Colenorton Cres. Eton W —3A 46
Coleridge Av. Yat —4C 118
Coleridge Clo. Crowt —6G 113
Coleridge Clo. Twy —1L 65
Coleridge Cres. Coln —7F 48
Coleridge La. Pang —1M 59

Coleridge Rd.—Deepdale

Coleridge Rd. Ashf —8M 73
Coleridge Way. W Dray —3M 49
Coley Av. Read —7F 62 (in two parts)
Coley Hill. Read —6F 62
Coley Pk. Rd. Read —6F 62
Coley Pl. Read —6G 62
Colham Av. W Dray —9M 25
Colham Grn. Rd. Uxb —6N 25
Colham Mill Rd. W Dray —1L 49
Colham Rd. Uxb —5N 25
Colham Roundabout. Uxb —7N 25
Colin Way. Slou —2D 46
Collaroy Rd. Cold A —4F 80
College Av. Egh —9C 72
College Av. M'head —7B 20
College Av. Slou —2G 46
College Cres. Col T —1J 119
College Cres. Wind —8D 46
College Glen. M'head —7A 20
College Piece. Mort —4G 106
College Ride. Bag —9D 114
College Ride. Camb —2N 119
College Rise. M'head —7A 20
College Rd. Brack —6N 91
College Rd. Cipp —9B 22
College Rd. Col T —2J 119
College Rd. M'head —6A 20
College Rd. Read —6M 63
College Way. Ashf —8N 73
Colleton Dri. Twy —9K 41
Collier Clo. M'head —5C 20
Colliers Way. Read —5B 62
Collingwood Wlk. Tile —5J 61
Collins Clo. Newb —7N 79
Collins Dri. Herm —6C 56
Collis St. Read —7H 63
Colliston Wlk. Calc —9N 61
Colmworth Clo. Lwr Ear —3N 87
Colnbrook By-Pass. Coln & W Dray —5D 48
Colnbrook Ct. Coln —7G 48
Coln Clo. M'head —6C 20
Colndale Rd. Coln —8F 48
Colne Av. W Dray —1K 49
Colnebridge Clo. Stai —8F 72
Colne Orchard. Iver —7G 25
Colne Pk. Caravan Site. W Dray —3K 49
Colne Reach. Stai —2G 73
Colne Way. Stai —6C 72
Coln Trading Est. Coln —7G 48
Colonial Rd. Slou —1J 47
Colston Clo. Calc —8L 61
Colthrop La. That —9L 81
Coltsfoot Clo. Bfld C —8J 85
Coltsfoot Dri. W Dray —7M 25
Columbia Ct. Wokgm —2K 111
Colwyn Clo. Yat —3A 118
Colyer Clo. Herm —4F 56
Colyton Way. Pur T —8K 37
Combermere Clo. Wind —8D 46
Combe Rd. Tile —5N 61
Combe View. Hung —7K 75
Comet Rd. Stai —4L 73
Comet Way. Wdly —5F 64
Comfrey Clo. Wokgm —3C 90
Commercial Rd. Read —2G 86
Commonfield La. B'ham —2G 110
Common Hill. Eng —8A 60
Common La. Bright & Farnb —2B 30
Common La. Eton C —4E 46
Common Rd. Dor —3M 45
Common Rd. Eton W —3B 46
Common Rd. Hdly —8H 103
Common Rd. Slou —3B 48
Commons Rd. Wokgm —2L 89
Common, The. W Dray —3K 49
Communications Rd. Green —5C 102
Compton Av. Tile —5J 61
Compton Clo. Brack —8J 91
Compton Clo. Ear —8B 64
Compton Clo. Sand —9G 113
Compton Ct. Burn —7A 22
Compton Dri. M'head —6L 19
Compton Ho. Comp —9G 13
Comsaye Wlk. Brack —7N 91
Concleve Clo. Aldm —3J 105
Concorde Clo. Uxb —3M 25
Concorde Rd. M'head —1A 44
Concorde Way. Slou —1E 46
Concorde Way. Wdly —5F 64
Condor Clo. Tile —1K 61
Conduit La. Dat —5N 47
Conegar Ct. Slou —9G 22
Conifer Clo. Baug —9G 104
Conifer Crest. Newb —5G 100
Conifer Dri. Tile —2J 61
Conifer La. Egh —9D 72
Conifers, The. Crowt —3E 112
Conifer Wlk. Wind —6M 45
Coningham Rd. Read —5J 87
Coningsby. Brack —6N 91
Coningsby Clo. M'head —2A 44
Coningsby La. Fif —8F 44
Conisboro Av. Cav —8E 38
Conisboro Way. Cav —8E 38
Coniston Clo. Mar —5A 4
Coniston Clo. That —8D 80
Coniston Clo. Wdly —7E 64
Coniston Ct. Light —9L 115
Coniston Ct. Newb —7L 79
Coniston Cres. Burn —6M 21
Coniston Dri. Tile —2N 61
Connaught Av. Ashf —8M 73
Connaught Clo. Crowt —7D 112
Connaught Clo. M'head —5B 20
Connaught Clo. Read —5D 62
Connaught Clo. Yat —3A 118
Connaught Rd. Bag —7F 114
Connaught Rd. Newb —8M 79
Connaught Rd. Read —5D 62
Connaught Rd. Slou —1K 47
Constable Way. Col T —3J 119
Constitution Rd. Read —4B 62
Consul Clo. Wdly —7E 64
Convent Rd. Wind —8C 46
Conway Dri. That —6E 80
Conway Rd. Calc —7K 61
Conway Rd. Tap —7L 21
Conygree Clo. Lwr Ear —2A 88
Cookham Clo. Sand —9G 113
Cookham Dean Bottom. Cook —7G 4
Cookham Rd. Brack —4J 91
Cookham Rd. M'head —4B 20
Coombe Ct. That —8H 81
Coombe Hill. Farnb —6M 9
Coombe Hill Ct. Wind —1N 69
Coombe La. Asc —6M 93
Coombe Pine. Brack —8A 92
Coombe Rd. Comp —3J 33
Coombe Rd. Yat —2A 118
Coombesbury La. Stcks —3A 78
Coombes La. Wokgm —7F 88
Coombe, The. Streat —8H 15
Cooper Clo. Read —4J 87
Cooper Rd. Hen T —3C 16
Cooper Rd. W'sham —6N 115
Coopers Clo. Stai —9F 72
Coopers Cres. That —7F 80
Coopers Hill La. Egh —7L 71 (in three parts)
Coopers Pightle. Kid E —2D 38
Coopers Row. Iver —5D 24
Cooper Way. Slou —2D 46
Cope Hall La. Newb —3F 100
Copenhagen Clo. Read —4J 87
Copenhagen Wlk. Crowt —6F 112
Copperage Rd. Farnb —5C 10
Copper Beech Clo. Wind —7N 45
Copperdale Clo. Ear —9M 63
Copperfield Av. Owl —8J 113
Copperfield Av. Uxb —6N 25
Coppermill Rd. Wray —3B 72
Coppice Clo. Baug —9F 104
Coppice Clo. Newb —2M 101
Coppice Dri. Wray —4M 71
Coppice Gdns. Crowt —5D 112
Coppice Gdns. Yat —4A 118
Coppice Grn. Brack —2K 91 (in two parts)
Coppice Rd. Wdly —8D 64
Coppice, The. W Dray —7M 25
Coppidbeech La. Brack —5F 90
Coppins La. Iver —6G 24
Copse Av. Cav —1K 63
Copse Barnhill La. Wokgm —5E 88
Copse Clo. Mar —5A 4
Copse Clo. Tile —1L 61
Copse Clo. Up Buck —3L 81
Copse Clo. W Dray —2L 49
Copse Dri. Wokgm —4M 89
Copse La. Eve —9M 111
Copse Mead. Wdly —3E 64
Copse, The. Tadl —9J 105
Copse, The. Warg —2K 41
Copse Way. Wokgm —3K 111
Copse Wood. Iver —2E 24
Copthorn Clo. M'head —1L 43
Copthorne Chase. Ashf —8N 73
Copthorne Dri. Light —9L 115
Corbett Gdns. Wdly —5D 64
Corbridge Rd. Read —8J 63
Corby Clo. Egh —1L 95
Corby Clo. Wdly —3F 64
Corby Dri. Egh —1L 95
Cordelia Croft. Warf —3B 92
Cordelia Gdns. Stai —4M 73
Cordelia Rd. Stai —4M 73
Corderoy Clo. That —9J 81
Cordwallis Pk. M'head —6B 20
Cordwallis Rd. M'head —6B 20
Cordwallis St. M'head —6B 20
Cores End Rd. Bour —4M 5
Corey Ho. Brack —4M 91
Corfe Gdns. Slou —8C 22
Corfe M. Cav —9L 39
Corfe Pl. M'head —7N 19
Corfield Clo. Finch —7K 111
Coriander Way. Ear —2M 87
Corinne Clo. Read —2H 87
Corinthian Way. Stanw —4L 73
Cormorant Pl. Col T —2J 119
Cornbunting Clo. Col T —2H 119
Corn Croft. Warf —2B 92
Cornfield. Yat —5A 118
Cornfield Clo. Uxb —3L 25
Cornfield Grn. Wokgm —3L 89
Cornfield Rd. Wdly —4F 64
Cornflower Clo. Wokgm —4J 89
Cornwall Av. Slou —5E 22
Cornwall Clo. Eton W —4A 46
Cornwall Clo. M'head —4B 20
Cornwall Clo. Tile —9J 37
Cornwall Clo. Warf —1C 92
Cornwall Clo. Wokgm —5J 89
Cornwall Rd. Uxb —1L 25
Cornwall Way. Stai —9F 72
Cornwell Rd. Old Win —3J 71
Cornwood Gdns. Read —9J 63
Coronation Av. G Grn —6N 23
Coronation Av. Wind —8J 47
Coronation Cotts. Hurst —8J 65
Coronation Rd. Asc —9K 93
Coronation Rd. L Grn —9F 18
Coronation Rd. Yat —2C 118
Coronation Sq. Read —8B 62
Coronation Sq. Wokgm —4B 90
Corporation Cottage. Newb —7K 79
Corrie Gdns. Vir W —9L 95
Corsair Clo. Stai —4L 73
Corsair Rd. Stai —4M 73
Corsham Rd. Calc —9N 61
Corsham Way. Crowt —5F 112
Corwen Rd. Tile —4L 61
Costa Clo. Newb —6H 79
Cotswold Clo. Farn —9J 119
Cotswold Clo. M'head —8E 20
Cotswold Clo. Slou —2E 46
Cotswold Clo. Stai —9H 73
Cotswold Clo. Uxb —2K 25
Cotswold Rd. Sand —9D 112
Cotswold Way. Tile —2J 61
Cottage La. Ping —1C 86
Cotterell Clo. Brack —2M 91
Cotterell Gdns. Twy —1L 65
Cottesbrooke Clo. Coln —7E 48
Cottesmore. Brack —9L 91
Cottesmore Rd. Wdly —6C 64
Coulson Way. Burn —6L 21
County La. Warf —1A 92
Course Rd. Asc —5K 93
Court Clo. M'head —3F 44
Court Cres. Slou —7F 22
Court Dri. M'head —3F 20
Court Dri. Uxb —2N 25
Courtenay Dri. Emm G —6H 39
Courtfield Dri. M'head —8N 19
Court Gdns. Camb —4N 119
Courthouse Rd. M'head —7N 19
Courtlands. M'head —8C 20
Courtlands Av. Slou —3M 47
Courtlands Hill. Pang —9D 36
Courtlands Rd. Newb —1M 101
Court La. Burn —4N 21
Court La. Dor —2L 45
Court La. Iver —9H 25 (in two parts)
Courtney Rd. Houn —9N 49
Court Rd. M'head —4F 20
Courts Rd. Ear —8A 64
Court, The. That —7G 81
Courtyards, The. Langl —1B 48
Courtyard, The. Thea —9F 60
Courtyard, The. Wokgm —6A 90
Cousins Clo. W Dray —8M 25
Coventry Rd. Read —4L 63
Coverdale Way. Slou —5A 22
Covert La. Brack —6N 91
Covert, The. Asc —9L 93
Covert, The. Farn —9J 119
Covey Clo. Farn —9L 119
Cow La. E Ils —7B 12
Cow La. Moul —4G 15
Cow La. Read —2E 62 (in two parts)
Cowley Bus. Pk. Cow —4K 25
Cowley Cres. Uxb —6K 25
Cowley Mill Rd. Uxb —3J 25
Cowley Mill Trading Est. Uxb —3J 25
Cowley Rd. Uxb —3K 25
Coworth Clo. Asc —7D 94
Coworth Pk. S'hill —6E 94
Coworth Rd. Asc —7C 94
Cowper Rd. Slou —5C 22
Cowper Way. Read —8D 62
Cowslade. Speen —6H 79
Cowslip Clo. Tile —6J 61
Cowslip Clo. Uxb —1M 25
Cowslip Cres. That —6H 81
Coxborrow Clo. Cook —8J 5
Coxeter Rd. Newb —7J 79
Cox Grn. Col T —3H 119
Cox Grn. La. M'head —2M 43
Cox Grn. Rd. M'head —1N 43
Cox's La. Midg —9M 81
Cox's La. Shalb —7E 96
Crabtree Clo. Herm —6C 56
Crabtree La. Cur —7B 56
Crabtree Rd. Camb —7M 119
Cradock Rd. Read —8G 63
Craig Av. Read —4B 62
Crail Clo. Wokgm —8M 89
Crake Pl. Col T —1H 119
Cranberry Wlk. B'water —6K 119
Cranborne Gdns. Read —2A 62
Cranbourne Av. Calc —8K 61
Cranbourne Av. Wind —8B 46
Cranbourne Clo. Slou —9E 22
Cranbourne Cotts. Wind —7L 69
Cranbourne Hall Cotts. Wind —5L 69
Cranbourne Rd. Slou —9E 22
Cranbrook Dri. M'head —5M 19
Cranbury Rd. Read —5D 62
Crane Ct. Col T —1H 119
Crane Wharf. Read —5H 63
Cranford Av. Stai —4M 73
Cranford Clo. Hurst —4L 65
Cranford Clo. Stai —4M 73
Cranford Pk. Dri. Yat —3B 118
Cranmer Clo. Tile —1J 61
Craufurd Ct. M'head —6B 20
Craufurd Rise. M'head —6B 20
Craven Clo. Kint —1G 99
Craven Dene. Newb —7M 79
Craven Rd. Ink —3N 97
Craven Rd. Newb —9J 79
Craven Rd. Read —6K 63
Craven Way. Kint —9G 77
Crawford Clo. Ear —9A 64
Crawford Gdns. Camb —4M 119
Crawford Pl. Newb —8K 79
Crawley Chase. Wink R —1E 92
Crawshay Dri. Emm G —6H 39
Crayle St. Slou —4C 22
Craysleaze. Kid E —2D 38
Crecy Clo. Wokgm —5K 89
Creden Clo. M'head —6A 20
Crediton Clo. Wdly —6F 64
Cree's Meadow. W'sham —7M 115
Creighton Ct. Read —8K 63
Cremyll Rd. Read —3F 62
Crendon Ct. Cav —2G 63
Crescent Dri. M'head —7B 20
Crescent Ho. Wdly —7D 64
Crescent Rd. Read —6L 63
Crescent Rd. Tile —3L 61
Crescent Rd. Wokgm —6A 90
Crescent, The. Ashf —9N 73
Crescent, The. B'water —5H 119
Crescent, The. Brack —6N 91
Crescent, The. Ear —8B 64
Crescent, The. Egh —1N 95
Crescent, The. Kint —9F 76
Crescent, The. Lwr P —7L 83
Crescent, The. M'head —7B 20
Crescent, The. Mort —4H 107
Crescent, The. S'lake —1G 40
Crescent, The. Slou —1G 46
Crescent, The. Thea —8F 60
Cressex Clo. Binf —1G 91
Cressida Chase. Warf —3B 92
Cressingham Rd. Read —9J 63
Cressington Pl. Bour —3L 5
Cress Rd. Slou —1D 46
Cresswell Rd. Newb —7A 80
Cresswells Mead. M'head —4E 44
Crest Clo. Rusc —7K 41
Creswell Clo. Read —5J 87
Cricketers La. Warf —9D 68
Cricketers La. W'sham —5N 115
Cricket Field Gro. Crowt —6H 113
Cricket Field Rd. Uxb —2L 25
Cricketfield Rd. W Dray —3K 49
Cricket Hill. Finch —8L 111
Cricket Hill. Yat —6C 118
Cricket Hill La. Yat —6B 118
Crimp Hill. Old Win & Egh —4H 71
Crisp Gdns. Binf —2J 91
Crispin Clo. Cav —8D 38
Crisp Rd. Hen T —3B 16
Crocker Clo. Asc —3J 93
Crockford Pl. Binf —2K 91
Crockhamwell Rd. Wdly —6D 64
Crocus Way. Wokgm —4J 89
Croft Clo. Uxb —1N 25
Croft Clo. Wokgm —9M 89
Crofters Clo. Sand —1E 118
Crofters, The. Old Win —3J 71
Crofthill Rd. Slou —5D 22
Croft La. Newb —7J 79
Croft La. Yat —2A 118
Crofton Clo. Brack —7B 92
Croft Rd. Gor —8L 15
Croft Rd. Hung —5K 75
Croft Rd. Mort —4G 107
Croft Rd. Newb —2K 101
Croft Rd. Spen W —9J 87
Croft Rd. Wokgm —9M 89
Croft, The. Brack —2M 91
Croft, The. Kint —9F 76
Croft, The. M'head —9N 19
Croft, The. Mar —4E 4
Croft, The. Wokgm —6B 90
Croft, The. Yat —2B 118
Cromer Clo. Tile —3K 61
Cromer Rd. W Houn —9N 49
Cromwell Clo. Hen T —6C 16
Cromwell Dri. Slou —7G 23
Cromwell Gdns. Mar —5C 4
Cromwell Pl. Newb —8L 79
Cromwell Rd. Asc —6L 93
Cromwell Rd. Camb —2N 119
Cromwell Rd. Cav —2H 63
Cromwell Rd. Hen T —6D 16
Cromwell Rd. M'head —7A 20
Cromwell Rd. Mar —5C 4
Cromwell Rd. Newb —6N 79
Cromwell Ter. Speen —6H 79
Crondall End. Yat —2A 118
Crondell Ct. Camb —5M 119
Cropper Clo. That —8K 81
Crosfields Clo. Read —3J 87
Cross Fell. Brack —6L 91
Cross Gates Clo. Brack —5C 92
Cross Keys Rd. S Sto —2L 15
Crossland Rd. Read —5H 63
Cross La. Ashmw —9N 117
Cross La. Graz —2B 108
Cross Oak. Wind —8C 46
Cross Rd. Asc —9B 94
Cross Rd. Uxb —1K 25
Cross St. Read —4H 63
Cross St. Uxb —1K 25
Cross St. Wokgm —5A 90
Crossway. Brack —4N 91
Crossways. Egh —9E 72
Crossways. Wdly —7D 64
Crossway, The. Uxb —3N 25
Crosthwaite Way. Slou —6N 21
Crouch La. Wink —4H 69
Crowfield Dri. That —8E 80
Crowle Rd. Lamb —3G 27
Crown Acre Clo. That —8F 80
Crown Ct. That —8F 80
Crown La. Farn R —3C 22
Crown La. M'head —7D 20
Crown La. Thea —9F 60
Crown La. Vir W —8M 95
Crown Mead. That —8F 80
Crown Meadow. Coln —6C 48
Crown Pl. Owl —9J 113
Crown Pl. Read —6J 63
Crown Rd. Mar —5B 4
Crown Rd. Vir W —8L 95
Crown Row. Brack —8A 92
Crown St. Egh —9B 72
Crown St. Read —6H 63
Crown Wlk. Uxb —1K 25
Crown Way. W Dray —9N 25
Crow Piece La. Farn R —1B 22
Crowsley Rd. S'lake —1F 40
Crowsley Way. Son C —1E 38
Crowthorne Rd. Brack —7L 91
Crowthorne Rd. Crowt & Brack —4H 113
Crowthorne Rd. Sand —1E 118
Crowthorne Rd. N. Brack —5M 91
Croxley Rise. M'head —8A 20
Cruch La. Tap —3B 68
Cruikshank Lea. Col T —3J 119
Crummock Clo. Slou —7M 21
Crutchley Rd. Wokgm —4B 90
Culford Clo. Lwr Ear —1C 88
Culham Dri. M'head —4B 20
Culham Ho. Brack —6B 92
Cullen Clo. Yat —4A 118
Cullerns Pas. M'head —8C 20
Culley Way. M'head —1L 43
Culloden Way. Wokgm —5K 89
Culvercroft. Binf —2J 91
Culver La. Ear —5N 63
Culver Rd. Newb —2K 101
Culver Rd. Owl —9H 113
Culver Rd. Read —6M 63
Culvert La. Uxb —3J 25
Cumberland Av. Slou —5E 22
Cumberland Dri. Brack —3A 92
Cumberland Rd. Ashf —7L 73
Cumberland Rd. Read —4K 63
Cumberland St. Stai —9E 72
Cumberland Way. Wokgm —5J 89
Cumbrae Clo. Slou —9J 23
Cumbria Clo. M'head —1N 43
Cumbrian Way. Uxb —1L 25
Cumnor Way. Brack —6B 92
Cunworth Ct. Brack —8K 91
Curlew Clo. That —8F 80
Curlew Dri. Tile —6K 61
Curling Way. Newb —7N 79
Curls La. M'head —1B 44
Curls Rd. M'head —1A 44
Curl Way. Wokgm —6M 89
Curly Bri. Clo. Farn —9K 119
Curnock Ct. Newb —1J 101
Curran Clo. Uxb —5K 25
Curridge Grn. Cur —8B 56
Curridge Piece. Cur —7C 56
Curridge Rd. Cur —9L 55
Curtis Rd. Calc —7K 61
Curzon Mall. Slou —1H 47
Curzon St. Read —4D 62
Cusden Wlk. Read —5G 62 (off Castle St.)
Cutbush Clo. Lwr Ear —3A 88
Cutbush La. Lwr Ear —3N 87
Cutbush La. Shin —5L 87
Cutting Hill. Hung —7F 96
Cuttings, The. Hamp N —8J 33
Cwmcarn. Cav —7F 38
Cygnet Clo. That —8E 80
Cygnet Way. Hung —4K 75
Cypress Clo. Wokgm —2M 111
Cypress Ho. Langl —4C 48
Cypress Rd. Wdly —6F 64
Cypress Wlk. Egh —1K 95
Cypress Way. B'water —4F 118
Cyril Vokins Rd. Newb —9B 80

Dacre Av. Cav —9L 39
Dagmar Rd. Wind —8F 46
Dagnall Cres. Uxb —6K 25
Dalby Cres. Green —2M 101
Dalcross. Brack —8B 92
Dale Clo. Asc —7C 94
Dale Ct. Chalv —1E 46
Dale Gdns. Sand —1E 118
Daleham Av. Egh —9B 72
Dale Lodge Rd. Asc —7C 94
Dale Rd. Read —7H 63
Dalley Ct. Col T —2H 119
Dalton Clo. Tile —4M 61
Damer Gdns. Hen T —6D 16
Danbridge Dri. Bour —4N 5
Dandridge Clo. Slou —3M 47
Danehill. Lwr Ear —3A 88
Danes Gdns. Cook —9K 5
Daniel's La. Hung —5G 96
Danvers Clo. That —9G 81
Danywern Dri. Winn —1H 89
Darby Grn. La. B'water —4F 118
Darby Grn. Rd. B'water —4E 118
Darell Rd. Cav —1F 62
Dark Dale. Asc —7D 92
Darkhole Ridge. Wind —1K 69
Dark La. Brad —5L 59
Dark La. E Ils —9K 11
Dark La. Hung —5N 75
Dark La. Pang —4N 59
Dark La. Tile —2J 61
Dark La. W'sham —6L 115
Darleydale Clo. Owl —8H 113
Darling's La. M'head —6J 19
Darrel Clo. Langl —3A 48
Darrell Charles Ct. Uxb —1M 25
Dart Clo. Finch —4L 111
Dart Clo. Slou —5C 48
Dart Clo. That —6E 80
Dartington Av. Wdly —8C 64
Dartington Clo. Tile —4N 61
Dartmouth Clo. Brack —5B 92
Dartmouth Ter. Read —6H 63
Darvills La. Slou —3D 66
Darvill's La. Slou —1F 46
Darwall Dri. Asc —4G 93
Darwin Clo. Read —2G 87
Darwin Rd. Slou —1A 48
Dashwood Clo. Brack —3A 92
Dashwood Clo. Slou —3L 47
Datchet Pl. Dat —7K 47
Datchet Rd. Hort —9A 48
Datchet Rd. Old Win —1J 71
Datchet Rd. Slou —3H 47
Datchet Rd. Wind —6F 46
Dauntless Rd. Bfld C —7J 85
Davenport Rd. Brack —3B 92
Daventry Clo. Coln —7G 48
Daventry Ct. Brack —3M 91
David Smith Ct. Calc —7N 61
Davis Clo. Mar —6C 4
Davis Clo. Winn —2G 89
Davis Gdns. Col T —2J 119
Davis St. Hurst —9H 65
Davis Way. Hurst —8J 65
Davy Clo. Wokgm —6A 90
Dawes E. Rd. Burn —5M 21
Dawes Moor Clo. Slou —7L 23
Dawe's Rd. Uxb —3M 25
Dawley Ride. Coln —7F 48
Dawlish Rd. Read —1J 87
Dawnay Clo. Asc —3J 93
Dawnay Rd. Camb —1M 119
Dawn Redwood Clo. Hort —9B 48
Dawson Clo. Wind —8C 46
Deacon Clo. Wokgm —3A 90
Deaconfield. S Sto —3L 15
Deacon's La. Herm —5F 56
Deacon Way. Tile —2A 62
Deadman's La. Gor H —2J 37
Deadmans La. Green —4M 101
Deadman's La. Thea —8E 60
Deadmoor La. Newt —8J 101
Deal Av. Slou —7B 22
Dean Clo. Uxb —1N 25
Dean Clo. Wind —9N 45
Deanfield Av. Hen T —5C 16
Deanfield Clo. Mar —4B 4
Deanfield Rd. Hen T —5B 16
Dean Gro. Wokgm —4A 90
Dean La. Cook —7F 4
Dean Pde. Camb —9C 114
Deans Clo. Stoke P —2K 23
Deans Ct. W'sham —7N 115
Deansgate. Brack —9M 91
Deansgate Rd. Read —6H 63
Dean St. Mar —5B 4
Deanswood Rd. Tadl —9J 105
Deanwood Ho. Stcks —6F 78
De Beauvoir Rd. Read —5L 63
De Bohun Rd. Read —3H 63
Decies Way. Stoke P —2J 23
Dedmere Ct. Mar —5D 4
Dedmere Rise. Mar —5C 4
Dedmere Rd. Mar —5C 4
Dedworth Dri. Wind —7B 46
Dedworth Rd. Wind —8M 45
Deena Clo. Slou —8A 22
Deepdale. Brack —6L 91

Deepdene Clo.—Evesham Wlk.

Deepdene Clo. Read —5E **62**
Deepfield. Dat —6K **47**
Deepfield Rd. Brack —4A **92**
Deerhurst Av. Winn —1H **89**
Deerhurst Clo. Calc —8M **61**
Dee Rd. Tile —6N **61**
Deer Rock Hill. Brack —8N **91**
Deerswood. M'head —5D **20**
Defford Clo. Wokgm —2L **89**
De Havilland Way. Stai —3M **73**
Delafield Dri. Calc —8K **61**
Delaford Clo. Iver —7H **25**
Delamere Rd. Ear —4A **64**
Delane Dri. Winn —2G **88**
Delaney Clo. Tile —4N **61**
Delft Clo. Tile —4N **61**
Deller St. Binf —2K **91**
Dellfield Cres. Uxb —5L **25**
Dell Rd. Crowt —7M **111**
Dell Rd. Finch —7M **111**
Dell Rd. Tile —2K **61**
Dell Rd. W Dray —3N **49**
Dell, The. M'head —2K **43**
Dell, The. Read —5J **63**
Dell, The. Yat —4A **118**
Delph, The. Lwr Ear —1D **88**
De Montfort Cres. Hung —7J **75**
De Montfort Rd. Read —3G **63**
De Montfort Rd. Speen —6J **79**
Dempsey Ho. Read —5N **61**
Denbridge Ind. Est. Uxb —1K **25**
Denbury Gdns. Read —3J **87**
Denby Way. Tile —3N **61**
Dencliffe. Ashf —9N **73**
Dene Clo. Brack —2N **91**
Dene Clo. Ear —9N **63**
Dene Way. Don —6K **79**
Denford La. Hung —3A **76**
Denham Clo. M'head —8N **19**
Denham Dri. Yat —4B **118**
Denham Gro. Brack —8N **91**
Denham Rd. Egh —8B **72**
Denham Rd. Iver —2E **24**
Denhose Clo. Lwr Ear —2N **87**
Denley Sq. Uxb —1K **25**
Denly Way. Light —9M **115**
Denmark Av. Wdly —3F **64**
Denmark Rd. Newb —9M **79**
Denmark Rd. Read —5K **63**
Denmark St. M'head —6B **20**
Denmark St. Wokgm —6A **90**
Denmead Ct. Brack —8B **92**
Dennisford Rd. Comp —2B **32**
Dennisford Rd. E Ils —9D **12**
Dennis Way. Slou —8N **21**
Denny Rd. Slou —3A **48**
Denton Clo. That —9F **80**
Denton Rd. Wokgm —5A **90**
Depot Rd. M'head —8C **20**
Derby Clo. Lamb —3G **26**
Derby Rd. Cav —1H **63**
Derby Rd. Newb —1K **101**
Derby Rd. Uxb —3K **25**
Derby St. Read —4F **62**
Derek Horn Ct. Camb —3M **119**
Derek Rd. M'head —6F **20**
Deridene Clo. Stai —3M **73**
De Ros Pl. Egh —9B **72**
Derrick Clo. Calc —8K **61**
Derry Rd. Farn —9K **119**
Derwent Av. Tile —2M **61**
Derwent Clo. Wokgm —5K **89**
Derwent Dri. M'head —6A **20**
Derwent Dri. Slou —6M **21**
Derwent Rd. Light —9L **115**
Derwent Rd. That —8D **80**
Desborough Cres. M'head —9N **19**
Desford Ct. Ashf —6N **73**
Desford Way. Ashf —6N **73**
Devenish Clo. S'hill —8N **93**
Devenish La. Asc —1N **115**
Devenish Rd. Asc —8M **93**
Devereux Rd. Wind —8F **46**
Deveron Dri. Tile —4A **62**
Devil's Highway, The. Crowt —5C **112**
De Vitre Grn. Wokgm —4D **90**
Devitt Clo. Read —2M **87**
Devon Av. Slou —7E **22**
Devon Chase. Warf —1B **92**
Devon Clo. Col T —2H **119**
Devon Clo. Wokgm —5K **89**
Devon Dri. Cav —9L **39**
Devonshire Clo. Farn R —3D **22**
Devonshire Gdns. Tile —1J **61**
Devonshire Grn. Farn R —3D **22**
Devonshire Pk. Read —1L **87**
Devon Way. Uxb —3N **25**
Dewberry Clo. That —7J **81**
Dhoon Rise. M'head —8C **20**
Diamedes Av. Stai —4L **73**
Diamond Rd. Slou —1J **47**
Diamond Way. Wokgm —4K **89**
Diana Clo. G Grn —7N **23**
Dianthus Pl. Wink R —1E **92**
Dickens Ct. Wokgm —5N **89**
Dickens Wlk. Newb —2L **101**
Dickens Way. Yat —4A **118**
Dieppe Clo. Wokgm —5K **89**
Digby Rd. Newb —7J **79**
Dines Way. Herm —5F **56**
Disraeli Ct. Coln —5C **48**
Ditchfield La. Wokgm —2K **111**
Ditchling. Brack —9L **91**
Ditton Pk. Rd. Slou —5N **47**
Ditton Rd. Dat —7M **47**
Ditton Rd. Langl —4A **48**
Dittons, The. Finch —4L **111**
Doctors La. Herm —5D **56**
Doddington Clo. Lwr Ear —2B **88**
Doddsfield Rd. Slou —4C **22**
Dodsells Well. Wokgm —2L **111**
Dogkennel La. S Faw —9H **9**
Dog La. Ash'd —7C **34**
Doles Hill. B'ham —8J **89**
Doles La. Wokgm —7K **89**
Dolman Rd. Newb —6L **79**
Dolphin Clo. Aldm —3H **105**
Dolphin Clo. Winn —2H **89**
Dolphin Ct. Brack —6N **91**
Dolphin Ct. Slou —1K **47**
Dolphin Ct. Stai —7H **73**
Dolphin Ct. N. Stai —7H **73**
Dolphin Rd. Slou —1K **47**
Doman Rd. Camb —5K **119**
Donaldson Way. Wdly —4F **64**
Doncastle Rd. Brack —5J **91**
Don Clo. Tile —4A **62**
Donegal Clo. Cav —1J **63**
Donkey La. W Dray —3K **49**
Donkin Hill. Cav —1J **63**
Donnington Clo. Camb —5M **119**
Donnington Gdns. Read —6K **63**
Donnington Lodge. Don —4K **79**
Donnington Pl. Winn —1J **89**
Donnington Rd. Read —5K **63**
Donnington Sq. Newb —6K **79**
Donnybrook. Brack —9L **91**
Dorcas Ct. Camb —6M **119**
Dorchester Clo. M'head —5M **19**
Dorchester Ct. Read —6C **62**
Dorchester Ct. Stai —8H **73**
Doreen Clo. Farn —9J **119**
Dorian Dri. Asc —3A **94**
Dorking Way. Calc —8H **61**
Dormer Clo. Crowt —5E **112**
Dormer Clo. Newb —4J **101**
Dornels. Slou —7L **23**
Dorney Reach Rd. Dor R —2J **45**
Dorney Wood Rd. Burn —2M **21**
Dorothy St. Read —6H **63**
Dorset Rd. Ashf —7L **73**
Dorset Rd. Wind —7E **46**
Dorset St. Read —4C **62**
Dorset Vale. Warf —1B **92**
Dorset Way. Uxb —3N **25**
Dorset Way. Wokgm —5K **89**
Doublet Clo. That —8D **80**
Douglas Ct. Ear —9N **63**
Douglas Grange. Hurst —8J **65**
Douglas La. Wray —2A **72**
Douglas Ride. Wool H —9C **100**
Douglas Rd. Cav —2K **63**
Douglas Rd. Slou —6F **22**
Douglas Rd. Stai —3L **73**
Douro Clo. Baug —9F **104**
Dove Clo. Lwr Ear —3M **87**
Dovecote Rd. Read —4H **87**
Dovedale Clo. Cav —1F **62**
Dovedale Clo. Owl —8H **113**
Dove Ho. Cres. Slou —4A **22**
Dover Rd. Slou —7B **22**
Dover St. Read —6G **62**
Doveton Way. Newb —7M **79**
Dowding Clo. Wdly —5F **64**
Dowding Ct. Crowt —4G **112**
Dowding Rd. Uxb —1N **25**
Dower Pk. Wind —1A **70**
Downend La. Chvly —1M **55**
Downfield La. Wal L & White —7F **42**
Downfield Rd. Wal L —9E **42**
Downham Ct. Read —2L **87**
Downing Path. Slou —5A **22**
Downing Rd. Tile —4L **61**
Downlands. E Gar —7B **28**
Downmill Rd. Brack —4K **91**
Down Pl. Water —5K **45**
Downs Clo. E'bury —6M **27**
Downshire. Gt Shef —9G **28**
Downshire Sq. Read —6E **62**
Downshire Way. Brack —4L **91**
(in two parts)
Downside. Brack —5M **91**
Downs La. Blew —1C **12**
Downs Rd. Comp —1K **33**
Downs Rd. Slou —1M **47**
Downs Way. Tile —2K **61**
Doyle Gdns. Yat —5A **118**
Drain Hill. Lamb —1G **26**
(in two parts)
Drake Av. Slou —3M **47**
Drake Av. Stai —9G **73**
Drake Clo. Brack —7M **91**
Drake Clo. Wokgm —3K **111**
Draper Clo. That —9G **81**
Drawback Hill. Hen T —7C **16**
Draycott. Brack —7B **92**
Drayhorse Dri. Bag —8H **115**
Drayton Clo. Brack —4A **92**
Drayton Gdns. W Dray —1M **49**
Drayton Rd. Read —4B **62**
Dresden Way. Tile —3N **61**
Drewett Clo. Read —5J **87**
Drift Hill. Ash'd —7F **34**
Drift Rd. M'head & Wink —1K **67**
Drift Rd. Wink —4K **69**
Drift Way. Coln —7D **48**
Driftway Clo. Lwr Ear —2C **88**
Drive, The. Bour —3K **5**
Drive, The. Dat —7K **47**
Drive, The. Ear —5N **63**
Drive, The. Newb —2J **101**
Drive, The. Slou —1N **47**
Drive, The. Vir W —7N **95**
Drive, The. Wray —2M **71**
Droitwich Clo. Brack —5A **92**
Drome Path. Winn —9F **64**
Dropmore Rd. Burn —2M **21**
Drove La. Cold A —1E **80**
Drovers Way. Brack —5C **92**
Drovers Way. Wdly —7D **64**
Drove, The. Hdly —9L **103**
Drove, The. Hung —6N **97**
Drove, The. Sil —8E **106**
Druce Way. That —8G **81**
Drummond Clo. Brack —3C **92**
Drury La. Mort —5G **107**
Dry Arch Rd. Asc —8B **94**
Dryden. Brack —9L **91**
Dryden Clo. That —6G **80**
Dryland Ho. Read —5N **61**
Duchess Clo. Whit T —6E **36**
Dudley Clo. Tile —3M **61**
Dudley Ct. Slou —2J **47**
Dudley M. Tile —2M **61**
Dudley Rd. Ashf —8N **73**
Duffield La. Stoke P —1H **23**
Duffield Pk. Stoke P —4J **23**
Duffield Rd. Son & Wdly —2D **64**
Dugdale Ho. Egh —9D 72
(off Pooley Grn. Rd.)
Duke of Cornwall Av. Camb —9A **114**
Dukesbridge Ct. Read —5H 63
(off Duke St.)
Dukes Covert. Bag —4H **115**
Dukeshill Rd. Brack —3M **91**
Dukes La. Asc —2C **94**
Dukes Meadow Ind. Est. Bour —4M **5**
Duke's Ride. Crowt —6C **112**
Dukes Ride. Sil —9B **106**
Duke St. Hen T —4D **16**
Duke St. Read —5H **63**
Duke St. Wind —6E **46**
Dukes Wood. Crowt —5F **112**
(in two parts)
Dulnan Clo. Tile —4A **62**
Dulverton Gdns. Read —1J **87**
Dumas Clo. Yat —4A **118**
Dumbarton Way. Cav —8L **39**
Dunaways Clo. Ear —9C **64**
Dunbar Clo. Slou —7J **23**
Dunbar Dri. Wdly —6F **64**
Duncan Dri. Wokgm —6B **90**
Duncan Gdns. Pur T —9K **37**
Duncannon Cres. Wind —9N **45**
Duncan Rd. Wdly —6D **64**
Duncroft. Wind —9B **46**
Dundas Clo. Brack —6M **91**
Dundee Rd. Slou —7B **22**
Dundela Clo. Wdly —6D **64**
Dunford Pl. Brack —2J **91**
Dungells Farm Clo. Yat —5B **118**
Dungells La. Yat —5A **118**
Dungrove Hill. M'head —3G **19**
Dunholme Clo. Lwr Ear —1D **88**
Dunholme End. M'head —2A **44**
Dunkirk Clo. Wokgm —5K **89**
Dunluce Gdns. Pang —8F **36**
Dunn Cres. Kint —1G **98**
Dunnock Way. Warg —2K **41**
Dunoon Clo. Calc —8M **61**
Dunromyn Caravan Pk. Bray —5H **45**
Dunsden Way. Bin H —4N **39**
Dunsfold Rd. Tile —5N **61**
Dunstall Clo. Tile —4L **61**
Dunstan Rd. That —7H **81**
Dunster Clo. Cav —7J **39**
Dunster Gdns. Slou —8C **22**
Dunt Av. Hurst —8K **65**
Dunt La. Hurst —7J **65**
Dunwood Ct. M'head —9N **19**
Durand Rd. Ear —2N **87**
Durham Av. Slou —7C **22**
Durham Clo. Read —3J **87**
Durham Clo. Wokgm —5K **89**
Durham Rd. Owl —8J **113**
Durley Mead. Brack —7C **92**
Dusseldorf Way. Read —5G **62**
Dutch Barn Clo. Stai —3L **73**
Dutch Elm Av. Wind —6H **47**
Dutton Way. Iver —7F **24**
Duval Pl. Bag —7H **115**
Dwyer Rd. Read —8N **61**
Dyson Clo. Wind —9D **46**
Dysons Clo. Newb —8J **79**
Dysonswood La. Tok G —5E **38**
Eagle Clo. Crowt —3E **112**
Eaglehurst Cotts. Binf —9G **67**
Eagles Nest. Sand —9E **112**
Earleydene. Asc —1L **115**
Earley Hill Rd. Read —7N **63**
Earley Pl. Read —5H **63**
Earlsfield. Holyp —3F **44**
Earlsfield Clo. Cav —9L **39**
Earlswood. Brack —9M **91**
Easington Dri. Lwr Ear —1D **88**
Eastbourne Rd. Slou —7B **22**
East Bri. Slou —9L **23**
E. Burnham La. Farn R —2C **22**
Eastbury Av. Tile —4J **61**
Eastbury Ct. Brack —2K **91**
Eastbury Pk. Winn —1J **89**
Eastbury Shute. Hung —2L **51**
Eastcourt Av. Ear —6N **63**
East Cres. Wind —7B **46**
Eastcroft. Slou —5D **22**
East Dri. Calc —7M **61**
East Dri. Stoke P —4G **22**
East Dri. Vir W —9K **95**
Eastern Av. Read —5L **63**
Eastern Ct. Read —6L **63**
Eastern Dri. Bour —3N **5**
Eastern La. Crowt —6K **113**
Eastern Rd. Brack —4A **92**
Eastfield Clo. Slou —2J **47**
Eastfield La. Whit T —6E **36**
Eastfield Rd. Burn —6K **21**
East Grn. B'water —5G **118**
Easthampstead Rd. Brack —4L **91**
Easthampstead Rd. Wokgm —5B **90**
Eastheath Av. Wokgm —7N **89**
Eastheath Gdns. Wokgm —8N **89**
East La. Chvly —3M **55**
East La. Rusc —7M **41**
Eastlyn Rd. Pam H —9N **105**
East Mall. Stai —8G **72**
Easton Hill. E'ton —8N **53**
East Ridge. Bour —3M **5**
East Rd. M'head —7B **20**
East Rd. W Dray —3N **49**
E. Stratton Clo. Brack —7C **92**
East St. Read —5H **63**
E. View Clo. Warg —3K **41**
E. View Rd. Warg —3K **41**
Eastwood Ct. Wdly —8D **64**
Eastwood Rd. Wdly —8D **64**
Eaton Ct. Read —5F 62
(off Oxford Rd.)
Eaton Pl. Read —5F **62**
Eaton Rd. Camb —5M **119**
Ebborne Sq. Lwr Ear —2B **88**
Ebsworth Clo. M'head —3F **20**
Eccles Clo. Cav —2J **63**
Eddington Hill. Edd —4L **75**
Eddington Rd. Brack —8J **91**
Eddystone Wlk. Stai —4M **73**
Eden Clo. Slou —4B **48**
Edenhall Clo. Tile —1L **61**
Edenham Clo. Lwr Ear —2D **88**
Edenham Cres. Read —7E **62**
Eden Way. Winn —2G **89**
Edgar Milward Clo. Tile —3A **62**
Edgar Rd. W Dray —8M **25**
Edgar Wallace Pl. Bour —2M **5**
Edgbarrow Ct. Crowt —7E **112**
Edgbarrow Rise. L Sand —8E **112**
Edgcumbe Pk. Dri. Crowt —5E **112**
Edgecombe La. Newb —6N **79**
Edgedale Clo. Crowt —6F **112**
Edgehill St. Read —7H **63**
Edgell Clo. Vir W —5N **95**
Edgell Rd. Stai —9G **73**
Edgewood Clo. Crowt —3E **112**
Edinburgh Av. Slou —6C **22**
Edinburgh Dri. Stai —9L **73**
Edinburgh Gdns. Wind —8F **46**
Edinburgh Rd. M'head —5B **20**
Edinburgh Rd. Mar —4C **4**
Edinburgh Rd. Read —5E **62**
Edith Rd. M'head —7L **19**
Edmonds Ct. Brack —3N **91**
Edmunds Way. Slou —6K **23**
Edneys Hill. Wokgm —8J **89**
Edward Av. Camb —4L **119**
Edward Ct. Stai —9K **73**
Edward Ct. Wokgm —6N **89**
Edward Rd. Charv —8G **40**
Edward Rd. W'sham —6N **115**
Edwards Ct. Slou —1G **46**
Edwards Hill. Lamb —3H **27**
Edward Way. Ashf —6N **73**
Edwin Clo. That —8J **81**
Eeklo Pl. Newb —1M **101**
Egerton Rd. Col T —3K **119**
Egerton Rd. Read —2L **87**
Egerton Rd. Slou —5A **22**
Egham By-Pass. Egh —9A **72**
Egham Hill. Egh —1M **95**
Egremont Dri. Lwr Ear —9C **64**
Egremont Gdns. Slou —9C **22**
Eight Acres. Burn —5L **21**
Eight Bells. Newb —9K **79**
Elan Clo. Tile —5N **61**
Elbow Meadow. Coln —7G **49**
Eldart Clo. Tile —5B **62**
Elder Clo. Tile —3K **61**
Elder Clo. W Dray —8M **25**
Elderfield Rd. Stoke P —1H **23**
Elder Way. Langl —1A **48**
Eldon Pl. Read —5J **63**
Eldon Rd. Read —5J **63**
Eldon Sq. Read —5K **63**
Eldon St. Read —5K **63**
Eldon Ter. Read —5K **63**
Elford Clo. Lwr Ear —2B **88**
Elgar Av. Crowt —3F **112**
Elgar Rd. Read —6G **63**
Elgar Rd. S. Read —7H **63**
Elgarth Dri. Wokgm —2L **111**
Eliot Clo. Cav —9G **39**
Eliot Clo. That —6F **80**
Eliot Dri. Mar —3D **4**
Elizabethan Clo. Stai —5L **73**
Elizabethan Way. Stai —5L **73**
Elizabeth Av. Bag —8J **115**
Elizabeth Av. Newb —3H **101**
Elizabeth Clo. Brack —6N **91**
Elizabeth Clo. Cook —8K **5**
Elizabeth Clo. Hen T —6A **16**
Elizabeth Ct. Slou —1J **47**
Elizabeth Ct. Thea —9F **60**
Elizabeth Ct. Tile —3L **61**
Elizabeth Ct. Warg —3J **41**
Elizabeth Ct. Wokgm —5N **89**
Elizabeth Gdns. Asc —7L **93**
Elizabeth Gdns. Kint —9G **77**
Elizabeth M. Read —5H **63**
Elizabeth Rd. Hen T —6A **16**
Elizabeth Rd. Mar —4C **4**
Elizabeth Rd. Wokgm —5B **90**
Elizabeth Rout Clo. Spen W —9J **87**
Elizabeth Wlk. Read —7H **63**
Elizabeth Way. Stoke P —2H **23**
Ellenborough Clo. Brack —3A **92**
Ellerton Clo. Thea —8F **60**
Ellesfield Av. Brack —6J **91**
Ellesmere Clo. Cav —1H **63**
Elliman Av. Slou —8G **23**
Elliman Sq. Slou —1H **47**
Ellington Gdns. Tap —7F **20**
Ellington Pk. M'head —5B **20**
Ellington Rd. Tap —7F **20**
Elliott Rise. Asc —4G **93**
Ellis Av. Slou —1G **46**
Ellison Clo. Wind —9B **46**
Ellison Way. Wokgm —5N **89**
Ellis Rd. Crowt —4E **112**
Ellis's Hill. Arbor —7E **88**
Elmar Grn. Slou —4C **22**
Elm Bank. Yat —2A **118**
Elmbank Av. Egh —1K **95**
Elm Clo. Farn C —1E **22**
Elm Clo. Stai —5L **73**
Elm Cotts. Wool H —9D **100**
Elm Ct. Owl —8J **113**
Elm Ct. Son C —1G **38**
Elm Croft. Dat —7L **47**
Elmcroft. Gor —9L **15**
Elmcroft Dri. Ashf —9N **73**
Elm Dri. Bfld —6J **85**
Elm Dri. Wink —5K **69**
Elm Gro. M'head —7B **20**
Elm Gro. That —6E **80**
Elm Gro. W Dray —8N **25**
Elmhurst Rd. Gor —7L **15**
Elmhurst Rd. Read —7K **63**
Elmhurst Rd. Slou —2B **48**
Elmhurst Rd. That —6D **80**
Elm La. Bour —2K **5**
Elm La. Lwr Ear —1M **87**
(in two parts)
Elm Lawn Clo. Uxb —1M **25**
Elmleigh Ct. Cav —1J **63**
Elmley Clo. Wokgm —2L **89**
Elm Lodge Av. Read —4D **62**
Elm Pk. S'dale —1N **115**
Elm Pk. Ct. Read —5D **62**
Elm Pk. Rd. Read —5D **62**
Elm Rd. Lwr Ear —1L **87**
Elm Rd. Tok G —6D **38**
Elm Rd. Wind —9D **46**
Elms Av. That —8H **81**
Elms Dri. Bour —4M **5**
Elmshott La. Slou —8A **22**
Elmsleigh Cen., The. Stai —8G **73**
Elmsleigh Rd. Stai —9G **72**
Elms Rd. Wokgm —6N **89**
Elms, The. B'water —5H **119**
Elms, The. Warf P —1D **92**
Elmstone Dri. Tile —3K **61**
Elmsway. Ashf —9N **73**
Elmwood. M'head —2E **20**
Elmwood Rd. Slou —8K **23**
Elruge Clo. W Dray —2L **49**
Elsinore Av. Stai —5M **73**
Elsley Rd. Tile —1L **61**
Elstow Av. Cav —7J **39**
Elstree Clo. Tile —2L **61**
Eltham Av. Cav —8L **39**
Elthorne Rd. Uxb —3L **25**
Elton Dri. M'head —6A **20**
Elton La. W'ton —3J **53**
Elvaston Way. Tile —5N **61**
Elveden Clo. Lwr Ear —1D **88**
Elvendon Rd. Gor —7L **15**
Elwell Clo. Egh —9B **72**
Ely Av. Slou —6E **22**
Elyham. Pur T —8J **37**
Ely Rd. Thea —1F **84**
Embankment, The. Wray —5L **71**
Ember Rd. Slou —2C **48**
Emblen Cres. Arbor X —9D **88**
Embrook Way. Calc —8H **61**
Emerald Clo. Wokgm —4K **89**
Emerald Ct. Slou —1G **47**
Emerson Ct. Crowt —5F **112**
Emery Acres. Up Bas —7J **35**
Emery Down Clo. Brack —5D **92**
Emma La. Warg —3K **41**
Emmbrook Ct. Read —1L **87**
Emmbrook Ga. Wokgm —3L **89**
Emmbrook Rd. Wokgm —3L **89**
Emmbrook Vale. Wokgm —2L **89**
Emm Clo. Wokgm —3L **89**
Emmer Grn. Ct. Cav —8J **39**
Emmer Grn. Rd. Bin H —4M **39**
Emmets Nest. Binf —1G **91**
Emmets Pk. Binf —1G **91**
Emmview Clo. Wokgm —4L **89**
Empress Rd. Calc —7K **61**
Enborne Clo. Tile —4K **61**
Enborne Ct. Newb —1H **101**
Enborne Gdns. Brack —2A **92**
Enborne Gro. Newb —9J **79**
Enborne Pl. Newb —9J **79**
Enborne Rd. Newb —1G **100**
Enborne St. Enb & Newb —6D **100**
Enborne Way. Brimp —4B **104**
Enfield Clo. Uxb —3L **25**
Engineers Rd. Green —5D **102**
Englefield Clo. Egh —1L **95**
Englefield Rd. Thea —8D **60**
Englehurst. Egh —1L **95**
Englemere Rd. Brack —2K **91**
English Gdns. Wray —2M **71**
Ennerdale. Brack —6L **91**
Ennerdale Cres. Slou —6M **21**
Ennerdale Rd. Read —9K **63**
Ennerdale Way. That —8D **80**
Ensign Clo. Stai —5L **73**
Ensign Way. Stai —5L **73**
Enstone Rd. Wdly —4F **64**
Enterprise Way. That —9K **81**
Epping Clo. Read —5F **62**
Epping Way. Brack —6C **92**
Epsom Clo. Camb —1N **119**
Epsom Ct. Read —6F **62**
Epsom Cres. Newb —1M **101**
Erfstadt Ct. Wokgm —6A **90**
Erica Clo. Slou —8A **22**
Erica Dri. Wokgm —6B **90**
Eric Av. Cav —7G **39**
Eriswell Clo. Lwr Ear —1D **88**
Erleigh Ct. Dri. Ear —5N **63**
Erleigh Ct. Gdns. Ear —5N **63**
Erleigh Dene. Newb —1K **101**
Erleigh Rd. Read —6K **63**
Ermine St. Stcks —5C **78**
Ermin Wlk. That —8E **80**
Errington Dri. Wind —7C **46**
Erskine Clo. Pam H —9A **106**
Eschle Ct. Slou —7G **23**
Esher Rd. Camb —9D **114**
Eskdale Gdns. M'head —3E **44**
Eskdale Rd. Uxb —3J **25**
Eskdale Rd. Winn —8F **64**
Eskin Clo. Tile —5A **62**
Essex Av. Slou —6E **22**
Essex Pl. Lamb —2H **27**
Essex Rise. Warf —2C **92**
Essex St. Newb —3G **101**
Essex St. Read —7H **63**
Essex Way. Son C —2G **38**
Ethel Rd. Ashf —9M **73**
Eton Clo. Dat —5J **47**
Eton Ct. Eton —6F **46**
Eton Ct. Stai —9G **73**
Eton Pl. Mar —5B **4**
Eton Rd. Dat —4H **47**
Eton Sq. Eton —6F **46**
Eton Wick Rd. Eton W —3A **46**
Eustace Cres. Wokgm —3B **90**
Evedon. Brack —9M **91**
Evelyns Clo. Uxb —7N **25**
Evendon's Clo. Wokgm —8M **89**
Evendon's La. Wokgm —9K **89**
Evenlode. M'head —6C **20**
Evenlode Way. Sand —1G **119**
Everard Av. Slou —1G **46**
Everest Rd. Camb —9A **114**
Everest Rd. Crowt —4F **112**
Everest Rd. Stai —4L **73**
Evergreen Ct. Stai —4L **73**
Evergreen Dri. Calc —8N **61**
Evergreen Oak Av. Wind —9J **47**
Evergreen Way. Stai —4L **73**
Evergreen Way. Wokgm —6L **89**
Everington La. Herm —4H **57**
Everitts Corner. Slou —8A **22**
Everland Rd. Hung —5K **75**
(in two parts)
Eversley Rd. Arbor X —9D **88**
Eversley Rd. Finch & Arbor X —5D **110**
Eversley St. Eve —9F **110**
Evesham Rd. Emm G —8H **39**
Evesham Wlk. Owl —9H **113**

Hankin's La.—Hithermoor Rd.

Hankin's La. Ham M —1J 99
Hanley Clo. Wind —7N 45
Hannibal Rd. Stai —4L 73
Hanningtons Way. Bfld C —8K 85
Hanover Clo. Egh —1K 95
Hanover Clo. Slou —2J 47
Hanover Clo. Wind —7B 46
Hanover Clo. Yat —2B 118
Hanover Ct. Cav —7J 39
Hanover Gdns. Brack —9K 91
Hanover Mead. Bray —2F 44
Hanover Mead. Newb —4H 101
Hanover Way. Wind —8B 46
Hanwood Clo. Wdly —4B 64
Hanworth Clo. Brack —8N 91
Hanworth Rd. Brack —1L 113
Harborough Clo. Slou —9N 21
Harbour Clo. Farn —9L 119
Harcourt Clo. Dor R —2H 45
Harcourt Clo. Egh —9D 72
Harcourt Clo. Hen T —5B 16
Harcourt Dri. Ear —1M 87
Harcourt Rd. Brack —8M 91
Harcourt Rd. Camb —4M 119
Harcourt Rd. Dor R —2J 45
Harcourt Rd. Wind —7A 46
Hardell Clo. Egh —9B 72
Harding Rd. Wdly —4B 64
Hardings Clo. Iver —4D 24
Hardings Row. Iver —4D 24
Hardwell Way. Brack —6B 92
Hardwick Clo. M'head —6K 19
Hardwick Rd. Tile —4N 61
Hardwick Rd. Whit T —6D 36
Hardy Av. Yat —5A 118
Hardy Clo. Cav —2J 63
Hardy Clo. Slou —9C 22
Hardy Clo. That —6F 80
Hardy Grn. Crowt —6F 112
Harebell Dri. That —7H 81
Harefield Clo. Winn —1H 89
Harefield Rd. M'head —7L 19
Harefield Rd. Uxb —1K 25
Hare Shoots. M'head —9B 20
Harewood Dri. Cold A —3F 80
Harewood Pl. Slou —2J 47
Hargrave Rd. M'head —6A 20
Hargreaves Wlk. Calc —8N 61
Hargreaves Way. Calc —8N 61 (off Bayford Dri.)
Harkness Rd. Burn —6L 21
Harlech Av. Cav —8L 39
Harlech Rd. B'water —5H 119
Harleyford La. Mar —7A 4
Harley Rd. Cav —2H 63
Harlington Rd. Uxb —4N 25
Harlton Clo. Lwr Ear —3B 88
Harman Ct. Winn —1G 89
Harman's Water Rd. Brack —7A 92
Harmar Clo. Wokgm —5C 90
Harmondsworth La. W Dray —5M 49
Harmondsworth Rd. W Dray —4M 49
Harness Clo. Read —5H 87
Harold Rd. Kint —9G 77
Harpesford Av. Vir W —7K 95
Harpsden Rd. Bin H —2N 39
Harpsden Rd. Hen T —6D 16
Harpsden Way. Hen T —6D 16
Harpton Clo. Yat —2B 118
Harpton Pde. Yat —2B 118
Harrier Clo. Wdly —6F 64
Harrington Clo. Lwr Ear —1B 88
Harrington Clo. Newb —9M 79 (King's Rd.)
Harrington Clo. Newb —6B 80 (Waller Dri.)
Harrington Clo. Wind —1B 70
Harris Arc. Read —4H 63
Harris Clo. Wdly —4G 65
Harrison Clo. Twy —1L 65
Harrison Way. Slou —9N 21
Harrogate Ct. Slou —4B 48
Harrogate Rd. Cav —9E 38
Harrow Bottom Rd. Vir W —8N 95
Harrow Clo. M'head —5B 20
Harrow Ct. Read —6F 62
Harrow La. M'head —5A 20
Harrow Rd. Felt —6N 73
Harrow Rd. Slou —2A 48
Hart Clo. Brack —2M 91
Hart Clo. Farn —9J 119
Hart Dyke Clo. Wokgm —9N 89
Hartford Rise. Camb —3N 119
Hartigan Pl. Wdly —4F 64
Hartin Clo. Uxb —3M 25
Hartland Clo. Slou —9F 22
Hartland Rd. Read —2H 87
Hartley Clo. B'water —4F 118
Hartley Clo. Stoke P —2L 23
Hartley Copse. Old Win —3J 71
Hartley Ct. Rd. Three M —5E 86
Hartleys. Sil —9C 106
Hartley Way. That —7H 81
Hartmead Rd. That —8H 81
Hartsbourne Rd. Ear —9M 63
Harts Clo. Arbor —9D 88
Harts Clo. Lamb —2H 27
Hartshill Rd. Tadl —9H 105
Harts Hill Rd. That & Up Buck —7H 81
Hart's La. Uft N —6C 84
Harts Leap Clo. Sand —9F 112
Harts Leap Rd. Sand —1E 118
Hartslock Ct. Pang —7C 36
Hartslock View. Lwr B —3N 35
Hartslock Way. Tile —2K 61
Hart St. Hen T —4D 16
Hart St. Read —4E 62
Harvard Clo. Wdly —4G 64
Harvard Rd. Owl —9J 113
Harvaston Pde. Tile —5N 61
Harvest Clo. Tile —6J 61
Harvest Clo. Yat —5A 118
Harvest Grn. Newb —1J 101
Harvest Hill. Bour & Wbrn G —5N 5
Harvest Hill Rd. M'head —1B 44
Harvest Ride. Brack —1L 91
Harvest Rd. Egh —9M 71
Harvey Ho. Read —6D 62
Harvey Rd. Slou —2C 48
Harvey Rd. Uxb —3N 25
Harwich Clo. Lwr Ear —2C 88
Harwich Rd. Slou —7C 22
Harwood Dri. Uxb —2N 25
Harwood Gdns. Old Win —4K 71
Harwood Rise. Wool H —8D 100 (in two parts)
Harwood Rd. Mar —6A 4
Haslemere Rd. Wind —7C 46
Hasting Clo. M'head —3F 44
Hastings Clo. Read —8A 62
Hatch Clo. Chap R —4E 82
Hatch End. W'sham —6M 115
Hatchet La. Asc & Wind —1K 93
Hatchet La. Wink —7L 69
Hatchets La. Fril —5L 57
Hatchgate Clo. Cold A —5F 80
Hatchgate Copse. Brack —8J 91
Hatchgate Gdns. Burn —4N 21
Hatch Ga. La. C Grn —7L 17
Hatch La. Chap R —3E 82
Hatch La. W Dray —6L 49
Hatch La. Wind —9C 46
Hatch Ride. Crowt —3E 112
Hatch Rd. Bfld —5L 85
Hatch, The. Wind —6M 45
Hatchway. Read —4J 87
Hatfield Clo. M'head —8N 19
Hatfield Ct. Calc —8J 61
Hatfield Rd. Slou —1J 47
Hatford Rd. Read —8B 62
Hatherley Rd. Read —6L 63
Hatherwood. Yat —4D 118
Hatt Clo. P'mre —6H 31
Hatton Av. Slou —5F 22
Hatton Gro. W Dray —1L 49
Hatton Hill. Ash'd —6D 34
Hatton Hill. W'sham —4L 115
Haughurst Hill. Baug —9E 104
Havelock Cres. M'head —7M 19
Havelock Rd. M'head —7M 19
Havelock Rd. Wokgm —5M 89
Havelock St. Wokgm —5M 89
Haven Ct. Read —5L 63
Haven, The. Kint —9F 76
Haversham Dri. Brack —8M 91
Hawkchurch Rd. Read —3K 87
Hawkedon Way. Lwr Ear —1C 88
Hawker Ct. Langl —2B 48
Hawker Way. Wdly —6F 64
Hawkesbury Dri. Calc —9M 61
Hawkes Clo. Wokgm —4M 89
Hawkes Leap. W'sham —4L 115
Hawkesworth Dri. Bag —9G 115
Hawkins Clo. Brack —4D 92
Hawkins Way. Wokgm —5C 90
Hawk La. Brack —6A 92
Hawkridge Ct. Brack —6B 92
Hawkridge Hill. Fril —6L 57
Hawks Hill. Bour —5N 5
Hawkshill Rd. Slou —4C 22
Hawks Way. Stai —7G 73
Hawkswood Gro. Ful —1A 24
Hawkswood Ho. Brack —3J 91
Hawksworth Rd. Bfld C —8J 85
Haw La. Hamp N & Ash'd —6A 34
Hawley Clo. Calc —8K 61
Hawley Ct. Farn —9J 119
Hawley Grn. B'water —6J 119
Hawley La. Farn —8L 119 (in two parts)
Hawley Rd. B'water —5H 119
Haws La. Stai —3H 73
Hawthorn Clo. Brack —3L 91
Hawthorn Clo. Mar —3C 4
Hawthorn Cotts. Graz —8C 86
Hawthorn Dri. Den —1K 25
Hawthorne Ct. Stai —4L 73 (off Hawthorne Way)
Hawthorne Cres. B'water —5J 119
Hawthorne Cres. Slou —7G 23
Hawthorne Cres. W Dray —1N 49
Hawthorne Rd. Cav —9L 39
Hawthorne Rd. Stai —8D 72
Hawthornes. Tile —1J 61
Hawthorne Way. Gt Shef —9G 28
Hawthorne Way. Stai —4L 73
Hawthorne Way. Wink —5L 69
Hawthorn Gdns. M'head —9B 20
Hawthorn Gdns. Read —1L 87
Hawthorn Hill Rd. M'head —1N 67
Hawthorn La. Brack —4B 68
Hawthorn La. Farn C —1B 22
Hawthorn La. Wind —4A 68
Hawthorn Rd. Newb —7L 79
Hawthorns, The. Charv —1F 64
Hawthorns, The. Coln —7G 48
Hawthorn Way. Son —2D 64
Hawtrey Clo. Slou —1K 47
Hawtrey Rd. Wind —8E 46
Haydon La. E Ils —7B 12
Hayes La. Wokgm —7G 89
Hayes Pl. Mar —6B 4
Hayfield Clo. Tile —4K 61
Hayfield Ct. E'bury —7M 27
Hayley Grn. Warf —9C 68
Haymaker Clo. Uxb —1N 25
Haymill Rd. Slou —5N 21
Haynes Clo. Slou —4A 48
Hay Rd. Read —7F 62
Hayse Hill. Wind —7N 45
Haywards Clo. Hen T —5B 16
Haywards Mead. Eton W —4B 46
Haywards, The. That —7G 81
Haywood. Brack —9N 91
Haywood Ct. Read —5M 63
Haywood Way. Read —7N 61
Hazel Av. W Dray —2N 49
Hazelbank. Finch —4J 111
Hazelby Cotts. N End —6M 99
Hazel Clo. Bfld —6J 85
Hazel Clo. Egh —1K 95
Hazel Clo. Mar —1A 4
Hazel Clo. Wokgm —6L 89
Hazel Cres. Read —1L 87
Hazelcroft Clo. Uxb —1N 25
Hazeldene. Chvly —3M 55
Hazel Dri. Wdly —7B 64
Hazel Grn. Baug —9F 104
Hazel Gro. That —6G 80
Hazelhurst Rd. Burn —3M 21
Hazell Clo. M'head —6C 20
Hazell Hill. Brack —5N 91
Hazell Way. Stoke P —1H 23
Hazelmoor La. Gall C —1C 38
Hazel Rd. Pur T —8K 37
Hazelwood Clo. Tile —3K 61
Hazelwood La. Binf —9K 67
Hazlemere Rd. Slou —9K 23
Heacham Clo. Lwr Ear —3N 87
Headington Clo. M'head —7L 19
Headington Clo. Wokgm —3B 90
Headington Dri. Wokgm —3B 90
Headington Rd. M'head —6L 19
Headley Clo. Wdly —4F 64
Headley Pk. Ind. Est. Wdly —5E 64
Headley Rd. Wdly —5D 64
Headley Rd. E. Wdly —5E 64
Head's La. Ink C —5F 98
Heardman Clo. That —9J 81
Hearmon Clo. Yat —3C 118
Hearne Dri. Holyp —4D 44
Hearn Rd. Wdly —7D 64
Hearn Wlk. Brack —3B 92
Hearsey Gdns. B'water —3F 118 (in two parts)
Heathacre. Coln —7E 48
Heath Clo. Stai —3K 73
Heath Clo. Vir W —6M 95
Heath Clo. Wokgm —7N 89
Heathcote. M'head —3E 44
Heathcote Rd. Camb —4N 119
Heathcote Way. W Dray —9L 25
Heath Ct. Bag —7H 115
Heath Ct. Baug —8G 105
Heath Croft. Cav —9H 39
Heath Dri. Bin H —4N 39
Heath End Rd. Baug —9F 104
Heather Clo. Uxb —6N 25
Heather Clo. Wokgm —3K 111
Heatherdale Rd. Camb —5N 119
Heatherdene Av. Crowt —6C 112
Heatherdene Clo. Read —4J 87
Heatherden Grn. Iver —2D 24
Heather Dri. Asc —9D 94
Heather Dri. Tadl —8H 105
Heather La. W Dray —7M 25
Heatherley Clo. Camb —4M 119
Heatherley Rd. Camb —4M 119
Heathermount. Brack —6B 92
Heathermount Dri. Crowt —4D 112
Heathermount Gdns. Crowt —4D 112
Heatherside Dri. Vir W —8J 95
Heathers, The. Stai —4N 73
Heatherway. Crowt —5E 112
Heathfield. Mort C —4H 107
Heathfield Av. Asc —7A 94
Heathfield Av. Bin H —4A 40
Heathfield Av. Tile —6L 61
Heathfield Clo. Bin H —4A 40
Heathfields. Chvly —4L 55
Heath Hanger La. Hung —1B 76
Heath Hill Rd. N. Crowt —5F 112
Heath Hill Rd. S. Crowt —5F 112
Heathlands. Baug —9G 104
Heathlands. Brack —6L 91
Heathlands Ct. Wokgm —2D 112
Heathlands Ct. Yat —5C 118
Heathlands Dri. M'head —8L 19
Heathlands Rd. Wokgm —8D 90
Heath La. Henw —6F 80
Heathmoors. Brack —7N 91
Heathpark Dri. W'sham —6N 115
Heath Pl. Bag —7H 115
Heath Ride. Wokgm —4N 111
Heath Rise. Vir W —6M 95
Heath Rd. Bag —7H 115
Heath Rd. Pam H —9N 105
Heath Rd. Read —7N 63
Heath Rd. South —1J 83
Heathrow Airport. Houn —8M 49
Heathrow Clo. W Dray —7J 49
Heathrow Copse. Baug —9F 104
Heathrow Summit Cen. W Dray —6L 49
Heathway. Asc —3H 93
Heathway. Iver —3E 24
Heathway. Tile —4K 61
Heathwood Clo. Yat —2B 118
Heavens Lea. Bour —5N 5
Hedge Way. Newb —7N 79
Hedingham M. M'head —7A 20
Hedsor Hill. Bour —5N 5
Hedsor Rd. Bour —5M 5
Heelas Rd. Wokgm —5M 89
Helena Rd. Wind —8F 46
Helen Ct. Read —7A 62
Hellas Rd. Wokgm —5M 89
Hellyer Way. Bour —4M 5
Helmsdale. Brack —7B 92
Helmsdale Clo. Read —4B 62
Helson La. Wind —7D 46
Helston Gdns. Read —2H 87
Helston La. Wind —7D 46
Hemdean Hill. Cav —1G 63
Hemdean Rise. Cav —1G 62
Hemdean Rd. Cav —2G 63
Hempson Av. Slou —2L 47
Hemsdale. M'head —5M 19
Hemwood Rd. Wind —9N 45
Hencroft St. Slou —2H 47
Hendons Way. Holyp —4E 44
Hendon Way. Stai —3L 73
Hengrove Clo. Lwr Ear —1D 88
Hengrove Cres. Ashf —7L 73
Henley Bri. Hen T —4D 16
Henley Clo. Farn —9J 119
Henley Gdns. Yat —4B 118
Henley Rd. Cav —1H 63
Henley Rd. M'head —6H 19
Henley Rd. Mar —7A 4
Henley Rd. Medm —1K 17
Henley Rd. Slou —7A 22
Henley Rd. Warg —8H 17
Henley Wood Rd. Ear —8C 64
Henry Rd. Slou —1F 46
Henrys, The. That —7G 80
Henry St. Read —6H 63
Henshaw Cres. Newb —2H 101
Hensworth Rd. Ashf —9L 73
Henwick Clo. Henw —5E 80
Henwick La. That —6D 80
Henwood Copse. Up Bas —7J 35
Hepplewhite Clo. Baug —9G 105
Hepworth Croft. Col T —3J 119
Herald Way. Wdly —5F 64
Herbert Clo. Brack —7M 91
Hercies Rd. Uxb —1N 25
Herewood Clo. Newb —7K 79
Heritage Clo. Uxb —5K 25
Heritage Ct. Read —5F 62
Hermes Clo. Wokgm —4G 89
Hermitage Clo. Slou —2L 47
Hermitage Dri. Asc —4H 93
Hermitage Dri. Twy —8J 41
Hermitage La. Wind —1C 70
Hermitage Pde. Asc —5L 93
Hermitage Rd. Cold A —9E 56
Hermitage, The. E'bury —5L 27
Hermitage, The. Uxb —1M 25
Hermits Clo. Bfld C —8J 85
Hermit's Hill. Bfld —7K 85
Herndon Clo. Egh —8B 72
Heroes Wlk. Read —4H 87
Heron Clo. Asc —3G 93
Herondale. Brack —9N 91
Heron Dri. Slou —3C 48
Heron Dri. Twy —7K 41
Heronfield. Egh —1K 95
Herongate. Hung —4K 75
Heron Island. Cav —3J 63
Heron Rd. Wokgm —5K 89
Heronsbrook. Asc —4A 94
Herons Ct. Light —9M 115
Heron Shaw. Gor —7L 15
Herons Pl. Mar —5C 4
Heron's Way. Wokgm —4C 90
Heron Way. Read —8E 62
Heron Way. That —8E 80
Herrings La. W'sham —5N 115
Herriot Clo. Yat —5A 118
Herschel Pk. Dri. Slou —1H 47
Herschel St. Slou —1H 47
Hertford Clo. Cav —7K 39
Hertford Clo. Wokgm —6K 89
Hetherington Clo. Slou —4B 22
Hever Clo. M'head —8N 19
Hewett Av. Cav —9D 38
Hewett Clo. Cav —9D 38
Hewgate Ct. Hen T —5D 16
Hewlett Pl. Bag —7J 115
Hexham Clo. Owl —8H 113
Hexham Rd. Read —9J 63
Heywood Av. M'head —4L 43
Heywood Ct. M'head —4L 43
Heywood Ct. Clo. M'head —3L 43
Heywood Gdns. M'head —4L 43
Hibbert Rd. M'head —2D 44
Hibbert's All. Wind —7F 46
Hicks La. B'water —4F 118
Higgs La. Bag —7G 114
High Beech. Brack —6C 92
Highbeeches Clo. Mar —1A 4
Highbridge Clo. Cav —8L 39
High Bri. Wharf. Read —5H 63
Highbury Rd. Tile —5H 61
Highclere. Asc —7N 93
Highclere Clo. Brack —4B 92
Highdown Av. Cav —7G 38
Highdown Hill Rd. Cav —6G 38
Higher Alham. Brack —9B 92
Highfield. Brack —8K 91
Highfield. Lwr Ear —1A 88
Highfield Av. Newb —9L 79
Highfield Clo. Egh —1L 95
Highfield Clo. Wokgm —5A 90
Highfield Ct. Bfld C —8J 85
Highfield Ct. Farn R —2D 22
Highfield Ct. Twy —9K 41
Highfield La. M'head —1L 43
Highfield Pk. Mar —6A 4
Highfield Rd. Bour —4M 5
Highfield Rd. M'head —6M 19
Highfield Rd. Newb —1K 101
Highfield Rd. Tile —9J 37
Highfield Rd. Wind —9B 46
High Fields. Asc —7B 94
Highgate Rd. Wdly —7C 64
Highgrove. Farn —9M 119
Highgrove Pk. M'head —6B 20
Highgrove St. Read —7J 63
Highgrove Ter. Read —6H 63
Highland Av. Wokgm —6H 89
Highmead Clo. Read —1L 87
High Meadow. Cav —1D 62
Highmoor Rd. Cav —1E 62
High Rd. Cook —8J 5
High Rd. Uxb —6K 25
High St. Bray, Bray —1F 44
High St. Eton, Eton —5F 46
High St. Iver, Iver —7F 24
High St. Ascot, Asc —5J 93
High St. Bagshot, Bag —7H 115
High St. Boxford, Box —2M 77
High St. Bracknell, Brack —4M 91
High St. Burnham, Burn —4M 21
High St. Camberley, Camb —3N 119
High St. Chalvey, Chalv —2E 46
High St. Chieveley, Chvly —4M 55
High St. Colnbrook, Coln —6D 48
High St. Compton, Comp —1G 33
High St. Cookham, Cook —8M 5
High St. Cowley, Cow —5K 25
High St. Crowthorne, Crowt —6G 112
High St. Datchet, Dat —7K 47
High St. East Ilsley, E Ils —8B 12
High St. Egham, Egh —9A 72
High St. Goring, Gor —8K 15
High St. Harmondsworth, Harm —5L 49
High St. Hungerford, Hung —6K 75
High St. Kintbury, Kint —9E 76
High St. Lambourn, Lamb —3H 27
High St. Langley, Langl —4A 48
High St. Little Bedwyn, L Bed —2A 96
High St. Little Sandhurst, L Sand —9D 112
High St. Maidenhead, M'head (in two parts) —7C 20
High St. Marlow, Mar —5B 4
High St. Pangbourne, Pang —8D 36
High St. Sandhurst, Sand —9D 112
High St. Slough, Slou —9H 23
High St. Sonning, Son —1C 64
High St. Staines, Stai —8G 72
High St. Stanwell, Stanw —3L 73
High St. Streatley, Streat —8H 15
High St. Sunningdale, S'dale —7C 94
High St. Sunninghill, S'hill —7N 93
High St. Taplow, Tap —5H 21
High St. Thatcham, That —8G 80
High St. Theale, Thea —9F 60
High St. Twyford, Twy —8J 41
High St. Upper Lambourn, Up Lamb —9D 6
High St. Uxbridge, Uxb —1K 25 (in two parts)
High St. Wargrave, Warg —4H 41
High St. W. Slou —1G 47
High St. Whitchurch on Thames, Whit T —6D 36
High St. Windsor, Wind —7F 46
High St. Wraysbury, Wray —3N 71
High St. Yiewsley, Yiew —8L 25
High Town Rd. M'head —8B 20 (in two parts)
High Tree Dri. Ear —6A 64
Highview. Calc —7J 61
Highview Cres. Camb —9C 114
Highway. Crowt —5E 112
Highway Av. M'head —7L 19
Highwayman's Ridge. W'sham —4L 115
Highway Rd. M'head —8M 19
Highwood. Shaw —5M 79
Highwood Clo. Yat —5B 118
Highwoods Clo. Mar —1A 4
Highwoods Dri. Mar —1A 4
Highworth Cotts. Baug —9E 104
Highworth Way. Tile —2J 61
Hilary Clo. Read —4J 87
Hilborn Way. Arbor X —1F 110
Hilbury Rd. Ear —9N 63
Hilcot Rd. Read —4D 62
Hildens Dri. Tile —5K 61
Hildesley Ct. E Ils —8B 12
Hilfield. Yat —4D 118
Hillary Dri. Crowt —4F 112
Hillary Rd. Slou —1N 47
Hillberry. Brack —9N 91
Hill Bottom Clo. Whit H —2F 36
Hillbrow. Read —2L 87
Hill Clo. Newb —3H 101
Hill Copse View. Brack —3B 92
Hill Cres. Woolh —8E 82
Hillcrest. Tadl —9K 105
Hillcrest Av. Cook —1B 20
Hillersdon. Slou —6K 23
Hill Farm La. Binf —7J 67
Hill Farm Rd. Binf —7J 67
Hill Farm Rd. Mar —1B 4
Hill Farm Rd. Tap —3H 21
Hill Gdns. Streat —8H 15
Hillgreen La. P'mre —7G 31
Hill Ho. Cav —9H 39
Hillhouse La. Hdly —9K 103
Hilliards Rd. Uxb —7L 25
Hilliary Dri. Crowt —4F 112
Hilliers Av. Uxb —4N 25
Hillingdon Av. Stai —5M 73
Hillingdon Hill. Uxb —3M 25
Hillingdon Rd. Uxb —2L 25
Hill Lands. Warg —3J 41
Hillmead Ct. Tap —6J 21
Hill Pl. Farn C —1D 22
Hill Rise. Slou —5B 48
Hill Rd. Arbor —1E 110
Hill Rd. Newb —7J 79
Hillside. Bfld C —8K 85
Hillside. Ear —9C 64
Hillside. M'head —9A 20
Hillside. Read —7J 63
Hillside. Sand —2K 119
Hillside. Slou —1G 46
Hillside. Vir W —8L 95
Hillside. Whit T —5E 36
Hillside Dri. Binf —1G 91
Hillside Pk. Asc —9B 94
Hillside Rd. Hung —7K 75
Hillside Rd. Mar —3C 4
Hills La. Cook —8G 5
Hill St. Read —6H 63
Hilltop Clo. Asc —4A 94
Hilltop Rd. Cav —8D 38
Hilltop Rd. Ear —5A 64
Hilltop Rd. Twy —6K 41
Hilltopr Rd. Ear —4A 64
Hilltop View. Yat —4A 118
Hillview Clo. Tile —2J 61
Hillview Rd. Wray —3M 71
Hilmanton. Lwr Ear —3M 87
Hilperton Rd. Slou —1G 46
Hilton Clo. Uxb —3J 25
Hindell Clo. Farn —9L 119
Hindhay La. M'head —3M 19
Hindhead Rd. Ear —9N 63
Hinksey Clo. Slou —2C 48
Hinton Clo. Crowt —3F 112
Hinton Dri. Crowt —3F 112
Hinton Rd. Hurst —4L 65
Hinton Rd. Slou —8A 22
Hinton Rd. Uxb —2K 25
Hirstwood. Tile —3M 61
Hirtes Av. Shin —6L 87
Hitcham La. Tap & Slou —4H 21
Hitcham Rd. Tap & Slou —7J 21
Hitherhooks Hill. Binf —3J 91
Hithermoor Rd. Stai —3G 73

Kimpton Clo.—London Rd.

Kimpton Clo. Lwr Ear —3L 87
Kinburn Dri. Egh —9N 71
King Acre Ct. Stai —7F 72
King Edward Ct. Wind —7F 46
King Edward's Clo. Asc —3H 93
King Edward VII Av. Wind —6G 46
King Edward's Rise. Asc —2H 93
King Edward's Rd. Asc —3H 93
King Edward St. Slou —1F 46
Kingfisher Ct. Slou —5D 22
Kingfisher Ct. Twy —1K 65
Kingfisher Ct. Ind. Est. Newb —8A 80
Kingfisher Dri. Stai —8G 72
Kingfisher Dri. Wdly —6B 64
Kingfisher Dri. Yat —3A 118
Kingfisher Pl. Read —4H 63
Kinghorn La. M'head —3A 20
Kinghorn Pk. M'head —3A 20
King James Way. Hen T —6B 16
King John's Clo. Stai —3L 71
Kingsbridge Cotts. Wokgm —3B 112
Kingsbridge Hill. Swal —4G 109
Kingsbridge Rd. Newb —8H 101
Kingsbridge Rd. Read —1J 87
Kingsbury Cres. Stai —8E 72
Kingsbury Dri. Old Win —4J 71
Kingsclear Pk. Camb —5N 119
Kings Clo. Hen T —4C 16
King's Cres. Camb —1N 119
Kingscroft La. Brack —6C 68
Kingsdown Clo. Ear —1A 88
Kings Dri. M'head —8B 20
Kingsfield. Wind —7N 45
Kingsford Clo. Wdly —7F 64
Kingsgate Pl. Read —5K 63
(off Kingsgate St.)
Kingsgate St. Read —5K 63
Kings Gro. M'head —8B 20
King's Keep. Sand —9F 112
Kingsland Cen. That —8G 81
Kingsland Grange. Newb —2J 101
Kings La. Cook —7F 4
Kings La. Egh —9J 71
Kings La. W'sham —5N 115
Kingsley Av. Camb —5N 119
Kingsley Av. Egh —1K 95
Kingsley Clo. Charv —8F 40
Kingsley Clo. Crowt —7F 112
Kingsley Clo. Read —4H 87
Kingsley Clo. Shaw —6M 79
Kingsley Dri. Mar —1A 4
Kingsley Path. Slou —5N 21
Kings Mead. Newb —5G 100
King's Meadow Rd. Read —4H 63
Kingsmere Rd. Brack —3K 91
Kings Reach Ct. Read —5H 63
(off Crane Wharf)
King's Ride. Asc —7F 92
Kings Ride. Camb —9A 114
King's Rd. Cav —2H 63
King's Rd. Crowt —6F 112
Kings Rd. Egh —8B 72
King's Rd. Hen T —4C 16
Kings Rd. Newb —9L 79
King's Rd. Read —5H 63
(in three parts)
King's Rd. Slou —2G 46
King's Rd. S'hill —7N 93
King's Rd. Uxb —3L 25
King's Rd. W Dray —1N 49
King's Rd. Wind —1F 70
Kings Rd. W. Newb —9L 79
Kingstable St. Eton —6F 46
Kingston Av. W Dray —8N 25
(in two parts)
Kingston Cres. Ashf —9K 73
Kingston Gdns. Read —1J 87
Kingston La. Sul'd —5D 84
Kingston La. Uxb —4M 25
Kingston La. W Dray —1N 49
Kingston Rd. Camb —9D 114
Kingston Rd. Stai & Ashf —8H 73
King St. M'head —7C 20
(in three parts)
King St. Mort C —4H 107
King St. Read —5H 63
King St. La. Winn —3G 88
Kingsvale Ct. W Dray —8L 25
King's Wlk. Col T —3K 119
Kings Wlk. Hen T —3C 16
King's Wlk. Read —5H 63
Kingsway. B'water —4H 119
Kingsway. Cav —7L 39
Kingsway. Iver —7F 24
Kingsway. Stai —5L 73
Kingswick Clo. Asc —6N 93
Kingswick Dri. Asc —6N 93
Kingswood Clo. Egh —8M 71
Kingswood Ct. M'head —9C 20
Kingswood Ct. Read —6D 62
Kingswood Creek. Wray —2M 71
Kingswood Ho. Slou —6E 22
Kingswood Pde. Mar —2B 4
Kingswood Rise. Egh —9M 71
Kinnaird Clo. Slou —7M 21
Kinross Av. Asc —7J 93
Kinross Ct. Asc —7J 93
Kinson Rd. Tile —3A 62
Kintbury Rd. Ink —4E 98
Kintbury Wlk. Read —8C 62
Kinver Wlk. Read —7H 63
Kipling Clo. That —6F 80
Kipling Clo. Yat —5A 118
Kipling Ct. Wind —8D 46
Kirkfell Clo. Tile —2K 61
Kirkham Clo. Cav —7L 39
Kirkham Clo. Owl —8H 113
Kirkstall Ct. Calc —8L 61
Kirkwall Spur. Slou —6G 22
Kirkwood Cres. Bfld C —8G 85
Kirton Clo. Read —5B 62
Kittiwake Clo. Wdly —5G 64
Kitwood Dri. Lwr Ear —2D 88
Klondyke. Mar —5B 4
Knappe Clo. Hen T —6B 16
Knapp Rd. Ashf —8N 73
Knapp, The. Ear —8A 64
Knighton Clo. Cav —1G 62
Knighton Way La. Den —1J 25
Knightsbridge Dri. Hdly —7E 102
Knights Clo. Wind —7N 45
Knights La. Bal H —7A 100
Knights Way. Emm G —8H 39
Knightswood. Brack —1M 113
Knole Wood. Asc —1N 115
Knollmead. Calc —8L 61
Knoll Rd. Camb —3N 119
Knoll, The. Tile —2J 61
Knoll Wlk. Camb —3N 119
Knollys Rd. Pam H —9A 106
Knolton Way. Slou —7K 23
Knossington Clo. Lwr Ear —1B 88
Knott La. Lwr P —7K 83
Knowle Clo. Cav —9D 38
Knowle Grn. Stai —9H 73
Knowle Gro. Vir W —9L 95
Knowle Gro. Clo. Vir W —9L 95
Knowle Hill. Vir W —9K 95
Knowle Pk. Av. Stai —9J 73
Knowle Rd. Wdly —8D 64
Knowles Av. Crowt —5D 112
Knowles Clo. W Dray —9M 25
Knowl Hill Comn. Know H —2C 42
Knowl Hill Ter. Know H —1C 42
Knowsley Clo. M'head —5L 19
Knowsley Rd. Tile —1J 61
Knox Grn. Binf —9G 66
Koya Ct. Wex —7K 23
Krooner Rd. Camb —6M 119
Kyle Clo. Brack —5M 91

Laburnham Rd. M'head —8A 20
Laburnum Av. W Dray —8N 25
Laburnum Clo. Mar —3C 4
Laburnum Gdns. Read —2L 87
Laburnum Gro. Newb —7L 79
Laburnum Gro. Slou —5C 48
Laburnum Pl. Egh —1K 95
Laburnum Rd. Winn —2H 89
Laburnums, The. B'water —4F 118
Laburnum Way. Stai —5N 73
Lackman's Hill. Brack —1M 91
Ladbroke Clo. Wdly —6E 64
Ladbrooke Rd. Slou —2E 46
Ladwell Clo. Newb —5H 101
Ladybank. Brack —1M 113
Ladyday Pl. Slou —9E 22
Lady Jane Ct. Cav —1H 63
Lady Margaret Rd. Asc —9B 94
Ladymask Clo. Calc —8N 61
Laffords, The. South —1J 83
Laggan Rd. M'head —4C 20
Laggan Sq. M'head —5C 20
Laird Ct. Bag —9H 115
Lake Av. Slou —8F 22
Lake End. Crowt —6E 112
Lake End Ct. Tap —7K 21
Lake End Rd. Tap —8L 21
Lake Rd. Vir W —6K 95
Lakeside. Brack —2N 91
Lakeside. Ear —9A 64
Lakeside. M'head —4E 20
Lakeside Dri. Stoke P —2G 23
Lakeside Est. Coln —6G 49
Lakeside Gdns. Farn —9H 119
Lakeside Rd. Coln —6G 49
Lakeside, The. B'water —5H 119
Lake View Caravan Site. Wink —5H 69
Lalande Clo. Wokgm —5K 89
Laleham Rd. Stai —9G 72
Lamb Clo. That —6F 80
Lambert Av. Slou —2N 47
Lambert Ct. Read —5N 61
Lambert Cres. B'water —5G 119
Lambfields. Thea —9E 60
Lambly Hill. Vir W —5N 95
Lamborne Clo. Sand —9E 112
Lambourn. Newb —6M 79
Lambourn Ct. Caravan Pk. Lamb —3H 27
Lambourne Clo. Tile —4L 61
Lambourne Ct. Uxb —2J 25
Lambourne Dri. Bag —8G 115
Lambourne Dri. M'head —2N 43
Lambourne Gdns. Ear —8C 64
Lambourne Gro. Brack —4B 92
Lambourn Pl. Lamb —2H 27
Lambourn Rd. Woods —5G 79
Lambridge La. Hen T —3A 16
Lambridge Wood Rd. Hen T —2A 16
Lamb's La. Spen W —4G 109
Lambswoodhill. Graz —1D 108
Lamerton Rd. Read —2J 87
Lammas Ct. Stai —6E 72
Lammas Ct. Wind —8E 46
Lammas Dri. Stai —8E 72
Lammas Mead. Binf —2J 91
Lammas Rd. Slou —6N 21
Lamorna Cres. Tile —3K 61
Lamp Acres. Shaw —6M 79
Lamplighters Wlk. Calc —8N 61
Lamsden Way. Bfld C —8J 85
Lanark Clo. Wdly —6F 64
Lancashire Hill. Warf —1C 92
Lancaster Av. Slou —5E 22
Lancaster Clo. Egh —9M 71
Lancaster Clo. Hung —7J 75
Lancaster Clo. Read —7J 63
Lancaster Clo. That —7F 80
Lancaster Gdns. Ear —9A 64
Lancaster Ho. Brack —7M 91
Lancaster Rd. M'head —6M 19
Lancaster Rd. Uxb —1L 25
Lancaster Sq. Hung —7K 75
Lancaster Way. Farn —9N 119
Lancastria M. M'head —7A 20
Lancelot Clo. Slou —1C 46
Lanchester Dri. Crowt —3G 113
Lancing Clo. Read —5D 62
Lancresse Clo. Uxb —1L 25
Landen Ct. Wokgm —7N 89
Landrake Cres. Read —2J 87
Landseer Clo. Col T —3J 119
Lane End Clo. Shin —5L 87
Laneswood. Mort —5F 106
Lane, The. Sil —9C 106
Lane, The. Vir W —5N 95
Langborough Rd. Wokgm —6A 90
Langdale Clo. M'head —8D 20
Langdale Dri. Asc —4H 93
Langdale Gdns. Ear —1M 87
Langford Clo. Cav —8J 39
Langham Pl. Egh —9A 72
Langhams Way. Warg —3K 41
Langley Broom. Slou —4A 48
Langley Bus. Cen. Langl —1B 48
Langley Bus. Pk. Langl —1A 48
Langley Comn. Rd. Arbor X & B'ham —1D 110
Langley Farm Cotts. Beed —7B 32
Langley Hill. Tile —6K 61
Langley Hill Clo. Tile —6K 61
Langley La. Arbor —5C 88
Langley Pk. Rd. Iver —8C 24
Langley Pk. Rd. Slou & Iver —1B 48
Langley Quay. Langl —1B 48
Langley Rd. Slou —1L 47
Langley Rd. Stai —9G 73
Langley Wlk. Mar —5A 4
Langton Clo. M'head —5A 20
Langton Clo. Slou —9N 21
Langworthy End. M'head —5E 44
Langworthy La. M'head —5D 44
Laniver Clo. Ear —2A 88
Lansdowne Av. Slou —9G 22
Lansdowne Ct. Slou —9G 23
Lansdowne Rd. Tile —5K 61
Lantern Wlk. M'head —7E 20
Lapwing Clo. Tile —6K 61
Larch Av. Asc —7A 94
Larch Av. Wokgm —4M 89
Larch Clo. Bfld —7J 85
Larch Clo. Camb —9B 114
Larch Clo. Slou —6D 22
Larch Clo. Speen —6H 79
Larch Dri. Wdly —7D 64
Larches, The. Warf P —2D 92
Larchfield Rd. M'head —9A 20
Larchside Clo. Spen W —9H 87
Larch Way. Frogm —4F 118
Larchwood. Brack —7C 92
Larchwood Dri. Egh —1K 95
Lardon Cotts. Streat —8J 15
Larges Bri. Dri. Brack —5N 91
Larges La. Brack —4N 91
Larissa Clo. Tile —3M 61
Lark Av. Stai —7G 72
Larkings La. Stoke P —2K 23
Larksfield. Egh —2L 95
Larks Meade. Ear —2N 87
Larkspur Clo. Wokgm —4J 89
Larkspur Gdns. That —7J 81
Larkswood Clo. Sand —9E 112
Larkswood Clo. Tile —1L 61
Larkswood Dri. Crowt —5F 112
La Roche Clo. Slou —2L 47
Lascelles Rd. Slou —2K 47
Lashbrook Mead. Lwr S —1G 40
Lashbrook Rd. Lwr S —1G 40
Lassell Ct. M'head —7E 20
Lassell Gdns. M'head —7E 20
Latimer. Brack —1M 113
Latimer Dri. Calc —8K 61
Latimer Rd. Wokgm —6N 89
Laud's Clo. Hen T —5B 16
Laud Way. Wokgm —5C 90
Launceston Av. Cav —7L 39
Launcestone Clo. Lwr Ear —1A 88
Laundry La. Col T —3J 119
Lauradale. Brack —6L 91
Laurel Av. Egh —9K 71
Laurel Av. Slou —1N 47
Laurel Clo. Camb —5N 119
Laurel Clo. Coln —6F 48
Laurel Clo. Wokgm —6L 89
Laurel Dri. Tile —4J 61
Laurel La. W Dray —3M 49
Laurels End. Iver —3E 24
Lauser Rd. Stai —4K 73
Lavender Rise. W Dray —1N 49
Lavender Rd. Uxb —6N 25
Lavenham Dri. Wdly —4E 64
Laverheath Clo. Lwr Ear —1D 88
Lawford Cres. Yat —3B 118
Lawkland. Farn R —4E 22
Lawn Av. W Dray —1K 49
Lawn Clo. Dat —6L 47
Lawn Rd. Uxb —1K 25
Lawnsend La. Charv —2G 65
Lawns, The. Asc —5G 92
Lawns, The. Coln —7F 48
Lawns, The. Read —9K 63
Lawrence Clo. Wokgm —5B 90
Lawrence Ct. Wind —8E 46
Lawrence Cres. W'sham —6N 115
Lawrence Gro. Binf —3H 91
Lawrence Mead. Kint —9F 76
Lawrence Rd. Tile —4A 62
Lawrences La. That —6G 80
Lawrence Way. Camb —5K 119
Lawrence Way. Slou —6N 21
Lawson Way. Asc —8D 94
Laxton Grn. M'head —2N 43
Layburn Cres. Slou —5C 48
Layland's Grn. Kint —1G 98
Layton Rise. Tile —1K 61
Lea Clo. Mar —1B 4
Lea Clo. Read —9A 62
Leacroft. Asc —7C 94
Lea Croft. Crowt —4F 112
Leacroft. Stai —9H 73
Leacroft Clo. Stai —8J 73
Leacroft Clo. W Dray —7M 25
Leacroft Rd. Iver —7F 24
Leafield Copse. Brack —6C 92
Leaholme Gdns. Slou —6M 21
Lea Rd. Camb —7M 119
Lea Rd. Son C —1F 38
Leas Dri. Iver —7F 24
Lea, The. Wokgm —2L 111
Leaver Rd. Hen T —5B 16
Leaves Grn. Brack —8A 92
Ledbury Clo. Read —4C 62
Ledbury Dri. Calc —8L 61
Ledger La. M'head —8G 45
Ledgers Rd. Slou —1F 46
Ledran Clo. Lwr Ear —2B 88
Leeds Rd. Slou —8G 22
Lee La. M'head —3J 19
Lees Clo. M'head —9M 19
Lees Gdns. M'head —9M 19
Leeson Gdns. Eton W —3A 46
Lees Wlk. Mar —5A 4
Leicester. Brack —9B 92
Leicester Clo. Hen T —3C 16
Leigh Field. Mort C —4G 107
Leigh Pk. Dat —6L 47
Leigh Rd. Slou —8D 22
Leigh Sq. Wind —8N 45
Leighton Ct. Ear —9L 63
Leighton Gdns. M'head —5E 20
Leiston Clo. Lwr Ear —2C 88
Leiston Spur. Slou —7G 22
Leith Clo. Crowt —3E 112
Lemart Clo. Tile —4M 61
Lemington Gro. Brack —8M 91
Lendore Rd. Frim —9N 119
Leney Clo. Wokgm —3B 90
Lenham Clo. Winn —2K 89
Lennox Clo. Calc —8J 61
Lennox Rd. Read —7N 63
Lent Grn. Burn —5L 21
Lent Grn. La. Burn —5L 21
Lent Rise Rd. Tap & Burn —7L 21
Leonard Clo. Frim —9N 119
Leonard Ct. Thea —9F 60
Leopold Wlk. Read —5K 63
Leppington. Brack —9M 91
Lerwick Dri. Slou —6G 22
Lesford Rd. Read —8E 62
Lesley Ct. Read —6D 62
Leslie Dunne Ho. Wind —8A 46
Leslie Southern Ct. Newb —7M 79
Lesters Rd. Cook —9H 5
Letcombe Sq. Brack —6B 92
Letcombe St. Read —5H 63
Letcomb Sq. Brack —6B 92
Leverton Cotts. Hung —3J 75
Leverton La. Chilt F —2G 75
Lewendon Rd. Speen —6J 79
Lewins Farm Ct. Cipp —8B 22
Lewins Way. Slou —8B 22
Lewisham Way. Owl —9H 113
Lewis Ho. Brack —8M 91
Lewis Wlk. Newb —4G 101
Lexington Av. M'head —9A 20
Lexington Gro. Read —5J 87
Leyburn Clo. Wdly —4F 64
Leycester Clo. W'sham —4L 115
Leyland Gdns. Shin —5L 87
Leylands La. Stai —1G 73
(in two parts)
Ley Rd. Farn —9L 119
Leys Gdns. Newb —7K 79
Ley Side. Crowt —5E 112
Lichfield Clo. Lwr Ear —2B 88
Lichfields. Brack —4B 92
Liddall Way. W Dray —9N 25
Liddell. Wind —9M 45
Liddell Clo. Finch —7K 111
Liddell Pl. Wind —9M 45
Liddell Sq. Wind —8M 45
Liddell Way. Asc —7J 93
Liddell Way. Wind —9M 45
Lidstone Clo. Lwr Ear —2C 88
Liebenrood Rd. Read —6C 62
Lightlands La. Cook —1C 20
Lightwater By-Pass. Light —8K 115
Lightwater Meadow. Light —9L 115
Lightwater Rd. Light —9M 115
Lightwood. Brack —8A 92
Liguel Clo. Hung —7K 75
Lilac Clo. Pur T —8K 37
Lilac Ct. Slou —4B 22
Lilac Pl. W Dray —8N 25
Lilacs, The. Wokgm —7J 89
Lilac Wlk. Calc —7K 61
Lilley Ct. Crowt —6F 112
Lillibrooke Cres. M'head —2L 43
Lily Hill Dri. Brack —4B 92
Lily Hill Rd. Brack —4B 92
Lima Ct. Read —6F 62
Lime Av. Asc —8E 92
Lime Av. W Dray —8N 25
Lime Av. Wind —7B 70
(Windsor Great Park)
Lime Av. Wind —7H 47
(Windsor)
Lime Clo. Newb —7A 80
Lime Clo. Wokgm —6L 89
Limecroft. Yat —4A 118
Limerick Clo. Brack —3L 91
Limes Clo. Ashf —9N 73
Limes Rd. Egh —9A 72
Limetree Rd. Gor —8K 15
Lime View. Newb —7L 79
(off Victoria Rd.)
Lime Wlk. Brack —6N 91
Lime Wlk. M'head —6L 19
Limmer Clo. Wokgm —7H 89
Limmerhill Rd. Wokgm —6K 89
Linchfield Rd. Dat —7L 47
Lincoln Clo. Winn —9F 64
Lincoln Ct. Newb —9K 79
Lincoln Gdns. Twy —8J 41
Lincoln Hatch La. Burn —5M 21
Lincoln Rd. M'head —6M 19
Lincoln Rd. Read —8J 63
Lincolnshire Gdns. Warf —2B 92
Lincoln Way. Slou —8N 21
Lindale Clo. Vir W —6H 95
Lindberg Way. Wdly —3G 64
Lind Clo. Ear —1A 88
Linden. Brack —7C 92
Linden Av. M'head —5A 20
Linden Clo. M'head —5E 44
Linden Clo. Newb —7K 79
Linden Clo. Wokgm —6L 89
Linden Ct. Egh —1K 95
Linden Dri. Farn R —2E 22
Linden Hill La. Kiln G —2A 42
Lindenhill Rd. Brack —3K 91
Linden Ho. Langl —4C 48
Linden Pl. Stai —8H 73
Linden Rd. Bis G —7C 102
Linden Rd. Read —1L 87
Linden Rd. Wdly —8C 64
Lindores Rd. Holyp —5E 44
Lindsay Clo. Stai —2L 73
Lindsey Clo. Wokgm —6K 89
Linear Way. Calc —8K 61
Lines Rd. Hurst —6K 65
Lingfield Caravan Pk. Wind —5G 45
Lingfield Rd. Green —2N 101
Lingholm Clo. M'head —8N 19
Lingholm Clo. Tile —7N 61
Lingwood. Brack —8N 91
Link Ho. Newb —9L 79
Link Rd. Dat —7L 47
Link Rd. Newb —9L 79
Links Dri. Tile —4A 62
Links Rd. Ashf —9M 73
Links, The. Asc —4H 93
Linkswood Rd. Burn —3M 21
Link, The. Slou —7K 23
Link, The. Yat —3A 118
Link Way. Arbor X —9D 88
Linkway. Camb —5N 119
Linkway. Crowt —5D 112
Link Way. That —7E 80
Linnet Clo. Tile —6J 61
Linnet La. Bis G —7C 102
(off Linden Rd.)
Linnet Wlk. Wokgm —5K 89
Linstead Rd. Farn —9J 119
Lintott Ct. Stanw —3L 73
Lip La. Elc —3J 77
(in three parts)
Lipscomb Clo. Herm —6E 56
Lipscombe Clo. Newb —9J 79
Liscombe. Brack —9M 91
Liscombe Ho. Brack —9M 91
Lisle Clo. Newb —6K 79
Lismore Clo. Wdly —8D 64
Lismore Pk. Slou —7H 23
Lissett Rd. M'head —8D 20
Lister Clo. Pur T —8K 37
Liston Ct. Mar —5B 4
Liston Rd. Mar —5B 4
Litcham Spur. Slou —7F 22
Litchfield Ho. Tadl —9K 105
Littington Clo. Lwr Ear —3B 88
Lit. Benty. W Dray —4L 49
Lit. Bowden La. Pang —9A 36
Littlebrook Av. Slou —6A 22
Lit. Buntings. Wind —9B 46
Little Clo. F Hth —1M 5
Lit. Copse. Yat —2B 118
Littlecote Dri. Read —6E 62
Littlecote Rd. Frox —6B 74
Lit. Croft. Yat —5B 118
Littlecroft Rd. Egh —9A 72
Lit. Croft Rd. Gor —9L 15
Littledale Clo. Brack —5B 92
Littledown Rd. Slou —9H 23
Littlefield Grn. White —7K 43
Lit. Fryth. Wokgm —4A 112
Lit. Glebe. Son —1D 64
Lit. Heath Rd. Tile —5H 61
Lit. Hill Rd. Hurst —8J 65
Littlejohn's La. Read —4C 62
(in two parts)
Little La. Up Buck —5M 81
Lit. London Rd. Sil —9C 106
Lit. Marlow Rd. Mar —5C 4
Lit. Moor. Sand —9G 112
Lit. Oaks Dri. Tile —4K 61
Lit. Paddock. Camb —9D 114
Littleport Spur. Slou —7G 22
Lit. Ringdale. Brack —6B 92
Littlestead Clo. Cav —7L 39
Little St. Read —4E 62
Lit. Sutton La. Slou —4D 48
Lit. Vigo. Yat —5A 118
Lit. Woodlands. Wind —9B 46
Liverpool Rd. Read —4L 63
Liverpool Rd. Slou —7D 22
Livery Clo. Read —5H 63
Livingstone Gdns. Wdly —7D 64
Livingstone Rd. Newb —9M 79
Llangar Gro. Crowt —5E 112
Llanvair Clo. Asc —8K 93
Llanvair Dri. Asc —8J 93
Loader's La. Arbor —4D 88
Lochinvar Clo. Slou —1D 46
Lochinver. Brack —9M 91
Lock Av. M'head —4F 20
Lock Bri. Rd. Bour —4L 5
Locke Gdns. Slou —1L 47
Lockets Clo. Wind —7N 45
Lock La. M'head —1N 43
Lock Mead. M'head —4F 20
Lock Path. Dor —5N 45
Lock Pl. Read —4K 63
Lockram Rd. Bfld C —1J 107
Lock Rd. Mar —5C 4
Locks Ride. Asc —2E 92
Lockstile Mead. Gor —7L 15
Lockstile Way. Gor —8L 15
Lockton Chase. Asc —5G 93
Lockwood Clo. Farn —9J 119
Loddon Bri. Rd. Wdly —7E 64
Loddon Dri. M'head —6A 20
Loddon Dri. Warg —5F 40
Loddon Hall Rd. Twy —7K 41
Loddon Rd. Bour —3L 5
Loddon Spur. Slou —8G 22
Loddon Vale Cen. Wdly —5F 64
Lodge Clo. Egh —9M 71
Lodge Clo. Mar —6C 4
Lodge Clo. Slou —1E 46
Lodge Clo. Uxb —5K 25
Lodge Gro. Yat —3D 118
Lodge Rd. Hurst —5K 65
Lodge Way. Ashf —6M 73
Lodge Way. Wind —9A 46
Logan Clo. Tile —5N 61
Lomond Av. Cav —8L 39
London Ct. Read —5H 63
London La. Fac —9H 117
London Rd. Asc & S'hill —5L 93
London Rd. Bag —9E 114
London Rd. B'water —7A 118
London Rd. Brack & Asc —4A 92
London Rd. Camb —4K 119
London Rd. Egh —4K 95
London Rd. Newb & That —7L 79
London Rd. Read —6J 63
London Rd. Slou —2L 47
London Rd. Stai & Ashf —8H 73
London Rd. S'dale —9B 94
London Rd. That —8H 81

London Rd.—Melksham Clo.

London Rd. Vir W —7G 94
London Rd. W'sham —4K 115
London Rd. Wokgm & Brack —5B 90
London St. Read —5H 63
London View. Twy —1K 65
Loneacre. W'sham —6N 115
Longacre. Newb —2H 101
Longbarn La. Read —9H 63
Longbridge Rd. That —9J 81
Longbridge Way. Cow —3J 25
Long Clo. Farn C —1D 22
Long Clo. Kint —9G 76
Longcroft Rd. That —9H 81
Longdon Rd. Winn —2G 89
Longdown Lodge. Sand —1F 118
Longdown Rd. Sand —9E 112
Long Dri. Burn —4M 21
Longfield Clo. Farn —9L 119
Longfield Rd. Twy —7J 41
Longford Av. Stai —5M 73
Longford Cir. W Dray —7J 49
Longford Way. Stai —5M 73
Long Furlong Dri. Slou —5A 22
Long Gro. Baug —8F 104
Long Gro. Up Buck —6L 81
Long Hedge. Lamb —4K 27
Long Hill Rd. Asc —4D 92
Longhurst Clo. Cav —1J 63
Long La. Bright —2C 30
Long La. M'head —9A 44
Long La. Shaw —5N 79
Long La. Stai —6N 73
Long La. Tile —3H 61
Longleat Dri. Tile —1J 61
Longleat Gdns. M'head —8A 20
Longmead. Wind —7A 46
Longmead. Wool H —9D 100
Longmead La. Burn —1N 21
Long Mickle. Sand —9E 112
Longmoor La. Mort C —3G 107
Longmoors. Brack —3J 91
Longmore Rd. Read —5K 87
Long Readings La. Slou —4D 22
Longridge Clo. Read —5B 62
Long Row. Chad —6M 29
Longshot Ind. Est. Brack —4J 91
Longshot La. Brack —5J 91
(in two parts)
Longstone Rd. Iver —3D 24
Long's Way. Wokgm —4C 90
Long Toll. Whit H —1H 37
Long Wlk. Hung —1D 96
Long Wlk., The. Wind —2F 70
Longwater La. Eve —9K 111
Longwater La. Finch —8K 111
Longwater Rd. Brack —8N 91
Longwater Rd. Eve —9K 111
Longworth Av. Tile —5J 61
Longworth Dri. M'head —5F 20
Lonsdale Clo. M'head —5D 20
Lonsdale Way. M'head —4F 44
Loosen Dri. M'head —2L 43
Lord Harris Ct. Sind —2F 88
Lord Knyvett Clo. Stai —3L 73
Lord Mayor's Dri. Farn C —1B 22
Lordswood. Sil —9B 106
Loring Rd. Wind —7B 46
Lorne Clo. Slou —2D 46
Lorne Ct. Chalv —2E 46
Lorne Pl. Read —5E 62
Lorne St. Read —5E 62
Lory Ridge. Bag —6H 115
Losfield Rd. Wind —7A 46
Lossie Dri. Iver —8C 24
Loughborough. Brack —8B 92
Loundeys Clo. That —7E 80
Lovatt Clo. Tile —5J 61
Lovedean Ct. Brack —8B 92
Love Grn. La. Iver —6E 24
Love Hill La. Slou —8B 24
Lovejoy La. Wind —8N 45
Lovelace Clo. Hur —1D 18
Lovelace Rd. Brack —6J 91
Love La. Don —5K 79
Love La. Iver —7E 24
Lovel La. Wink —8L 69
Lovell Clo. Hen T —6B 16
Lovells Clo. Light —9L 115
Lovel Rd. Wink —8J 69
Loverock Rd. Read —3C 62
Love's Clo. Bfld C —8H 85
Loves Wood. Mort C —5G 107
Lovett Gdns. M'head —3E 20
Lovett Rd. Stai —8D 72
Lovibonds Av. W Dray —7N 25
Lowbrook Dri. M'head —2L 43
Lowbury. Brack —6B 92
Lowdell Clo. W Dray —7M 25
Lwr. Armour Rd. Tile —3L 61
Lwr. Boyndon Rd. M'head —8B 20
Lwr. Britwell Rd. Slou —5N 21
Lwr. Broadmoor Rd. Crowt —6G 112
Lwr. Brook St. Read —6G 63
Lwr. Charles St. Camb —3N 119
Lwr. Church Rd. Sand —9C 112
Lwr. Cippenham La. Slou —9A 22
Lwr. Common. Eve —9D 110
Lwr. Cookham Rd. M'head —2E 20
Lwr. Earley Way. Lwr Ear —3A 88
Lwr. Earley Way N. Winn —1E 88
Lwr. Earley Way W. Read & Lwr Ear —4L 87
Lwr. Elmstone Dri. Tile —3K 61
Lwr. Farm Ct. That —1C 102
Lwr. Field Rd. Read —6G 62
Lwr. Henley Rd. Cav —2J 63
Lwr. Lees Rd. Slou —4C 22
Lwr. Mead. Iver —4E 24
Lwr. Meadow Rd. Read —1K 87
Lwr. Mill Field. Bag —8G 115
Lwr. Moor. Yat —4B 118
Lwr. Mount. Read —7J 63
Lwr. Nursery. Asc —7C 94
Lwr. Pound La. Mar —8A 4
Lwr. Ridge. Bour —3M 5
Lower Rd. Cook —8J 5
Lwr. Sandhurst Rd. Finch & Sand —8L 111
Lwr. Village Rd. Asc —7L 93
Lower Way. That —8B 80
Lwr. Wokingham Rd. Wokgm & Crowt —4B 112
Lowes Clo. S'lake —1G 40
Lowestoft Clo. Lwr Ear —1C 88
Lowestoft Dri. Slou —7N 21
Lowfield Grn. Cav —9L 39
Lowfield Rd. Cav —8J 39
Lowlands Dri. Stai —2L 73
Lowlands Rd. B'water —5G 119
Low La. Calc —8N 61
Lowry Clo. Col T —3H 119
Lowther Clo. Wokgm —3L 89
Lowther Rd. Wokgm —2K 89
Loxwood. Ear —1B 88
Lucas Clo. Yat —4B 118
Lucas Dri. Yat —4B 118
Lucey Clo. Tile —1J 61
Luckley Path. Wokgm —5A 90
Luckley Rd. Wokgm —8N 89
Luckley Wood. Wokgm —8N 89
Luckmore Rd. Ear —9N 63
Luddington Av. Vir W —4N 95
Ludlow. Brack —9M 91
Ludlow Clo. Newb —7B 80
Ludlow Rd. M'head —8B 20
Luff Clo. Wind —9A 46
Luker Av. Hen T —3B 16
Lulworth Clo. Farn —9L 119
Lulworth Rd. Read —3J 87
Lunds Farm Rd. Wdly —4F 64
Lundy La. Read —5C 62
Lupin Clo. Bag —9F 114
Lupin Clo. W Dray —4L 49
Lupin Ride. Crowt —3F 112
Luscombe Clo. Cav —2K 63
Lutman La. M'head —4C 20
Lutman's Haven. Know H —8B 18
Lutterworth Clo. Brack —2N 91
Lutton Clo. Lwr Ear —3M 87
Lych Ga. Clo. Sand —1D 118
Lycroft Clo. Gor —7L 15
Lydbury. Brack —5C 92
Lydford Av. Slou —6F 22
Lydford Rd. Read —7L 63
Lydney. Brack —9M 91
Lydsell Clo. Slou —4C 22
Lye Copse Av. Farn —9M 119
Lyefield Ct. Emm G —7H 39
Lyell. Wind —9M 45
Lyell Pl. E. Wind —9M 45
Lyell Pl. W. Wind —9M 45
(off Lyell)
Lyell Wlk. E. Wind —9M 45
Lyell Wlk. W. Wind —9M 45
Lyme Gro. Tile —3L 61
Lymington Av. Yat —4A 118
Lymington Ga. Cav —8E 38
Lynch Clo. Uxb —1K 25
Lynch Hill La. Slou —5A 22
Lynch La. Lamb —2H 27
Lynch, The. Shalb —8F 96
Lynch, The. Uxb —1K 25
Lynden M. Read —7H 63
Lyndhurst Av. B'water —3G 118
Lyndhurst Av. Cook —9J 5
Lyndhurst Clo. Brack —5D 92
Lyndhurst Rd. Asc —6K 93
Lyndhurst Rd. Gor —8L 15
Lyndhurst Rd. Tile —3N 61
Lyndwood Dri. Old Win —3J 71
Lyne Clo. Vir W —8N 95
Lyneham Gdns. M'head —5M 19
Lyneham Rd. Crowt —5F 112
Lyne Rd. Vir W —8M 95
Lynmouth Ct. Read —3H 63
Lynmouth Rd. Read —3G 63
Lynton Clo. Wdly —7B 64
Lynton Ct. Newb —7L 79
Lynton Grn. M'head —7B 20
Lynwood Av. Egh —1N 95
Lynwood Av. Slou —2M 47
Lynwood Chase. Brack —2N 91
Lynwood Cres. Asc —8A 94
Lyon Clo. That —9J 81
Lyon Rd. Crowt —4G 112
Lyon Sq. Tile —4A 62
Lyon Way. Frim —8N 119
Lysander Clo. Wdly —4F 64
Lysander Mead. M'head —6F 20
Lytchett Minster Clo. Brack —6C 92
Lytham. Brack —8J 91
Lytham Clo. Read —8C 62
Lytham Ct. S'hill —7M 93
Lytham End. Tile —1J 61
Lytham Rd. Wdly —5D 64

Macadam Av. Crowt —3G 113
Macbeth Ct. Warf —3B 92
McCarthy Way. Wokgm —2L 111
McCrae's Wlk. Warg —3J 41
Macdonald Rd. Light —9K 115
Mace Clo. Ear —2N 87
Mackay Clo. Calc —9M 61
McKay Trading Est. Coln —8F 48
Mackenzie Mall. Slou —1H 47
McKernan Ct. Sand —1D 118
Macklin Clo. Hung —6K 75
McNair Clo. Lwr Ear —2N 87
Macphail Clo. Wokgm —3C 90
Macrae Rd. Yat —3A 118
Maddle Rd. Up Lamb —6C 6
Madeira Wlk. Wind —7F 46
Madingley. Brack —1M 113
Madox Brown End. Col T —2J 119
Mafeking Rd. Wray —6C 72
Magdalene Rd. Owl —8K 113
Magill Clo. Spen W —9H 87
Magna Carta La. Wray —5M 71
Magna Rd. Egh —1K 95
Magnolia Clo. Owl —9H 113
Magnolia Ct. Wdly —5F 64
Magnolia Gdns. Slou —2L 47
Magnolia St. W Dray —4L 49
Magnolia Way. Wokgm —6L 89
Magpie Clo. That —8E 80
Magpie Way. Slou —5A 22
Magpie Way. Tile —6J 61
Maiden Erlegh Dri. Ear —8A 64
Maidenfield. Winn —1J 89
Maidenhead Bus. Campus, The. White —3J 43
Maidenhead Ct. Pk. M'head —2E 20
Maidenhead Rd. Binf —6M 67
Maidenhead Rd. Cook —1B 20
Maidenhead Rd. M'head —2B 20
Maidenhead Rd. Wind —6M 45
Maidenhead Rd. Wokgm —9B 66
Maiden La. Cen. Lwr Ear —2C 88
Maiden Pl. Lwr Ear —1B 88
Maiden's Grn. Wink —6E 68
Main Dri. Brack —2C 92
Main Dri. Iver —3F 48
Mainprize Rd. Brack —3B 92
Main Rd. Wind —6M 45
Main St. Green —5D 102
Main St. Yat —2B 118
Maisie Webster Clo. Stai —4K 73
Maitland Rd. Read —5E 62
Maize La. Warf —1A 92
Majendie Clo. Speen —6H 79
Majors Farm Rd. Dat —6M 47
Makepiece Rd. Brack —2M 91
Maker Clo. Read —7B 62
Makins Rd. Hen T —6A 16
Malders La. M'head —3L 19
Maldon Clo. Read —6D 62
Malet Clo. Egh —9E 72
Malham Fell. Brack —6L 91
Malham Rd. That —8F 80
Mallard Clo. Ear —9N 63
Mallard Clo. Twy —1K 65
Mallard Dri. Slou —8B 22
Mallard Row. Read —6G 63
Mallards. Spen W —1G 109
Mallards, The. Gt Shef —1F 52
Mallards Way. Light —9K 115
Mallard Way. Yat —3A 118
Mallory Av. Cav —7K 39
Mallowdale Rd. Brack —9B 92
Mallow Pk. M'head —5N 19
Malone Rd. Wdly —6C 64
Malpas Rd. Slou —8K 23
Maltby Way. Lwr Ear —3M 87
Malt Clo. Wick —7J 53
Malt Hill. Egh —9N 71
Malt Hill. Warf —8B 68
Malt Ho. Clo. Old Win —4K 71
Malthouse Clo. That —9J 81
Malthouse La. Read —4F 62
Maltings Pl. Read —5G 63
Maltings, The. Stai —8F 72
Maltings, The. That —9J 81
Maltings, The. W Ils —5M 11
Malton Av. Slou —7D 22
Malt Shovel La. Lamb —1F 26
Malvern Clo. Wdly —6E 64
Malvern Ct. Coln —5B 48
Malvern Ct. Newb —1K 101
Malvern Ct. Read —6K 63
Malvern Rd. M'head —5A 20
Malvern Way. Twy —6J 41
Manchester Rd. Read —4L 63
Mandarin Ct. Newb —9N 79
Mandela Ct. Read —5K 63
Mander Ct. Cav —1H 63
Mandeville Clo. Tile —7N 61
Mandeville Ct. Egh —8B 72
Manea Clo. Lwr Ear —3B 88
Manfield Clo. Slou —4C 22
Manners Rd. Wdly —4C 64
Mannock Way. Wdly —4G 64
Manor Clo. Brack —2L 91
Manor Cotts. Fac —8H 117
Manor Cres. Comp —1G 33
Manorcrofts Rd. Egh —9B 72
Manor Farm Clo. Wind —9B 46
Manor Farm Ct. Egh —9B 72
Manor Farm La. Egh —9B 72
Manor Farm La. Tid —2D 60
Manor Farm Rd. Read —1H 87
Manor Gro. Fif —7G 45
Manor Ho. Ct. Read —7N 63
Manor Ho. Dri. Asc —2K 93
Manor Ho. La. Dat —6K 47
Manor La. Brimp —3N 103
Manor La. Chvly —3M 55
Manor La. Herm —3E 56
Manor La. Leck —8C 30
Manor La. M'head —1B 44
Manor La. Newb —6B 80
Manor Leaze. Egh —9C 72
Manor Pk. Clo. Tile —6K 61
Manor Pk. Dri. Finch —4J 111
Manor Pk. Dri. Yat —4B 118
Manor Pl. Speen —6H 79
Manor Pl. Stai —9J 73
Manor Rd. Ashf —9N 73
Manor Rd. Gor —8K 15
Manor Rd. Hen T —6C 16
Manor Rd. M'head —1B 44
Manor Rd. Shur R —3E 66
Manor Rd. Want —1H 9
Manor Rd. Whit T —6D 36
Manor Rd. Wind —8A 46
Manor Rd. Wokgm —9M 89
Manor Way. Bag —8H 115
Manor Way. Holyp —5D 44
Manor Waye. Uxb —2L 25
Manor Wood Ga. Lwr S —1F 40
Mansel Clo. Slou —6K 23
Mansell Clo. Wind —7A 46
Mansell Ct. Read —1L 87
Mansell Dri. Newb —5G 101
Mansfield Clo. Asc —3G 93
Mansfield Cres. Brack —8M 91
Mansfield Hall. Read —6J 63
Mansfield Pl. Asc —4G 93
Mansfield Rd. Read —6F 62
Mansfield Rd. Wokgm —6L 89
Man's Hill. Bfld C —8K 85
Mansion Ho. St. Newb —8L 79
Mansion La. Iver —9D 24
Manston Dri. Brack —8N 91
Manstone La. Hamp N —9N 33
Maple Av. W Dray —8M 25
Maple Bank. Rusc —7K 41
Maple Clo. B'water —4G 118
Maple Clo. M'head —9N 19
Maple Clo. Sand —9D 112
Maple Clo. Son C —1G 38
Maple Clo. Winn —9J 65
(off Meadow View)
Maple Ct. Brack —6C 92
Maple Ct. Egh —1K 95
Maple Ct. Gor —8K 15
Maple Cres. Newb —6L 79
Maple Cres. Slou —8K 23
Mapledene. Cav —1E 62
Maple Dri. Crowt —3G 112
Maple Dri. Light —9J 115
Mapledurham Dri. Pur T —8K 37
Mapledurham View. Tile —2L 61
Mapledurham Wlk. M'head —3B 20
Maple Gdns. Read —1L 87
Maple Gdns. Stai —6M 73
Maple Gdns. Yat —4B 118
Maple Pl. W Dray —9M 25
Maple Rise. Mar —4C 4
Maplin Pk. Slou —1C 48
Marathon Clo. Wdly —4G 64
Marbeck Clo. Wind —7N 45
Marchwood Av. Cav —5J 39
Marconi Rd. Newb —7M 79
Marcus Clo. Tile —5B 62
Marefield. Lwr Ear —1B 88
Marefield Rd. Mar —5B 4
Mare La. Binf —3J 67
(in two parts)
Marescroft Rd. Slou —5A 22
Marfleet Clo. Lwr Ear —1D 88
Margaret Clo. Read —4J 87
Margaret Sq. Uxb —2K 25
Maria Ct. Read —6D 62
Marigold Clo. Crowt —3D 112
Marina Way. Finch —4F 110
Marina Way. Iver —8H 25
Marina Way. Slou —8N 21
Mariners La. South —8J 59
Marish Ct. Langl —2B 48
Marish Wharf. Mid —1N 47
Markby Way. Lwr Ear —1C 88
Market La. Hen T —4C 16
Market La. Slou & Iver —2D 48
Market Pl. Brack —4M 91
Market Pl. Hen T —4C 16
Market Pl. Lamb —3H 27
Market Pl. Newb —8L 79
Market Pl. Read —5H 63
Market Pl. Wokgm —5A 90
Market Sq. Stai —8F 72
Market Sq. Uxb —1K 25
Market St. Brack —4M 91
Market St. M'head —7C 20
Market St. Newb —9L 79
Market St. Wind —7F 46
Market Way. Read —5H 63
Marks Rd. Wokgm —3M 89
Marlborough Av. Read —7K 63
Marlborough Clo. M'head —8L 19
Marlborough Cotts. Tile —3J 61
Marlborough Ct. Read —6F 62
Marlborough Ct. Wokgm —4B 90
Marlborough Ho. Read —8K 63
Marlborough Rd. Ashf —9L 73
Marlborough Rd. M'head —8L 19
Marlborough Rd. Slou —3M 47
Marlborough Way. Calc —8J 61
Marlin Ct. Mar —6B 4
Marling Clo. Tile —2K 61
Marlow Bottom. Mar —1A 4
Marlow Bri. La. Mar —7C 4
Marlow Ct. Read —6K 63
Marlowes, The. Newb —2K 101
Marlow Rd. Bish —9B 4
Marlow Rd. Hen T —3D 16
Marlow Rd. L Mar & Bour —3E 4
Marlow Rd. M'head —7B 20
Marlow Rd. M'head —1H 19
(Pinkeys Green)
Marlow Rd. Mar —1A 4
Marlston Rd. Herm —6E 56
Marmion Rd. Hen T —6D 16
Marquis Pl. Read —5L 63
Marsack St. Cav —2J 63
Mars Clo. Wokgm —5K 89
Marshall Clo. Farn —9K 119
Marshall Clo. Pur T —9L 37
Marshall Rd. Col T —2H 119
Marshalls Ct. Speen —6H 79
Marsham Ho. Brack —2M 91
Marshaw Ct. Read —9J 63
Marsh Ct. Read —5D 62
Marshfield. Dat —7M 47
Marshland Sq. Emm G —8H 39
Marsh La. Cav —1N 63
Marsh La. Cur —7N 55
Marsh La. Hung —6H 75
Marsh La. Newb —8L 79
Marsh La. Tap & Wind —9H 21
Marsh Rd. That —7H 81
Marshwood Rd. Light —9N 115
Marston Dri. Farn —9M 119
Marston Way. Asc —4H 93
Marten Pl. Tile —1K 61
Martin Clo. Wind —7M 45
Martin Clo. Wdly —6D 64
Martindale. Iver —5E 24
Martineaux La. Hurst —5K 65
Martin Rd. M'head —6C 20
Martin Rd. Slou —2G 46
Martins Clo. B'water —5H 119
Martin's Dri. Wokgm —3N 89
Martin's La. Brack —5B 92
Martins Plain. Stoke P —4H 23
Martins, The. That —9J 81
Marunden Grn. Slou —4B 22
Mary Drew Almshouses. Egh —1M 95
Maryland Clo. Wokgm —2K 111
Mary Lyne Almshouses. Read —7N 61
(off New La. Hill)
Mary Mead. Warf —1A 92
Mary Morgan Ct. Slou —6F 22
Maryside. Slou —1N 47
Mascoll Path. Slou —4B 22
Masefield Rd. That —7F 80
Masefield Way. Stai —5N 73
Mason Clo. Yat —4C 118
Mason Ct. Wool H —9D 100
Mason Pl. Sand —1D 118
Masons Ct. Cipp —8A 22
Masons Rd. Slou —2B 22
Mason St. Read —4E 62
Master Clo. Wdly —4G 64
Mathews Chase. Brack —2K 91
Mathisen Way. Coln —7F 48
Matlock Rd. Cav —9E 38
Matson Dri. Rem —4E 16
Matthews Clo. That —7E 80
Matthews Ct. Asc —6N 93
Matthewsgreen Rd. Wokgm —3M 89
Matthews La. Stai —8G 73
Matthews Rd. Camb —1N 119
Mattland Rd. Read —5E 62
Maultway Clo. Camb —9E 114
Maultway Cres. Camb —9E 114
Maultway N. Camb —9D 114
Maultway, The. Camb —9E 114
Mawbray Clo. Lwr Ear —1B 88
Maxine Clo. Sand —9F 112
Maxwell Clo. Wdly —4D 64
Maxwell Rd. W Dray —3N 49
Maybrick Clo. Sand —9D 112
Maybury Clo. Frim —9N 119
Maybury Clo. Slou —7N 21
May Clo. Owl —1H 119
Mayfair. Tile —5L 61
Mayfair Dri. Newb —1J 101
Mayfield Av. Calc —8J 61
Mayfield Caravan Pk. W Dray —2K 49
Mayfield Cotts. Comp —1F 32
Mayfield Dri. Cav —1K 63
Mayfield Rd. Camb —8M 119
May Fields. Sind —2F 88
Maygoods Clo. Uxb —6L 25
Maygoods Grn. Uxb —6L 25
Maygoods La. Uxb —6L 25
Maygoods View. Cow —6K 25
Maying, The. Read —5H 87
Maynard Clo. That —6F 80
Maynard Ct. Stai —8H 73
Mayow Clo. That —9J 81
May Pk. Calc —8M 61
Maypole Rd. Tap —6K 21
Mays Croft. Brack —6L 91
May's Hill. B Hill —3E 108
Mays La. Ear —7A 64
(in two parts)
May's La. Pad C —3B 106
May's La. Stcks —8N 77
May's Rd. Wokgm —5C 90
May Tree Clo. Mar —1A 4
Meachen Ct. Wokgm —5A 90
Mead Av. Slou —1C 48
Mead Clo. Egh —9C 72
Mead Clo. Mar —4D 4
Mead Clo. Slou —1C 48
Mead Clo. Tile —6J 61
Meade Ct. Bag —7J 115
Meadfield Av. Slou —1B 48
Meadfield Rd. Slou —2B 48
Mead La. Up Bas —8K 35
Meadow Bank. Bour —4M 5
Meadowbank Rd. Light —9M 115
Meadow Brook Clo. Coln —7G 48
Meadow Clo. B'water —5H 119
Meadow Clo. Gor —8L 15
Meadow Clo. Mar —6D 4
Meadow Clo. Old Win —2K 71
Meadow Clo. That —8F 80
Meadow Ct. Stai —7F 72
Meadowcroft Rd. Read —3J 87
Meadow Gdns. Stai —9E 72
Meadow La. Eton —5D 46
Meadow La. Pang —8E 36
Meadow La. Stai —8G 73
Meadow Rd. Ear —9C 64
Meadow Rd. Hen T —5D 16
Meadow Rd. Newb —2K 101
Meadow Rd. Read —3F 62
Meadow Rd. Slou —2N 47
Meadow Rd. Vir W —7G 94
Meadow Rd. Wokgm —5M 89
Meadowside. Stai —9H 73
Meadowside Rd. Pang —8E 36
Meadows, The. Camb —4J 119
Meadowsweet Dri. That —7H 81
Meadow View. Mar —1C 4
Meadowview. Stai —2H 73
Meadow View. Winn —9J 65
Meadow View La. Holyp —5B 44
Meadow Wlk. Bour —2L 5
Meadow Wlk. Wokgm —5M 89
Meadow Way. B'water —4G 119
Meadow Way. Brack —2L 91
Meadow Way. Dor R —1J 45
Meadow Way. Fif —7G 45
Meadow Way. Old Win —3K 71
Meadow Way. Thea —9E 60
Meadow Way. Wokgm —6M 89
Mead Rd. Uxb —1L 25
Meads, The. Uxb —5M 25
Mead, The. Gt Shef —1G 52
Mead Wlk. Slou —1C 48
Meadway. Ashf —8N 73
Mead Way. Slou —6N 21
Meadway Precinct. Tile —6A 62
Meadway, The. Tile —5M 61
Mearings, The. Bfld —6N 85
Measham Way. Lwr Ear —2B 88
Meavy Gdns. Read —1H 87
Medallion Pl. M'head —7E 20
Mede Clo. Wray —5M 71
Mede Ct. Stai —7F 72
Mediar Ct. Slou —9L 23
Medina Clo. Wokgm —4K 89
Medlar Dri. B'water —6K 119
Medman Clo. Uxb —3K 25
Medway Clo. That —6E 80
Medway Clo. Wokgm —4K 89
Melbourne Av. Slou —7E 22
Melbourne Av. Winn —2H 89
Meldreth Way. Lwr Ear —2B 88
Meldrum Clo. Newb —4G 100
Melford Grn. Cav —7L 39
Melksham Clo. Lwr Ear —3L 87
Melksham Clo. Owl —9H 113

Melling Clo.—Normanstead Rd.

Melling Clo. Ear —9D 64
Mellor Wlk. Read —7H 63
Melody Clo. Winn —9H 65
Melrose. Brack —1M 113
Melrose Av. Read —7N 63
Melrose Gdns. Arbor X —9D 88
Membury Wlk. Brack —6B 92
Memorial Av. S'lake X —3E 40
Mendip Clo. Charv —9G 41
Mendip Clo. Slou —4B 48
Mendip Dri. Tile —6H 61
Mendip Rd. Brack —7B 92
Mendip Rd. Farn —9J 119
Menpes Rd. Tile —9K 37
Mentone Cotts. Wal L —8C 42
Meon Clo. Tadl —9J 105
Mercer Wlk. Uxb —1K 25
Merchants Pl. Read —4G 63
Mercian Way. Slou —9N 21
Mercia Rd. M'head —1M 43
Mercury Av. Wokgm —5K 89
Mere Clo. Mar —5D 4
Mereoak La. Graz —8E 86
Mere Rd. Slou —2H 47
Mereside Pl. Vir W —9J 95
(Knowle Hill)
Mereside Pl. Vir W —7M 95
(Virginia Water)
Meridian Ct. S'dale —1L 115
Merlewood. Brack —7A 92
Merlin Clo. Slou —5C 48
Merlin Clove. Wink R —1E 92
Merrivale Gdns. Read —2J 87
Merrivale M. W Dray —9L 25
Merron Clo. Yat —4A 118
Merryfields. Uxb —3M 25
(in two parts)
Merryhill Chase. Winn —9H 65
Merryhill Grn. La. Winn —9J 65
Merryhill Rd. Brack —2L 91
Merryman Dri. Crowt —4D 112
Merryweather Clo. Finch —1L 111
Mersey Way. That —6E 80
Merton Clo. M'head —2N 43
Merton Clo. Owl —8K 113
Merton Rd. Slou —2J 47
Merton Rd. N. Read —2H 87
Merton Rd. S. Read —2H 87
Merwin Way. Wind —8N 45
Meteor Clo. Wdly —5F 64
Metro Cen., The. Wokgm —1M 89
Mews, The. Read —6L 63
Mews, The. Slou —2G 47
Mey Clo. Calc —7K 61
Meyrick Dri. Newb —5G 100
Micawber Av. Uxb —5N 25
Michael Clo. M'head —9N 19
Michaelmas Clo. Yat —5B 118
Michael's Path. M'head —5H 19
Micheldever Way. Brack —8C 92
Michelet Clo. Light —9L 115
Micklands Rd. Cav —9K 39
Mickle Hill. Sand —9E 112
Micro Cen., The. Read —9H 63
Midas Ind. Est. Cow —3J 25
Midcroft. Slou —5D 22
Middle Clo. Newb —3H 101
Middlefields. Rusc —7K 41
Middlefields Ct. Rusc —7K 41
Middle Gordon Rd. Camb —4N 119
Middle Grn. Slou —9N 23
Middlegreen Rd. Slou —1M 47
Middle Hill. Egh —8L 71
Middleton Ct. Newb —6B 80
Middle Wlk. Burn —4L 21
Midsummer Meadow. Cav —7F 38
Mid Winter Clo. Tile —4M 61
Milbanke Ct. Brack —4K 91
Milbanke Way. Brack —4K 91
Milburn Dri. W Dray —7M 25
Mildenhall Clo. Lwr Ear —1C 88
Mildenhall Rd. Slou —7G 22
Mile Elm. Mar —4E 4
Milestone Av. Charv —9F 40
Milestone Cres. Charv —9F 40
Milestone Way. Cav —7K 39
Miles Way. Wdly —5F 64
Milford Ct. Slou —1J 47
Milford Rd. Read —3F 62
Milkhouse Rd. Stcks —8A 78
Milkingbarn La. Shin —8N 87
Mill Av. Uxb —3K 25
Mill Bank. Kint —8F 76
Millbank Cres. Wdly —6E 64
Millboard Rd. Bour —4M 5
Mill Bri. Rd. Yat —1A 118
Millbrook Way. Coln —8F 48
Mill Clo. W Dray —2L 49
Mill Clo. Wokgm —4L 89
Mill Ct. Slou —9H 23
Milldown Av. Gor —7L 15
Milldown Rd. Gor —7L 15
Millenium Ct. Read —1H 87
Millers Clo. Gor —7K 15
Millers Clo. Stai —9J 73
Millers Ct. Egh —9E 72
Miller's Field. Gt Shef —1F 52
Millers Gro. Calc —8M 61
Miller's La. Old Win —3H 71
Millers Rd. Tadl —9K 105
Milley La. Hare H —5M 41
Milley Rd. Wal L —6B 42
Mill Field. Bag —7G 115
Millfield. Lamb —3H 27
Mill Grn. Brack —2J 91
Mill Grn. Cav —3J 63
(in two parts)
Millgreen La. Hdly —8J 103
Mill Ho. La. Stai —9E 72
Millins Clo. Owl —9J 113
Mill La. Asc —4B 94
Mill La. Brack —6K 91
Mill La. Calc —9M 61
Mill La. Cook —8M 5
Mill La. Ear —9D 64
(in two parts)
Mill La. Hen T —6E 16
Mill La. Hort —9C 48
Mill La. Hur —1D 18
Mill La. Lamb —3J 27
Mill La. Lwr P —8L 83
Mill La. Newb —8L 79
Mill La. Read —5H 63
(in two parts)
Mill La. S'lake —3E 40
Mill La. Sind —2E 88
Mill La. Tap —7F 20
Mill La. Tok G —4C 38
Mill La. Wind —6C 46
Mill La. Yat —1B 118
Mill Mead. Stai —8G 72
Mill Mead. Wokgm —4M 89
Millmere. Yat —2B 118
Mill Pl. Dat —8M 47
Mill Pond Rd. W'sham —4L 115
Mill Reef Clo. That —8C 80
Mill Ride. Asc —3G 92
Mill Rd. Bfld —2M 85
Mill Rd. Cav —3J 63
Mill Rd. Gor —6L 15
Mill Rd. Lwr S —3G 40
Mill Rd. Mar —6C 4
Mill Rd. W Dray —2K 49
Mill Side. Bour —4N 5
Mills Spur. Old Win —4K 71
Millstream La. Slou —9A 22
Mill St. Coln —6E 48
Mill St. Slou —9H 23
Millworth La. Shin —7L 87
Milman Clo. Brack —4D 92
Milman Rd. Read —7H 63
Milner Rd. Burn —6K 21
Milsom Clo. Shin —6L 87
Milton Clo. Brack —8M 91
Milton Clo. Hen T —5C 16
Milton Clo. Hort —9B 48
Milton Ct. Wokgm —4N 89
Milton Dri. Wokgm —4N 89
Milton Gdns. Stai —5N 73
Milton Gdns. Wokgm —5N 89
Milton Rd. Ear —5N 63
Milton Rd. Egh —9A 72
Milton Rd. Slou —5F 22
Milton Rd. Wokgm —3N 89
Milton Way. Rusc —8L 41
Milton Way. W Dray —3N 49
Milverton Clo. M'head —2M 43
Milward Gdns. Binf —4G 91
Mina Av. Slou —1M 47
Minchin Grn. Binf —9G 67
Minden Clo. Wokgm —5K 89
Minerva Clo. Stai —2H 73
Minerva Ho. Read —4H 63
(off Valpy St.)
Ministry Rd. Green —5D 102
Minley La. Yat —7B 118
Minley Mnr. B'water —9C 118
Minley Rd. B'water & Fleet —9A 118
Minley Rd. Farn —9D 118
(in two parts)
Minniecroft Rd. Burn —4L 21
Minstead Clo. Brack —5C 92
Minstead Dri. Yat —4A 118
Minster Ct. Camb —5K 119
Minster St. Read —5H 63
Minster Way. Slou —1A 48
Mint Clo. Ear —2M 87
Minton Clo. Tile —4N 61
Minton Rise. Tap —7L 21
Mirador Cres. Slou —8K 23
Mire La. Wal L —8B 42
Misbourne Ct. Langl —3B 48
Misbourne Rd. Uxb —2N 25
Missenden Gdns. Burn —7L 21
Mistletoe Rd. Yat —5B 118
Mitcham Clo. Read —7H 63
Mitcham Rd. Camb —9D 114
Mitchell Clo. Slou —2C 46
Mitchell Way. Wdly —5G 64
Mitford Clo. Read —3K 87
Moat Dri. Slou —6L 23
Modbury Gdns. Read —1J 87
Moffat Clo. Wdly —6F 64
Moffatts Clo. Sand —1E 118
Moffy Hill. M'head —4B 20
Mohawk Way. Wdly —4G 64
Mole Rd. Sind —7E 88
Moles Clo. Wokgm —6B 90
Mollison Clo. Wdly —4G 65
Molly Millars Bri. Wokgm —7N 89
Molly Millars Clo. Wokgm —7N 89
Molly Millar's La. Wokgm —6M 89
Molyneux Rd. W'sham —6N 115
Monarch Ho. Read —3G 62
Monck Ct. Read —6D 62
Money La. W Dray —2L 49
Moneyrow Grn. Holyp —7C 44
Monkey Island La. Bray —2G 45
Monkley Ct. Cav —3J 63
Monks All. Binf —9F 66
Monks Clo. Asc —8L 93
Monks Dri. Asc —8L 93
Monksfield Way. Slou —5C 22
Monks Hollow. Mar —2C 4
Monks Hood Clo. Wokgm —4C 90
Monk's La. Newb —3J 101
Monks Rd. Vir W —6M 95
Monks Rd. Wind —8N 45
Monks Wlk. Asc —8L 93
Monks Way. Read —7D 62
Monks Way. W Dray —5M 49
Monkswood Clo. Newb —3H 101
Monmouth Ct. Read —4F 62
(North St.)
Monmouth Ct. Read —3G 62
(off Northfield Rd.)
Mons Clo. Wokgm —5K 89
Monsell Gdns. Stai —9F 72
Mons Wlk. Egh —9D 72
Montacute Dri. That —9J 81
Montague Clo. Camb —4M 119
Montague Clo. Light —9K 115
Montague Pas. Uxb —1L 25
Montague Rd. Slou —8H 23
Montague Rd. Uxb —1L 25
Montague St. Cav —2J 63
Montague St. Read —5K 63
Montague Ter. Newb —2L 101
Montagu Rd. Dat —7K 47
Monteagle La. Yat —4A 118
Montem La. Slou —9F 22
Montgomery Clo. Sand —1F 118
Montgomery Dri. Spen W —9H 87
Montgomery of Alamein Ct. Brack —3A 92
Montgomery Pl. Slou —7L 23
Montgomery Rd. Newb —2J 101
Montpelier Ct. Wind —8E 46
Montpelier Dri. Cav —8K 39
Montrose Av. Dat —6L 47
Montrose Av. Slou —7D 22
Montrose Dri. M'head —8L 19
Montrose Ter. W Dray —8L 25
Montrose Wlk. Calc —8N 61
Montrose Way. Dat —7M 47
Monycrower Dri. M'head —7B 20
Moorbridge Rd. M'head —7D 20
Moor Clo. Owl —9J 113
Moor Clo. Wokgm —3K 111
Moor Copse Clo. Ear —9A 64
Moorcroft La. Uxb —6N 25
Moordale Av. Brack —3J 91
Moore Clo. Slou —1D 46
Moore Gro. Cres. Egh —1N 95
Moor End. M'head —4F 44
Moores Grn. Wokgm —3C 90
Moores La. Eton W —3B 46
Moore's Pl. Hung —6J 75
Moorfield Rd. Uxb —7L 25
Moorfield Ter. M'head —6D 20
Moorland Rd. W Dray —5K 49
Moorlands Dri. M'head —6K 19
Moorlands Pl. Camb —4L 119
Moorlands Rd. Camb —5M 119
Moor La. Brack —5G 91
Moor La. M'head —5C 20
Moor La. Newb —8H 79
Moor La. Stai —5E 72
Moor La. W Dray —5K 49
Moormead Cres. Stai —8G 73
Moor Pk. Ho. Brack —8J 91
Moor Pl. W'sham —5L 115
Moor Rd. Farn —9L 119
Moor Rd. Stai —3H 73
Moors Ct. Winn —9F 64
(off Ditchfield La.)
Moorside Clo. Farn —8L 119
Moorside Clo. M'head —5C 20
Moors, The. Pang —8E 36
Moors, The. That —8F 80
Moorstown Ct. Slou —1G 47
Moor, The. Mar —3G 5
Moray Av. Col T —1H 119
(in two parts)
Moray Dri. Slou —7J 23
Mordaunt Dri. Wel C —7F 112
Morden Clo. Brack —6C 92
Moreau Wlk. G Grn —7N 23
Morecambe Av. Cav —8E 38
Moreland Av. Coln —6D 48
Moreland Clo. Coln —6D 48
Moreleigh Clo. Read —3J 87
Morella Clo. Vir W —6M 95
Moretaine Rd. Ashf —7L 73
Moreton Way. Slou —9N 21
Morgan Rd. Read —7J 63
Moriston Clo. Read —4B 62
Morlais. Cav —8G 38
Morland Clo. W Ils —4L 11
Morlands Av. Read —7A 62
Morley Clo. Slou —1A 48
Morley Pl. Hung —6K 75
Mornington Av. Wokgm —2L 111
Mornington Clo. Baug —9F 104
Morpeth Clo. Read —8J 63
Morrice Clo. Slou —3A 48
Morriss Ct. Read —5K 63
(off Orts Rd.)
Mortimer Clo. Read —4J 87
Mortimer La. Mort —2L 107
Mortimer La. Strat S —9L 107
Mortimer Rd. Slou —2M 47
Morton Ct. Read —7K 63
Morton Pl. Thea —8F 60
Moss Clo. Cav —1J 63
Mossy Vale. M'head —5A 20
Mostyn Ho. Brack —2M 91
(off Merryhill Rd.)
Moulsham Copse La. Yat —2A 118
Moulsham Grn. Yat —2A 118
Moulsham La. Yat —2A 118
Mountain Ash. Mar —1B 4
Mountbatten Clo. Newb —6M 79
Mountbatten Clo. Slou —2J 47
Mountbatten Rise. Sand —9D 112
Mountbatten Sq. Wind —7E 46
Mount Clo. Newb —1L 101
Mount Clo., The. Vir W —8M 95
Mountfield. Gor —7L 15
Mount Hill. Wink —6M 69
Mount La. Brack —5N 91
Mount La. Chad —5L 29
Mt. Lee. Egh —9A 72
Mt. Pleasant. Been —5H 83
Mt. Pleasant. Brack —5N 91
(in two parts)
Mt. Pleasant. L Sand —9E 112
Mt. Pleasant. Read —6H 63
Mt. Pleasant. Tadl —9J 105
Mt. Pleasant. Wokgm —5M 89
Mt. Pleasant Clo. Light —9K 115
Mt. Pleasant Dri. Tadl —9J 105
Mt. Pleasant Gro. Read —6H 63
Mount Rd. That —7G 81
Mountsfield Clo. Stai —3H 73
Mounts Hill. Wind —6M 69
Mount St. Read —7H 63
(in two parts)
Mount, The. Cav —1F 62
Mount, The. Read —7K 63
Mount, The. Vir W —8M 95
Mt. View. Hen T —4C 16
Mowbray Cres. Egh —9B 72
Mowbray Dri. Tile —4A 62
Mower Clo. Wokgm —4D 90
Moyleen Rise. Mar —6A 4
Muddy La. Slou —6G 23
Mud La. Eve —9E 110
Mud La. P'mre —7G 31
Muirfield Clo. Read —5K 63
Muirfield Ho. Brack —8J 91
Mulberry Av. Stai —5M 73
Mulberry Av. Wind —9H 47
Mulberry Bus. Pk. Wokgm —7M 89
Mulberry Clo. Crowt —6G 113
Mulberry Clo. Owl —1H 119
Mulberry Clo. Wdly —6D 64
Mulberry Ct. Brack —7B 92
Mulberry Ct. Wokgm —5A 90
Mulberry Cres. W Dray —1N 49
Mulberry Dri. Slou —4N 47
Mulberry Ho. Brack —2M 91
Mulberry Pde. W Dray —2N 49
Mulberry Wlk. M'head —6N 19
Mulberry Way. Thea —9F 60
Mulfords Hill. Tadl —9K 105
Mullens Rd. Egh —9D 72
Mullens Ter. Chaz H —5D 38
Mumbery Hill. Warg —4K 41
Muncaster Clo. Ashf —8N 73
Munces Rd. Mar —1B 4
Munday Ct. Binf —2J 91
Mundaydean La. Mar —3A 4
Mundesley Spur. Slou —7G 22
Mundesley St. Read —6H 63
(off Southampton St.)
Munkle Marsh. That —8K 81
Munnings Dri. Col T —3H 119
Munro Av. Wdly —8E 64
Murdoch Clo. Stai —9H 73
Murdoch Rd. Wokgm —6A 90
Murray Ct. Asc —7M 93
Murray Rd. Wokgm —5M 89
Murrellhill La. Binf —2G 90
Murrells La. Camb —6M 119
Murrin Rd. M'head —6N 19
Mushroom Castle. Brack —1E 92
Mustard La. Son —3D 64
Mustard Mill Rd. Stai —8F 72
Muswell Clo. Thea —9F 60
Mutton Hill. Brack —3G 91
Mutton Oaks. Binf —3H 91
Myddleton Rd. Uxb —2K 25
Mylne Sq. Wokgm —5B 90
Myrke, The. Dat —3H 47
Myrtle Clo. Bfld C —8J 85
Myrtle Clo. Coln —7F 48
Myrtle Clo. Tile —1K 61
Myrtle Clo. Uxb —6N 25
Myrtle Clo. W Dray —2N 49
Myrtle Cres. Slou —8H 23
Myrtle Dri. B'water —4J 119
Myton Wlk. Thea —9F 60

Nabbs Hill Clo. Tile —7K 61
Nalderhill Rd. Stcks —3N 77
Napier Clo. Crowt —5G 113
Napier Clo. W Dray —2N 49
Napier Ct. Trading Est. Read —4H 63
Napier Rd. Crowt —6G 112
Napier Rd. Houn —7L 49
Napier Rd. M'head —8M 19
Napier Rd. Read —4H 63
Napper Clo. Asc —4F 92
Narromine Dri. Calc —8N 61
Naseby. Brack —1M 113
Nash Clo. Ear —9N 63
Nashdom La. Burn —1K 21
Nash Gdns. Asc —4H 93
Nash Gro. La. Wokgm —9K 89
Nashgrove Ride. Wokgm —9H 89
Nash Pk. Binf —1F 90
Nash Rd. Slou —3A 48
Nash's Yd. Uxb —1L 25
Navahoe Rd. Finch —4F 110
Neath Gdns. Tile —5N 61
Needham Clo. Wind —7A 46
Nell Gwynne Clo. Asc —6N 93
Nelson Clo. Brack —3B 92
Nelson Clo. Slou —3M 47
Nelson Rd. Ashf —9M 73
Nelson Rd. Cav —2J 63
Nelson Rd. H'row A —7N 49
Nelson Rd. Wind —9B 46
Nelson's La. Hurst —7N 65
Nelson Way. Camb —5K 119
Neptune Clo. Wokgm —5K 89
Netherton. Brack —6L 91
Netley Clo. Cav —7L 39
Nettlecombe. Brack —8A 92
Nevelle Clo. Binf —3H 91
Nevil Ct. That —9G 80
Neville Clo. Stoke P —1H 23
Neville Clo. Wal L —7D 42
Neville Ct. Burn —4M 21
Neville Dri. That —8H 81
Neville Duke Rd. Farn —9K 119
Nevis Rd. Tile —1L 61
Newalls Rise. Warg —3K 41
Newark St. Read —6H 63
New Bath Rd. Charv —8G 40
Newberry Cres. Wind —8N 45
Newbery Clo. Tile —3L 61
Newbery Way. Slou —1F 46
Newbold Rd. Speen —6H 79
Newbolt Clo. That —6F 80
New Bright St. Read —6G 63
Newbury Bus. Pk. Newb —7N 79
Newbury Dri. M'head —8E 20
Newbury Hill. Hamp N —8J 33
Newbury La. Comp —1G 32
Newbury Racecourse. Green —1A 102
Newbury Rd. Gt Shef —1F 52
Newbury Rd. Herm —6D 56
Newbury Rd. Houn —7N 49
Newbury Rd. Lamb —3J 27
Newbury St. Kint —9G 76
Newbury St. Lamb —3H 27
Newcastle Rd. Read —8J 63
Newchurch Rd. Slou —6B 22
Newchurch Rd. Tadl —9J 105
Newcombe Rise. W Dray —7M 25
New Cotts. Fac —9G 116
New Ct. Mar —5C 4
Newcourt. Uxb —6K 25
Newcroft Clo. Uxb —6N 25
New Cut. Slou —5K 21
Newell's La. Cav —7B 38
Newfield Gdns. Mar —4D 4
Newfield Rd. Mar —5D 4
Newfield Way. Mar —5D 4
New Forest Ride. Brack —9B 92
New Garden Dri. W Dray —1M 49
Newhaven Spur. Slou —5D 22
New Hayward Farm Cotts. Hung —1K 75
New Hill. Pur T —8K 37
Newhurst Gdns. Warf —9A 68
Newlands Av. Cav —1H 63
Newlands Clo. Yat —4B 118
Newlands Cotts. Wokgm —4E 88
Newlands Dri. Coln —9F 48
Newlands Dri. M'head —7L 19
Newlands Rd. Camb —8M 119
New La. Hill. Tile —5M 61
Newlyn Gdns. Read —2H 87
Newmarket Clo. Lwr Ear —1C 88
New Meadow. Asc —3G 93
New Mile Rd. Asc —4L 93
New Mill La. Eve —8D 110
New Mill Rd. Eve —8D 110
Newnham Clo. Slou —9J 23
New Pde. Ashf —8N 73
New Peachey La. Uxb —7L 25
Newport Clo. Newb —7M 79
Newport Rd. Houn —7N 49
Newport Rd. Newb —7M 79
Newport Rd. Read —3G 62
Newport Rd. Slou —5A 22
New Rd. Asc —2H 93
New Rd. Bag & W'sham —7J 115
New Rd. B'water —5J 119
New Rd. Bour —4M 5
New Rd. Brack —4A 92
New Rd. Bfld C —9M 85
New Rd. Chvly —1K 55
New Rd. Cook —8J 5
New Rd. Crowt —5G 112
New Rd. Dat —7M 47
New Rd. Green —1N 101
New Rd. Hur —3D 18
New Rd. Langl —2B 48
New Rd. M'head —5E 44
New Rd. Mar —1B 4
New Rd. Read —7K 63
New Rd. Rusc —7L 41
New Rd. Sand —1E 118
New Rd. S'lake —3E 40
New Rd. Stai —9D 72
New Rd. Twy —6J 41
New Rd. Hill. Midg —7D 82
New Sq. Slou —1H 47
New St. Hen T —4D 16
New St. Stai —8H 73
New St. Strat S —9A 108
Newton Av. Cav —8K 39
Newton Clo. Slou —1A 48
Newton Ct. Old Win —3J 71
Newton La. Old Win —3K 71
Newton Rd. Houn —7M 49
Newton's La. Bagn —4G 79
Newton's M. Hung —5K 75
Newtown. Tadl —9J 105
Newtown Gdns. Hen T —6D 16
Newtown Rd. Den —1J 25
Newtown Rd. Hen T —6E 16
Newtown Rd. Mar —4D 4
Newtown Rd. Newb —1L 101
Newtown Rd. Sand —1F 118
New Villas. Bal H —7N 99
New Way. South —1J 83
New Windsor St. Uxb —2K 25
New Wokingham Rd. Crowt —3E 112
Niagara Rd. Hen T —6D 16
Nicholas Ct. Read —5F 62
(off Prospect St.)
Nicholas Rd. Hen T —6A 16
Nicholls. Wind —9M 45
Nicholls Wlk. Wind —9M 45
Nicholson M. Egh —9B 72
(off Nicholson Wlk.)
Nicholsons La. M'head —7C 20
Nicholsons Wlk. M'head —7C 20
Nicholson Wlk. Egh —9B 72
Nideggen Clo. That —8G 81
Nightingale Cres. Brack —7N 91
Nightingale Gdns. Sand —1F 118
Nightingale La. M'head —3A 20
Nightingale La. Mort —3J 107
Nightingale Pk. Farn C —1B 22
Nightingale Rd. Wdly —7B 64
Nightingales, The. Newb —2M 101
Nightingales, The. Stai —5N 73
Nimrod Clo. Wdly —5G 64
Nimrod Way. Read —7H 63
Nine Elms Av. Uxb —6L 25
Nine Elms Clo. Uxb —6L 25
Nine Mile Ride. Read —9H 93
Nine Mile Ride. Crowt & Brack —1K 113
Nine Mile Ride. Finch —4G 111
Nine Mile Ride. Wokgm —4M 111
Niven Ct. S'hill —6N 93
Nixley Clo. Slou —1J 47
Noakes Hill. Ash'd —6D 34
Nobles Way. Egh —1N 95
Nodmore. Chadw —6N 29
Nonsuch Clo. Wokgm —4N 89
Norcot Rd. Tile —4M 61
Norden Clo. M'head —1N 43
Norden Rd. M'head —9N 19
Norelands Dri. Burn —3M 21
Nores Rd. Read —4K 87
Norfolk Av. Slou —6E 22
Norfolk Chase. Warf —2C 92
Norfolk Clo. Wokgm —5K 89
Norfolk Pk. Cotts. M'head —6C 20
Norfolk Rd. M'head —6B 20
Norfolk Rd. Read —5C 62
Norfolk Rd. Uxb —1L 25
Norlands. That —6F 80
Norman Av. Hen T —5D 16
Normandy Wlk. Egh —9D 72
Normanhurst. Ashf —9N 73
Norman Rd. Cav —9J 39
Normans Clo. Uxb —5N 25
Normanstead Rd. Tile —4K 61

Peel Cen., The—Rawling Ct.

Peel Cen., The. Brack —4L 91
Peel Clo. Cav —2K 63
Peel Clo. Wind —9D 46
Peel Clo. Wdly —4G 64
Peel Ct. Slou —6E 22
Peel Way. Uxb —6M 25
Pegasus Clo. That —7D 80
Pegasus Ct. Lamb —3H 27
Pegasus Ct. Tile —5K 61
Pegasus Rd. Farn —9K 119
Peggotty Pl. Owl —8J 113
Peg's Grn. Clo. Read —6B 62
Pelham Ct. Read —6D 62
Pelican La. Newb —7K 79
Pelican Rd. Pam H —8N 105
Pelling Hill. Old Win —4K 71
Pell St. Read —6H 63
Pemberton Gdns. Calc —8L 61
Pemberton Rd. Slou —5A 22
Pembroke. Brack —9K 91
Pembroke B'way. Camb —4N 119
Pembroke Clo. Asc —7N 93
Pembroke Clo. Bfld C —8K 85
Pembroke Ho. Cav —3J 63
Pembroke M. Asc —7N 93
Pembroke Pde. Yat —3C 118
Pembroke Pl. Cav —1J 63
Pembroke Rd. Newb —8K 79
Pendals Clo. Hamp N —8J 33
Pendennis Av. Cav —7L 39
Pendine Pl. Brack —7M 91
Pendlebury. Brack —9L 91
Pendragon Ct. Read —7D 62
Pendred Rd. Read —5K 87
Pendry's La. Binf —3L 67
Penling Clo. Cook —9J 5
Penn Clo. Cav —7G 38
Penn Clo. Uxb —5L 25
Pennfields. Rusc —7K 41
Pennine Clo. Tile —6J 61
Pennine Rd. Slou —6C 22
Pennine Way. Charv —9G 40
Pennine Way. Farn —9J 119
Penn Meadow. Stoke P —2H 23
Penn Rd. Dat —7M 47
Penn Rd. Slou —5F 22
Penn Rd. Speen —6H 79
Pennylets Grn. Stoke P —1H 23
Penny Piece. Gor —7L 15
Pennyroyal Ct. Read —6G 62
Penny's La. C Grn —8J 17
Penrith Clo. Uxb —1L 25
Penroath Av. Read —6C 62
Penrose Av. Wdly —6D 64
Penrose Clo. Newb —6K 79
Penrose Ct. Egh —1L 95
Pensford Clo. Crowt —3F 112
Penshurst Rd. M'head —9A 20
Pentangle, The. Newb —7L 79
Pentland Clo. Read —7N 61
Pentland Rd. Slou —6C 22
Pentridge Ho. Read —3J 87
Penwood Ct. M'head —7M 19
Penwood Gdns. Brack —8H 91
Penwood Heights. Burc —9E 100
Penwood La. Mar —6A 4
Penyston Rd. M'head —7N 19
Penzance Spur. Slou —5D 22
Peplow Clo. W Dray —9L 25
Peppard La. Hen T —7C 16
Peppard Rd. Cav —1H 63
Peppard Rd. Son C —1G 38
Pepper La. Ear —8L 63
Pepys Clo. Slou —5C 48
Perch Clo. Mar —7A 4
Percy Av. Ashf —9N 73
Percy Pl. Dat —7K 47
Peregrine Clo. Brack —7M 91
Peregrine Clo. Wokgm —6L 89
Periam Clo. Hen T —6B 16
Perimeter Rd. Wind —7F 46
Perimeter Rd. Wdly —4F 64
Perkins Ct. Ashf —9N 73
Perkins Way. Wokgm —6M 89
Perrin Clo. Ashf —9N 73
Perring Av. Farn —9J 119
Perrycroft. Wind —9A 46
Perryfields. Burn —5M 21
Perryhill Dri. Sand —9D 112
Perryman Way. Slou —4B 22
Perry Oaks. Brack —4B 92
Perry Oaks Dri. W Dray & Houn —8J 49
Perry Way. Brack —4B 92
Perseverance Hill. Hen T —9A 16
Perth Av. Slou —7D 22
Perth Clo. Wdly —3F 64
Perth Trading Est. Slou —6D 22
Peterhead M. Langl —4B 48
Peterhouse Clo. Owl —8K 113
Petersfield Av. Slou —9J 23
Petersfield Av. Stai —9K 73
Petersfield Rd. Stai —9K 73
Peters La. Holyp —5E 44
Petrel Clo. Wokgm —6K 89
Petworth Av. Read —9N 61
Petworth Ct. Read —6E 62
Pevensey Av. Cav —8L 39
Pevensey Rd. Slou —6C 22
Pewsey Vale. Brack —7C 92
Pheasant Clo. Winn —1H 89
Pheasant La. Bis G —7C 102
Pheasants Croft. M'head —1L 43
Pheasants Rise. Mar —1A 4
Philip Dri. F Hth —1N 5
Phillimore Rd. Cav —5J 39
Phillips Clo. Wdly —3G 65
Philpots Clo. W Dray —8L 25
Phipps Clo. M'head —3L 43
Phipps Rd. Slou —6N 21
(in three parts)
Phoebe Ct. Read —6G 63
Phoenix Bus. Pk. Brack —4G 91
Phoenix Clo. Wokgm —5K 89
Phoenix Wlk. Newb —4G 101
(off Glendale Av.)
Phyllis Ct. Dri. Hen T —3D 16
Pickering. Brack —6L 91
Picket Post Clo. Brack —5C 92
Picketts La. Pang —9N 35
Pickins Piece. Hort —8B 48
Pickwell Clo. Lwr Ear —2B 88
Picton Way. Cav —9H 39
Pield Heath Av. Uxb —5N 25
Pield Heath Rd. Uxb —5M 25
Pierce Field. Calc —8K 61
Pierce's Hill. Tile —3K 61
Pierson Rd. Wind —7N 45
Pigeonhouse La. Wink —7G 69
Pigeon's Farm Rd. Green —3A 102
Piggott's Rd. Cav —3J 63
Pightle, The. Graz —8N 85
Pigott Rd. Wokgm —3B 90
Pike Clo. Uxb —2N 25
Pikeshaw Way. Tile —2K 61
Pike St. Newb —7M 79
Pills La. Ham —7J 97
Pimento Dri. Ear —2M 87
Pimpernell Pl. That —7J 81
Pincents Kiln Trading Est. Tile —8H 61
Pincents La. Tile —8G 61
Pinchcut. Bfld C —8H 85
Pinchington La. Green —3L 101
Pindar Pl. Newb —6B 80
Pine Av. Camb —5N 119
Pine Clo. M'head —7M 19
Pine Clo. Sand —2J 119
Pinecote Dri. Asc —9B 94
Pine Ct. Brack —6B 92
Pinecroft. Mar —4B 4
Pine Croft Rd. Wokgm —9M 89
Pine Dri. B'water —6J 119
Pine Dri. Mort C —4G 107
Pine Dri. Wokgm —3M 111
Pinefields Clo. Crowt —5F 112
Pine Gro. Twy —8J 41
Pine Gro. W'sham —6N 115
Pinehill Rise. Sand —1G 118
Pinehill Rd. Crowt —6F 112
Pinehurst. S'hill —7N 93
Pine Mt. Rd. Camb —5N 119
Pine Ridge. Newb —6N 79
Pine Ridge Rd. Bfld C —8H 85
Pine Tree Ct. Emm G —8G 39
Pine Trees Bus. Pk. Stai —9F 72
Pine Way. Egh —1K 95
Pinewood Av. Crowt —4G 112
Pinewood Av. Uxb —7N 25
Pinewood Caravan Pk. Wokgm —2G 112
Pinewood Clo. Baug —9F 104
Pinewood Clo. Iver —1D 24
Pinewood Clo. Sand —1D 118
Pinewood Dri. Stai —9H 73
Pinewood Gdns. Bag —7F 114
Pinewood Grn. Iver —1D 24
Pinewood M. Stai —3L 73
Pinewood Pk. Farn —9G 119
Pinewood Rd. Iver —1C 24
Pinewood Rd. Vir W —6J 95
Pinfold La. Ash'd —8D 34
Pingewood Rd. Ping —3N 85
Pinglestone Clo. W Dray —6M 49
Pink La. Burn —3L 21
Pinkneys Dri. M'head —7J 19
Pinkneys Rd. M'head —5L 19
Pink's La. Baug —8G 105
Pinn Clo. Uxb —7L 25
Pipers Clo. Burn —4M 21
Pipers Ct. That —9K 81
Piper's End. Vir W —5M 95
Pipers La. That —1J 103
Pipers Way. That —9J 81
Pipers Way Ind. Est. That —9J 81
Pipit Clo. That —8E 80
Pippins Clo. W Dray —2L 49
Pipson La. Yat —4B 118
Pipsons Clo. Yat —3B 118
Pitch Pl. Binf —9H 67
Pitcroft Av. Read —6N 63
Pitfield La. Mort —6K 107
Pitford Rd. Wdly —4F 64
Pitts Clo. Binf —1H 91
Pitts La. Ear —5A 64
Pitts Rd. Slou —9E 22
Plackett Way. Slou —9N 21
Plain Ride. Wind —5M 69
Plantation Clo. Cur —7C 56
Plantation Rd. Tadl —8H 105
Plantation Row. Camb —4M 119
Plateau, The. Warf P —2D 92
Players Grn. Wdly —7D 64
Playhatch Rd. Play —8N 39
Play Platt. Thea —8E 60
Play Platt Houses. Thea —8E 60
Pleasant Hill. Tadl —9K 105
Ploughlands. Brack —3K 91
Plough La. S'lake —3C 40
Plough La. Stoke P —2K 23
Plough La. Wokgm —4D 90
Plough Lees La. Slou —8G 23
Plough Rd. Yat —2C 118
Plover Clo. Stai —7G 72
Plover Clo. Wokgm —6L 89
Plowden Way. S'lake X —4D 40
Plummery, The. Read —5J 63
(off Blakes Cotts.)
Plumpton Rd. Green —1N 101
Plumtrees. Ear —1A 88
Plymouth Av. Wdly —7B 64
Plymouth Rd. Slou —6A 22
Plympton Clo. Ear —9D 64
Pococks La. Eton —4G 46
Poffley Pl. That —8K 81
Pointers Clo. Chvly —2M 55
Points, The. M'head —2M 43
Polden Clo. Farn —9J 119
Polehampton Clo. Twy —9J 41
Polehampton Ct. Twy —9J 41
Pollard Clo. Old Win —2K 71
Pollard Cotts. Bal H —7N 99
Pollardrow Av. Brack —3K 91
(in two parts)
Pollards Way. Calc —8K 61
Polsted Rd. Tile —3L 61
Polyanthus Way. Crowt —2F 112
Polygon Bus. Cen. Coln —8G 48
Pond Clo. Newb —3H 101
Pond Croft. Yat —3C 118
Pond Head La. Ear —8C 64
Pond La. Herm —5F 56
Pond La. Map —6N 37
Pond Moor Rd. Brack —7M 91
Pond Rd. Egh —9D 72
Poole Clo. Tile —5N 61
Pooley Av. Egh —9C 72
Pooley Grn. Clo. Egh —9D 72
Pooley Grn. Rd. Egh —9C 72
Pool La. Slou —6B 22
Pool La. Wal L —8E 42
Poolmans Rd. Wind —9N 45
Popes Clo. Coln —6C 48
Popes La. Cook —7G 5
Popeswood Rd. Binf —2H 91
Popham Clo. Brack —7C 92
Poplar Av. Tile —7N 61
Poplar Av. W Dray —8N 25
Poplar Av. W'sham —4K 115
Poplar Clo. Baug —9F 104
Poplar Clo. Coln —7F 48
Poplar Gdns. Read —2L 87
Poplar Ho. Langl —4A 48
Poplar La. Hurst —3L 65
Poplar La. Winn —9J 65
Poplar Pl. Newb —6L 79
Poplars Gro. M'head —4E 20
Poplars, The. Asc —7K 93
Poppy Dri. That —7J 81
Poppy Pl. Wokgm —5N 89
Poppy Way. Calc —7K 61
Porchester. Asc —6K 93
Porchester Rd. Newb —1L 101
Porchfield Clo. Ear —2N 87
Porlock Clo. That —9G 80
Porlock Pl. Calc —8J 61
Portal Clo. Uxb —1M 25
(in two parts)
Porter Clo. Lwr Ear —3B 88
Porter End. Green —2M 101
Porters Way. W Dray —2N 49
Portesbery Rd. Camb —3N 119
Portia Gro. Warf —3B 92
Portland Bus. Cen. Dat —7K 47
(off Manor Ho. La.)
Portland Clo. Slou —5N 21
Portland Gdns. Tile —5K 61
Portland Rd. Ashf —7M 73
Portlands. Mar —6B 4
Portlock Rd. M'head —7N 19
Portman Clo. Brack —3L 91
Portman Gdns. Uxb —1N 25
Portman Rd. Read —3B 62
Portmeirion Gdns. Tile —3N 61
Portnall Dri. Vir W —8G 94
Portnall Rise. Vir W —7H 95
Portnall Rd. Vir W —7H 95
Portrush Clo. Wdly —6C 64
Portsmouth Ct. Slou —8G 23
Portsmouth Rd. Frim & Camb —8N 119
Portswood. Tadl —9M 105
Portway. Baug —9F 104
Portway. Rise —8J 109
Portway Clo. Read —6E 62
Post Horn Pl. Calc —8N 61
Posting Ho. M. Newb —7J 79
Post Meadow. Iver —4E 24
Post Office La. G Grn —7M 23
Post Office Rd. Ink —6D 98
Potley Hill Rd. Yat —3D 118
Potters Cross. Iver —4F 24
Pottery La. Ink —5C 98
Pottery Rd. Tile —3N 61
Poulcott. Wray —3N 71
Pound Cres. Mar —6A 4
Poundfield La. Cook —8K 5
Poundfield Way. Twy —1L 65
Pound La. Hurst —7M 65
Pound La. Mar —7A 4
Pound La. Newb —7H 79
Pound La. Son —2D 64
Pound La. That —8D 80
Pound La. W'sham —6M 115
Pound Piece. Hung —5J 75
Pound St. Newb —9K 79
Pound, The. Burn —5N 21
Pound, The. Cook —8K 5
Powis Clo. M'head —1M 43
Powney Rd. M'head —7N 19
Poyle Clo. Coln —8F 48
Poyle Gdns. Brack —3A 92
Poyle Ind. Est. Coln —9G 48
Poyle La. Burn —2L 21
Poyle Rd. Coln —9F 48
Poyle Technical Cen. Coln —8F 48
Poyle Trading Est. Coln —9F 48
Poynings, The. Iver —3G 48
Precincts, The. Burn —5L 21
Precinct, The. Cav —8J 39
Precinct, The. Egh —9B 72
Prentice Clo. Farn —9M 119
Prescott. Brack —9K 91
Prescott Rd. Coln —8F 48
Press Rd. Uxb —1L 25
Preston Rd. Read —7H 63
Preston Rd. Slou —8L 23
Prestwood. Slou —7K 23
Prides Crossing. Asc —2K 93
Priest Av. Wokgm —6D 90
Priest Hill. Cav —1G 62
Priest Hill. Egh & Old Win —7L 71
Priestwood Av. Brack —3K 91
Priestwood Ct. Brack —3L 91
Priestwood Ct. Rd. Brack —3L 91
Priestwood Sq. Brack —3L 91
Priestwood Ter. Brack —3L 91
Primrose Clo. Pur T —8K 37
Primrose La. M'head —7D 44
Primrose La. Winn —9H 65
Primrose Wlk. Brack —7N 91
Primrose Wlk. Yat —3A 118
Primrose Way. Sand —9F 112
Prince Albert Dri. Asc —6G 93
Prince Albert's Wlk. Wind —7J 47
Prince Andrew Clo. M'head —6E 20
Prince Andrew Rd. M'head —5E 20
Prince Andrew Way. Asc —4G 93
Prince Charles Cres. Farn —9M 119
Prince Consort Cotts. Wind —8F 46
Prince Consort Dri. Asc —6G 92
Prince Consort's Dri. Wind —3B 70
Prince Dri. Sand —9E 112
Prince of Wales Av. Read —5D 62
Prince of Wales Wlk. Camb —3N 119
Princes Clo. Eton W —4B 46
Prince's La. P'mre —7H 31
Princes Rd. Ashf —9N 73
Princes Rd. Bour —4N 5
Princes Rd. Egh —9A 72
Princess Av. Wind —9D 46
Princess Marina Dri. Arbor X
(in two parts) —1F 110
Princess Sq. Brack —4M 91
Princess St. M'head —8C 20
Prince's St. Read —5J 63
Princes St. Slou —1K 47
Princess Way. Camb —3N 119
Princes Way. Bag —9H 115
Prince William Dri. Tile —3K 61
Priors Clo. Farn —9L 119
Priors Clo. M'head —3E 44
Priors Ct. Slou —2J 47
Priors Ct. Rd. Herm —4N 55
Prior's La. B'water —4E 118
Priors Rd. Tadl —8J 105
Priors Rd. Wind —9N 45
Priors Way. M'head —3E 44
Priors Wood. Crowt —6B 112
Priory Av. Cav —2G 62
Priory Av. Hung —7K 75
Priory Clo. Asc —9C 94
Priory Clo. Hung —7K 75
Priory Ct. Camb —4K 119
Priory Ct. Winn —9H 65
Priory Grn. Stai —9J 73
Priory La. Warf —2N 91
(in two parts)
Priory M. Stai —9J 73
Priory Pl. Hung —6K 75
(off Tarrant's Hill)
Priory Rd. Chav D —3E 92
Priory Rd. Hung —7K 75
Priory Rd. Newb —1L 101
Priory Rd. Slou —6M 21
Priory Rd. S'dale —9C 94
Priory, The. Winn —9H 65
Priory Wlk. Brack —6C 92
Priory Way. Dat —6K 47
Priory Way. W Dray —5M 49
Proctors Rd. Wokgm —5D 90
Progress Bus. Cen. Burn —7N 21
Promenade Rd. Cav —2G 62
Prospect Ct. Read —6B 62
Prospect La. Egh —9J 71
Prospect Pl. Hur —3D 18
Prospect Pl. Newb —1L 101
Prospect Pl. Stai —9G 73
Prospect Rd. Hung —6K 75
Prospect Rd. Mar —5A 4
Prospect St. Cav —2G 63
Prospect St. Read —5F 62
Providence Pl. M'head —7C 20
Providence Rd. W Dray —9M 25
Prune Hill. Egh —2M 95
Pudding Hill. War R —8B 18
Pudding La. Arbor —8C 88
Pudding La. Bright —4C 30
Puffers Way. Newb —9J 79
Pumpkin Hill. Farn C —1A 22
Pump La. Asc —3A 94
Pump La. Graz —8C 86
Pump La. N. Mar —1D 4
Pump La. S. Mar —2E 4
Pundles La. White —7G 43
Purbeck Ho. Read —3J 87
Purbrook Ct. Brack —8B 92
Purcell Rd. Crowt —3F 112
Purfield Dri. Warg —3K 41
Purley La. Pur T —8K 37
Purley Village. Pur T —8K 37
Purley Way. Pang —8F 36
Purslane. Wokgm —6B 90
Purssell Clo. M'head —2L 43
Purton Ct. Farn C —1E 22
Purton La. Farn R —1E 22
Putman Pl. Hen T —5D 16
Pyegrove Chase. Brack —9B 92
Pyke's Hill. Ash'd C —9F 34

Quadrant Ct. Brack —5B 92
Qualitas. Brack —1K 113
Quantock Av. Cav —8K 39
Quantock Clo. Charv —9G 40
Quantock Clo. Slou —4B 48
Quantocks, The. That —9G 80
Quarrington Clo. That —9H 81
Quarrydale Dri. Mar —5D 4
Quarry La. Yat —4C 118
Quarry Wood. Cook —7E 4
Quarry Wood Rd. Mar & Cook D —7C 4
Quartz Clo. Wokgm —4J 89
Quaves Rd. Slou —2K 47
Quebec Gdns. B'water —5H 119
Quebec Rd. Hen T —6D 16
Queen Adelaide's Ride. Wind —3N 69
Queen Anne's Ga. Cav —2J 63
Queen Anne's Ride. Asc & Wind —1C 94
Queen Anne's Rd. Wind —1E 70
Queen Ann's Ct. Wind —7E 46
Queen Clo. Hen T —5D 16
Queen Elizabeth Rd. Camb —9A 114
Queen Elizabeth's Wlk. Wind —8G 47
Queen Mary Av. Camb —4L 119
Queens Acre. Wind —1F 70
Queensborough Dri. Cav —8E 38
Queensbury Pl. B'water —6G 119
Queen's Clo. Asc —2H 93
Queen's Clo. Old Win —2J 71
Queen's Cotts. Read —5H 63
Queens Ct. Newb —1L 101
Queens Ct. Slou —8H 23
Queen's Dri. Slou —3A 24
Queen's Dri., The. Ear —8L 63
Queens Hill Rise. Asc —5M 93
Queens La. Ashf —8N 73
Queens Lawns. Read —6K 63
Queensmead. Dat —7K 47
Queensmere. Slou —1H 47
Queensmere Rd. Slou —1J 47
Queens Pine. Brack —8B 92
Queens Pl. Asc —5K 93
Queen's Rd. Asc —7N 93
Queens Rd. Camb —5M 119
Queen's Rd. Cav —3H 63
Queen's Rd. Dat —6K 47
Queen's Rd. Egh —9A 72
Queens Rd. Eton W —4B 46
Queen's Rd. Mar —5B 4
Queen's Rd. Newb —9M 79
Queen's Rd. Read —5H 63
(in two parts)
Queen's Rd. Slou —8H 23
Queen's Rd. Uxb —4K 25
Queens Rd. W Dray —1N 49
Queen's Rd. Wind —8E 46
Queen St. Cav —1G 62
Queen St. Hen T —5D 16
Queen St. M'head —8C 20
(in three parts)
Queen's Wlk. Ashf —8L 73
Queens Wlk. Read —5G 62
Queensway. Brack —3K 91
Queensway. Cav —7K 39
Queens Way. Kint —9G 77
Queensway. M'head —5B 20
Queen Victoria St. Read —4H 63
Queen Victoria's Wlk. Col T —3K 119
Queen Victoria Wlk. Wind —7G 47
Quelmans Head Ride. Wind —6N 69
Quelm La. Brack —1M 91
Quentin Rd. Wdly —6C 64
Quentin Way. Vir W —6K 95
Quinbrookes. Wex —7L 23
Quince Clo. S'hill —6M 93
Quincy Rd. Egh —9B 72
Quintilis. Brack —1K 113
(in two parts)
Quoitings Dri. Mar —5A 4
Quoiting Sq. Mar —5B 4

Rabbs Mill Ho. Uxb —3K 25
Racecourse Rd. Newb —1M 101
Raceview Bus. Cen. Newb —9M 79
Rachael's Lake View. Warf —2B 92
Rackstraw Rd. Camb —9G 113
Radbourne Rd. Calc —8L 61
Radcliffe Way. Brack —3J 91
Radcot Av. Langl —2C 48
Radcot Clo. M'head —3B 20
Radcot Clo. Wdly —3D 64
Radical Ride. Wokgm —3L 111
Radley Bottom. Newt —3B 76
Radnor Clo. Hen T —4D 16
Radnor Gro. Uxb —3N 25
Radnor Rd. Brack —5C 92
Radnor Rd. Ear —9B 64
Radnor Way. Slou —3N 47
Radstock La. Ear —9N 63
Radstock Rd. Read —5L 63
Raeburn Way. Col T —3H 119
Ragdale. Bfld C —8H 85
Raggett's La. Far H —4N 109
Raggleswood Clo. Ear —9B 64
Raghill. Aldm —4M 105
Raglan Ct. Read —1K 87
Raglan Gdns. Cav —9J 39
Raglan Ho. Slou —9H 23
Ragley M. Cav —7K 39
Ragstone Rd. Slou —2F 46
Railside Cotts. Midg —9H 83
Railton Clo. Read —4K 87
Railway Cotts. Bag —6H 115
Railway Cotts. Gor —8L 15
Railway Cotts. Graz —8C 86
Railway Rd. Newb —9M 79
Railway Ter. Hamp N —7J 33
Railway Ter. Slou —9H 23
Railway Ter. Stai —9E 72
Rainbow Ind. Est. W Dray —8L 25
Rainsborough Chase. M'head —2M 43
Raleigh Clo. Slou —9C 22
Raleigh Ct. Stai —8H 73
Ralph's Ride. Brack —5B 92
(in two parts)
Rambler Clo. Tap —7L 21
Rambler La. Slou —2L 47
Ramsay Rd. W'sham —5N 115
Ramsbury Clo. Brack —8J 91
Ramsbury Dri. Ear —8N 63
Ramsey Ct. Slou —5N 21
Ramslade Cotts. Brack —5N 91
Ramslade Rd. Brack —6A 92
Ranald Ct. Asc —1K 93
Rances La. Wokgm —6C 90
Randall Clo. Slou —4A 48
Randall Mead. Binf —1F 90
Randell Clo. B'water —8J 119
Randell Ho. Hawl —8J 119
Randolph Rd. Read —3G 62
Randolph Rd. Slou —2N 47
Ranelagh Cres. Asc —3F 92
Ranelagh Dri. Brack —5N 91
Range Ride. Sand —2K 119
Range Rd. Wokgm —3N 111
Range View. Col T —1J 119
Rangewood Av. Read —9N 61
Rapley Grn. Brack —8N 91
Ratby Clo. Lwr Ear —1B 88
Ratcliffe Clo. Uxb —4L 25
Ratcliffe Rd. Farn —9K 119
Raven Clo. Yat —3A 118
Ravenglass Clo. Lwr Ear —9B 64
Ravensbourne Av. Stai —5M 73
Ravensbourne Dri. Wdly —4D 64
Ravenscroft Rd. Hen T —4C 16
Ravensdale Ho. Stai —9J 73
Ravensdale Rd. Asc —7K 93
Ravensfield. Egh —1L 95
Ravensfield. Slou —1M 47
Ravenshoe Clo. Bour —4L 5
Ravenswood Av. Crowt —5C 112
Ravensworth Rd. Mort —4F 106
Ravensworth Rd. Slou —4C 22
Rawling Ct. Read —4J 87

Rawlinson Rd.—St Margarets Clo.

Rawlinson Rd. Camb —3L **119**
Ray Dri. M'head —7E **20**
Ray Lea Clo. M'head —6E **20**
Ray Lea Rd. M'head —5E **20**
Rayleigh Clo. Wdly —7D **64**
Ray Mead Ct. M'head —5F **20**
Ray Mead Rd. M'head —7F **20**
Ray Mill Rd. E. M'head —5D **20**
Ray Mill Rd. W. M'head —6C **20**
Raymond Clo. Coln —7F **48**
Raymond Rd. M'head —7A **20**
Raymond Rd. Slou —2B **48**
Rayners Clo. Coln —6D **48**
Ray Pk. Av. M'head —5E **20**
Ray Pk. La. M'head —7E **20**
Ray Pk. Rd. M'head —6E **20**
Ray's Av. Wind —6B **46**
Ray St. M'head —7E **20**
Reade's La. Gall C —1C **38**
Reading Link Retail Pk. Read —7G **62**
Reading Retail Pk. Read —3B **62**
Reading Rd. Arbor —7A **88**
Reading Rd. Bfld —6L **85**
Reading Rd. Bfld C —1G **107**
Reading Rd. Chol —1J **15**
Reading Rd. Finch —5D **110**
Reading Rd. Gor —8L **15**
Reading Rd. Hen T —5D **16**
Reading Rd. Pang —8E **36**
Reading Rd. Streat —8J **15**
Reading Rd. Winn & Wokgm —1H **89**
Reading Rd. Wdly —4B **64**
Reading Rd. Yat —2A **118**
Reckitt Ho. Read —1L **87**
Recreation La. Spen W —9H **87**
Recreation Rd. Bour —4M **5**
Recreation Rd. Bfld C —9H **85**
Recreation Rd. Tile —4M **61**
Recreation Rd. Warg —3K **41**
Rectory Clo. Brack —6N **91**
Rectory Clo. Farn R —4E **22**
Rectory Clo. Newb —9K **79**
Rectory Clo. Sand —1D **118**
Rectory Clo. Wind —7C **46**
Rectory Clo. Wokgm —5A **90**
Rectory La. Brack —7M **91**
Rectory La. W'sham —6M **115**
Rectory Rd. Cav —2G **63**
Rectory Rd. Pad C —2A **106**
Rectory Rd. Streat —7D **14**
Rectory Rd. Tap —5G **21**
Rectory Rd. Wokgm —5A **90**
Rectory Row. Brack —6M **91**
Redberry Clo. Cav —8K **39**
Red Cottage Dri. Calc —8K **61**
Red Cottage M. Slou —2L **47**
Red Ct. Slou —9G **22**
Red Cross Rd. Gor —8L **15**
Reddington Dri. Slou —3N **47**
Redditch. Brack —9A **92**
Redfern Clo. Uxb —2K **25**
Redfield Ct. Newb —7A **80**
Redford Rd. Wind —7N **45**
Redford Way. Uxb —1L **25**
Redgauntlet. Finch —4J **111**
Redhatch Dri. Ear —1M **87**
Red Hill. Bin H —1M **39**
Redhouse Clo. Lwr Ear —3A **88**
Red Ho. Dri. Son C —1G **38**
Redlake Hill. Aldm —4L **105**
Redlands Rd. Read —6J **63**
Red La. Aldm —4L **105**
Redlane Ct. Read —7K **63**
Redlane Rd. P'mre —1K **31**
Redriff Clo. M'head —8A **20**
Red Rose. Binf —9G **67**
Redruth Gdns. Read —2H **87**
Redshots Clo. Mar —3C **4**
Red Shute Hill. Herm —8D **56**
Redvers Rd. Brack —7M **91**
Redwood. Burn —3L **21**
Redwood Av. Wdly —7F **64**
Redwood Dri. Asc —8D **94**
Redwood Gdns. Slou —8F **22**
Redwood Way. Tile —1L **61**
Reed Clo. Iver —7F **24**
Reeds Av. Ear —9M **63**
Reed's Hill. Brack —7M **91**
Reeve Rd. Holyp —5E **44**
Reeves Way. Wokgm —7M **89**
Reform Rd. M'head —7E **20**
Regency Heights. Cav —9E **38**
Regent Clo. Hung —6J **75**
Regent Clo. Lwr Ear —2B **88**
Regent Ct. Bag —8J **115**
Regent Ct. M'head —7C **20**
Regent Ct. Read —4G **62**
Regent Ct. Slou —7G **22**
Regents Ga. Read —6H **63**
Regents Pl. Sand —1G **118**
Regent St. Read —5L **63**
Regents Wlk. Asc —9M **93**
Regis Clo. Read —4K **87**
Regnum Dri. Shaw —6M **79**
Reid Av. M'head —9A **20**
Rembrandt Clo. Wokgm —5J **89**
Rembrandt Way. Read —7E **62**
Remembrance Rd. Newb —9J **79**
Remenham Chu. La. Rem —2F **16**
Remenham La. Rem —4E **16**
Renault Rd. Wdly —6F **64**
Rennie Clo. Ashf —7L **73**
Repton Clo. M'head —2N **43**
Repton Rd. Ear —9B **64**
Restwold Clo. Read —8C **62**
Retford Clo. Wdly —3E **64**
Retreat, The. Egh —9M **71**
Retreat, The. M'head —6G **45**
Revesby Clo. M'head —2A **44**
Reynards Clo. Tadl —9K **105**
Reynards Clo. Winn —1H **89**
Reynolds Ct. That —8G **80**
Reynolds Grn. Col T —3H **119**
Rhigos. Cav —7F **38**
Rhodes Clo. Ear —9D **64**
Rhodes Clo. Egh —9D **72**
*Rhodes Ct. Egh —9D **72** (off Pooley Grn. Clo.)*
Rhododendron Clo. Asc —2H **93**
Rhododendron Ride. Egh —1H **95**
Rhododendron Wlk. Asc —2H **93**
Ribbleton Clo. Ear —9D **64**
Ribstone Rd. M'head —2M **43**
Ricardo Rd. Old Win —3K **71**
*Richard Nevill Ct. Cav —2J **63** (off Nelson Rd.)*
Richards Clo. Uxb —2N **25**
Richborough Clo. Ear —1A **88**
Richfield Av. Read —3E **62**
Richings Way. Iver —2F **48**
Richmond Cres. Slou —9J **23**
Richmond Cres. Stai —9G **73**
Richmond Ho. Col T —2J **119**
Richmond Rise. Wokgm —4K **89**
Richmond Rd. Cav —9E **38**
Richmond Rd. Col T —1J **119**
Richmond Rd. Read —4D **62**
Richmond Rd. Stai —9G **73**
Richmondwood. Asc —9D **94**
Rickard Clo. W Dray —2L **49**
Rickman Clo. Arbor X —1D **110**
Rickman Clo. Brack —8N **91**
Rickman Clo. Wdly —7C **64**
Rickman's La. Stoke P —1G **23**
Riddings La. Hdly —8M **103**
Rider's La. Graz —7A **86**
Rideway Clo. Camb —5M **119**
Ridgebank. Slou —8B **22**
Ridge Hall Clo. Cav —1E **62**
Ridgemead Rd. Egh —7J **71**
Ridgemount Clo. Tile —2J **61**
Ridge Mt. Rd. Asc —9C **94**
Ridge, The. Cold A —2F **80**
Ridge, The. Pang —5A **36**
Ridge Way. Iver —8G **24**
Ridge Way. Warg —3J **41**
Ridgeway Clo. Herm —5E **56**
Ridgeway Clo. Light —9K **115**
Ridgeway Clo. Mar —3C **4**
Ridgeway, The. Brack —5N **91**
Ridgeway, The. Cav —1H **63**
Ridgeway, The. Light —9L **115**
Ridgeway, The. Mar —3C **4**
Ridgeway, The. Wdly —7E **64**
Ridgeway Trading Est. Iver —8G **24**
Riding Ct. Rd. Dat —6L **47**
Ridings, The. Emm G —5J **39**
Ridings, The. Iver —3G **49**
Ridings, The. M'head —8L **19**
Riding Way. Wokgm —5J **89**
Ridlington Clo. Lwr Ear —1D **88**
Riley Rd. Mar —5B **4**
Riley Rd. Tile —4N **61**
Ringmead. Brack —7J **91**
Ring, The. Brack —4N **91**
Ringwood. Brack —9K **91**
Ringwood Clo. Asc —6L **93**
Ringwood Rd. B'water —3G **118**
Ringwood Rd. Tile —3A **62**
Ripley Av. Egh —1N **95**
Ripley Clo. Slou —3N **47**
Ripley Rd. Tile —3A **62**
Ripplesmere. Brack —6A **92**
Ripplesmore Clo. Sand —1F **118**
Risborough Rd. M'head —6B **20**
Riseley Rd. M'head —7A **20**
Rise Rd. Asc —7A **94**
Rise, The. Cav —9H **39**
Rise, The. Cold A —4F **80**
Rise, The. Crowt —5D **112**
Rise, The. S'dale —8A **94**
Rise, The. Uxb —3N **25**
Rissington Clo. Tile —1M **61**
Rivacres. Whit H —2F **36**
Rivar Rd. Shalb —8E **96**
Riverbank. Stai —9G **73**
Riverbank, The. Wind —6D **46**
Riverdene Dri. Winn —9E **64**
Riverfield Rd. Stai —9G **73**
River Gdns. Bray —1G **45**
River Gdns. Pur T —8L **37**
Rivermead. That —1J **103**
Rivermead Ct. Mar —7C **4**
Rivermead Rd. Camb —7M **119**
Rivermead Rd. Wdly —7E **64**
River Pk. Newb —8M **79**
River Pk. Av. Stai —8E **72**
Riverpark Dri. Mar —6D **4**
River Rd. Cav —1D **62**
River Rd. Read —6G **63**
River Rd. Tap —8F **20**
River Rd. Wind —6M **45**
River Rd. Yat —1A **118**
Riversdale. Bour —6M **5**
Riversdale Ct. Read —4L **63**
Riverside. Bour —4M **5**
Riverside. Brad —6L **59**
Riverside. Egh —7B **72**
Riverside. Stai —9G **72**
Riverside. Wray —4L **71**
Riverside Av. Light —9M **115**
Riverside Caravan Pk. Read —2A **62**
Riverside Ct. Cav —2G **63**
Riverside Dri. Stai —9F **72** (Chertsey La.)
Riverside Pk. Camb —6L **119**
Riverside Pk. Coln —8F **48**
Riverside Pl. Stai —3L **73**
Riverside Rd. Stanw —2L **73**
Riverside Way. Camb —6L **119**
Riverside Way. Cow —2J **25**
River St. Wind —6F **46**
River Ter. Hen T —4D **16**
Riverview Rd. Pang —7D **36**
Riverway. Gt Shef —1F **52**
Riverwoods Dri. Mar —6E **4**
River Yd. Twy —8H **41**
Rixman Clo. M'head —9A **20**
Rixon Clo. G Grn —7N **23**
Roasthill La. Eton W —5N **45**
Roberts Clo. Stai —3K **73**
Roberts Clo. W Dray —9M **25**
Robertsfield. That —8C **80**
Roberts Gro. Wokgm —7L **89**
Robertson Clo. Green —2M **101**
Roberts Rd. Camb —3L **119**
Roberts Way. Egh —2L **95**
Robin Clo. Bfld C —8J **85**
Robindale Av. Ear —9C **64**
Robin Hood Clo. Farn —9L **119**
Robin Hood Clo. Slou —9B **22**
Robin Hood La. Winn —1H **89**
Robin Hood Way. Winn —9H **65**
Robin La. Bis G —7C **102**
Robin La. Sand —1F **118**
Robin's Bow. Camb —5M **119**
Robins Clo. Newb —3K **101**
Robins Clo. Uxb —6K **25**
Robins Gro. Cres. Yat —3A **118**
Robins Hill. Ink —4D **98**
Robin Way. Stai —7G **72**
Robin Way. Tile —6J **61**
Robin Willis Way. Old Win —3J **71**
Robinwood Gro. Uxb —5N **25**
Rochester Av. Wdly —3D **64**
Rochester Rd. Stai —9E **72**
Rochfords Gdns. Slou —9L **23**
Rochford Way. Tap —8K **21**
Rockall Ct. Slou —2C **48**
Rockbourne Gdns. Tile —3A **62**
Rockfel Rd. Lamb —3G **27**
Rockfield Way. Col T —1H **119**
Rockingham Clo. Uxb —2K **25**
Rockingham Pde. Uxb —1K **25**
Rockingham Rd. Newb —9K **79**
Rockingham Rd. Uxb —2J **25**
Rodney Ct. Read —6G **62**
Rodney Way. Coln —7F **48**
Rodway Rd. Tile —2M **61**
Roebuck Est. Binf —2G **91**
Roebuck Grn. Slou —9A **22**
Roebuts Clo. Newb —2K **101**
Roger's La. E Gar —7A **28**
Roger's La. Stoke P —1H **23**
Rokeby Clo. Brack —3A **92**
Rokeby Clo. Newb —3L **101**
Rokeby Dri. Tok G —5C **38**
Rokesby Rd. Slou —4B **22**
Rollington Clo. Lwr Ear —1D **88**
Rolls La. Holyp —5B **44**
Romana Ct. Stai —8H **73**
Roman Fields. Sil —9C **106**
Roman Lea. Cook —8K **5**
Roman Ride. Crowt —5B **112**
Romans Ga. Pam H —9A **106**
Roman Way. Bour —3L **5** (in two parts)
Roman Way. Ear —9C **64**
Roman Way. That —7D **80**
Romany Clo. Tile —3A **62**
Romany La. Tile —4N **61** (in two parts)
Romeo Hill. Warf —3C **92**
Romney Ho. Brack —6B **92**
Romney Lock Rd. Wind —6F **46**
Romsey Clo. B'water —3G **119**
Romsey Clo. Ear —9D **64**
Romsey Clo. Slou —2A **48**
Romsey Rd. Tile —3A **62**
Rona Ct. Read —4B **62**
Ronaldsay Spur. Slou —6G **22**
Rood Hill. E'ton —7N **53**
Rook Clo. Wokgm —6K **89**
Rookery Clo. Finch —4F **110**
Rookery Ct. Mar —5B **4**
Rookery Rd. Stai —9J **73**
Rooksfield. Bis G —8D **102**
Rooksnest La. Kint —5F **98**
Rookswood. Brack —2M **91**
Rookwood Av. Owl —8J **113**
Rope Wlk. That —8F **80**
Rosary Gdns. Yat —3B **118**
Roseary Clo. W Dray —3L **49**
Rosebank Clo. Cook —8J **5**
Rosebay. Wokgm —3C **90**
Rosebery Rd. Tok G —6D **38**
Rose Clo. Wdly —5G **64**
Rose Ct. Wokgm —5A **90**
Rosecroft Way. Shin —6L **87**
Rosedale. Binf —9G **67**
Rosedale Cres. Ear —4N **63**
Rosedale Gdns. Brack —7L **91**
Rosedale Gdns. That —9F **80**
Rosedene La. Col T —3H **119**
Rosefield Rd. Stai —8H **73**
Rose Gdns. Stai —4L **73**
Rose Gdns. Wokgm —5A **90**
Rose Hill. Binf —9G **67**
Rose Hill. Burn —2K **21**
Rosehill Ct. Slou —2J **47**
Rosehill Houses. Cav —6J **39**
Rosehill Pk. Cav —6H **39**
Rose Ind. Est. Bour —4M **5**
Rose Kiln La. Read —6G **62**
Rose La. C Grn —7M **17**
Roseleigh Clo. M'head —7L **19**
Rosemary Av. Ear —2M **87**
Rosemary Clo. Uxb —6N **25**
Rosemary Gdns. B'water —4G **119**
Rosemary La. B'water —3G **118**
Rosemary Ter. Newb —9J **79**
Rosemead Av. Tile —1J **61**
Rosen Ct. That —8H **81**
Rose Rd. M'head —9A **20**
Rosery, The. Bour —4L **5**
Roses La. Wind —8N **45**
Rose St. Wokgm —5A **90**
Rose Ter. Newb —1K **101**
Rose Wlk. Read —5G **63**
Rose Wlk. Slou —6D **22**
Rosewood. Wdly —7C **64**
Rosier Clo. That —9J **81**
Rosken Gdns. Farn R —3D **22**
Roslyn Rd. Wdly —6C **64**
Rossendale Rd. Cav —1K **63**
Rossett Clo. Brack —6M **91**
Rossington Pl. Read —3J **87**
Rossiter Clo. Slou —3N **47**
Ross Rd. M'head —9A **20**
Ross Rd. Read —3G **62**
Rostrevor Gdns. Iver —3E **24**
Rother Clo. Sand —1G **119**
Rotherfield Av. Wokgm —4L **89**
Rotherfield Clo. Thea —8G **60**
Rotherfield Rd. Hen T —7C **16**
Rotherfield Way. Cav —9G **39**
Rothwell Gdns. Wdly —3E **64**
Rothwell Ho. Crowt —6G **113**
Rothwell Wlk. Cav —2K **63**
Rotten Row Hill. Tut C —9H **59**
Roughgrove Copse. Binf —1F **90**
Roundabout La. Winn —3J **89**
Round Clo. Yat —4D **118**
Round End. Newb —5H **101**
Roundfield. Up Buck —5L **81** (in two parts)
Roundhead Rd. Thea —9E **60**
Roundway. Egh —9D **72**
Routh La. Tile —6M **61**
Rowallan Clo. Cav —7K **39**
Rowan. Brack —7C **92**
Rowan Av. Egh —9D **72**
Rowan Clo. Camb —9C **114**
Rowan Clo. Son C —1F **38**
Rowan Clo. Wokgm —6L **89**
Rowan Dri. Crowt —3G **112**
Rowan Dri. Newb —6L **79**
Rowan Dri. Wdly —4D **64**
Rowan Gdns. Iver —3D **24**
Rowan Rd. W Dray —3L **49**
Rowans Clo. Farn —8J **119**
Rowan Way. Bfld —7J **85**
Rowan Way. Slou —6D **22**
Rowanwood. Finch —4F **110**
Rowcroft Rd. Arbor X —3E **110**
Rowe Ct. Read —4B **62**
Rowland Clo. Wind —9N **45**
Rowland Way. Ear —1M **87**
Row La. D'den —5L **39**
Rowles Paddock. W Ils —4L **11**
Rowley Clo. Brack —5B **92**
Rowley La. Wex —2L **23**
Rowley Rd. Read —8H **63**
Rowlheys Pl. W Dray —2M **49**
Roxborough Way. M'head —1K **43**
Roxwell Clo. Slou —9A **22**
Royal Av. Calc —8J **61**
Royal Clo. Uxb —7N **25**
Royal Ct. Read —5J **63**
Royal La. Uxb & W Dray —6N **25**
Royal Mans. Hen T —5D **16**
Royal M. Wind —7F **46**
Royal Sta. Ct. Twy —9J **41**
Royal Victoria Gdns. S Asc —6K **93**
Roy Clo. Herm —6C **56**
Roycroft La. Wokgm —2K **111**
Royston Clo. Tile —5N **61**
Royston Gdns. Wokgm —4M **111**
Royston Way. Slou —6M **21**
Ruby Clo. Slou —2C **46**
Ruby Clo. Wokgm —4J **89**
Ruddlesway. Wind —7N **45** (in three parts)
Rudland Clo. That —9G **80**
Rudsworth Clo. Coln —6E **48**
Rugby Clo. Owl —9J **113**
Ruggles-Brise Rd. Ashf —9L **73**
Runnemede Rd. Egh —8B **72**
Runnymede Ct. Egh —8B **72**
Rupert Clo. Hen T —3D **16**
Rupert Rd. Newb —2K **101**
Ruperts La. Hen T —3D **16**
Rupert Sq. Read —5K **63**
Rupert St. Read —5K **63**
Rupert Wlk. Read —5K **63**
Ruscombe Gdns. Dat —5J **47**
Ruscombe La. Rusc —8K **41**
Ruscombe Pk. Ind. Est. Rusc —8K **41**
Ruscombe Rd. Twy —8K **41**
Rushall Clo. Lwr Ear —4L **87**
Rusham Ct. Egh —9B **72**
Rusham Pk. Av. Egh —9A **72**
Rusham Rd. Egh —9A **72**
Rushbrook Rd. Wdly —5B **64**
Rushden Dri. Read —2L **87**
Rushes M. Uxb —2K **25**
Rushes, The. M'head —8E **20**
Rushey Way. Lwr Ear —3M **87**
Rushington Av. M'head —8C **20**
Rushmoor Gdns. Calc —8J **61**
Ruskin Ct. Crowt —6C **112**
Ruskin Way. Wokgm —5J **89**
Russell Ct. B'water —4H **119**
Russell Ct. M'head —7C **20**
Russell Dri. Stai —3L **73**
Russell Gdns. W Dray —4N **49**
Russell Rd. Newb —9J **79**
Russell Rd. Tok G —6D **38**
Russell St. Read —5F **62**
Russell St. Wind —7F **46**
Russell Way. Winn —2G **89**
Russet Clo. Stai —3G **73**
Russet Glade. Bfld C —9J **85**
Russet Glade. Cav —6J **39**
Russet Rd. M'head —2N **43**
Russley Grn. Wokgm —1M **111**
Rustington Clo. Ear —2A **88**
Ruston Way. Asc —4H **93**
Rutherford Clo. Wind —7B **46**
Rutherford Wlk. Tile —5H **61**
Rutland Av. Slou —6E **22**
Rutland Pl. M'head —8N **19**
Rutland Rd. M'head —8A **20**
Rutland Rd. Read —5D **62**
Rutters Clo. W Dray —1N **49**
Ryan Mt. Sand —1E **118**
Ryans Mt. Mar —5A **4**
Rycroft. Wind —9B **46**
Rycroft Clo. Warg —2K **41**
Rydal Av. Tile —2N **61**
Rydal Dri. That —8D **80**
Rydal Pl. Light —9L **115**
Ryde Gdns. Yat —3A **118**
Rydings. Wind —9B **46**
Rye Clo. Brack —2A **92**
Rye Clo. M'head —1L **43**
Rye Ct. Slou —2J **47**
Ryecroft Clo. Wdly —3C **64**
Ryecroft Gdns. B'water —5J **119**
Rye Gro. Light —9N **115**
Ryehurst La. Binf —8J **67**
Ryeish La. Spen W —8J **87**
Ryeland Clo. W Dray —7M **25**
Ryemead La. Wink —7F **68**
Ryhill Way. Lwr Ear —3L **87**
Rylstone Clo. M'head —2N **43**
Rylstone Rd. Read —4D **62**
Ryvers Rd. Slou —2A **48**

Sabah Ct. Ashf —8N **73**
Sackville St. Read —4G **62**
Saddleback Rd. Camb —9B **114**
Saddlewood. Camb —5N **119**
Sadlers Ct. Winn —3J **89**
Sadlers End. Sind —4G **89**
Sadlers La. Winn —3J **89**
Sadlers M. M'head —7E **20**
Sadlers Rd. Ink —5M **97**
Saffron Clo. Dat —7K **47**
Saffron Clo. Ear —8B **64**
Saffron Clo. Newb —8K **79**
Saffron Rd. Brack —6M **91**
Sage Clo. Ear —2N **87**
Sagecroft Rd. That —6F **80**
Sage Rd. Tile —1K **61**
Sage Wlk. Warf —2A **92**
Sailing Club La. Bour —4L **5**
St Adrians Clo. M'head —1M **43**
St Agnes Ter. Lamb —3H **27**
St Alban's Clo. Wind —7F **46**
St Alban's St. Wind —7F **46**
St Andrews. Brack —8J **91**
St Andrew's Av. Wind —8B **46**
St Andrew's Clo. Crowt —4D **112**
St Andrew's Clo. Old Win —3J **71**
St Andrews Clo. Wray —3N **71**
St Andrew's Ct. Read —5K **63**
St Andrew's Cres. Wind —8B **46**
St Andrew's Hall. Read —6J **63**
St Andrew's Rd. Cav —9F **38**
St Andrews Rd. Hen T —6B **16**
St Andrew's Rd. Uxb —2M **25**
St Andrew's Way. Slou —8N **21**
St Anne's Av. Stai —4L **73**
St Annes Clo. Hen T —5C **16**
St Annes Glade. Bag —7G **114**
St Anne's Rd. Cav —2G **62**
St Anthonys Clo. Brack —3L **91**
St Barnabas Rd. Cav —7G **39**
St Barnabas Rd. Read —2M **87**
St Bartholomews Rd. Read —5M **63**
St Bernards Rd. Slou —2L **47**
St Birinus Rd. Calc —7K **61**
St Catherine's Clo. Sind —2F **88**
St Catherines Ct. Stai —8H **73**
St Cecelia Ct. Read —1J **87**
St Chads Rd. M'head —1M **43**
St Christopher Rd. Uxb —7L **25**
St Christophers Gdns. Asc —3G **92**
St Clement Clo. Uxb —7L **25**
St Clements Clo. Lwr Ear —2B **88**
St Cloud Way. Tap —7C **20**
St Columbus Clo. M'head —1M **43**
St Cuthberts Clo. Egh —9M **71**
St David Clo. Uxb —6L **25**
St David's Clo. Cav —8F **38**
St David's Clo. Farn —9K **119**
St David's Clo. Iver —2E **24**
St Davids Clo. M'head —1L **43**
St David's Rd. Newb —9K **79**
St Donats Pl. Newb —9L **79**
St Edwards Rd. Read —6N **63**
St Elizabeth Clo. Read —4H **87**
St Elmo Clo. Slou —5F **22**
St Elmo Cres. Slou —5F **22**
St George's Av. Newb —9J **79**
St Georges Clo. Wind —7A **46**
St Georges Ct. Owl —8J **113**
St George's Cres. Slou —8N **21**
St George's Hall. Read —7K **63**
St George's Ind. Est. Camb —6M **119**
St George's La. Asc —5L **93**
St George's Rd. Read —4B **62**
St George's Ter. Read —4B **62**
St Giles Clo. Read —6H **63**
*St Giles Ct. Read —6H **63** (off Southampton St.)*
St Helen Clo. Uxb —6L **25**
St Helens Cres. Sand —1F **118**
St Helier Clo. Wokgm —8N **89**
St Hilda's Av. Ashf —9M **73**
St Ives Clo. Thea —1E **84**
St Ives Rd. M'head —7D **20**
St James Clo. Pang —7D **36**
St James Clo. Twy —8K **41**
*St James' Courtyard. Mar —5B **4** (off Claremont Gdns.)*
St James Pl. Slou —7M **21**
St James Rd. Wokgm —2K **111**
St James Wlk. Iver —1F **48**
St Johns Clo. Uxb —2J **25**
St Johns Clo. Wdly —4E **64**
St John's Ct. Egh —9B **72**
St John's Dri. Wind —8C **46**
*St Johns Gdns. Newb —1K **101** (off Old Newbury Rd.)*
*St Johns Ga. Read —4H **63** (off Valpy St.)*
St John's Hill. Read —5J **63**
St John's Rd. Asc —2J **93**
St John's Rd. Cav —2J **63**
St John's Rd. Mort C —5H **107**
St John's Rd. Newb —1L **101**
St John's Rd. Read —5J **63**
St John's Rd. Sand —2F **118**
St Johns Rd. Slou —8J **23**
St John's Rd. That —8F **80**
St John's Rd. Uxb —2J **25**
St John's Rd. Wind —8C **46**
St John's St. Read —5J **63**
*St Joseph's Ct. Newb —7M **79** (off Charlton Pl.)*
St Jude's Clo. Egh —9L **71**
St Jude's Rd. Egh —8L **71**
St Katherine's Rd. Hen T —7C **16**
St Laurence Clo. Uxb —6K **25**
St Laurence Way. Slou —2J **47**
St Lawrence Sq. Hung —6J **75**
St Leger Ct. Newb —7J **79**
St Leonard's Av. Wind —8E **46**
St Leonard's Hill. Wind —1N **69**
St Leonard's Rd. Wind —3M **69** (Windsor Safari Park)
St Leonard's Rd. Wind —9C **46** (Windsor)
St Leonards Wlk. Iver —2G **48**
St Luke Clo. Uxb —7L **25**
St Lukes Ct. Cav —9H **39**
St Luke's Rd. M'head —7C **20**
St Luke's Rd. Old Win —3J **71**
St Luke's Rd. Uxb —1M **25**
St Lukes Way. Cav —9H **39**
St Margarets Av. Uxb —5N **25**
St Margarets Clo. Iver —3E **24**

St Margarets Ga.—South Pl.

St Margarets Ga. Iver —3E **24**
St Margarets Rd. M'head —7L **19**
St Mark's Clo. Eng —7C **60**
St Marks Clo. That —8F **80**
St Mark's Cres. M'head —7M **19**
St Marks Pl. Wind —8E **46**
St Mark's Rd. Binf —2G **91**
St Mark's Rd. Hen T —6C **16**
St Mark's Rd. M'head —7N **19**
St Marks Rd. Wind —8E **46**
St Martin Clo. Uxb —7L **25**
St Martin's Cen. Cav —2G **63**
St Martins Clo. Lwr Ear —2B **88**
St Martin's Clo. W Dray —2L **49**
St Martin's Ct. Ashf —9K **73**
St Martin's Rd. W Dray —2L **49**
St Mary's Av. Pur T —8K **37**
St Mary's Av. Stai —4L **73**
St Mary's Butts. Read —5G **63**
St Mary's Clo. Hen T —6A **16**
St Mary's Clo. M'head —7C **20**
St Mary's Clo. Sand —1G **119**
St Mary's Clo. Stai —4L **73**
St Mary's Cres. Stai —4L **73**
St Mary's Gdns. Bag —7H **115**
St Mary's Hill. Asc —8M **93**
St Mary's La. Wink —7G **68**
St Mary's Rd. Asc —9L **93**
St Mary's Rd. Camb —3N **119**
St Mary's Rd. Langl —9N **23**
St Mary's Rd. Mort C —5H **107**
St Mary's Rd. Newb —7L **79**
St Mary's Rd. Sind —3G **88**
St Mary's Way. Bfld C —8J **85**
St Matthew Clo. Uxb —7L **25**
St Michaels Clo. Lamb —3G **27**
St Michael's Ct. Rusc —7K **41**
St Michaels Ct. Slou —5N **21**
St Michael's Rd. Camb —4M **119**
St Michael's Rd. Newb —9K **79**
St Michael's Rd. Sand —1D **118**
St Michael's Rd. Tile —4L **61**
St Nazaire Clo. Egh —9E **72**
St Neot's Rd. Eve —9E **110**
St Nicholas Clo. Uxb —7L **25**
St Nicholas's Rd. Newb —9K **79**
St Patrick's Av. Charv —8F **40**
St Patricks Clo. E Ils —7B **12**
St Patricks Clo. M'head —1M **43**
St Patrick's Hall. Read —8K **63**
St Paul Clo. Uxb —6L **25**
St Pauls Av. Slou —8H **23**
St Paul's Ct. Read —6G **62**
St Paul's Ga. Wokgm —4M **89**
St Paul's Rd. Stai —9E **72**
St Peter's Av. Cav —9E **38**
St Peter's Clo. Burn —5L **21**
St Peter's Clo. Old Win —2J **71**
St Peter's Clo. Stai —9G **73**
St Peter's Gdns. Yat —3B **118**
St Peter's Hill. Cav —1F **62**
St Peter's Rd. M'head —4A **20**
St Peter's Rd. Read —6N **63**
St Peters Rd. Uxb —6L **25**
St Peter St. Mar —6C **4**
St Ronan's Rd. Read —4B **62**
St Saviour's Rd. Read —7F **62**
St Saviours Ter. Read —6F **62**
St Sebastian's Clo. Wokgm —3C **112**
St Stephen's Clo. Cav —2G **63**
St Stephens Ct. Read —5K 63
(off Rupert St.)
St Stephen's Rd. W Dray —9L **25**
St Swithins Clo. Wick —8J **53**
St Swithin's Ct. Twy —9J **41**
St Thomas Wlk. Coln —6E **48**
Salamanca. Crowt —5C **112**
Salcombe Dri. Ear —8A **64**
Salcombe Rd. Ashf —8M **73**
Salcombe Rd. Newb —1J **101**
Salcombe Rd. Read —9K **63**
Saleby Clo. Lwr Ear —1D **88**
Sale Garden Cotts. Wokgm —6A **90**
Salford Clo. Read —4J **87**
Salisbury Av. Slou —5E **22**
Salisbury Clo. Wokgm —9M **89**
Salisbury Rd. B'water —5G **119**
Salisbury Rd. Hung —8J **75**
Salisbury Rd. Read —4E **62**
Salisbury Rd. Uxb —3J **25**
Salmon Clo. Spen W —9H **87**
Salmond Rd. Read —5J **87**
Salters Clo. M'head —7D **20**
Saltersgate Clo. Lwr Ear —1C **88**
Salters Rd. M'head —7E **20**
Salt Hill Av. Slou —9E **22**
Salt Hill Dri. Slou —9E **22**
Salt Hill Mans. Slou —9E **22**
Salt Hill Way. Slou —9E **22**
Salwey Clo. Brack —8M **91**
Samian Pl. Binf —2J **91**
Sampage Clo. Read —5J **87**
Sampson Pk. Binf —3H **91**
Sampson's Grn. Slou —4B **22**
Sanctuary Clo. Tile —4M **61**
Sandcroft Rd. Cav —7E **38**
Sanden Clo. Hung —6J **75**
Sandford Down. Brack —7C **92**
Sandford Dri. Wdly —3E **64**
Sandford La. Wdly & Hurst —5G **65**
Sandford Rd. Tadl —9J **105**
Sandgate Av. Tile —2N **61**
Sand Hill Ct. Farn —9M **119**
Sandhills Ct. Vir W —7N **95**
Sandhills La. Vir W —7N **95**
Sandhills Way. Calc —8M **61**
Sandhurst-Crowthorne By-Pass. Col T —4J **119**
Sandhurst-Crowthorne By-Pass. Crowt —3J **113**
Sandhurst La. B'water —3F **118**
Sandhurst Rd. Crowt —7F **112**
Sandhurst Rd. Wokgm —2N **111**
Sandhurst Rd. Yat —2D **118**
Sandisplatt Rd. M'head —8L **19**
Sandleford Clo. Read —5J **87**
Sandleford Rise. Newb —3L **101**
Sandlers End. Slou —5D **22**
Sandown Av. Calc —8J **61**
Sandown Clo. B'water —4H **119**
Sandown Rd. Slou —6B **22**
Sandown Way. Green —1N **101**
Sandpit Hill. Newb —6G **101**
Sandpit La. D'den —5M **39**
Sandpit La. Far H —6N **109**
Sandringham Ct. Slou —7N **21**
Sandringham Dri. Ashf —8L **73**
Sandringham Rd. H'row A —2M **73**
Sandringham Rd. M'head —4B **20**
Sandringham Way. Calc —8J **61**
Sands Drove. Hung —5A **98**
Sands Farm Dri. Burn —5M **21**
Sandstone Clo. Winn —2H **89**
Sandygate Clo. Mar —4B **4**
Sandygate Rd. Mar —4B **4**
Sandy La. Brack —3N **91**
Sandy La. Chvly —2B **56**
Sandy La. Cur —8C **56**
Sandy La. Farn —9J **119**
Sandy La. N Asc —3F **92**
Sandy La. Sand —9D **112**
Sandy La. Shalb —9D **96**
Sandy La. S'dale —7C **94**
Sandy La. Vir W —6N **95**
Sandy La. Wokgm —7H **89**
Sandy Mead. M'head —4F **44**
Sandy Ride. S'hill —6A **94**
Sapphire Clo. Wokgm —4K **89**
Sargeants Clo. Uxb —4L **25**
Sarsby Dri. Stai —6B **72**
Sarum. Brack —1K **113**
Sarum Complex. Uxb —4J **25**
Sarum Cres. Wokgm —4B **90**
Sarum Rd. Tadl —9J **105**
Sarum Way. Hung —7K **75**
Saturn Clo. Wokgm —5K **89**
Saturn Croft. Wink R —1D **92**
Saunders Ct. Pur T —8J **37**
Saunders Rd. Uxb —1N **25**
Savernake Clo. Tile —5N **61**
Savernake Way. Brack —8B **92**
Savill Way. Mar —5D **4**
Savory Wlk. Binf —1F **90**
Savoy Gro. B'water —6H **119**
Sawpit Rd. Hurst —5K **65**
Sawtry Clo. Lwr Ear —1D **88**
Sawyers Clo. M'head —3L **43**
Sawyers Clo. Wind —6A **46**
Sawyers Cres. M'head —3L **43**
Saxby Clo. Bfld C —8J **85**
Saxon Clo. Slou —1A **48**
Saxon Clo. Uxb —6N **25**
Saxon Gdns. Tap —5G **21**
Saxon Ho. Cotts. Lamb —1F **26**
Saxon Way. Old Win —3K **71**
Saxon Way. W Dray —5K **49**
Saxony Way. Yat —5A **118**
Sayers Clo. Green —2M **101**
Scafell Clo. Tile —2J **61**
Scafell Rd. Slou —5B **22**
Scampton Rd. Houn —3N **73**
Scania Wlk. Wink R —1E **92**
Scarborough Way. Slou —2D **46**
Scarletts La. Kiln G —5N **41**
Scholars Clo. Cav —1F **62**
Scholars Clo. Gt Shef —1F **52**
School Allotment Ride. Wind —4L **69**
School Cotts. Asc —3G **93**
Schoolfields. S'lake X —3D **40**
School Grn. Shin —7L **87**
School Hill. Crowt —6H **113**
School Hill. Sand —9E **112**
School Hill. Warg —4J **41**
School La. Bag —8G **115**
School La. Box —8B **54**
School La. Bfld C —8G **85**
School La. Cav —2G **63**
School La. Cook —8L **5**
School La. Cook D —8F **4**
School La. Egh —9B **72**
School La. Emm G —8H **39**
School La. L Bed —1A **96**
School La. L Mar —2G **5**
School La. M'head —5B **20**
School La. Stoke P —1K **23**
School La. Warg —3J **41**
School La. W'sham —5N **115**
School La. Yat —3A **118**
School Rd. Arbor X & B'ham —9D **88**
School Rd. Asc —7N **93**
School Rd. B'ham —5B **90**
School Rd. Bfld —5K **85**
School Rd. Chvly —3J **55**
School Rd. Comp —1H **33**
School Rd. Hurst —5L **65**
School Rd. Pad —1A **106**
School Rd. Rise —6L **109**
School Rd. Tile —4L **61**
School Rd. W Dray —5L **49**
School Rd. W'sham —4K **115**
School Ter. Read —4L **63**
School Wlk. Slou —8K **23**
Schroder Ct. Egh —9K **71**
Scotland Hill. Sand —9E **112**
Scotlands Dri. Farn C —1D **22**
Scots Clo. Stanw —5L **73**
Scots Dri. Wokgm —3K **89**
Scottalls La. Hamp N —8J **33**
Scott Clo. Emm G —8G **39**
Scott Clo. W Dray —3N **49**
Scott Clo. Wdly —5F **64**
Scott's Ct. Farn —9M **119**
Scott Ter. Brack —3B **92**
Scours La. Tile —3B **62**
Scratchface La. Brad —4E **58**
Scrivens Mead. That —8J **81**
Scutley La. Light —8N **115**
Seacourt Rd. Slou —3C **48**
Seaford Gdns. Wdly —6D **64**
Seaford Rd. Houn —2L **73**
Seaford Rd. Wokgm —5B **90**
Sealand Rd. Houn —3N **73**
Searles Farm La. Read —2B **86**
Seaton Dri. Ashf —6M **73**
Seaton Gdns. Read —1J **87**
Seaton Rd. Camb —4M **119**
Second Cres. Slou —6E **22**
Second St. Green —5C **102**
Sedgefield Rd. Green —2N **101**
Seebys Oak. Col T —3J **119**
Sefton Clo. Stoke P —2H **23**
Sefton Paddock. Stoke P —1J **23**
Sefton Way. Uxb —7K **25**
Segsbury Gro. Brack —6B **92**
Selborne Clo. B'water —3G **119**
Selborne Ct. Read —5J **63**
Selborne Gdns. Read —3A **62**
Selcourt Clo. Wdly —4C **64**
Sellafield Way. Lwr Ear —1B **88**
Selsdon Av. Wdly —4E **64**
Selsey Way. Lwr Ear —3A **88**
Selva Ct. Read —6J **63**
Selwood Clo. Stai —3K **73**
Selwood Gdns. Stai —3K **73**
Selwyn Dri. Yat —3A **118**
Selwyn Pl. Cipp —8B **22**
Send Rd. Cav —2J **63**
September Ct. Uxb —3L **25**
Sermed Ct. Slou —9L **23**
Setley Way. Brack —5C **92**
Seton Dri. Calc —8N **61**
Settringham Clo. Lwr Ear —1D **88**
Sett, The. Yat —4A **118**
Seven Hills Rd. Iver —1E **24**
Sevenoaks Dri. Spen W —8G **87**
Sevenoaks Rd. Ear —9A **64**
Seventh St. Green —5C **102**
Severalls, The. Ham —7J **97**
Severn Clo. Sand —1G **119**
Severn Clo. That —6E **80**
Severn Cres. Slou —4C **48**
Severn Way. Tile —6N **61**
Sewell Av. Wokgm —3M **89**
Sewell Clo. Cold A —2E **80**
Seymour Av. Shin —6L **87**
Seymour Clo. M'head —2M **43**
Seymour Ct. Crowt —6C **112**
Seymour Ct. Rd. Mar —2A **4**
Seymour Pk. Rd. Mar —4B **4**
Seymour Plain. Mar —2A **4**
Seymour Rd. Slou —1F **46**
Shackleton Rd. Slou —8H **23**
Shackleton Way. Wdly —5F **64**
Shaftesbury Clo. Brack —7A **92**
Shaftesbury Ct. Slou —1G **47**
Shaftesbury Ct. Wokgm —4B **90**
Shaftesbury Mt. B'water —6H **119**
Shaftesbury Rd. Read —4B **62**
Shaggy Calf La. Slou —8J **23**
Shakespeare Clo. Cav —8K **39**
Shakespeare Rd. That —7F **80**
Shakespeare Way. Warf —3B **92**
Shalbourne Clo. Hung —6H **75**
Sharney Av. Slou —2C **48**
Sharnwood Dri. Calc —7N **61**
Sharpethorpe Clo. Lwr Ear —2A **88**
Shaw Ct. Old Win —2J **71**
Shaw Farm Rd. Newb —4M **79**
Shawfield Ct. W Dray —2M **49**
Shaw Hill. Newb —6M **79**
Shaw Pk. Crowt —7F **112**
Shaw Rd. Newb —7M **79**
Shaw Rd. Read —7F **62**
Shaw, The. Cook —1B **20**
Sheehy Way. Slou —8K **23**
Sheepcote La. M'head —9N **43**
Sheepcote Rd. Eton W —4C **46**
Sheepcote Rd. Wind —8A **46**
Sheepcot La. Bfld C —9N **85**
Sheepdrove Rd. Lamb —2J **27**
Sheephouse Rd. M'head —5E **20**
Sheephouse Way. Chad —8M **29**
Sheep Leaze La. Catm —2E **30**
Sheepridge La. Mar —1J **5**
Sheep Wlk. Cav —9H **39**
Sheepwash. Newt —8K **101**
Sheepways La. Tok G —5B **38**
Sheerlands Rd. Arbor —3E **110**
Sheet St. Wind —8F **46**
Sheet St. Rd. Wind —8N **69**
Sheffield Rd. Slou —7E **22**
Shefford Cres. Wokgm —3B **90**
Shefford Lodge. Newb —9L **79**
Sheldon Gdns. Read —2J **87**
Shelgate Wlk. Wdly —5B **64**
Shelley Av. Brack —4B **92**
Shelley Clo. Slou —4B **48**
Shelley Clo. Wdly —8D **64**
Shelley Ct. Camb —4N **119**
Shelley Rd. Mar —4D **4**
Shelley Rd. That —7F **80**
Shelley Wlk. Yat —4A **118**
Shelton Ct. Slou —2L **47**
Shenstone Clo. Wokgm —2M **111**
Shenstone Dri. Burn —5N **21**
Shenstone Pk. S'hill —6A **94**
Shenstone Rd. Read —8H **63**
Shepherd's Av. Ear —4A **64**
Shepherds Chase. Bag —8H **115**
Shepherds Clo. Hur —3D **18**
Shepherds Clo. Uxb —5K **25**
Shepherds Hill. Brack —3N **91**
Shepherds Hill. Comp —2H **33**
Shepherds Hill. Ear —4A **64**
Shepherd's Ho. La. Read —4N **63**
Shepherd's La. Brack —2L **91**
Shepherds La. Cav —7D **38**
Shepherds La. Hur —3B **18**
Shepherds Mt. Comp —2H **33**
Shepherds Rise. Comp —1H **33**
Shepherds Wlk. Farn —9J **119**
Shepherds Wlk. Wdly —4B **64**
Shepherds Way. Crowt —6C **112**
Shepherdton La. Graz —9C **86**
Shepley Dri. Asc —8E **94**
Shepley Dri. Read —8C **62**
Shepley End. Asc —7E **94**
Sheraton Clo. B'water —5J **119**
Sheraton Dri. Tile —3J **61**
Sherborne Clo. Coln —7F **48**
Sherbourne Dri. Asc —7F **94**
Sherbourne Dri. M'head —2N **43**
Sherbourne Dri. Wind —1B **70**
Sherbourne Dri. Wdly —4E **64**
Sherfield Clo. Read —8K **63**
Sherfield Dri. Read —8K **63**
Sherfield Hall. Read —8K **63**
Shergold Way. Cook —9K **5**
Sheridan Av. Cav —8F **38**
Sheridan Ct. Cipp —8A **22**
Sheridan Ct. Newb —8N **79**
Sheridan Cres. Baug —9G **104**
Sheridan Rd. Frim —9N **119**
Sheridan Way. Wokgm —6K **89**
Sheringham Ct. Read —7J **63**
Sherman Pl. Read —6H **63**
Sherman Rd. Read —6H **63**
Sherman Rd. Slou —6G **23**
Sherrardmead. Shaw —6M **79**
Sherring Clo. Brack —2N **91**
Sherwin Cres. Farn —9M **119**
Sherwood Clo. Brack —4D **92**
Sherwood Clo. Slou —2N **47**
Sherwood Ct. Coln —4A **48**
Sherwood Dri. M'head —8L **19**
Sherwood Gdns. Hen T —6B **16**
Sherwood Pl. Pur T —9J **37**
Sherwood Rise. Pur T —9J **37**
Sherwood Rd. Winn —1H **89**
Sherwood St. Read —4C **62**
Shifford Cres. M'head —4B **20**
Shinfield Ct. Three M —6J **87**
Shinfield Rise. Read —2L **87**
Shinfield Rd. Read —8K **63**
Shiplake Ho. Brack —6C **92**
Shiplake Row. S'lake —4B **40**
Shipley Clo. Wdly —3F **64**
Shipton Clo. Tile —2K **61**
Shire Clo. Bag —8H **115**
Shireshead Clo. Read —6D **62**
Shires, The. Wokgm —7K **89**
Shires Way. Yat —2B **118**
Shirley Av. Read —4J **87**
Shirley Av. Wind —7B **46**
Shirley Rd. M'head —9N **19**
Shoesmiths Ct. Read —4G 63
(off Merchants Pl.)
Shootersbrook La. Uft N —9B **84**
Shooter's Hill. Pang —6C **36**
Shop La. Leck —8D **30**
Shop La. Newb —5K **79**
Shoppenhangers Rd. M'head —2M **43**
Shop Rd. Wind —6M **45**
Shoreham Rise. Slou —5N **21**
Shoreham Rd. E. H'row A —2M **73**
Shoreham Rd. W. H'row A —2M **73**
Shortfern. Slou —7L **23**
Shortheath La. Sul'd —8E **84**
Shortlands Hill. Chol —2E **14**
Short La. Stai —4N **73**
Short Rd. Houn —3M **73**
Short St. Cav —2H **63**
Short St. Pang —8E **36**
Short St. Read —6H **63**
Short, The. Pur T —8L **37**
Shortwood Av. Stai —7J **73**
Shrewsbury Ter. Newb —1K **101**
Shrivenham Clo. Col T —1H **119**
Shropshire Gdns. Warf —2C **92**
Shrubbs Hill La. S'dale —8E **94**
Shrubland Dri. Read —8A **62**
Shute End. Wokgm —5N **89**
Shyshack La. Baug —9G **105**
Sibley Pk. Rd. Ear —1N **87**
Sibson. Lwr Ear —1B **88**
Sidbury Clo. Asc —7C **94**
Sidestrand Rd. Newb —2J **101**
Sidings, The. Stai —8J **73**
Sidmouth Grange Clo. Ear —5A **64**
Sidmouth Grange Rd. Ear —5A **64**
Sidmouth St. Read —5J **63**
(in two parts)
Sidney Harrison Ho. Lwr S —2G **40**
Sidney Rd. Stai —8H **73**
Sidney Rd. Wind —9M **45**
Silbury Clo. Calc —8H **61**
Silchester Rd. Pam H —9K **105**
Silchester Rd. Read —8C **62**
Silco Dri. M'head —8B **20**
Silton Clo. Ear —9D **64**
Silver Birches. Wokgm —8H **89**
Silver Clo. M'head —9L **19**
Silverdale Ct. Stai —8J **73**
Silverdale Rd. Ear —9A **64**
Silverdale Rd. Tadl —9K **105**
Silverdale Rd. Warg —4K **41**
Silver Fox Cres. Wdly —6C **64**
Silver Glades. Yat —5A **118**
Silver Hill. Col T —1J **119**
Silver La. Pad C —1A **106**
Silver St. Read —6H **63**
Silver St. Flats. Read —6H 63
(off Silver St.)
Silverthorne Dri. Cav —7D **38**
Silvertrees Dri. M'head —9M **19**
Silwood. Brack —1J **113**
Silwood Clo. Asc —4N **93**
Silwood Rd. Asc —6B **94**
Simkin's Clo. Wink R —1E **92**
Simmonds Clo. Brack —3J **91**
Simmonds St. Read —5G **63**
Simmons Clo. Slou —3B **48**
Simmons Field. That —7J **81**
Simmons Pl. Stai —9F **72**
Simmons Rd. Hen T —3C **16**
Simms Farm La. Mort —6G **107**
Simons Clo. Tile —9K **37**
Simon's La. Wokgm —5H **89**
(in two parts)
Simons Wlk. Egh —2L **95**
Simpson Clo. M'head —6E **20**
Sindlesham Rd. Arbor —8D **88**
Sine Clo. Farn —9M **119**
Singers Clo. Hen T —6D **16**
Singers La. Hen T —6D **16**
Singret Pl. Cow —5K **25**
Sinhurst Rd. Camb —5M **119**
Sinkins Ho. Chalv —9E **22**
Sipson Clo. W Dray —5N **49**
Sipson La. W Dray —5N **49**
Sipson Rd. W Dray —2N **49**
Sir Henry Peeks Dri. Farn C —1D **22**
Sirius Clo. Wokgm —5K **89**
Six Acre La. Hung —4F **96**
Sixth St. Green —5C **102**
Skeffling Clo. Lwr Ear —1D **88**
Skerries Ct. Langl —3B **48**
Skerrit Way. Pur T —9L **37**
Skilman Dri. That —8J **81**
Skilton Rd. Tile —1K **61**
Skimerdale Way. Ear —9D **64**
Skimped Hill La. Brack —4L **91**
Skinners Grn. La. Newb —2F **100**
Skydmore Path. Slou —4B **22**
Skye Clo. Calc —8M **61**
Skye Lodge. Slou —9G **22**
Skylings. Newb —7N **79**
Skyport Dri. Harm —6L **49**
Skyway Trading Est. Coln —9G **48**
Slaidburn Grn. Brack —9B **92**
Slanting Hill. Herm —9E **56**
Sloane Clo. Gor —8L **15**
Slopes, The. Cav —2K **63**
Slough By-Pass. Slou —3F **46**
Slough Ind. Est. Slou —7C **22**
Slough Rd. Dat —4J **47**
Slough Rd. Eton C & Slou —5F **46**
Slough Rd. Iver —4D **24**
Slough Trading Est. Slou —6B **22**
Smallmead Rd. Read —2D **86**
(in two parts)
Smewins Rd. White —7H **43**
Smitham Bri. Rd. Hung —6J **75**
Smithfield Rd. M'head —2K **43**
Smith's Hill. Let B —1D **8**
Smith's La. Wind —8A **46**
Smith Sq. Brack —4A **92**
Smiths Wlk. Wokgm —5L **89**
Smithy's Grn. W'sham —6N **115**
Snape Spur. Slou —7G **22**
Snipe La. Bis G —8C 102
(off Willow Rd.)
Snowball Hill. M'head —5M **43**
Snowberry Clo. Wokgm —6L **89**
Snowden Dri. Tile —6H **61**
Snowdon Clo. That —9G **80**
Snowdon Clo. Wind —1N **69**
Snowdon Rd. Farn —9J **119**
Snowdrop Copse. That —7J **81**
Snowdrop Gro. Winn —9H **65**
Snows Paddock. W'sham —3L **115**
Snows Ride. W'sham —5L **115**
Sodom La. Ash'd C —9G **35**
Soham Clo. Lwr Ear —3B **88**
Soho Cres. Wbrn G —3N **5**
Soke Rd. Sil —6N **105**
Soldiers Rise. Wokgm —3B **112**
Solent Ct. Read —6H **63**
Solent Rd. Houn —3N **73**
Somerford Clo. M'head —6E **20**
Somersby Cres. M'head —2B **44**
Somerset Clo. Hung —6J **75**
Somerset Clo. Wokgm —5J **89**
Somerset Wlk. Tile —6J 61
(off Barton Rd.)
Somerset Way. Iver —1G **49**
Somerstown Ct. Read —5F **62**
Somerton Gdns. Ear —1N **87**
Somerton Gro. That —9F **80**
Somerville Clo. Wokgm —7J **89**
Somerville Cres. Yat —3C **118**
Somerville Rd. Eton —4E **46**
Sonninge Clo. Col T —1H **119**
Sonning La. Son —2C **64**
Sonning Meadows. Son —3B **64**
Sopwith Clo. Wdly —5F **64**
Sorrel Clo. Bfld C —8J **85**
Sorrel Clo. Newb —6A **80**
Sorrel Clo. Wokgm —3C **90**
Sospel Ct. Farn R —3E **22**
Southampton Clo. B'water —3G **119**
Southampton Rd. H'row A —3M **73**
Southampton St. Read —6H **63**
South Av. Hen T —6D **16**
Southbourne Dri. Bour —4L **5**
Southbury La. Rusc —8L **41**
South Clo. Slou —8N **21**
South Clo. W Dray —2N **49**
South Clo. Wokgm —5A **90**
(Peach St.)
South Clo. Wokgm —7B **90**
(South Dri.)
S. Common Rd. Uxb —1M **25**
Southcote Farm La. Read —7D **62**
Southcote La. Read —8A **62**
Southcote Lodge. Read —8A **62**
Southcote Rd. Read —6D **62**
South Croft. Egh —9K **71**
Southcroft. Slou —5D **22**
Southdown Rd. Ben H —8C **80**
Southdown Rd. Emm G —8H **39**
Southdown Rd. Tadl —9J **105**
South Dri. Read —1L **87**
South Dri. Son —3B **64**
South Dri. Sul'd —4E **84**
South Dri. Vir W —9J **95**
South Dri. Wokgm —6A **90**
Southend. Cold A —5F **80**
South End Rd. South —2H **83**
Southern Cotts. Stai —2H **73**
Southern Ct. Read —5H **63**
Southerndene Clo. Tile —2L **61**
Southern Hill. Read —7K **63**
Southern Perimeter Rd. H'row A —2J **73**
Southern Rd. Camb —3N **119**
S. Farm La. Bag —8K **115**
Southfield Clo. Dor —2M **45**
Southfield Gdns. Burn —6L **21**
Southfields. Box —9A **54**
Southfields. Chvly —4M **55**
Southgate Ho. M'head —7C **20**
Southglade. Read —3K **87**
South Grn. Slou —8G **23**
South Groves. Chilt F —1G **74**
S. Hill Rd. Brack —8L **91**
S. Lake Cres. Wdly —7D **64**
Southlands Clo. Wokgm —6B **90**
Southlands Rd. Wokgm —7B **90**
Southlea Rd. Dat & Old Win —7K **47**
S. Lynn Cres. Brack —7M **91**
South Mall. Stai —8G **72**
S. Meadow. Crowt —7H **113**
(in three parts)
S. Meadow La. Eton —5E **46**
S. Path. Wind —7E **46**
South Pl. Mar —6C **4**

South Rd.—Tay Rd.

South Rd. Crowt —7J **113**
South Rd. Egh —1L **95**
South Rd. M'head —8B **20**
South Rd. W Dray —2N **49**
South Rd. Wokgm —9H **91**
South St. Cav —2H **63**
South St. Read —5H **63**
South St. Stai —9G **72**
South View. Brack —5H **91**
South View. Hung —6K **75**
S. View Av. Cav —2H **63**
Southview Clo. Twy —7K **41**
S. View Gdns. Newb —7M **79**
S. View Pk. Cav —2J **63**
Southview Rd. Mar —3C **4**
Southwark Clo. Yat —3A **118**
Southway. Camb —5M **119**
Southwell Pk. Rd. Camb —4M **119**
Southwick. Bag —9H **115**
Southwick Ct. Brack —8B **92**
Southwold. Brack —1J **113**
Southwold Clo. Lwr Ear —2C **88**
Southwold Spur. Slou —1D **48**
Southwood. Wokgm —7B **90**
Southwood Gdns. Bfld C —8H **85**
Southwood Gdns. Cook —1B **20**
Southwood Rd. Cook —1B **20**
Sovereign Ct. Asc —9D **94**
Sovereign Way. Calc —7K **61**
Sowbury Pk. Chvly —4L **55**
Spackman Clo. That —9G **81**
Spackmans Way. Slou —2E **46**
Span Hill. Son —6A **40**
Sparrowbill. Bright —3C **30**
Sparrow Clo. Wokgm —6K **89**
Sparvell Way. Camb —3N **119**
Speedwell Way. That —7J **81**
Speenhamland Ct. Newb —7L **79**
Speen Hill Clo. Newb —7J **79**
Speen La. Newb —6G **79**
Speen Lodge Ct. Speen —7J **79**
Speen Pl. Speen —7J **79**
Spencer Clo. Pam H —9N **105**
Spencer Clo. Uxb —4K **25**
Spencer Clo. Wokgm —5J **89**
Spencer Gdns. Egh —9M **71**
Spencer Rd. Brack —3K **91**
Spencer Rd. Newb —4H **101**
Spencer Rd. Read —4H **87**
Spencer Rd. Slou —2A **48**
Spencers Clo. M'head —6A **20**
Spencers La. Cook —9J **5**
Spencers Rd. M'head —6A **20**
Spens. M'head —6C **20**
Spenwood Clo. Spen W —9H **87**
Sperling Rd. M'head —5C **20**
Spey Rd. Tile —5A **62**
Spinfield La. Mar —6A **4**
Spinfield La. W. Mar —6A **4**
Spinfield Mt. Mar —6A **4**
Spinfield Pk. Mar —6A **4**
Spinis. Brack —1K **113**
Spinner Grn. Brack —7M **91**
Spinners Wlk. Mar —6A **4**
Spinners Wlk. Wind —7E **46**
Spinney. Slou —9D **22**
Spinney Clo. Emm G —6H **39**
Spinney Clo. W Dray —8M **25**
Spinney La. Wink —5L **69**
Spinney, The. Asc —7A **94**
Spinney, The. Calc —8M **61**
Spinney, The. Wokgm —2L **111**
Spinney, The. Yat —2B **118**
Spinningwheel La. Binf —4G **67**
Spital St. Mar —5B **4**
Spitfire Way. Wdly —5F **64**
Splash, The. Binf —1M **91**
Spode Clo. Tile —4M **61**
Spout La. Stai —1H **73**
Spout La. N. Stai —1J **73**
Spray La. Bright —4A **30**
Spray Rd. Ham —7J **97**
Spray Rd. Hung —7N **97**
Spriggs Clo. That —9G **81**
Springate Field. Slou —1N **47**
Spring Av. Egh —1N **95**
Spring Clo. M'head —4C **20**
Spring Clo. Up Bas —8M **35**
Springcross Av. B'water —6H **119**
Springdale. Ear —1A **88**
Springdale. Wokgm —2K **111**
Springfield. Light —9N **115**
Springfield Clo. Wind —8D **46**
Springfield Ct. Twy —8K **41**
Springfield End. Gor —6L **15**
Springfield La. Newb —2M **101**
Springfield Pk. M'head —4E **44**
Springfield Pk. Twy —8K **41**
Springfield Rd. Ashf —9N **73**
Springfield Rd. Binf —4G **91**
Springfield Rd. Pam H —9N **105**
Springfield Rd. Slou —6C **48**
Springfield Rd. Wind —8D **46**
Spring Gdns. Asc —6L **93**
Spring Gdns. Bour —3L **5**
Spring Gdns. Mar —4C **4**
Spring Gdns. N Asc —2H **93**
Spring Gdns. Spen W —9H **87**
Spring Gro. Read —6H **63**
Spring Hill. M'head —2B **44**
Springhill Ct. Brack —6M **91**
Springhill Rd. Gor —6L **15**
Spring La. Cold A —3F **80**
Spring La. Cook D —9F **4**
Spring La. Farn R —1D **22**
Spring La. Mort —3H **107**
Spring La. Rise —7G **108**
Spring La. Slou —9B **22**
Spring La. Son —7A **40**
Springmead Ct. Owl —9J **113**
Spring Meadow. Brack —3A **92**
Spring Meadows. Gt Shef —9G **29**
Spring Rise. Egh —1N **95**
Spring Ter. Bin H —5N **39**
Spring Ter. Read —7H **63**
Spring Wlk. Warg —3J **41**
Spring Wood La. Bfld C —9H **85**
Spring Woods. Sand —9G **112**
Spring Woods. Vir W —6K **95**
Spruce Ct. Slou —2H **47**
Spruce Rd. Wdly —6F **64**
Spurcroft Rd. That —8G **81**
Spur, The. Slou —6N **21**
Spur, The. Warg —2K **41**
Square, The. Bag —7H **115**
Square, The. Bis G —7D **102**
Square, The. Brack —6B **92**
Square, The. Camb —3N **119**
Square, The. Ear —3N **87**
Square, The. Light —9M **115**
Square, The. Spen W —9H **87**
Square, The. W Dray —7J **49**
Squirrel Clo. Sand —1F **118**
Squirrel Dri. Wink —5L **69**
Squirrel La. Wink —5L **69**
Squirrel Rise. Mar —1B **4**
Squirrels Clo. Uxb —1N **25**
Squirrels Drey. Crowt —5D **112**
Squirrels Way. Ear —1A **88**
Stable Clo. Bfld C —8H **85**
Stable Ct. Newb —5M **79**
Stable Croft. Bag —8G **115**
Stables Ct. Mar —6A **4**
Stable View. Yat —2B **118**
Staddlestone Clo. Tile —2K **61**
Stadium Way. Tile —3B **62**
Stadium Way Ind. Est. Read —3B **62**
Staff College. Camb —3N **119**
Staff College Rd. Camb —3L **119**
Stafferton Way. M'head —8C **20**
Stafford Av. Slou —5E **22**
Stafford Clo. Tap —7L **21**
Stafford Clo. Wdly —4E **64**
Staffordshire Clo. Read —4N **61**
Staffordshire Croft. Warf —1C **92**
Stag Hill. Chilt F —2G **74**
Stainash Cres. Stai —9J **73**
Stainash Pde. Stai —9J 73
(off Kingston Rd.)
Stainby Clo. W Dray —2M **49**
Staines Bri. Stai —9F **72**
Staines By-Pass. Stai —6D **72**
Staines Central Trading Est. Stai —8F **72**
Staines Rd. Wray —4N **71**
Stamford Rd. M'head —8N **19**
Stanbrook Clo. South —1J **83**
Stanfield. Tadl —9K **105**
Stanham Rd. Tile —4N **61**
Stanhope Heath. Stai —3K **73**
Stanhope Rd. Camb —5K **119**
Stanhope Rd. Read —9K **63**
Stanhope Rd. Slou —7N **21**
Stanhope Way. Stai —3K **73**
Stanlake La. Rusc —9L **41**
Stanley Clo. Mar —4D **4**
Stanley Clo. Uxb —2L **25**
Stanley Cotts. Slou —9H **23**
Stanley Grn. Langl —3A **48**
Stanley Gro. Read —4E **62**
Stanley Rd. Ashf —9M **73**
Stanley Rd. Newb —9M **79**
Stanley Rd. Wokgm —5C **90**
Stanley St. Read —4F **62**
Stanley Wlk. Brack —4N **91**
Stanmore Clo. Asc —6K **93**
Stanmore Gdns. Mort C —5G **107**
Stanmore Rd. Beed —3M **31**
Stanmore Rd. E Ils —7B **12**
Stanshawe Rd. Read —4G **62**
Stanstead Rd. Houn —3N **73**
Stanton Clo. Ear —8B **64**
Stanton Way. Slou —3N **47**
Stanway Cotts. Read —6M **63**
Stanwell Clo. Stai —3L **73**
Stanwell Gdns. Stai —3L **73**
Stanwell Moor Rd. Stai & W Dray —7H **73**
Stanwell New Rd. Stai —7H **73**
Stanwell Rd. Ashf —8M **73**
Stanwell Rd. Hort —9B **48**
Stapleford Rd. Read —8C **62**
Staplehurst. Brack —9J **91**
Stapleton Clo. Mar —3D **4**
Stapleton Clo. Newb —4G **101**
Star La. Know H —8A **18**
Star La. Read —5H **63**
Starling Clo. Wokgm —6L **89**
Starlings Dri. Tile —7J **61**
Starmead Dri. Wokgm —6B **90**
Star Post Rd. Camb —9B **114**
Star Rd. Cav —2J **63**
Starting Gates. Newb —1N **101**
Startins La. Cook —7G **4**
Starwood Ct. Slou —2L **47**
Statham Ct. Brack —3J **91**
Station App. Ashf —8N **73**
Station App. B'water —5J **119**
Station App. Frim —9N **119**
Station App. M'head —8C **20**
Station App. Mar —5C **4**
Station App. Read —4G **63**
Station App. Vir W —6M **95**
Station App. W Dray —9M **25**
Station App. Wind —7F **46**
Station Cres. Ashf —7L **73**
Station Hill. Asc —5K **93**
Station Hill. Cook —8K **5**
Station Hill. Hamp N —7J **33**
Station Hill. Read —4G **63**
Station Ind. Est. Wokgm —5N **89**
Station Pde. Ashf —8N **73**
Station Pde. Cook —8K **5**
Station Pde. S'dale —9C **94**
Station Pde. Vir W —6M **95**
Station Path. Stai —8G **73**
Station Rise. Mar —5C **4**
Station Rd. Ashf —8N **73**
Station Rd. Bag —6H **115**
Station Rd. Bour —4L **5**
Station Rd. Brack —4M **91**
Station Rd. Cipp —7A **22**
Station Rd. Cook —8K **5**
Station Rd. Ear —8B **64**
Station Rd. E Gar —7B **28**
Station Rd. E Wood —8D **100**
Station Rd. Egh —9B **72**
Station Rd. Frim —8N **119**
Station Rd. Gor —8K **15**
Station Rd. Gt Shef —1F **52**
Station Rd. Hen T —5D **16**
Station Rd. Hung —6K **75**
Station Rd. Kint —9G **76**
Station Rd. Lamb —3H **27**
Station Rd. Langl —2B **48**
Station Rd. Lwr S —1F **40**
Station Rd. Mar —6C **4**
Station Rd. Midg —9E **82**
Station Rd. Mort —5M **107**
Station Rd. Newb —9L **79**
Station Rd. Pang —7D **36**
Station Rd. Read —4G **63**
Station Rd. Speen —6H **79**
Station Rd. S'dale —8C **94**
Station Rd. Tap —7J **21**
Station Rd. That —8G **81**
Station Rd. Thea —9F **60**
Station Rd. Twy —9J **41**
Station Rd. Uxb —5K **25**
Station Rd. Warg —4H **41**
Station Rd. W Dray —1M **49**
Station Rd. Wokgm —5N **89**
Station Rd. Wray —3A **72**
Station Rd. N. Egh —9B **72**
Staunton Rd. Slou —6F **22**
Staverton Clo. Brack —2M **91**
Staverton Clo. Wokgm —5D **90**
Staverton Rd. Read —9J **63**
Stayne End. Vir W —6J **95**
Steeple Wlk. Lwr Ear —3M **87**
Steerforth Copse. Owl —8J **113**
Stephanie Chase Ct. Wokgm —4B **90**
Stephen Clo. Twy —1L **65**
Stephens Clo. Mort C —4G **106**
Stephens Firs. Mort —4F **106**
Stephenson Ct. Slou —1H **47**
Stephenson Dri. Wind —6D **46**
Stephenson Rd. Arbor —3F **110**
Stephen's Rd. Mort C —4G **107**
Stephens Rd. Tadl —9L **105**
Sterling Cen. Brack —4A **92**
Sterling Way. Read —3A **62**
Stevens Hill. Yat —4C **118**
Stevenson Dri. Binf —9G **66**
Stewart Av. Slou —6H **23**
Stewart Clo. M'head —7G **44**
Stile Rd. Slou —2M **47**
Stilwell Clo. Yat —3C **118**
Stirling Clo. Cav —7K **39**
Stirling Clo. Uxb —4K **25**
Stirling Clo. Wind —8N **45**
Stirling Gro. M'head —6L **19**
Stirling Rd. Houn —3N **73**
Stirling Rd. Slou —6C **22**
Stirling Way. That —7F **80**
Stockbridge Way. Yat —5B **118**
Stockbury Clo. Ear —2A **88**
Stockdales Rd. Eton W —3B **46**
Stockley Rd. Uxb & W Dray —7N **25**
Stockton Rd. Read —2H **87**
Stockwells. Tap —5G **20**
Stoke Cotts. Slou —9H **23**
Stoke Ct. Read —2H **87**
Stoke Ct. Dri. Stoke P —2G **23**
Stokeford Clo. Brack —7C **92**
Stoke Gdns. Slou —9G **23**
Stoke Grn. Stoke P —5J **23**
Stoke Ho. Tadl —9K **105**
Stoke Pk. Av. Farn R —4E **22**
Stoke Poges La. Slou —9G **22**
Stoke Rd. Slou —9H **23**
Stokesay. Slou —8H **23**
Stokes View. Pang —8D **36**
Stompits Rd. Holyp —5E **44**
Stomp Rd. Burn —6L **21**
Stonea Clo. Lwr Ear —3B **88**
Stonebridge Field. Eton —4D **46**
Stone Clo. W Dray —9N **25**
Stonecroft Av. Iver —7F **24**
Stonefield Pk. M'head —7N **19**
Stoneham Clo. Tile —6A **62**
Stonehaven Dri. Wdly —6F **64**
Stonehill Rd. Light —9K **115**
Stone Ho. La. Cook —6G **5**
Stone St. Read —3B **62**
Stoney Clo. Yat —5B **118**
Stoney Drove. Link —9A **116**
Stoneyfield. Been —5J **83**
Stoneylands Ct. Egh —9A **72**
Stoneylands Rd. Egh —9A **72**
Stoney La. Farn C —2C **22**
Stoney La. Newb & That —6A **80**
Stoney La. That —8H **81**
Stoney Meade. Slou —9D **22**
Stoney Rd. Brack —3L **91**
Stoney Ware. Mar —7C **4**
Stoney Ware Clo. Mar —7B **4**
Stony La. Wood M —8J **27**
Stour Clo. Slou —2D **46**
Stour Clo. Tile —4A **62**
Stovell Rd. Wind —6D **46**
Stowe Clo. Lwr Ear —1C **88**
Stowe Rd. Slou —8A **22**
Stowmarket Clo. Lwr Ear —1C **88**
Straight La. Hung —1L **51**
Straight Mile, The. Shur R & Wokgm —3B **66**
Straight Rd. Old Win —2J **71**
Strande Pk. Cook —1C **20**
Strande View Wlk. Cook —1C **20**
Strand La. Cook —1C **20**
Strand Way. Lwr Ear —2A **88**
Stranraer Rd. Houn —3M **73**
Stratfield. Brack —1J **113**
Stratfield Ct. M'head —6E **20**
Stratfield Rd. Slou —1J **47**
Stratford Av. Uxb —3N **25**
Stratford Clo. Slou —5N **21**
Stratford Dri. Wbrn G —3N **5**
Stratford Gdns. M'head —1N **43**
Stratford Way. Tile —6H **61**
Strathdean Pl. Read —4F **62**
Strathmore Ct. Camb —3N **119**
Strathmore Dri. Charv —9F **40**
Strathy Clo. Read —4B **62**
Stratton Gdns. Read —2J **87**
Strawberry Hill. Newb —7K **79**
Strawberry Hill. Warf —1B **92**
Streatley Hill. Streat —8G **15**
Street, The. Aldm —3J **105**
Street, The. Eng —7C **60**
Street, The. Mort —4H **107**
Street, The. Shur R —2E **66**
Street, The. S Sto —2K **15**
Street, The. Swal —4J **109**
Street, The. Tid —2E **60**
Street, The. Wal L —7D **42**
Stretton Clo. South —2J **83**
Strode's Cres. Stai —9K **73**
Strode St. Egh —8B **72**
Strongrove Ct. Cipp —8N **21**
Strongrove Hill. Hung —5H **75**
Strood La. Asc —1M **93**
Stroud Clo. Wind —9N **45**
Stroud Farm Rd. Holyp —5E **44**
Strouds, The. Been —5H **83**
Stuart Clo. Emm G —8H **39**
Stuart Clo. Wind —8B **46**
Stuart Rd. Newb —4H **101**
Stuart Way. Vir W —6J **95**
Stuart Way. Wind —8A **46**
Stubbles. Ash'd —8E **34**
Stubbles La. Cook —9F **4**
Stubbs Folly. Col T —2H **119**
Stubbs Hill. Binf —8J **67**
Studland Clo. Read —4J **87**
Studland Ind. Est. Bal H —6A **100**
Sturbridge Clo. Lwr Ear —2B **88**
Sturges Rd. Wokgm —6A **90**
Sturt Grn. M'head —5B **44**
Suck's La. Ash'd C —2E **58**
Suffolk Clo. Bag —8H **115**
Suffolk Clo. Slou —7A **22**
Suffolk Clo. Wokgm —5J **89**
Suffolk Rd. M'head —1A **44**
Suffolk Rd. Read —5D **62**
Sulham Hill. Sul —3F **60**
Sulham La. Sul —1F **60**
Sulhamstead Hill. Sul'd —5D **84**
Sulhamstead Rd. Sul'd —7E **84**
Sulhamstead Rd. Uft N —7H **85**
Sulham Wlk. Read —8B **62**
Sullivan Rd. Camb —4L **119**
Sumburgh Way. Slou —6G **22**
Summerfield Clo. Wokgm —2L **89**
Summerfield Rise. Gor —7M **15**
Summerhouse La. W Dray —5L **49**
Summerlea. Slou —9D **22**
Summerleaze Rd. M'head —5D **20**
Summers Rd. Burn —4M **21**
Summit Clo. Wokgm —3L **111**
Sunbury Rd. Eton —5F **46**
Sun Clo. Eton —5F **46**
Sunderland Clo. Wdly —4G **65**
Sunderland Ct. Stanw —3M **73**
Sunderland Pl. That —7F **80**
Sunderland Rd. Houn —3M **73**
Sunderland Rd. M'head —6M **19**
Sundew Clo. Light —9N **115**
Sundew Clo. Wokgm —3C **90**
Sundon Cres. Vir W —7K **95**
Sun Gdns. Bfld C —9H **85**
Sun Hill Cotts. Midg —9H **83**
Sun La. M'head —7B **20**
Sun La. Rise —8H **109**
Sunning Av. Asc —9A **94**
Sunninghill Clo. Asc —6N **93**
Sunninghill Ct. Asc —6N **93**
Sunninghill Rd. Asc —3B **94**
Sunninghill Rd. S'hill —7N **93**
Sunninghill Rd. W'sham —3K **115**
Sunninghill Rd. Wind & Asc —9N **69**
Sunnybank. Mar —3A **4**
Sun Pas. Wind —7F **46**
Sunray Av. W Dray —1L **49**
Sun Ray Est. Sand —1E **118**
Sun St. Read —5K **63**
Surbiton Rd. Camb —9D **114**
Surley Row. Cav —7G **39**
(in three parts)
Surly Hall Wlk. Wind —7B **46**
Surrey Av. Camb —5L **119**
Surrey Av. Slou —6E **22**
Surrey Ct. Warf —2C **92**
Surrey Rd. Read —8H **63**
Surridge Ct. Bag —8H **115**
Sussex Clo. Slou —1K **47**
Sussex Gdns. Wdly —5D **64**
Sussex Keep. Slou —1K **47**
Sussex La. Spen W —9J **87**
Sussex Pl. Slou —1J **47**
Sutcliffe Av. Ear —8C **64**
Sutherland Chase. Asc —4G **93**
Sutherland Gro. Calc —8M **61**
Sutherlands. Newb —3J **101**
Sutherlands Av. Read —7J **63**
Sutton Av. Slou —1L **47**
Sutton Clo. Cook —8M **5**
Sutton Clo. M'head —8N **19**
Sutton La. Coln —5C **48**
Sutton Pl. Slou —5C **48**
Sutton Rd. Camb —9D **114**
Sutton Rd. Cook —8M **5**
Sutton Rd. Speen —6H **79**
Suttons Bus. Pk. Read —4M **63**
Suttons Pk. Av. Read —4L **63**
Sutton Wlk. Read —7J **63**
Swabey Rd. Slou —3B **48**
Swains Clo. W Dray —1M **49**
Swainstone Rd. Read —7H **63**
Swaledale. Brack —7L **91**
Swallow Clo. Stai —8G **72**
Swallow Clo. Tile —6K **61**
Swallow Clo. Yat —3A **118**
Swallowdale. Iver —4E **24**
Swallowfield. Egh —1K **95**
Swallowfield Dri. Read —5H **87**
Swallowfield Gdns. Thea —8F **60**
Swallowfield Rd. Arbor —9B **88**
Swallowfield Rd. Far H & Arbor —3N **109**
Swallowfield St. Swal —3J **109**
Swallow St. Iver —4E **24**
Swallow Way. Wokgm —6K **89**
Swanbrook Ct. M'head —7D **20**
Swancote Grn. Brack —7M **91**
Swan Ct. Newb —8K **79**
Swangate. Hung —4K **75**
Swanholm Gdns. Calc —8N **61**
Swan La. Sand —2F **118**
Swanmore Clo. Lwr Ear —2D **88**
Swann Ct. Chalv —2G **46**
Swan Pl. Read —5G **63**
Swan Rd. Iver —7G **25**
Swan Rd. W Dray —1L **49**
Swans Ct. Twy —1K **65**
Swansdown Wlk. That —8E **80**
Swansea Cotts. Tile —3M **61**
Swansea Rd. Read —3G **62**
Swansea Ter. Tile —3M **61**
Swanston Field. Whit T —6E **36**
Swan Ter. Wind —6D **46**
Sweeps La. Egh —9A **72**
Sweetbriar. Crowt —3E **112**
Sweet Briar Dri. Calc —8K **61**
Sweetcroft La. Uxb —1N **25**
Sweetwell Rd. Brack —4J **91**
Sweetzer's Piece. Mort —4F **106**
Swepstone Clo. Lwr Ear —1B **88**
Swift Clo. Wokgm —6K **89**
Swift La. Bag —7J **115**
Swinbrook Clo. Tile —1L **61**
Swing Brook Clo. Tile —1L **61**
Swinley Rd. Asc —5F **92**
Swinley Rd. Bag —4G **114**
Swiss Cotts. Clo. Tile —4K **61**
Swiss Farm Caravan Site. Hen T —2C **16**
Switchback Clo. M'head —4A **20**
Switchback Rd. N. M'head —2B **20**
Switchback Rd. S. M'head —4A **20**
Sycamore Clo. Bfld —6J **85**
Sycamore Clo. M'head —1N **43**
Sycamore Clo. Sand —1F **118**
Sycamore Clo. W Dray —8N **25**
Sycamore Clo. Wdly —7B **64**
Sycamore Cotts. Camb —6M 119
(off Frimley Rd.)
Sycamore Ct. Pang —7D **36**
Sycamore Dri. Mar —2B **4**
Sycamore Dri. Twy —8J **41**
Sycamore Rise. Brack —5A **92**
Sycamore Rise. Newb —6N **79**
Sycamore Rd. Read —1L **87**
Sycamores, The. B'water —4F **118**
Sycamore Wlk. Egh —1K **95**
Sycamore Wlk. G Grn —7N **23**
Sydings, The. Speen —6H **79**
Sydney Clo. Crowt —3G **112**
Sydney Clo. That —8H **81**
Sydney Gro. Slou —7E **22**
Sykecluan. Iver —1F **48**
Sykeings. Iver —2F **48**
Sykes Dri. Stai —9J **73**
Sykes Rd. Slou —7D **22**
Sylvana Clo. Uxb —2N **25**
Sylvan Ridge. Sand —9E **112**
Sylvanus. Brack —9K **91**
Sylvan Wlk. Read —8C **62**
Sylverns Ct. Warf —2A **92**
Sylvester Clo. Speen —6J **79**
Sylvester Rd. M'head —4B **20**
Symondson M. Binf —8G **66**
Sympson Rd. Tadl —9M **105**

Tachbrook Rd. Uxb —3K **25**
Tachbrook Rd. W Dray —9M **25**
Tadcroft Wlk. Calc —9M **61**
Tadham Pl. That —9F **80**
Tadley Comn. Rd. Tadl —9L **105**
Taff Way. Tile —5A **62**
Tagg La. D'den —5M **39**
Tag La. Hare H —4M **41**
Talbot Av. Slou —1A **48**
Talbot Clo. Cav —2K **63**
Talbot Clo. Newb —6J **79**
Talbot Ct. Read —5G **62**
Talbot Pl. Bag —7H **115**
Talbot Pl. Dat —7L **47**
Talbot Rd. Ashf —9M **73**
Talbots Dri. M'head —8M **19**
Talbot Way. Tile —1K **61**
Talfourd Av. Read —7N **63**
Talisman Clo. Crowt —5B **112**
Tallis La. Read —8D **62**
Tall Trees. Coln —7E **48**
Tamar Gdns. Read —9J **63**
Tamarind Way. Ear —2M **87**
Tamarisk Av. Read —2L **87**
Tamarisk Ct. That —7J **81**
Tamarisk Rise. Wokgm —4A **90**
Tamarisk Way. Slou —1D **46**
Tamar Way. Slou —4C **48**
Tamar Way. Wokgm —5K **89**
Tamworth. Brack —9A **92**
Tamworth Clo. Lwr Ear —2B **88**
Tanfield. Read —9J **63**
Tangier Ct. Eton —5F **46**
Tangier La. Eton —5F **46**
Tanglewood. Wokgm —3M **111**
Tangley Dri. Wokgm —7N **89**
Tanhouse La. Wokgm —6M **89**
Tank Rd. Camb —4K **119**
Tanners Clo. Bfld C —9G **85**
Tanners La. Chalk —5F **38**
Tanners Yd. Bag —7H **115**
Tape La. Hurst —4L **65**
Tapling Trading Est. W Dray —8L **25**
Taplow Comn. Rd. Burn —1J **21**
Taplow Rd. Tap —7K **21**
Tarbat Clo. Owl —1H **119**
Tarbay La. Oak G —9L **45**
Target Hill. Warf —2A **92**
Target Ct. Winn —1G **89**
Tarlton Ct. Tile —6N **61**
Tarmac Way. W Dray —6J **49**
Tarnbrook Way. Brack —9B **92**
Tarn La. Newb —2K **101**
Tarragon Clo. Ear —2M **87**
Tarragon Way. Bfld C —8J **85**
Tarrant's Hill. Hung —6K **75**
Tatchbrook Clo. M'head —6D **20**
Tattersall Clo. Wokgm —6C **90**
Tavistock Clo. M'head —6L **19**
Tavistock Rd. Read —9H **63**
Tavistock Rd. W Dray —9L **25**
Tawfield. Brack —9J **91**
Tawny Croft. Owl —1J **119**
Taylor Ct. Read —5E **62**
Taylor's Bushes Ride. Wind —6M **69**
Taylor's Clo. Mar —5D **4**
Taylors Ct. M'head —6M **19**
Taylor's La. Rise —6H **109**
Taynton Wlk. Read —7H **63**
Tay Rd. Tile —4A **62**

Tazewell Ct.—Wallcroft Clo.

Tazewell Ct. Read —6F 62
Tealgate. Hung —4K 75
Tebbit Clo. Brack —4A 92
Technology Cen. Thea —1F 84
Tedder Clo. Uxb —1N 25
Teesdale Rd. Slou —6B 22
Tekels Av. Camb —4N 119
Telford Av. Crowt —3G 112
Telford Cres. Wdly —3E 64
Telford Dri. Slou —1C 46
Telston Clo. Bour —2L 5
Templar Clo. Sand —1E 118
Temple La. Bish —1G 18
Temple M. Wdly —5E 64
Temple Mill Island. Mar —1F 18
Temple Pk. Hur —3D 18
Temple Pk. Uxb —4N 25
Temple Pl. Read —6G 63
Temple Rd. Wind —8E 46
Templeton Gdns. Read —2J 87
Temple Way. Brack —2J 91
Tenaplas Dri. Up Bas —8H 35
Tenby Av. Cav —8K 39
Tenby Dri. Asc —7N 93
Tennyson Rd. Ashf —9M 73
Tennyson Rd. That —7F 80
Tennyson Rd. Wdly —8D 64
Tennyson Way. Slou —5A 22
Tern Clo. Tile —5A 62
Terrace Rd. N. Binf —9G 66
Terrace Rd. S. Binf —1G 90
Terrace, The. Asc —7N 93
Terrace, The. Bray —2F 44
Terrace, The. Crowt —5J 113
Terrace, The. Sand —4L 119
Terrace, The. Wokgm —5N 89
Terrington Hill. Mar —5A 4
Terry Pl. Cow —6K 25
Terry's La. Cook —6J 5
Tessa Rd. Read —3F 62
Test Clo. Tile —4A 62
Test Way. Link —7B 116
Testwood Rd. Wind —7N 45
Tetbury Ct. Read —5E 62
Teviot Rd. Tile —5M 61
Textile Est. Yat —2B 118
Thames Av. Pang —7E 36
Thames Av. Read —3G 63
Thames Av. Wind —6F 46
Thames Bank S. Whit T —6E 36
Thamesbourne M. Bour —4L 5
(off Station Rd.)
Thames Clo. Bour —3L 5
Thames Cres. M'head —4E 20
Thames Dri. Charv —7E 40
Thamesfield Gdns. Mar —6C 4
Thames Ind. Est. Mar —5D 4
Thames Mead. Wind —7A 46
Thames Reach. Pur T —9L 37
Thames Rd. Gor —8K 15
Thames Rd. Slou —3B 48
Thames Rd. That —6E 80
Thames Rd. Wind —6M 45
Thames Side. Hen T —4D 16
(in two parts)
Thames Side. Read —3G 63
(in two parts)
Thames Side. Wind —6F 46
Thames Side Promenade. Read —2F 62
Thames St. Son —9C 40
Thames St. Stai —9G 72
Thames St. Wind —7F 46
Thames Ter. Son —9C 40
Thames Valley Bus. Pk. Cav —3N 63
Thames Valley Pk. Dri. Cav —4M 63
Thanington Way. Lwr Ear —1A 88
Thanksgiving La. Bin H —3M 39
Thatcher Clo. W Dray —1M 49
Thatchers Dri. M'head —9L 19
Theal Clo. Col T —1H 119
Theale Commercial Est. Thea —9G 60
Theale Rd. Bfld —4J 85
Theobald Dri. Tile —9L 37
Thetford M. Cav —7K 39
Thetford Rd. Ashf —8M 73
Thibet Rd. Sand —1G 118
Thicket Gro. M'head —7K 19
Thicket Rd. Tile —4M 61
Thicket, The. W Dray —7M 25
Third Cres. Slou —6E 22
Third St. Green —5C 102
Thirkleby Clo. Slou —9E 22
Thirlmere Av. Slou —6M 21
Thirlmere Av. Tile —2N 61
Thirtover. Cold A —2E 80
Thistledown. Tile —3K 61
Thistleton Way. Lwr Ear —1D 88
Thomas Dri. Warf —2B 92
Thomas La. Wokgm —2K 111
Thomas Rd. Wbrn G —3N 5
Thompkins La. Farn R —1B 22
Thompson Clo. Herm —6C 56
Thompson Clo. Slou —3A 48
Thompson Dri. That —9H 81
Thompson Rd. Uxb —2M 25
Thomson Wlk. Calc —8M 61
Thorburn Chase. Col T —3J 119
Thornbank Clo. Stai —2H 73
Thornbers Way. Charv —8G 40
Thornbridge Rd. Iver —2D 24
Thornbridge Rd. Read —3H 87
Thornbury Clo. Crowt —5F 112
Thornbury Grn. Twy —8J 41
Thorncroft. Egh —2L 95
Thorndike. Slou —6C 22
Thorndown La. W'sham —7N 115
Thorn Dri. G Grn —7N 23
Thorne Clo. Crowt —3E 112
Thorney Clo. Lwr Ear —1D 88
Thorney La. N. Iver —7G 25
Thorney La. S. Iver —1G 49
Thorney Mill Rd. Iver & W Dray —2H 49
Thornfield. Hdly —7G 103
Thornfield Grn. B'water —6K 119
Thornford Rd. Crook C —6E 102
Thornford Rd. Hdly —8G 103
Thornhill. Brack —6B 92
Thorn La. Read —5H 63
Thorn St. Read —5G 62
Thornton Av. W Dray —2N 49
Thornton Clo. W Dray —2N 49
Thornton M. Read —4D 62
Thornton Rd. Read —4C 62
Thorn Wlk. Read —4F 62
(off Weldale St.)
Thorp Clo. Binf —9G 67
Thorpe Clo. Wokgm —8M 89
Thorpe Lea Rd. Egh —9D 72
Thorpe Rd. Stai —9E 72
Thrale M. Read —4B 62
Three Acre Rd. Newb —2K 101
Three Firs Way. Bfld C —1G 106
Three Gables La. Streat —7J 15
Threepost La. Lamb —2H 27
(off Big La.)
Threshfield. Brack —7L 91
Thrift La. M'head —3N 43
(in two parts)
Thrush Clo. Bfld C —8J 85
Thurlby Way. M'head —2A 44
Thurlestone Gdns. Read —1J 87
Thurnscoe Clo. Lwr Ear —3M 87
Thurso Clo. Tile —4A 62
Thurston Rd. Slou —7G 22
Thyme Clo. Ear —2M 87
Tichborne Clo. B'water —4H 119
Tickenor Dri. Wokgm —3L 111
Tickhill Clo. Lwr Ear —4M 87
Tickleback Row. Warf —6M 67
Ticklecorner La. Mort —8K 107
Tidmarsh La. Tid —2A 60
Tidmarsh Rd. Pang —1E 60
Tidmarsh St. Read —3B 62
Tidwells Lea. Warf —3B 92
Tierney Ct. Mar —6C 4
Tiffany Clo. Wokgm —5J 89
Tiger Clo. Wdly —5G 64
Tigerseye Clo. Wokgm —4J 89
Tilbury Clo. Cav —1J 63
Tilebarn Clo. Hen T —5B 16
Tilebarn La. Hen T —5B 16
Tile Barn Row. Wool H —9C 100
Tilecotes Clo. Mar —5B 4
Tilehurst La. Binf —9G 67
Tilehurst Rd. Read —6B 62
Tilling Clo. Tile —2J 61
Tillington Way. That —5F 80
Tillys La. Stai —8G 72
Tilney Way. Lwr Ear —3M 87
Tilstone Av. Eton W —4A 46
Tilstone Clo. Eton W —4A 46
Timbers Wlk. M'head —9M 19
Timline Grn. Brack —4C 92
Timsway. Stai —9G 72
Tindal Clo. Yat —3B 118
Tinkers La. S'dale —8D 94
Tinkers La. Wind —8N 45
Tinsey Clo. Egh —9B 72
Tinsley Clo. Lwr Ear —3M 87
Tintagel Rd. Wokgm —2N 111
Tintern Clo. Slou —2E 46
Tintern Cres. Read —7F 62
Tippett Rise. Read —7H 63
Tippings La. Wdly —3F 64
Tippits Mead. Brack —3H 91
Tippitts Mead. Brack —3J 91
Tiree Ho. Slou —5D 22
Titcombe Way. Kint —9F 76
Tite Hill. Egh —9M 71
Tithe Barn Dri. M'head —4G 45
(in two parts)
Tithebarn Gro. Calc —8N 61
Tithe Clo. M'head —4F 44
Tithe Ct. Slou —3B 48
Tithe La. Wray —3B 72
Tithe Meadows. Vir W —8L 95
Titness Pk. S'hill —5C 94
Tiverton Clo. Wdly —3D 64
Tiwell Clo. Lwr Ear —1D 88
Toad La. B'water —5J 119
Tockington Ct. Yat —3B 118
Tockley Rd. Burn —4L 21
Tofrek Ter. Read —5C 62
Tokersgreen La. Kid E —6D 38
Tokers Grn. Rd. Tok G —4D 38
Toll Gdns. Brack —5C 92
Tollgate. M'head —8L 19
Tolpuddle Way. Yat —4D 118
Tomlin Rd. Slou —5A 22
Tomlinson Dri. Wokgm —3M 111
Topaz Clo. Slou —9D 22
Topaz Clo. Wokgm —4K 89
Top Common. Warf —2A 92
Tope Cres. Arbor —3E 110
Tope Rd. Arbor —2E 110
Topping La. Uxb —4L 25
Torcross Gro. Calc —8J 61
Torin Ct. Egh —9L 71
Torquay Spur. Slou —4D 22
Torridge Rd. Slou —5C 48
Torrington Rd. Read —1J 87
Toseland Way. Lwr Ear —9D 64
Totnes Rd. Read —1J 87
Tottenham Wlk. Owl —9H 113
Totterdown. Bfld C —9G 85
Touchen End Rd. M'head —7A 44
Toutley Clo. Wokgm —2K 89
Toutley Rd. Wokgm —1L 89
Tower Clo. Cav —5J 39
Towerhill. Chad —5M 29
Tower Ho. Chalv —2G 46
Tower Ho. Iver —7F 24
Tower Ride. Wind —7A 70
Towers Dri. Crowt —6F 112
Town Farm Way. Stanw —4L 73
Town La. Stai —3L 73
(in two parts)
Town La. Wbrn G —3N 5
Town Mills. Newb —8K 79
Town Pl. Read —5K 63
Townsend Clo. Brack —7B 92
Townsend Rd. Aldw —1A 34
Townsend Rd. Ashf —9M 73
Townsend Rd. Streat —7J 15
Town Sq. Brack —4N 91
Tozer Wlk. Wind —9N 45
Trafalgar Clo. Wokgm —5K 89
Trafalgar Ct. Read —6D 62
Trafalgar Ho. Read —3F 62
Trafalgar Way. Camb —5K 119
Trafford Rd. Frim —9N 119
Trafford Rd. Read —3E 62
Travic Rd. Slou —4B 22
Travis Ct. Farn R —4D 22
Travis La. Sand —2G 118
Treacher Ct. Twy —8K 41
Tredegar Rd. Cav —8F 38
Tree Clo. Tile —4L 61
Treeside Clo. W Dray —3L 49
Treesmill Dri. M'head —2M 43
Trees Rd. Bour —4M 5
Trefoil Clo. Wokgm —4C 90
Trefoil Drove. That —7J 81
Treforgan. Cav —8F 38
Trelawney Av. Slou —2M 47
Trelawney Dri. Tile —3J 61
Trelleck Rd. Read —7F 62
Trenchard Rd. Holyp —5E 44
Trenches La. Slou —8B 24
Trent Clo. Wokgm —4K 89
Trent Cres. That —6E 80
Trenthams Clo. Pur T —8J 37
Trent Rd. Slou —5C 48
Trevelyan. Brack —9J 91
Trewarden Av. Iver —3E 24
Treyarnon Ct. Read —6L 63
Triangle, The. Tile —4L 61
Triangle, The. Up Bas —8K 35
Trident Ind. Est. Coln —9F 48
Trindledown. Brack —1L 91
Tring Rd. Tile —1K 61
Trinity. Owl —8J 113
Trinity Av. Mar —4B 4
Trinity Clo. Hen T —5C 16
Trinity Clo. Stai —3K 73
Trinity Ct. Wokgm —4L 89
Trinity Cres. Asc —7C 94
Trinity Pl. Read —5F 62
Trinity Pl. Wind —8E 46
Trinity Rd. Mar —5B 4
Triptree Clo. Lwr Ear —3M 87
Troon Ct. Brack —8J 91
Troon Ct. Read —5K 63
Troon Ct. S'hill —7M 93
Trotsworth Av. Vir W —6N 95
Trotsworth Ct. Vir W —6M 95
Trotwood Clo. Owl —8J 113
Troutbeck Clo. Slou —8H 23
Troutbeck Clo. Twy —7J 41
Trout Clo. Mar —7A 4
Trout La. Uxb —4J 25
Trout Rd. W Dray —9L 25
Trout Wlk. Newb —7N 79
Trowe's La. B Hill —5C 108
Trowe's La. Swal —4J 109
Trumbull Rd. Brack —2L 91
Trumper Way. Uxb —1K 25
Trumpsgreen Av. Vir W —8M 95
Trumpsgreen Clo. Vir W —7N 95
Trumpsgreen Rd. Vir W —9L 95
Trumps Mill La. Vir W —8N 95
Truro Clo. M'head —7L 19
Truss Hill Rd. Asc —7M 93
Trust Corner. Hen T —6D 16
Trusthorpe Clo. Lwr Ear —1D 88
Tubbs Farm Clo. Lamb —3H 27
Tubwell Rd. Stoke P —2K 23
Tudor Clo. Ashf —8M 73
Tudor Clo. Wokgm —6D 90
Tudor Ct. M'head —4F 20
Tudor Ct. Stanw —3M 73
Tudor Ct. Tadl —9K 105
Tudor Dri. Yat —5B 118
Tudor Gdns. Slou —7M 21
Tudor Ho. Brack —7M 91
Tudor La. Old Win —4L 71
Tudor Rd. Newb —1L 101
Tudor Rd. Read —4G 62
Tudor Way. Uxb —1N 25
Tudor Way. Wind —7A 46
Tuns Hill Cotts. Read —7N 63
Tuns La. Hen T —4D 16
Tuns La. Slou —2E 46
Tupsley Rd. Read —7F 62
Turks Clo. Uxb —4N 25
Turk's La. Mort C —5G 107
Turmeric Clo. Ear —2M 87
Turnberry. Brack —8J 91
Turnberry Ct. Read —5K 63
(off Muirfield Clo.)
Turnbridge Clo. Lwr Ear —3A 88
Turner Pl. Col T —3H 119
Turner Rd. Slou —1L 47
Turners Clo. Stai —9J 73
Turners Dri. That —8H 81
Turnery, The. That —8F 80
Turnfields. That —8G 81
Turnoak Pk. Wind —1A 70
Turnpike Ind. Est. Newb —6B 80
Turnpike La. Uxb —4M 25
Turnpike Rd. Brack —4H 91
Turnpike Rd. Newb —7A 80
Turnstone Clo. Winn —9G 64
Turnvill Clo. Light —9K 115
Turpins Grn. M'head —9L 19
Turpins Rise. W'sham —4L 115
Turton Way. Slou —2F 46
Tuscam Way. Camb —5K 119
Tuscan Clo. Tile —3M 61
Tuscany Way. Yat —5A 118
Tuxford M. Read —5B 62
Tweed Ct. Tile —5B 62
Tweed Rd. Slou —5C 48
Twinches La. Slou —9D 22
Twin Oaks. Emm G —7H 39
Two Tree Hill. Hen T —6A 16
Twyford Rd. Binf —3N 89
Twyford Rd. Twy —6J 41
Twyford Rd. Wokgm —3N 89
Twynham Rd. Camb —4N 119
Twynham Rd. M'head —7M 19
Tyberton Pl. Read —7F 62
Tydehams. Newb —3J 101
Tyle Pl. Old Win —2J 71
Tyler Clo. Cav —8E 38
Tyle Rd. Tile —4L 61
Tyler's La. Bckby —2L 81
Tylers Pl. Tile —4N 61
Tylorstown. Cav —8F 38
Tyne Way. That —6E 80
Tyrell Gdns. Wind —9B 46
Tyrrel Ct. Read —5J 63
Tytherton. Brack —4N 91

Uffington Clo. Tile —4K 61
Uffington Dri. Brack —6B 92
Uffoot Clo. Lwr Ear —3M 87
Ufton Ct. Yd. Bour —3M 5
Ullswater. Brack —9J 91
Ullswater Clo. Slou —6M 21
Ullswater Clo. That —8D 80
Ullswater Dri. Tile —1L 61
Ulster Clo. Cav —8K 39
Ulswater Clo. Light —9L 115
Ulswater Rd. Light —9L 115
Umberville Way. Slou —4B 22
Uncles La. Wal L —1D 66
Underhill. Moul —3H 15
Underhill Clo. M'head —8B 20
Underwood. Brack —8J 91
Underwood Ct. Binf —1G 91
Underwood Rd. Read —8N 61
Union Clo. Owl —8J 113
Union Rd. Brad —9L 59
Union St. Read —4G 63
Unity Clo. Emm G —8H 39
Unity Ct. Emm G —8H 39
Uong La. Cook D —1N 19
Upavon Dri. Read —7E 62
Upavon Gdns. Brack —7C 92
Upcroft. Wind —9D 46
Updown Hill. W'sham —6N 115
Upland Rd. Camb —2N 119
Uplands. Hung —6J 75
Uplands. Mar —1B 4
Uplands Clo. Sand —1F 118
Uplands Rd. Cav —8E 38
Up. Bray Rd. Bray —3F 44
Up. Broadmoor Rd. Crowt —5G 113
Up. Charles St. Camb —3N 119
Up. College Ride. Camb —9C 114
Up. Crown St. Read —6H 63
Up. Culham Rd. C Grn —4H 17
Up. Eddington. Edd —4L 75
Upper End. Chadw —5M 29
Up. Gordon Rd. Camb —4N 119
Up. Lambourn Rd. Lamb —1G 26
Up. Lees Rd. Slou —4D 22
Up. Meadow Rd. Read —1K 87
Up. Nursery. S'dale —7C 94
Up. Park Rd. Camb —4N 119
Up. Raymond Almshouses. Newb
(off Newtown Rd.) —9K 79
Up. Red Cross Rd. Gor —8L 15
Up. Redlands Rd. Read —7K 63
Up. Star Post Ride. Crowt —3M 113
Up. Verran Rd. Camb —6N 119
Up. Village Rd. Asc —7M 93
Up. Warren Av. Cav —1C 62
Up. Woodcote Rd. Cav —8D 38
Uppingham Dri. Wdly —3E 64
Uppingham Gdns. Cav —7K 39
Upshire Gdns. Brack —6C 92
Upton Clo. Hen T —5D 16
Upton Clo. Slou —2H 47
Upton Ct. Rd. Slou —2J 47
Upton Lea Pde. Slou —8K 23
Upton Pk. Slou —2G 47
Upton Rd. Slou —2J 47
Upton Rd. Tile —5B 62
Urquhart Rd. That —1G 103
Usk Rd. Tile —6N 61
Uxbridge Ind. Est. Uxb —3J 25
Uxbridge Rd. Slou —1J 47
Uxbridge Rd. Uxb & Hay —4N 25

Vachel Rd. Read —4G 62
Vale Cres. Tile —3M 61
Vale Gro. Slou —2G 47
Valentia Clo. Read —4D 62
Valentia Rd. Read —4D 62
Valentine Clo. Read —2M 87
Valentine Cres. Cav —9J 39
Valerie Ct. Read —6E 62
Vale Rd. Camb —5L 119
Vale Rd. Wind —6B 46
Vale View Dri. B Hill —5D 108
Valley Clo. Cav —9G 38
Valley Clo. Gor —8L 15
Valley Cres. Wokgm —3M 89
Valley Rd. Bfld C —8H 85
Valley Rd. Hen T —6A 16
Valley Rd. Newb —1J 101
Valley Rd. Uxb —3M 25
Valley Way. Pam H —9N 105
Valon Rd. Arbor —1D 110
Valpy St. Read —4H 63
Valroy Clo. Camb —3N 119
Vanbrugh Ct. Read —5K 63
Vandyke. Brack —8J 91
Vanlore Way. Calc —7K 61
Vanners La. Enb —5B 100
Vansittart Est. Wind —6E 46
Vansittart Rd. Bish —8C 4
Vansittart Rd. Wind —7D 46
Vantage Rd. Slou —9D 22
Vanwall Bus. Pk. M'head —9N 19
Vanwall Rd. M'head —1N 43
Vastern Ct. Read —3G 63
Vastern Rd. Read —3G 63
Vaughan Gdns. Eton W —3B 46
Vaughan Way. Slou —5A 22
Vauxhall Dri. Wdly —6E 64
Vegal Cres. Egh —9L 71
Venetia Clo. Cav —6J 39
Venning Rd. Arbor —2E 110
Ventnor Rd. Tile —4L 61
Venus Clo. Wokgm —5L 89
Verbena Clo. W Dray —4L 49
Verbena Clo. Winn —9F 64
Verey Clo. Twy —1L 65
Vermont Rd. Slou —5B 22
Vermont Woods. Wokgm —3K 111
Verney Clo. Mar —5B 4
Verney M. Read —5C 62
Verney Rd. Slou —3B 48
Vernon Cres. Read —4H 87
Vernon Dri. Asc —4G 93
Verona Clo. Uxb —6K 25
Verran Rd. Camb —6N 119
Vicarage Av. Egh —9C 72
Vicarage Clo. Cook —8M 5
Vicarage Ct. Egh —9C 72
Vicarage Cres. Egh —9C 72
Vicarage Dri. M'head —1F 44
Vicarage Gdns. Asc —7K 93
Vicarage La. Cold A —3F 80
Vicarage La. Crowt & Bag —5D 114
Vicarage La. Wray —5N 71
Vicarage La. Yat —2A 118
Vicarage Meadow. Been —5H 83
Vicarage Pl. Slou —2J 47
Vicarage Rd. Bag —7F 114
Vicarage Rd. B'water —5J 119
Vicarage Rd. Egh —9B 72
Vicarage Rd. Hen T —5D 16
Vicarage Rd. M'head —6C 20
Vicarage Rd. Read —7J 63
Vicarage Rd. Stai —7F 72
Vicarage Rd. Yat —2A 118
Vicarage Wlk. Bray —1F 44
Vicarage Way. Coln —6D 48
Vicarage Wood. Tile —2J 61
Vickers Clo. Shin —7M 87
Vickers Clo. Wdly —6G 64
Victor Clo. M'head —6M 19
Victoria Av. Camb —4L 119
Victoria Ct. Bag —9H 115
Victoria Ct. Hen T —5D 16
Victoria Ct. Mar —5C 4
(off Victoria Rd.)
Victoria Cres. Iver —8G 25
Victoria Dri. B'water —5G 119
Victoria Gdns. Newb —7L 79
Victoria M. Read —3D 62
Victoria Rd. Asc —7K 93
Victoria Rd. Cav —1G 62
Victoria Rd. Eton W —3A 46
Victoria Rd. Mar —5C 4
Victoria Rd. Mort —4G 106
Victoria Rd. Owl —9J 113
Victoria Rd. Slou —9K 23
Victoria Rd. Stai —7F 72
Victoria Rd. Tile —4L 61
Victoria Rd. Uxb —1K 25
Victoria Rd. Warg —3K 41
Victoria Sq. Read —5K 63
Victoria St. Egh —1L 95
Victoria St. Read —5K 63
Victoria St. Slou —1H 47
Victoria St. Wind —7F 46
Victoria Way. Read —5K 63
Victor Pl. Woolh —9E 82
Victor Rd. That —8H 81
Victor Rd. Wind —9E 46
Victor Way. Wdly —5F 64
Vigo La. Yat —4A 118
Viking. Brack —7J 91
Village Clo. Read —5H 87
Village Rd. Dor —2L 45
Village, The. Finch —7K 111
Village Way. Ashf —8N 73
Village Way. Yat —2B 118
Villa M. Read —5L 63
Villiers Mead. Wokgm —5M 89
Villiers Rd. Slou —6F 22
Villier St. Uxb —4L 25
Villiers Wlk. Newb —4G 101
Villiers Way. Newb —4G 100
Vincent Clo. Wdly —6E 64
Vincent Dri. Uxb —2N 25
Vincent Rise. Brack —5B 92
Vincent Rd. That —7H 81
Vine Clo. Stai —2H 73
Vine Clo. W Dray —3N 49
Vine Ct. Newb —1M 101
Vine Cres. Read —8A 62
Vine Gro. Uxb —1N 25
Vine La. Hil —2N 25
Vineries Clo. W Dray —5N 49
Vinery, The. Warg —3J 41
Vines, The. Wokgm —8H 89
Vine St. Uxb —2L 25
Vineyard Dri. Bour —2L 5
Viola Av. Stai —5M 73
Viola Croft. Warf —3C 92
Violet Av. Uxb —6N 25
Virginia Av. Vir W —7L 95
Virginia Beeches. Vir W —5L 95
Virginia Dri. Vir W —7L 95
Virginia Way. Read —8B 62
Viscount Ind. Est. Coln —9F 48
Viscount Rd. Stai —5M 73
Viscount Way. Wdly —5E 64
Vivien Clo. Cook —9K 5
Voller Dri. Tile —6K 61
Volunteer Rd. Thea —1E 84
Vo-Tec Cen. Newb —9C 80
Vulcan Clo. Sand —2E 118
Vulcan Clo. Wdly —3G 64
Vulcan Way. Sand —2F 118

Waborne Rd. Bour —3M 5
Wade Dri. Slou —9C 22
Wadham. Owl —9K 113
Wagbullock Rise. Brack —8N 91
Waggoners Hollow. Bag —8H 115
Wagner Clo. M'head —2K 43
Wagtail Clo. Twy —9K 41
Waingels Rd. Land E —3F 64
Wakefield Cres. Stoke P —1H 23
Wakeford Clo. Pam H —9N 105
Wakeford Ct. Pam H —8N 105
Wakelins End. Cook —8J 5
Wakeman Rd. Bour —4L 5
Wakemans. Up Bas —9M 35
Walbury. Brack —6B 92
Waldeck Rd. M'head —7D 20
Waldeck St. Read —7H 63
Walden Av. Arbor —8B 88
Waldens Clo. Bour —4L 5
Waldorf Heights. B'water —6H 119
Waldron Hill. Brack —3C 92
Waleys Pl. Cav —2J 63
Walford Rd. Uxb —3K 25
Walgrove Gdns. White —6H 43
Walker Rd. M'head —1D 44
Walker's La. Lamb —2H 27
Walkers Pl. Read —5C 62
Walk, The. Eton W —4C 46
Wallace Clo. Mar —3D 4
Wallace Clo. Wdly —7C 64
Wall Clo. Uxb —3M 25
Wallcroft Clo. Binf —2K 91

AREAS COVERED BY THIS ATLAS
with their map square reference

Names in this index shown in CAPITAL LETTERS, followed by its Postcode district, are Postal addresses.

Areas covered by this Atlas

Printed and bound in Great Britain by
Butler & Tanner Ltd, Frome and London